Modern Piracy

Legal Challenges and Responses

Edited by

Douglas Guilfoyle

Reader in Law, Faculty of Laws, University College London, UK

Edward Elgar

Cheltenham, UK • Northampton, MA, USA

Published by
Edward Elgar Publishing Limited
The Lypiatts
15 Lansdown Road
Cheltenham
Glos GL50 2JA
UK

Edward Elgar Publishing, Inc.
William Pratt House
9 Dewey Court
Northampton
Massachusetts 01060
USA

A catalogue record for this book is available from the British Library

Library of Congress Control Number: 2012952652

This book is available electronically in the ElgarOnline.com Law Subject Collection, E-ISBN 978 1 84980 493 6

ISBN 978 1 84980 484 4

Typeset by Columns Design XML Ltd, Reading
Printed by MPG PRINTGROUP, UK

Contents

PART III   PIRACY AND PRIVATE LAW

PART IV   CONCLUSIONS

Contributors

Robert Beckman is the Director of the Centre for International Law (CIL), a university-wide research centre at the National University of Singapore (NUS) which was established in 2009. In addition to serving as Director of the Centre, he also heads its ocean law and policy programme and its research projects on the South China Sea and International Maritime Crimes. Professor Beckman received his J.D. from the University of Wisconsin and his LL.M. from Harvard Law School. He is an Associate Professor at the NUS Faculty of Law, where he has taught for more than 30 years. He currently teaches Ocean Law & Policy in Asia and Public International Law at the NUS Faculty of Law. Professor Beckman is an expert on the issues of law of the sea in Southeast Asia, including piracy and maritime security. He served for several years as a regional resource person in the workshops on Managing Potential Conflicts in the South China Sea. He has represented Singapore in various CSCAP meetings on maritime security, and has worked for many years on the legal and policy issues relating to the Straits of Malacca and Singapore. Professor Beckman lectures in the summer diploma programme at the Rhodes Academy of Oceans Law & Policy in Rhodes, Greece. Professor Beckman is also an Adjunct Senior Fellow in the Maritime Security Programme at the S Rajaratnam School of International Studies (RSIS), Nanyang Technological University (NTU).

Christian Bueger is lecturer in International Relations at Cardiff University. Before joining Cardiff he was a Leverhulme fellow at the Greenwich Maritime Institute and obtained a PhD in international relations from the European University Institute. The focus of his research is counter-piracy governance, maritime security, international organizations, international political sociology and practice theory. Further information is available at <http://bueger.info>.

Håkan Friman is Deputy Director-General in the Swedish Ministry of Justice (on leave), and former head of the division for international judicial cooperation and criminal cases. He is a Visiting Professor, University College London, Faculty of Laws, United Kingdom, and a

Visiting Scholar, George Washington University, Washington DC, USA. Håkan Friman is former Associate Judge of Appeal, Svea Court of Appeal, Sweden, and former E.o. Professor, Department of Procedural Law, University of Pretoria, South Africa. He has long been involved in international and national work in the area of international criminal law. He has published extensively in this field and is co-author of a leading textbook: *An Introduction to International Criminal Law and Procedure* (2nd edn, Cambridge University Press, 2010).

Douglas Guilfoyle is a Reader in Law at the Faculty of Laws, University College London where he teaches public international law, international criminal law and the international law of the sea. He completed his LLM and doctorate at the University of Cambridge, where he held a British Council Chevening Scholarship and a Gates Cambridge Trust Scholarship. He holds undergraduate degrees from the Australian National University. He has also worked as a litigation solicitor and as a judge's associate in the Federal Court of Australia. In 2009 he prepared a report on treaty-based jurisdiction over pirates for Working Group 2 of the Contact Group on Piracy off Somalia and he remains involved in its work. In 2011–2012 he acted as Specialist Advisor to the House of Commons Foreign Affairs Committee inquiry into Somali piracy. He is also author of *Shipping Interdiction and the Law of the Sea* (Cambridge University Press, 2009) as well as numerous articles and book chapters on the law of piracy. He is married to Zoë and will be a new father at the time of printing.

James Kraska is Howard S. Levie Chair of Operational Law, member of the faculty of the International Law Department and senior associate in the Center for Irregular Warfare and Armed Groups at the US Naval War College in Newport, Rhode Island. An elected member of the International Institute of Humanitarian Law in San Remo, Italy, Kraska is a commander in the US Navy Judge Advocate General's Corps, and also serves as a Senior Fellow at the Foreign Policy Research Institute in Philadelphia, Pennsylvania and as a guest investigator with the Marine Policy Center, Woods Hole Oceanographic Institution. Commander Kraska served in four Pentagon assignments, including as Oceans Law & Policy Adviser and also as office director for international treaty negotiations, both on the Joint Staff. Commander Kraska earned a doctor of juridical science (S.J.D.) and master of laws (LL.M.) from the University of Virginia School of Law and the doctor of jurisprudence (J.D.) from Indiana University Maurer School of Law in Bloomington.

Jens Lindborg is a judge in Sweden. He has worked as a legal advisor to the Swedish Ministry of Justice, Division for Criminal Cases and International Legal Co-operation, with international negotiations and legislative drafting. He has served as a legal advisor to the Commanding Officer of the Swedish Armed Forces in Afghanistan taking part in the International Security Assistance Force (ISAF) and as a legal advisor to the Force Commander of EU NAVFOR conducting Operation Atalanta. Jens Lindborg is happily married to Åsa and proud father of Anton.

Peter MacDonald Eggers QC is a barrister practising at 7 King's Bench Walk, Temple, London. He specializes in all aspects of commercial law, with a particular emphasis on insurance, commodities and shipping. Peter MacDonald Eggers is a Visiting Professor at University College London. He is co-author of *Good Faith and Insurance Contracts*, a contributor to *Marine Insurance: The Law in Transition* and *Reforming Marine and Commercial Insurance Law*, author of *Deceit: The Lie of the Law*, and is a Contributing Editor of *Chitty on Contracts*. Peter MacDonald Eggers has been involved in a number of piracy cases, most recently in *Masefield v Amlin* and *Osmium Shipping Corporation v Cargill International*.

Keith Michel was educated at Bradfield College and Cambridge University and qualified as a solicitor in 1973. He was a partner at Holman Fenwick Willan for 25 years where he specialized in contracts of carriage, energy contracts and war risks insurance. He has contributed to journals and has been a conference speaker for many years and is the author of *War, Terror and Carriage by Sea* (Informa, 2004). Recently he has taught maritime law at University College London where he is a Visiting Professor.

Andrew Murdoch is currently a legal adviser at the UK's Foreign and Commonwealth Office. He previously served in the UK Royal Navy from 1990–2011 both ashore and at sea. He qualified as a barrister in 2000 and practised at the Chambers of Michael Lawson QC for a year where he specialized in criminal law. In 2001 he served as the Assistant Chief Naval Judge Advocate, prosecuting and defending at courts-martial, before joining a destroyer in 2003 where he saw service during the Iraq conflict. After two years as the legal adviser to shore establishments, he advised the surface and submarine fleet and deployed to support maritime operations in the Middle East and Lebanon. He was promoted to Commander in 2007 before obtaining an LLM at University College London, being awarded the Georg Schwarzenberger Prize in International Law by the Institute of Advanced Legal Studies for performance in international law. He has served in Bahrain as the Coalition Maritime Force/UK Maritime Component Commander legal adviser and as the Royal Navy's principal source of advice on international law. He is the author of the Royal Navy's legal guidance to Commanding Officers on Maritime Security Operations and has written several articles on matters of international law.

Martin N. Murphy is an internationally recognized expert on piracy and unconventional conflict at sea. Dr Murphy is a Senior Fellow at the Atlantic Council of the United States, Visiting Fellow at the Corbett Centre for Maritime Policy Studies at King's College London and Adjunct Professor at Georgetown University. In addition to book chapters and journal articles his published works include three books: *Somalia, the New Barbary? Piracy and Islam in the Horn of Africa* (2011), *Small Boats, Weak States, Dirty Money: Piracy and Maritime Terrorism in the Modern World* (2009), both issued by Hurst/Columbia University Press and recognized by the US Naval Institute as amongst the most important naval titles published in their respective years; and *Contemporary Piracy and Maritime Terrorism* (2007), an Adelphi Paper for the London-based International Institute for Strategic Studies. He is currently engaged on two more books: *Piracy, Terrorism and Unconventional Warfare at Sea: Navies Confront the 21st-Century* and *The Maritime Trinity: A History of Piracy, Trade and War*.

Tullio Treves is Professor of International Law at the University of Milan and served as a Judge of the International Tribunal for the Law of the Sea from 1996 to 2011, including as President of the Seabed Disputes Chamber. He has an extensive record of publication in international law, principally in the fields of the international law of the sea and international environmental law. He obtained his doctorate from the University of Milan in 1964 and has taught at the University of Sassari (1969–1973), the University of Turin (1974–1980) and the University of Milan (1980–present). He is a frequent guest lecturer and course leader at other institutions. In addition he has been active in international diplomatic practice as a member of the Italian delegations to the Third UN Conference on the Law of the Sea (1974–1982) and numerous other conferences and negotiations. He is a member of the Institut de droit international and of the Curatorium of the Hague Academy of International Law. He acts as counsel and as arbitrator in international law of the sea cases.

Captain Brian Wilson, JAGC, US Navy (Retired) is the Deputy Director of the Global Maritime Operational Threat Response Coordination

Center (GMCC). The GMCC is a Department of Homeland Security office within the US Coast Guard and operates as the primary US coordination center for the Maritime Operational Threat Response Plan of the US President's Maritime Security Policy. Captain Wilson is also an adjunct professor at the United States Naval Academy, where he teaches *Piracy, Maritime Terrorism, and Law of the Sea.* Captain Wilson served on active duty in the US Navy Judge Advocate General's Corps for 21 years, retiring in the rank of Captain. Navy assignments included serving as Staff Judge Advocate for USS *Kitty Hawk* and commands in Bahrain, Japan and McMurdo Station, Antarctica (Operation Deep Freeze). His Pentagon postings included serving as Oceans Policy Advisor in the Office of the Under-Secretary of Defense and on the Joint Staff. A graduate of Florida State University (Bachelor of Science), Captain Wilson also earned degrees at the University of Florida (Juris Doctorate), George Washington University (Master of Laws), and US Naval War College (Master of Arts).

Preface

This volume reflects the work of the Modern Laws of High Seas Piracy Project, a group of lawyers from academia and government or private practice drawn from Europe, North America and Southeast Asia. The aim of the project was to bring together a range of academics and practitioners, as well as both public and private lawyers, to produce a study that considers the modern law of maritime piracy in the round and in context.

As editor, I must express our gratitude first and foremost to the Leverhulme Trusts International Networks Grants that provided financial assistance to bring us together for a highly productive workshop in London in September 2011. Thanks are also due to the administrative team at the UCL Faculty of Laws for their support at that meeting in a variety of ways.

I am grateful to all the contributors for taking the time away from their ordinary commitments and in many cases for taking the time required to travel, and I must also express my thanks to their institutions for supporting that time away and/or travel. I must also thank the contributors for their diligence, timeliness and good humour throughout the entire process. It is a blessing, though perhaps a mixed one, when the contributors are more efficient than their editor.

In assembling the present volume, we have drawn on some work which has been previously published (though it appears here in updated or substantially revised form). I would like to acknowledge the permission of the following publishers to use and/or revise this work in whole or part:

- Douglas Guilfoyle, 'Somali Pirates as Agents of Change in International Law-making and Organisation' (2012) 1 *Cambridge Journal of International and Comparative Law* 81.
- Tullio Treves, 'Piracy, Law of the Sea, and Use of Force: Developments off the Coast of Somalia' (2009) 20 *European Journal of International Law* 399.
- Douglas Guilfoyle and Andrew Murdoch, 'The Use of Lethal

Force in Counter-piracy Operations off Somalia', in Simon Bron-
itt, Miriam Gani and Saskia Hufnagel (eds), *Shooting to Kill:
Socio-Legal Perspectives on the Use of Lethal Force* (Hart, 2012).
- Brian Wilson, 'Interagency Collaboration on the High Seas' (2011)
2 *InterAgency Journal* 58.

Finally, thanks are due to Dr Arman Sarvarian and Mr Chris Hall for
their exemplary editorial assistance at various phases of the project,
making my own work as editor much easier. Any remaining editorial
errors, of course, remain my own.

Douglas Guilfoyle
London

Abbreviations

AU	African Union
ASEAN	Association of Southeast Asian Nations
BIMCO	Baltic and International Maritime Council
BMP	Best Management Practices
CGPCS or The Contact Group	United Nations Contact Group on Piracy off the Coast of Somalia
CMF	Combined Maritime Forces
CMI	Comité Maritime International
DCoC	Djibouti Code of Conduct
EAW	European arrest warrant
ECCAS	Economic Community of Central African States
ECHR	European Convention on Human Rights (Convention for the Protection of Human Rights and Fundamental Freedoms 1950)
ECOWAS	Economic Community of West African States
EEZ	Exclusive Economic Zone
EU NAVFOR	EU Naval Force
FNDIC	Federation of Niger Delta Ijaw Communities
FSA	UN Fish Stocks Agreement (The United Nations Agreement for the Implementation of the Provisions of the United Nations Convention on the Law of the Sea of 10 December 1982 relating to the Conservation and Management of Straddling Fish Stocks and Highly Migratory Fish Stocks 1995)
GCC	Gulf Cooperation Council
GGC	Gulf of Guinea Commission
GUARDCON	A Standard Contract for the Employment of Security Guards on Ships
HRA	High Risk Area
IAMSAP	International Association of Maritime Security Professionals
ICC	International Chamber of Commerce
ICoC	International Code of Conduct for Private Security Service Providers

IGAD	East African Intergovernmental Authority on Development
IHL	International Humanitarian Law
IMB	International Maritime Bureau
IMO	International Maritime Organization
IMO-MSC	International Maritime Organization Maritime Safety Committee
INTERTANKO	International Association of Independent Tanker Owners
IOC	International Oil Company
IPTA	International Parcel Tankers Association
IRTC	Internationally Recommended Transit Corridor
ISC	Information Sharing Centre
ISO	International Organization for Standardization
ITLOS	International Tribunal for the Law of the Sea
JTF	Joint Task Force (Nigeria)
MEND	Movement for the Emancipation of the Niger Delta
MLA	mutual legal assistance
MOSOP	Movement for the Emancipation of the Ogoni People
MOTR	Maritime Operational Threat Response
MOU	memorandum of understanding
MOWCA	Maritime Organization of West and Central Africa
MSC	Maritime Safety Committee
MSC-HOA	Maritime Security Center Horn of Africa
MSPA	Maritime Security Patrol Area
MSPWG	IMO Working Group on Maritime Security including Piracy and Armed Robbery against Ships
NATO	North Atlantic Treaty Organization
NDPVF	Niger Delta People's Volunteer Force
NDV	Niger Delta Vigilantes
NDVF	Niger Delta Volunteer Force
NGO	Non-Governmental Organization
NNOC	Nigeria National Oil Company
OPEC	Organization of Petroleum Exporting Countries
PCASP	Privately Contracted Armed Security Personnel
PD	Presidential Directive
PDP	People's Democratic Party (Nigeria)
PER	Perceived Enhanced Risk
PMSC	private maritime security companies
PRC	Piracy Reporting Centre
PSC	private security companies

ReCAAP	Regional Cooperation Agreement on Combating Piracy and Armed Robbery against Ships in Asia 2004
ROE	rules of engagement
RPG	rocket-propelled grenade
SADC	Southern African Development Community
SAMI	Security Association for the Maritime Industry
SHADE	Shared Awareness and Deconfliction Mechanism or Meetings
SUA or SUA Convention	Convention for the Suppression of Unlawful Acts against the Safety of Maritime Navigation 1988
TFG	Transitional Federal Government of Somalia
UN	United Nations
UN Basic Principles	United Nations Basic Principles for the Use of Force and Firearms by Law Enforcement Officials 1990
UNCLOS	United Nations Convention on the Law of the Sea 1982
UNDP	United Nations Development Programme
UNODC	United Nations Office on Drugs and Crime
UNPOS	United Nations Political Office for Somalia
UNSC	United Nations Security Council
UNSCR	United Nations Security Council Resolution
UNTOC	United Nations Convention against Transnational Organized Crime 2000
VLCC	very large crude carrier
VPD	Vessel Protection Detachment
WFP	World Food Program

1. Introduction: piracy, law and lawyers

Douglas Guilfoyle

1.1 OUR APPROACH

This book considers the legal challenges posed by piracy, and in doing so attempts to bring together the perspectives of both public and private lawyers. These two groups of practitioners and scholars have a number of common interests when it comes to piracy, but frequently risk speaking past rather than with each other. One aim of the present book is to considering piracy 'in the round': to examine piracy in context and from both public and private law perspectives. The substantive chapters of this book are therefore divided into three parts: Part I deals with piracy in context, Part II considers the legal issues from the perspective of state and government actors, and Part III examines the law as it relates to private actors. Each of these sections is outlined below. The aim is to examine a selection of key questions in detail, while remaining throughout as accessible as possible to the non-specialist.

A preliminary distinction to make is one of definition. When we discuss piracy, are we always talking about the same thing? The simple answer that emerges from this volume is 'no'. First, viewed in context, every major instance of piracy is always factually different – piracy is a single label for a diverse phenomenon which is highly contingent on local conditions. Second, lawyers do not have a single definition of piracy. For the public international lawyer, piracy principally refers to an act of violence, detention or depredation committed on the high seas by a private vessel against another vessel for private ends.[1] Acts occurring within the territorial sea or internal waters (ports, rivers, etc.) are thus usually referred to as 'armed robbery against ships'. The commercial lawyer is likely familiar with a broader concept of piracy which will encompass the international law definition but which also extends to

---

[1]   United Nations Convention on the Law of the Sea (adopted 10 December 1982, entered into force 16 November 1994) 1833 UNTS 397, Art. 101(a).

attacks in port, or even attacks originating from the shore.[2] Thus an armed group attacking vessels in Nigeria's internal waterways may constitute 'pirates' in common parlance and commercial law, but would not be 'pirates' in international law. Some of the consequences of these distinctions are explored in later chapters.

1.2 PART I: CONTEXT

The first section of this book considers the regions currently most affected by piracy, and the nature of the international response. Chapters in Part I thus deal with the differing forms of maritime violence found in Southeast Asia, off the coast of Somalia and within and off the coast of Nigeria; a final chapter provides an overview of counter-piracy practices and the organisations involved.

In Chapter 2 Robert Beckman considers piracy and armed robbery in Southeast Asia, which was as recently as 2000 the area of the world that saw the greatest number of attacks against shipping.[3] Superficially at least, Southeast Asia is the great counter-piracy success story. After a period of rising attacks between 1998 and 2004, measures taken by regional states and the international community, including through the establishment of a regional Information Sharing Centre, appear to have significantly reduced the number of attacks. Beckman's analysis eschews a direct cause and effect relationship between those governance measures and the subsequent fact of piracy attacks 'coming under control', and further outlines a number of important differences between piracy in this region and off Somalia.

I discuss Somali piracy in Chapter 3. My chapter begins with an extended account of the history of Somali piracy and its context, presenting Somali piracy as a highly adaptive business. It is worth understanding the facts of Somali piracy and its business model(s) for a number of reasons. First, given the obvious topicality of Somali piracy, it forms a recurrent example or case study in later chapters. Second, understanding how Somali piracy is shaped by its context cautions us against concluding either that Somali-style piracy may 'spread' elsewhere or that approaches that appear to have contained piracy elsewhere will translate readily to the Somali context. A further theme of the chapter

---

[2] See Chapter 11.4.

[3] R. Beckman, 'Combating Piracy and Armed Robbery Against Ships in Southeast Asia: The Way Forward' (2002) 33 *Ocean Development and International Law* 317–341, 317.

will be the impact of Somalia on international law and organisation. The main argument will be that while the response to Somali piracy has not changed the substantive public international law applicable to piracy, that response has generated new models of cooperation and soft law.

Chapter 4 by Martin Murphy deals with the often overlooked phenomenon of West African piracy, in particular Nigerian maritime violence. Acts of depredation against ships and oil platforms frequently occur on the inland and coastal waters of Nigeria but have also ranged on occasion over 100 miles out to sea. Indeed, in the context of the Nigerian oil industry Murphy suggests that Nigerian 'piracy' may inflict 'far greater financial losses and [have] a far wider [global] economic impact' than piracy anywhere else.[4] Murphy's chapter conducts a thorough historical and political survey of the sobering causes of conflict in the Niger delta and offers a stern warning as to how difficult it may be to combat disorder in oil rich states. Setting strict law to one side, this chapter more than any other may prompt us to ask who the real pirates may be.

Stepping back a little, in Chapter 5 Christian Bueger provides a concise overview of the 'myriad of governmental and non-governmental actors, UN agencies and international organizations [that] have become active in counter-piracy'.[5] The task of understanding contemporary counter-piracy is made complex by the fact that it is now characterised by a plurality of actors and agencies with overlapping mandates and missions. At best, these various activities are horizontally coordinated; at worse they are duplicating effort. Bueger's chapter helpfully illuminates this field by addressing the various strands of international practice in counter-piracy: 'includ[ing] governance, epistemic, military, law enforcement, development, and humanitarian practices'.[6] Without such a thematic mental map, the organisational terrain of counter-piracy can be next to incomprehensible. This is important background when considering the later chapters dealing with counter-piracy practice from the perspective of states (and their lawyers).

1.3 PART II: PIRACY AND PUBLIC LAW

The focus of Part II is not simply the public international law of piracy, but also the practicalities of counter-piracy operations as viewed by government lawyers. While they are all writing in a personal capacity, the

---

4 Chapter 4.1.
5 Chapter 5.1.
6 *Ibid.*

present volume benefits greatly from the practical perspective of a number of contributors in government service. It also has the benefit of commencing with an authoritative exposition of the basic law.

Judge Tullio Treves, in Chapter 6, introduces the public international law of piracy and outlines the major debates. The focus is upon Somali piracy in particular, which has been the crucible for contemporary international law developments. The chapter thus serves as an introduction to the rest of Part II, in which some of the particular themes outlined by Judge Treves are taken up in further detail. The chapter begins by reviewing the scope and limitations of the general public international law definition of piracy and the jurisdictional rules applicable to states' counter-piracy efforts. It then turns to the tailored regime created by a succession of UN Security Council resolutions to deal with the phenomenon of Somali piracy, and the extent to which these both broaden the traditional rules and contain their own limitations. The legal framework applicable to prosecuting pirates is introduced, in particular the difficult questions attendant on capturing warships transferring Somali piracy suspects to third jurisdictions for prosecution. This discussion provides important context for Chapter 8, in particular. The possibility of using the Convention for the Suppression of Unlawful Acts against the Safety of Maritime Navigation[7] as a counter-piracy instrument is also explored, as are the fundamental rules governing the use of force against pirates by warships.

The role of warships in counter-piracy is the crux of Chapter 7 by Andrew Murdoch and me (though it is principally the work of the former). International law gives vessels (or aircraft) on government service unique positive authorisation to intervene against pirates. One of the most visible and discussed aspects of such operations off Somalia is what happens when a naval vessel encounters a suspect pirate craft which is either attacking a merchant vessel or threatening to use force against a naval vessel or personnel. The question becomes how much force naval vessels or personnel may use either to deter or disrupt an attack or to capture suspects and what law applies to such actions. While the chapter focuses principally on such maritime activities, the law applicable to counter-piracy operations ashore is also noted. Chapter 7 also considers the framework for cooperation between the various national and multinational missions deployed off Somalia and how the law works in an operational context, particularly through the adoption of military Rules of

---

[7]   (Adopted 10 March 1988, entered into force 1 March 1992) 1678 UNTS 221.

Engagement. The latter is an important and understudied issue, explored through two case-studies of real counter-piracy incidents involving lethal force.

Chapter 8 by Håkan Friman and Jens Lindborg goes on to consider more generally the impact of (and rationale for) conducting counter-piracy operations within a paradigm of law-enforcement and prosecution. In this context, it explores the practical legal difficulties for navies at the moment they capture suspect pirates and become part of a criminal justice process. This involves often complex questions of mutual legal assistance between states, as well as the problems that can follow from the length of time that may pass between capturing possible pirates and a decision being made either to transfer them (usually to another state) for prosecution or to release them. As a practical matter, it is not entirely clear that the states or international organisations involved have entirely shaken off the intellectual baggage of treating counter-piracy as first and foremost a military deployment. Thus, Chapter 8 concludes that if 'piracy is to be treated [successfully]...as a criminal problem, much more attention must be given to the resulting legal challenges. States detailing military forces to collective operations must ensure that they have the legal tools necessary to perform a law-enforcement job efficiently.'[8]

Chapter 9, by Brian Wilson, in turn suggests that if maritime law-enforcement operations are to be effective then they require the coordination of assets and expertise within states (i.e., between departments and agencies). This is especially the case if timely decisions are to be made. Thus, '[w]hile the onus of resolving maritime threats traditionally has rested with naval assets, the spectrum of responses now extends into diplomatic, investigative and judicial venues. The intersection of agencies with separate command structures, operating procedures and authorities poses considerable coordination challenges.'[9] In the United States, such inter-agency coordination is achieved through the Maritime Operational Threat Response (MOTR) Plan. Chapter 9 examines the MOTR plan's origins, implementation, and the potential lessons learned both for piracy and maritime law-enforcement more generally.

Part II thus starts at the highest level of generality, with a detailed account of the general legal framework. It then moves through the legal challenges inherent in states' conduct of counter-piracy operations and states' efforts to cooperate in piracy prosecutions, before concluding with an examination of *intra*-state concerns in maritime security coordination.

---

[8]   Chapter 8.9.
[9]   Chapter 9.1.

1.4 PART III: PIRACY AND PRIVATE LAW

Broadly, Part III deals with two important and complex questions which can be opaque to the non-specialist. The first is the legal framework governing the relatively recent rise of private armed security as a counter-piracy defence aboard merchant ships. The second is the general law of marine insurance as it relates to piracy, including: the definition of piracy (as a question of commercial law); insurance against the risk of piracy (under ship or cargo policies) and the payment of ransoms; and the question of piracy under contracts for the carriage of goods by sea. The essential theme of Part III, then, concerns the role of law in the allocation of, and protection against, risk by and among private parties. On questions of commercial law, the treatment in this volume is largely from the perspective of common law jurisdictions and that of the United Kingdom in particular.

In Chapter 10, James Kraska explores the legal issues surrounding the use of private contracted armed security personnel (PCASP) in protecting merchant vessels. In particular, he notes that, through the work of the International Maritime Organization, the shipping industry and flag states 'standards and rules are emerging for employment of PCASP to guard ships transiting the High Risk Area threatened by Somali pirates in the western Indian Ocean'.[10] The issues involved include: the division of authority between master and PCASP aboard; appropriate rules for the use of force; questions of liability arising from any use of force; and the potential difficulties involved when a ship carries weapons into foreign ports. While many of these issues can be regulated by the flag state, many will also fall within the jurisdiction of other states, including port states. Despite the potential complexities involved, and the potential for liability if and when things go wrong, there has been a steady shift in the position of the major shipping industry associations in favour of the use of armed guards – at least in certain cases. That said, PCASP will never be a panacea; rather they are one more possible tool as part of a larger package of state and private measures designed to shave the odds against successful piracy attack.

Of course, when there is a successful piracy attack, costs follow. In some types of piracy, especially that prevalent in Southeast Asia, the losses involved may be little more than the theft of readily moveable property – essentially burglary at sea. In Somali piracy the costs may run to millions of dollars, including ransom of the vessel and crew, delay of

---

[10]   Chapter 10.1.

the vessel's voyage, etc. Commercial parties will be keen to mitigate such losses and the laws of insurance and carriage of goods by sea both have implications for how such losses are allocated – or avoided in the first place.

In Chapters 11 and 12, Peter MacDonald Eggers outlines the fundamental questions relating to insurance law and piracy. Chapter 11 examines the common law definition of piracy in historical perspective. Clear definitions are an essential aspect of the law of piracy just as much in the commercial as in the public sphere. The purpose of defining words used in commercial contracts is, of course, 'to give effect to the understanding of those words shared by the "ordinary commercial community"'.[11] The point being that while the commercial concept of piracy encompasses those acts that would be piracy at public international law, the commercial definition is – as noted above – much broader.

Chapter 12 introduces the law applicable to marine insurance: that is, contractual promises by an insurer to compensate for loss caused by an insured against peril. Questions of who bears the risk of piracy will be relevant to a range of commercial actors involved in the voyage of a ship and its cargo ('a maritime adventure') including ship owners, cargo owners and crew members, among others. Though other legal interests (such as profits or the crews' lives) may be insured, a ship will usually be insured under a 'hull and machinery' policy and its cargo under a 'cargo' policy. If a pirate attack occurs, those interested in a maritime adventure will almost invariably involve their insurers. What then follows requires an understanding of the basic principles of insurance law and the common forms of maritime insurance: what losses can be attributed to piracy and when are such losses covered by insurance policies? In answering such questions four issues will be critical. First, the contract itself may contain certain conditions or exclusions. Second, insured perils may be defined in differing ways, with implications for piracy-related claims. Third, as a fundamental principle, there must be a loss caused by the insured against peril. Further, the classification of any loss (i.e., as a partial loss, an actual total loss or a constructive total loss) arising from piracy will have important legal consequences. Thus in ransom cases '[w]here pirates seize a vessel and decide to keep the vessel, there may well be a total loss, an actual total loss if the deprivation is irretrievable and a constructive total loss if the recovery of possession [of the vessel]

---

[11] Chapter 11.6.

is unlikely within a reasonable time'.[12] Fourth, the insured party is usually under an obligation to take reasonable measures to avert or minimise any loss. Thus, if paying a ransom is not contrary to English law or public policy, it may be positively required under an insurance contract in situations where such payment is reasonable. It may therefore be that an insured does not have a good claim for total loss of a vessel where there is a reasonable prospect of recovering it through a ransom payment. It is thus unsurprising that UK courts have recently had to consider the question of such ransom payments in marine insurance law.[13]

In Chapter 13, Keith Michel reviews the law of carriage of goods by sea as it applies to piracy. (The definition of piracy used under such contracts is essentially the same as that discussed in Chapter 11.) This includes an examination of various commonly used contractual clauses either drafted specifically to deal with piracy or potentially relevant to piracy. Particular attention is paid to the relationship between standard clauses dealing with war risk ('war risk clauses') and piracy specific clauses (the latter are often based on principles found in the former). An interesting point arises, then, in terms of the definition of 'war' under war risk clauses. English courts have typically adopted a wide view of 'an act of war', such that some acts of maritime violence – even those not attributable to a state – may be covered by a war risk clause. War risks may thus in some cases already cover certain acts of piracy. By contrast, the definition of piracy is rather more tightly prescribed. Of particular interest is the chapter's consideration of the practical impact of piracy on contracts of carriage. Piracy may cause, in relation to a contractually covered voyage, either loss of time (e.g., through taking a longer route to avoid pirate-prone areas) or delay (e.g., by being captured for ransom). With regard to the former, who should meet the costs of any lost time will depend on whether or not a so-called off-hire clause applies. Regrettably, the case law in this field remains limited. The chapter therefore outlines how other elements of the law of carriage of goods by sea might apply in the piracy context. Relevant considerations may include the law determining responsibility for the chosen route on a contractual voyage (e.g., under the contract may the master vary the route taken to minimise exposure to possible pirate attacks?). For those of us

---

[12]   Chapter 12.5.4.

[13]   *Masefield AG v Amlin Corporate Member Ltd* [2010] EWHC 280 (Comm); [2011] EWCA Civ 24. The editor is pleased to note that our author on this point, Peter McDonald Eggers QC, appeared successfully for the insurers in this case.

who are not specialists, these questions are important if we are to understand the behaviour and incentives of the commercial actors affected by piracy.

1.5 PART IV: CONCLUSIONS

The final chapter of this volume draws together a number of recurrent themes. First, there is – as noted above – the problem of definition. A second, and closely related, observation is that piracy is always situated and contingent. It is more useful to talk of *piracies* than piracy. Third, efforts to repress piracy off Somalia raise questions about the tension between efficiency and justice in attempting to conduct law-enforcement through a multinational military deployment. Our fourth theme is that the legal response to piracy always involves a delicate balance between state sovereignty or jurisdiction on the one hand and collective responses on the other. Finally, we can ask the intriguing question: 'when State repression fails, does the market intervene?'

PART I

Context

2. Piracy and armed robbery against ships in Southeast Asia

Robert Beckman

2.1 INTRODUCTION

This chapter will analyze piracy and armed robbery against ships in Southeast Asia, the area of the world which had the greatest number of incidents of attacks against ships in 2000.[1] It will first examine the nature of attacks on ships in Southeast Asia and explain that the majority of attacks are not considered 'piracy' under international law but rather 'armed robbery against ships'. It will then discuss attacks on ships in Southeast Asia between 1998 and 2008. It will examine the reasons for the rise in the number of attacks between 1998 and 2004 and the measures taken by states in Southeast Asia as well as the international community to bring the number of attacks under control. It will then examine the relative increase in attacks in 2010 and 2011, including the increase in the number of incidents which would either constitute 'piracy' as defined in Article 101 of the United Nations Convention on the Law of the Sea (UNCLOS)[2] or offences under the 1988 Convention for the Suppression of Unlawful Acts against the Safety of Maritime Navigation (SUA Convention).[3] Finally, it will examine fundamental differences between piracy in Somalia and piracy in Southeast Asia, before focusing on the steps that should be taken by states in Southeast Asia to combat piracy and armed robbery against ships in Southeast Asia.

---

[1] International Maritime Bureau (IMB), *Piracy and Armed Robbery Against Ships Annual Report 1 January – 31 December 2000,* in R. Beckman, 'Combating Piracy and Armed Robbery Against Ships in Southeast Asia: The Way Forward' (2002) 33 *Ocean Development and International Law* 317, 317.

[2] United Nations Convention on the Law of the Sea (adopted 10 December 1982, entered into force 16 November 1994) 1833 UNTS 397 (UNCLOS).

[3] Convention for the Suppression of Unlawful Acts against the Safety of Maritime Navigation (adopted 10 March 1988, entered into force 1 March 1992) 1678 UNTS 222 (SUA Convention).

2.2 CATEGORISING THE ATTACKS ON SHIPS IN SOUTHEAST ASIA

Under UNCLOS, piracy can only be committed against ships on the high seas[4] or in the exclusive economic zones (EEZ)[5] of states. Consequently, attacks against ships located in the territorial sea of a state do not constitute piracy. While attacks on ships in Southeast Asia are commonly described as 'piracy', in most cases, this is inaccurate. Most attacks on ships in Southeast Asia occur in port, in internal waters, in the territorial sea, in straits used for international navigation (such as the Malacca Strait or Singapore Strait) or in the archipelagic waters of Indonesia.[6] Since these attacks occur in maritime zones under the sovereignty of the coastal state, they are not acts of piracy governed by the UNCLOS regime[7] but are classified as 'armed robbery against ships'. This is defined by the International Maritime Organization (IMO) as:

> any illegal act of violence or detention or any act of depredation, or threat thereof, other than an act of piracy, committed for private ends and directed against a ship or against persons or property on board such ship, within a state's internal waters, archipelagic waters and territorial sea.[8]

Attacks on ships in maritime zones under the sovereignty of the coastal states are not crimes under international law, but are only crimes under the laws of the coastal state, and possibly the laws of the flag state and the state of nationality of the perpetrators.[9] The coastal state has the exclusive right to exercise the power of arrest over persons in maritime zones under its sovereignty.[10] Foreign warships have no power to patrol in maritime zones under the sovereignty of a coastal state, and they have

---

[4]   UNCLOS, Art. 101.

[5]   UNCLOS, Art. 58(2).

[6]   R. Beckman, 'The 1988 SUA Convention and the 2005 SUA Protocol: Tools to Combat Piracy, Armed Robbery and Maritime Terrorism', in S. Bateman *et al.* (eds), *Lloyd's MIU Handbook of Maritime Security* (2008), 187–213.

[7]   UNCLOS, Art. 101.

[8]   IMO, *Code of Practice for the Investigation of Crimes of Piracy and Armed Robbery against Ships,* IMO Assembly Resolution A. 1025 (26), 18 December 2009.

[9]   For a general overview of criminal jurisdiction, see A. Watts and R. Jennings (eds), *Oppenheim's International Law* (Vol 1) (9th edn, 1996), 456.

[10]   R. Beckman and T. Davenport, 'Maritime Terrorism and the Law of the Sea: Basic Principles and New Challenges' (Centre for International Law Working Paper, 2010) <http://cil.nus.edu.sg/wp/wp-content/uploads/2010/12/

no power to board ships or arrest persons without the consent of the coastal state.[11] The upper half of the Straits of Malacca and the South China Sea are the only areas in Southeast Asia in which attacks take place outside of territorial waters[12] where the UNCLOS piracy provisions are applicable.

The distinction between piracy and armed robbery against ships is important because it limits the types of cooperative measure which can be taken to enhance the security of sea lanes and combat attacks against vessels. The countries in Southeast Asia jealously guard their sovereignty and they oppose any suggestions for cooperative regimes which could undermine their sovereignty.[13] They are very unlikely to agree to other states patrolling waters or exercising police power in maritime zones under their sovereignty. They are likely to insist that any proposal for cooperative measures recognize their sovereignty and be consistent with the principles and rules of international law, especially UNCLOS.

2.3   ATTACKS IN SOUTHEAST ASIA, 1998 TO 2008

2.3.1   Increase in Attacks from 1998 to 2004

Attacks on ships passing through Southeast Asian waters have been a problem since ancient times.[14] Between 1998 and 2004, attacks on ships became a particular problem in Southeast Asia.[15] Among the reasons for

---

Beckman-and-Davenport-Maritime-Terrorism-31-Jan-2011-Final.pdf>   accessed 21 December 2011.

[11]   *Ibid.*, citing *SS Lotus (France v Turkey)*, PCIJ Rep Ser. A No 10 [1927] 18.

[12]   R. Beckman, *supra* note 1, 326.

[13]   E. Barrios, 'Casting a Wider Net: Addressing the Maritime Piracy Problem in Southeast Asia' (2005) 28(1) *Boston College International and Comparative Law Review* 149–163, 160; R. Beckman, 'The Establishment of a Cooperative Mechanism for the Straits of Malacca and Singapore under Article 43 of the United Nations Convention on the Law of the Sea', in A. Chircop *et al.* (eds), *The Future of Ocean Regime-Building: Essays in Tribute to Douglas M. Johnston* (Maritunus Nijhoff 2009), 233–260.

[14]   M. Richardson, 'The Threats of Piracy and Maritime Terrorism in Southeast Asia' (2004) 139 *Maritime Studies* 18–21. See also R. Beckman *et al.*, 'Acts of Piracy in the Malacca and Singapore Straits' (1994) 1(4) *Maritime Briefing* 1, 3: 'Piracy existed in the waters of Southeast Asia long before the advent of the Europeans into the Indian Ocean Basin c. 1450 AD.'

[15]   For example, the number of attacks on ships in Indonesia increased from 60 in 1998, to 121 in 2003 and 93 in 2004, and the number of attacks on ships in

this were the 1997 Asian Economic Crisis and the period of instability in Indonesia following the fall of the Suharto Government in 1998.[16] This was exacerbated by the independence movement in the Indonesian province of Aceh, as it was reported that the rebels in Aceh were responsible for some of the more serious attacks, including hijacking of ships and holding crew members hostage for ransom.[17]

In 2000, the Annual Report of the International Maritime Bureau (IMB) reported that the largest number of reported attacks in the world took place in Southeast Asia.[18] Indonesian waters were reported to be the most dangerous in the world, with 86 reported actual attacks and 31 reported attempted attacks in 2000.[19] This accounts for almost 25 percent of the total reported attacks. In addition, there were 75 reported incidents in the Malacca Straits in 2000, up from only two reported incidents in 1999.[20] As a result, the 2000 IMB Annual Report stated that the Malacca Straits was the most dangerous area for piracy attacks in the world after Indonesia.[21]

2.3.2 New Cooperative Mechanism for the Straits of Malacca and Singapore

After the terrorist attacks against the United States on 11 September 2001, there was increased concern in the international shipping community regarding maritime terrorism. Maritime security became a high priority at the IMO and the IMO adopted measures to enhance the

---

the Malacca Straits increased from one in 1998, to 28 in 2003, and 37 in 2004. International Chamber of Commerce (ICC) International Maritime Bureau, *Piracy and Armed Robbery Against Ships Annual Report 1 January–31 December 2004*, 4.

[16] J. Dela Pena, 'Maritime Crime in the Straits of Malacca: Balancing regional and extra-regional concerns' (2009) 10(2) *Stanford Journal of International Relations*, 1–8, 3.

[17] ICC IMB, *Piracy and Armed Robbery Against Ships Annual Report 1 January–31 December 2004*, 16.

[18] ICC IMB, *Piracy and Armed Robbery Against Ships Annual Report 1 January–31 December 2000*. It should be noted that the IMB Annual Reports do not distinguish between 'piracy' as defined in UNCLOS and 'armed robbery against ships'.

[19] *Ibid.*

[20] *Ibid.*

[21] *Ibid.*

security of ships and ports.[22] At its 92nd session in June 2004, the IMO Council addressed concerns about the security of vital shipping lanes and requested that the Secretary-General work on the issue in collaboration with the parties concerned.[23] The IMO Secretariat undertook a study of vital shipping lanes and gave special consideration to the Straits of Malacca and Singapore.[24]

At the IMO Council's 93rd session in October 2004, the Secretary-General submitted a document on the key issues involved in protecting vital shipping lanes against terrorist attacks.[25] The document included a profile of the Straits of Malacca and Singapore.[26] The IMO Council agreed that the organization had and could play a role in protecting shipping lanes of strategic importance and significance.[27] In March 2005, the IMO Secretary-General delivered the keynote address at the ASEAN Regional Forum on Confidence Building Measures in Singapore.[28] The Secretary-General stated that, as part of his efforts to push forward collaboration on maritime security in the region, he had initiated a round

---

[22]   IMO, 'Maritime Security' <http://www.imo.org/OurWork/Security/Guide_to_Maritime_Security/Pages/Default.aspx> accessed 22 December 2011: 'A comprehensive security regime for international shipping entered into force on 1 July 2004. The mandatory security measures, adopted in December 2002, include a number of amendments to the 1974 Safety of Life at Sea Convention (SOLAS), the most far-reaching of which enshrines the new International Ship and Port Facility Security Code (ISPS Code), which contains detailed security-related requirements for Governments, port authorities and shipping companies in a mandatory section (Part A), together with a series of guidelines about how to meet these requirements in a second, non-mandatory section (Part B).'

[23]   IMO, 'Council – 92nd session: 21–25 June 2004' <http://www.imo.org/blast/mainframe.asp?topic_id=114&doc_id=3580> accessed 21 December 2011.

[24]   *Ibid.*

[25]   'Note by the Secretary-General, Protection of Vital Shipping Lanes', IMO Doc. C93/15 (7 October 2004) in Beckman, *supra* note 13, 246. Document includes: Annex, 'Profile of the Straits of Malacca and Singapore'.

[26]   *Ibid.*

[27]   *Ibid.*

[28]   E. Mitropolous, 'Regional Co-operation in Maritime Security' (2 March 2005) *ASEAN Regional Forum Conference*, IMO, 'Speeches by the Secretary-General – Archives' <http://www.imo.org> accessed 22 December 2011, in Beckman, *supra* note 13, 246: 'I consider this latter meeting a unique opportunity for us all to work together and make progress in producing an outcome conducive to the building of confidence in the safety of navigation and the overall security in the Strait. This should be endeavoured with full respect to the sovereign rights and the territorial integrity of the littoral States and the relevant provisions of international law, including the UN Convention on the Law of the Sea.'

of consultations with the three littoral states and selected user states.[29] He referred to the planned IMO-sponsored meeting to be hosted by Indonesia in September 2005 and stated that this gathering would provide a 'unique opportunity' for the coastal states, user states and other stakeholders to work to enhance the safety of navigation, environmental protection and overall security in the Strait.[30]

In August 2005, one month before the IMO-sponsored meeting in Jakarta, the foreign ministers of the three littoral states met in Batam, Indonesia, to discuss these topics.[31] This was the fourth trilateral ministerial meeting of the three littoral states on matters relating to the Straits of Malacca and Singapore and the first since 1977.[32]

In the resulting 2005 Batam Statement, the foreign ministers of Indonesia, Malaysia and Singapore set out the principles for cooperation with user states and other stakeholders with respect to the Straits of Malacca and Singapore.[33] The agreed principles included the following: (1) that the littoral states have sovereignty and sovereign rights in the Straits; (2) that the littoral states have primary responsibility over the safety, environmental protection and security of the Straits; and (3) that any measures adopted or taken on these matters must be in accordance with international law, including UNCLOS.[34]

The IMO convened three meetings on the Enhancement of Safety, Security and Environmental Protection in the Straits of Malacca.[35] The first was in Jakarta, Indonesia, in September 2005; the second was in

---

[29]   *Ibid.* The term 'littoral State' is used to refer to those states bordering straits used for international navigation.

[30]   *Supra* note 28.

[31]   *The Batam Statement of the 4th Tripartite Ministerial Meeting on the Straits of Malacca and Singapore*, IMO Doc. IMO/SGP 1/INF.3, Annex 3 (Batam 1–2 August 2005); Singapore Ministry of Foreign Affairs, 'The Batam Joint Statement of the 4th Tripartite Ministerial Meeting of the Littoral States on the Straits of Malacca and Singapore' (Press Release: 2 August 2005) <http://www.mfa.gov.sg/content/mfa/media_centre/press_room/if/2005/200508/infocus_20050802_02.html> accessed 4 November 2012, in Beckman, *supra* note 13, 247–248.

[32]   *Ibid.*

[33]   *Ibid.*

[34]   *Ibid.*

[35]   IMO, *2005 Jakarta Statement on Enhancement of Safety, Security and Environmental Protection in the Straits of Malacca and Singapore*, IMO Doc IMO/JKT 1/2 (Jakarta, 8 September 2005); IMO, 'Council – 97th Session', *2006 Kuala Lumpur Statement on Enhancement of Safety, Security and Environmental Protection* (Kuala Lumpur, 18–20 September 2006) <http://www.imo.org/blast/mainframe.asp?topic_id=114&doc_id=6698> accessed 22 December 2011; IMO,

Kuala Lumpur, Malaysia, in September 2006; and the third was in Singapore in September 2007. The result was the establishment of a new cooperative mechanism for the Straits of Malacca and Singapore.[36] However, despite the fact that the impetus for the mechanism was driven by concerns about security, it is limited to measures to enhance navigational safety and environmental protection, and the 'primary responsibility' for such measures 'lies with the littoral States'.[37]

2.3.3   Measures in 2004 and 2005 to Suppress Attacks

Even though the new mechanism to enhance cooperation in the Straits of Malacca and Singapore is limited to safety and environmental protection, other measures were taken at the regional and sub-regional level in 2004 and 2005 to enhance the security of shipping in the major sea lines of communication in Southeast Asia. The need to cooperate to reduce the number of attacks became especially important after June 2005 when the Joint War Committee of Lloyd's Market Association, the influential London-based insurance trade association, included the Straits of Malacca and adjacent ports in Indonesia as a 'war-risk area', thereby threatening to increase the cost of sending ships through the Malacca Strait.[38]

2007 Singapore Statement on Enhancement of Safety, Security and Environmental Protection in the Straits of Malacca and Singapore, IMO Doc IMO/SGP 1/4 (Singapore, 6 September 2007) <http://www.mpa.gov.sg/sites/pdf/spore_statement.pdf> accessed 22 December 2011; International Maritime Organization, 'Milestone Agreement reached on co-operation over the Straits of Malacca and Singapore' (*Briefing*: 18 September 2007) <http://www.imo.org/blast/mainframe.asp?topic_id=1472&doc_id=8471> accessed 22 December 2011.

[36]   IMO *2007 Singapore Statement, supra* note 35.

[37]   *Ibid.* 'Affirming the sovereignty, sovereign rights, jurisdiction and territorial integrity of the littoral States over the Straits, as provided for under international law, in particular UNCLOS, and that the primary responsibility over the safety of navigation, environmental protection and maritime security in the Straits lies with the littoral States.'

[38]   IMO, 'Information Resources on Piracy and Armed Robbery at Sea' (*IMO Library Services External Relations Office Information Sheet No. 28*, 12 December 2007) <http://www.imo.org/KnowledgeCentre/InformationResourcesOnCurrentTopics/InformationResourcesOnCurrentTopicsArchives/Documents/PIRACY%20(13%20December%202007).pdf> accessed 22 December 2011; Beckman, *supra* note 13, 245.

Beginning in 2004, Indonesia, Malaysia, and Singapore took steps to combat piracy and armed robbery against ships.[39] All three states made significant efforts to enhance their ability to secure their waters. Malaysia established a new Maritime Enforcement Agency with functions similar to a coast guard.[40] Indonesia received substantial assistance from Japan and the United States in the form of patrol boats and radar stations.[41] The three states also took three new measures to cooperate to suppress attacks. First, they enhanced the system of trilateral Malacca Straits Sea Patrols in which each state patrols within its own waters but in a coordinated manner and with enhanced information sharing.[42] Second, they began to conduct 'Eyes in the Sky' aerial patrols in the Straits.[43] Third, these arrangements were formalized by Defense Chiefs of the three states agreeing to written Malacca Straits Patrols Standard Operating Procedures.[44] The sea patrols permit 'hot pursuit' across territorial sea boundaries, but they contain a 'hand-off mechanism' to deal with cross-boundary enforcement.[45] In addition, Indonesia and Singapore have been collaborating since 2005 to share information in order to enhance surveillance and security along their common border in the Singapore Strait.[46]

At the regional level, the Japanese Government led an initiative in 2002 and 2003 to establish a regional mechanism to combat piracy and armed robbery against ships. The resulting agreement was the Regional Cooperation Agreement on Combating Piracy and Armed Robbery

---

[39]   R. Beckman, 'Singapore Strives to Enhance Safety, Security, and Environmental Protection in its Port and in the Straits of Malacca and Singapore' (2009) 14(2) *Ocean and Coastal Law Journal* 167, 183.

[40]   Malaysian Maritime Enforcement Agency (MMEA), 'About MMEA: Background' <http://www.mmea.gov.my/index.php?option=com_content&view=article&id=43&Itemid=56&lang=en> accessed 21 December 2011.

[41]   R. Beckman, 'Piracy off Somalia: the Challenges for International Law', in (2009) *Proceedings of the 103rd Annual Meeting of the American Society of International Law: International Law as Law*, 89.

[42]   Beckman, *supra* note 39, 183.

[43]   *Ibid.* See also Chew Men Leong, 'Navies and Maritime Security – A Republic of Singapore Navy Perspective' (2007) 33(3) *Pointer* 5, 7.

[44]   IMO, *Singapore Statement on Enhancement of Safety, Security and Environmental Protection in the Straits of Malacca and Singapore*, IMO Doc. IMO/SGP 1/4 (6 September 2007) <http://www.mpa.gov.sg/sites/pdf/spore_statement.pdf> accessed 22 December 2011.

[45]   Beckman, *supra* note 39, 183.

[46]   I. Lim, 'Comprehensive Maritime Domain Awareness – An Idea Whose Time Has Come?' (2007) 33(3) *Pointer* 13, 19.

against Ships in Asia 2004 (ReCAAP).[47] An Information Sharing Centre (ISC) based in Singapore was established under the Agreement and has been entered into by 17 states parties.[48] Unfortunately, neither Indonesia nor Malaysia has ratified the Agreement, though both have indicated that they would cooperate with the ISC.[49] The reasons for failing to ratify the Agreement have not been publicly stated but it is understood that both Indonesia and Malaysia have been cooperating with the ISC, to some degree, at an operational level.[50]

Other measures or events may also have contributed to the decrease in attacks. Indonesia received aid and financial assistance to help it defend its waters, including patrol vessels from Japan and the United States and radar stations from the United States.[51] The tsunami which struck the Indian Ocean in December 2004 caused devastating damage in the Indonesian province of Aceh and may have destroyed many pirate vessels and killed many pirates. Also, attacks from Aceh stopped almost completely after the Indonesian Government reached a formal peace agreement with the Aceh rebels in August 2005.[52]

---

[47]   *2004 Regional Cooperation Agreement on Combating Piracy and Armed Robbery against Ships in Asia* (ReCAAP) (adopted 11 November 2004, entered into force 4 September 2006) <http://www.recaap.org/Portals/0/docs/About%20ReCAAP%20ISC/ReCAAP%20Agreement.pdf> accessed 21 December 2011.

[48]   ReCAAP Information Sharing Centre, 'About ReCAAP' (*Background Information*) <http://www.recaap.org/AboutReCAAPISC.aspx> accessed 22 December 2011. The 17 countries are: the People's Republic of Bangladesh, Brunei Darussalam, the Kingdom of Cambodia, the People's Republic of China, the Kingdom of Denmark, the Republic of India, the Republic of Indonesia, Japan, the Republic of Korea, the Lao People's Democratic Republic, Malaysia, the Union of Myanmar, the Republic of the Philippines, the Republic of Singapore, the Democratic Socialist Republic of Sri Lanka, the Kingdom of Thailand and the Socialist Republic of Viet Nam.

[49]   Chew Men Leong, *supra* note 43. In para. 9 of the *The Batam Joint Statement*, *supra* note 31, the Ministers took note of the establishment of the ReCAAP Information Sharing Centre in Singapore. The Statement also states that '[i]n this regard, the Ministers of Indonesia and Malaysia indicated their countries' preparedness to cooperate with the Centre'.

[50]   Beckman, *supra* note 39.

[51]   Beckman, *supra*, note 41.

[52]   ICC IMB, *supra* note 17, 16: 'In the past, these attacks were believed to be solely the work of Aceh rebels, though there are now increasing indications that crime syndicates are also operating from fishing boats and are staging copycat kidnaps which they see as an easy way to make money. It appears that when authorities increased patrols in the hotspots, the attacks moved to another area. However, after the tsunami wreaked havoc in these areas on 26 December

As a result of these measures, the number of attacks on ships was gradually reduced between 2005 and 2008. In its 2008 Annual Report, the IMB noted that there had been a decline in the number of attacks in Southeast Asia:

> Indonesia, for example, should be applauded for their tireless efforts in curbing piracy and armed robbery in its waters. Compared to 2003 when 121 attacks had been reported, there has been a continued year on year decline in Indonesia with 28 incidents reported in 2008. The majority have been opportunistic in nature. The Malacca Straits has seen a further reduction in the number of incidents reported, only two in 2008 compared to seven in 2007. Incidents in the Singapore Straits are however up from three in 2007 to six in 2008. Malaysia has seen a slight increase in the number of incidents with three vessels being hijacked and seven boarded as compared to nine boarded in 2007.

> This welcome reduction has been the cumulative effort of increased vigilance and patrolling by the littoral states and the continued precautionary measures on board ships.[53]

The measures to suppress the attacks on ships in Southeast Asia came from the coastal states themselves and were consistent with the position of the three littoral states that any assistance from outside powers must respect their territorial sovereignty and independence, must be consistent with UNCLOS and should be focused on helping them secure their own waters.[54]

2.4   ATTACKS IN SOUTHEAST ASIA, 2010 TO 2011

The IMB reported that in 2010 the number of attacks on ships in Indonesia increased from ten in 2008 to 15 in 2009, and to 40 in 2010.[55] It also reported an increase in the number of attacks on ships in the South

---

2004, the attacks had halted. It may be that some pirates were killed in the tsunami, but certainly it is the case that their equipment like boats and weapons may have been lost or destroyed. Similarly, the increased presence of naval ships off Aceh may be a deterrent factor [...].'

[53]   ICC IMB, *Piracy and Armed Robbery Against Ships Annual Report 1 January–31 December 2008*, 26–27.

[54]   Beckman, *supra,* note 13.

[55]   ICC IMB, *Piracy and Armed Robbery Against Ships Annual Report 1 January–31 December 2010*, 5–6.

China Sea, from no attacks in 2008, to 13 in 2009 and to 31 in 2010.[56] In addition, the number of attacks in Malaysia increased from ten in 2008, to 16 in 2009, and to 18 in 2010.[57] There were only two attacks per year from 2008 to 2010 in the Malacca Strait.[58] In the Singapore Strait there were six attacks in 2008, nine in 2009 and three in 2010.[59] The ReCAAP Piracy Reporting Centre reports similar statistics.[60]

Although attacks on ships in Southeast Asia are not nearly as high as they were in 2002 and 2003, there are indications of at least two trends which give rise to concern. In a paper presented in January 2011 at a Workshop on International Maritime Crimes organized by the Centre for International Law (CIL) at the National University of Singapore, Karsten von Hoesslin of Risk Intelligence analyzed the attacks in Southeast Asia and identified certain trends.[61]

Von Hoesslin confirms that the most common type of attack in Southeast Asia is the same as it has been for many years. It is on-board theft against ships at anchor within territorial waters.[62] Targeted vessels are usually boarded at night. Perpetrators armed with long knives (parangs) use the element of surprise. They generally seek to steal engine parts, crew effects, cash or other portable high-value items.[63]

---

[56]   *Ibid.*

[57]   *Ibid.*

[58]   *Ibid.*

[59]   *Ibid.*

[60]   ReCAAP Information Sharing Centre (*Incident Reports 2006–2011*) <http://www.recaap.org/AlertsReports/IncidentReports.aspx?EntryId=11> accessed 22 December 2011.

[61]   K. von Hoesslin, 'International Maritime Crimes in the ASEAN Region: Incidents and Trends', Centre for International Law Workshop on International Maritime Crimes: Legal Issues and Prospects for Cooperation (Singapore, 17–18 January 2011). Information on the Conference, including the Report of the Conference, is available on the website of the Centre for International Law <http://cil.nus.edu.sg/research-projects/international-maritime-crimes/> accessed 21 December 2011. The paper was subsequently published in R. Beckman and J. Roach (eds), *Piracy and International Maritime Crimes in ASEAN: Prospects for Cooperation* (Edward Elgar 2012).

[62]   *Ibid.*; ReCAAP Information Sharing Centre, 'Special Report on Hijacked/Missing Tug boats and barges in Asia March–June 2011' <http://www.recaap.org/Portals/0/docs/Reports/Special%20Report%2029%20Jun%2011.pdf> accessed 21 December 2011.

[63]   Von Hoesslin, *supra* note 61. For detailed reports of five specific incidents in 2011, including the nature of the attack, the weapons carried and how the crew are treated, see ReCAAP Report *supra* note 60.

Von Hoesslin also identified two trends which are more worrying.[64] First, he asserts that since 2008, a sophisticated campaign of piracy and armed robbery at sea has been waged off the Anambas Islands of Indonesia, orchestrated by experienced criminal syndicates. He states that the attacks off the Anambas Islands are seasonal. They commonly occur during the transitional monsoon period between March and the end of October. As the rainy season begins in early-to-mid November, incidents taper off due to stronger winds and greater wave heights, both of which make nocturnal boarding significantly more difficult.[65]

Von Hoesslin argues that the attackers off the Anambas Islands are engaged in what he calls 'cluster piracy'.[66] He maintains that from the period 2008 to 2010, there have been 57 reported incidents involving cluster piracy within the Anambas/Natuna/Tembalan corridor in Indonesian waters.[67] Cluster piracy entails a group of pirates operating within a specific maritime area in a short time period and systematically attacking a number of vessels. Some of these attacks are taking place in the archipelagic waters or territorial sea of Indonesia, but others take place in Indonesia's exclusive economic zone, which is outside its territorial sovereignty.[68]

The second trend von Hoesslin identifies is an increased number of ship-hijackings in Southeast Asia.[69] Von Hoesslin maintains that since 2008, there have been six successful hijackings of tugboats in Southeast Asia.[70] Tugboats are being hijacked, renamed and supplied to a pre-arranged buyer. They are usually hijacked off the coast of Malaysia, near the northern entrance to the Singapore Strait. The modus operandi in the tug hijackings is the same. The tugboats are boarded by a well-organized group of hijackers who immediately assume control of the vessel and detain the crew. The crew are not injured or mistreated. They are tied up and then released in a life raft, usually within the central South China

---

[64]   Von Hoesslin, *supra* note 61.

[65]   *Ibid.*

[66]   *Ibid.*

[67]   *Ibid.* The ReCAAP Report, *supra* note 62, does not document as many incidents, perhaps due to its record of those incidents which are reported to it (see para. 5).

[68]   Von Hoesslin *supra* note 61.

[69]   *Ibid.*

[70]   *Ibid.* The ReCAAP Report, *supra* note 62, 2–3 (paras 1, 5) states that between 2008 and 2011, 11 hijacking and 'missing vessel incidents' were reported to it – '[…] two incidents in 2008, one incident in 2009, three incidents in 2010 and five incidents (from March–June) in 2011'.

Sea. The tugboats then proceed to their final destinations while under-going re-painting and re-naming to prevent identification. Von Hoesslin suspects that the group responsible for the tugboat hijackings could be the same group behind the Anambas piracy incidents.[71]

Von Hoesslin reports that there were no incidents in Southeast Asia of ships being hijacked for ransom or crew members being held hostage for ransom.[72]

2.5 SOMALI PIRACY AND SOUTHEAST ASIA

The major concern which has arisen in the wake of the attacks against ships in the Horn of Africa is the fear that the 'business model' of Somali pirates hijacking vessels and kidnapping crew for ransom could be adopted by pirates in Southeast Asia. However, there is no evidence that the Somali model is being imported to Southeast Asia and it is highly doubtful that it could be for practical reasons.[73] Somali pirates hijack large vessels and hold the vessel and crew members for ransom with the support of local coastal communities. They are also highly organized and tied in with sophisticated networks of negotiators and persons willing to launder ransom payments. Syndicates in Southeast Asia do not appear so large or well organized, and there are no areas where there has been a breakdown of law and order where local communities would provide support to the hijackers, as is the case in Somalia.[74]

As mentioned above, the majority of attacks in Southeast Asia are conducted against ships at anchor in waters under territorial sovereignty. Attacks on ships at anchor became a particular problem after the 2008 global financial crisis resulted in many ships being laid up. Hundreds of vessels anchored in waters near the Singapore Strait, especially in the territorial sea of Malaysia. Since they were manned by only a skeletal crew, these vessels were ripe for attack by robbers. As discussed above, such attacks are armed robbery against ships, not piracy. They are a threat to the safety of crew members, but they are not a threat to international navigation on major shipping routes through Southeast Asia.

---

[71] Von Hoesslin *supra* note 61.

[72] *Ibid.*

[73] K. von Hoesslin, 'Piracy and armed robbery against ships in the ASEAN region: incidents and trends', in R. Beckman and J. Roach (eds), *Piracy and International Maritime Crimes in ASEAN: Prospects for Cooperation* (Edward Elgar 2012) 137.

[74] *Ibid.*, 138.

The closest analogy in Southeast Asia to Somali piracy is the hijacking of tugboats.[75] However, the tugboats are not being hijacked for ransom, but for sale to pre-arranged buyers.[76] Also, in the majority of cases, the crew members have been released with food and water, and have not been threatened or harmed. Nevertheless, these are clear cases of ship-hijacking.

In addition, it is not possible to completely exclude the possibility of the Somali 'business model' being adopted by criminal syndicates in Southeast Asia. Certain aspects, particularly those which do not require a large degree of organization or resources, such as the kidnapping of crew for ransom, may well be considered to be lucrative and sufficiently low-risk by syndicates in Southeast Asia.

As explained earlier, the littoral states in Southeast Asia can be expected to strongly resist anti-piracy measures similar to those that have been adopted to combat attacks against ships in the Horn of Africa. For example, the gravity of the problem posed by Somali pirates in the Horn of Africa prompted the United Nations Security Council, acting under Chapter VII of the United Nations Charter, to make exceptions to the normal rules governing piracy. In a series of resolutions on Somali piracy, the Security Council has provided that the forces cooperating with the Transitional Federal Government of Somalia (TFG) can apply the piracy rules to attacks on ships in waters under Somali territorial sovereignty, allowing such forces to enter Somali territorial waters and arrest suspected pirate ships.[77] Such a radical departure from generally accepted principles of international law would not be readily accepted by states in Southeast Asia. Southeast Asian states jealously guard their sovereignty and strongly resist authorizing any foreign warships to exercise police powers within their territorial sea or archipelagic waters.[78] It was for this reason that Indonesia insisted that the UN Security Council Resolutions relating to Somali piracy include a paragraph stating that such resolutions are an exception which cannot be interpreted as evidence of a rule of customary law. The standard paragraph in such resolutions is as follows:

> *Affirms* that the authorizations provided in this resolution apply only with respect to the situation in Somalia and shall not affect the rights or obligations

---

[75]   ReCAAP Report, *supra* note 60.

[76]   ICC IMB Report, *supra* note 55, 26.

[77]   E.g., United Nations Security Council (UNSC) Res. 1816 (2 June 2008), UN Doc. S/RES/1816.

[78]   Beckman, *supra* note 13.

or responsibilities of Member States under international law, including any rights or obligations under the Convention, with respect to any other situation, and underscores in particular that this resolution shall not be considered as establishing customary international law; and *affirms further* that such authorizations have been provided only following the receipt of the 20 November letter conveying the consent of the TFG.[79]

The international response to Somali piracy is discussed further in Chapters 6 to 8.

2.6 COMBATING PIRACY AND ARMED ROBBERY AGAINST SHIPS IN SOUTHEAST ASIA: THE WAY FORWARD

From the above discussion, it is clear that current incidents of piracy and armed robbery against ships in Southeast Asia are not as serious as they were in 1998–2004 and it is unlikely that the Somali 'business model' of hijacking ships and kidnapping crew for ransom will be adopted on a large scale in Southeast Asia.[80] However, attacks against ships in Southeast Asian waters remain a serious problem, especially in light of the recent trends highlighted by von Hoesslin of 'cluster piracy' and tugboat hijackings.[81] Further, it is not possible to completely discount the possibility that certain aspects of the Somali 'business model' could be adopted in Southeast Asia. Accordingly, several steps should be taken to address these problems, which will be dealt with below.

2.6.1 Enhancing Information Sharing and Capacity-building

Effective prevention of and enforcement against attacks on ships in Southeast Asia face several obstacles. First, as mentioned above, the vast majority of attacks on ships in Southeast Asia take place within waters under territorial sovereignty. Traditional enforcement mechanisms recognized under UNCLOS, such as the right to arrest ships suspected of engaging in piracy[82] and the right to board vessels suspected of engaging in piracy,[83] will not apply to the majority of attacks that occur in

---

[79] UNSC Res. 1846 (2008), para. 1 (2 December 2008), UN Doc. S/RES/ 1846.
[80] Von Hoesslin, *supra* note 73.
[81] Von Hoesslin, *supra* note 61; ReCAAP Report, *supra* note 62.
[82] UNCLOS, Art. 105.
[83] UNCLOS, Art. 110.

Southeast Asia. As foreign vessels will not be able to exercise such powers in maritime zones under the territorial sovereignty of coastal states, it will be up to the coastal states concerned to prevent and arrest perpetrators of attacks against vessels.

Many of the attacks in Southeast Asia occur in Indonesian waters under the territorial sovereignty of Indonesia. Indonesia is a very large country with vast maritime zones and limited enforcement capacity. It has many maritime security problems, including illegal unregulated and unreported fishing, the smuggling of goods, people, timber and weapons, and so on. The international community sometimes seems to expect Indonesia to devote most of its limited naval and coast guard resources to protecting international shipping, without considering the fact that Indonesia may have other maritime security issues to which it gives higher priority.

Second, it is highly unlikely that Indonesia, or any other country in Southeast Asia for that matter, would consent to naval or coast guard vessels from other states patrolling its waters. Therefore, the most that can be expected is for it to agree to 'hot pursuit' into its waters by vessels from neighbouring states, provided that the perpetrators are turned over to the Indonesian authorities if they are its nationals.[84] A further issue preventing effective cooperation is the belief that the majority of attacks against ships in Indonesian waters, the Straits of Malacca and Singapore, in Malaysian waters and in the South China Sea are committed by Indonesian nationals. Therefore, the Indonesian Government is naturally cautious about calls for cooperation that target its nationals. Given this situation, the best way to cooperate with Indonesia to combat piracy and armed robbery against ships may be to exchange information and to provide Indonesia with training as well as vessels and equipment to better secure its waters. Indonesia should also be given incentives to investigate the activities of syndicates suspected of being engaged in piracy. Pirate gangs are more likely to be discovered through good police work on the ground than by arresting the perpetrators in the course of an attack at sea.

2.6.2 Enhancing Cooperation through Ratification and Implementation of Relevant International Conventions

Another measure that can be taken in the region to suppress attacks on ships is to use the international conventions which are already in place to combat attacks on ships of a more serious nature, such as those involving

---

[84]   Barrios, *supra* note 13; Beckman, *supra* note 13.

the hijacking of a ship, the use of violence against crew members, or the taking of crew members hostage for ransom. This was the focus of the Workshop on International Maritime Crimes: Legal Issues and Prospects for Co-operation in ASEAN on 17 and 18 January 2011 organized by the CIL at the National University of Singapore.[85] The objective of the Workshop was to examine whether ASEAN states can better combat serious maritime crimes such as piracy, ship-hijacking and hostage-taking of crew by ratifying and effectively implementing various relevant global and regional instruments.

The CIL issued a Workshop Report (CIL Workshop Report)[86] which made several relevant recommendations. First, the CIL Workshop Report recommended that ASEAN states should be willing to use the powers provided in UNCLOS to combat acts of piracy. Second, it recommended that ASEAN states should also be willing to enter into the international cooperative regimes in the SUA Convention and the Hostages Convention[87] in order to combat serious attacks and the holding of crew members for ransom.

There are at least three types of attacks on ships in which the international regimes may come into play. First, some of the attacks on ships off the Anambas Islands take place in Indonesia's EEZ and constitute piracy under UNCLOS. International ships transiting this area to and from the Straits of Malacca and Singapore should be advised not to pass through the territorial sea or archipelagic waters of Indonesia. Foreign warships have a right under international law to conduct anti-piracy patrols or escort vulnerable vessels in the sea lanes off Anambas which pass through the EEZ of Indonesia. However, it would be wise to consult Indonesia before conducting such patrols and to seek its cooperation by having it conduct coordinated patrols in the same area within its territorial sea and archipelagic waters.

Second, some of the attacks in Southeast Asia are offences under the SUA Convention because they involve either the taking control of a ship or the use of violence against crew members which endanger the safety

---

[85] Centre for International Law, 'Workshop on International Maritime Crimes: Legal Issues and Prospects for Cooperation' (Workshop Report) (Singapore 17–18 January 2011) <http://cil.nus.edu.sg/programmes-and-activities/past-events-old/international-maritime-crimes-legal-issues-and-prospects-for-co-operation-in-asean/> accessed 21 December 2011.

[86] *Ibid.*

[87] International Convention against the Taking of Hostages (adopted 17 December 1979, entered into force 17 December 1979) 1316 UNTS 206 (Hostages Convention).

of navigation.[88] If all of the states in the region could be persuaded to become parties to the SUA Convention, it would provide a useful tool for combating some of the more serious attacks on ships, including the hijacking of tugboats. For example, if a tugboat flying a Singapore flag were hijacked by Indonesians in the territorial sea of Malaysia and then taken to the Philippines, the SUA Convention would come into play.[89] If it discovered the presence of the hijackers in its territory, the Philippines would be obliged to take them into custody. The Philippines would then be under an obligation to either extradite the hijackers to the flag state (Singapore), to the state in whose territorial sea the act took place (Malaysia), or to the state of nationality of the offenders (Indonesia). The SUA Convention could be used as legal basis for the extradition. If the Philippines decided not to extradite the hijackers to any of the three states, it would be under an obligation to prosecute them in the Philippines for a SUA offence. In addition, regardless of which state the perpetrators were prosecuted in, the other states would be under an obligation to provide legal assistance.

Third, cases could arise in which crew members or passengers are taken hostage and held for ransom either at sea or in another state. Such actions would be offences under the Hostages Convention.[90] If all the states in the region were parties to this Convention, they would be under an obligation to cooperate in the same manner as in the case of SUA offences described above.[91]

However, as noted by the CIL Workshop Report, many ASEAN member states are not in a position to use the SUA Convention and the Hostages Convention to deal with cases of ship-hijacking and hostage-taking of crew members. Three key states in Southeast Asia have not become parties to the SUA Convention – Indonesia, Malaysia and Thailand.[92] In addition, Indonesia and Vietnam are not parties to the

---

[88]   SUA Convention, Art. 3 which sets out SUA offences.

[89]   SUA Convention, Arts 6 (jurisdictional obligation), 7 (general custodial obligation), 10 (obligation to submit case for prosecution), 11 (obligation to extradite) and 12 (mutual assistance obligation).

[90]   Hostages Convention, Arts 1–2.

[91]   Hostages Convention, Arts 4 (exchange of information), 5 (jurisdictional obligation), 6 (general custodial obligation) and 8 (obligation to extradite or submit the case for prosecution).

[92]   IMO, 'Status of Multilateral Instruments in respect of which the International Maritime Organization or its Secretary-General performs Depositary or other functions' <http://www.imo.org/about/conventions/statusofconventions/documents/status%20-%202012.pdf> accessed 31 July 2012.

Hostages Convention.[93] Further, some ASEAN states, such as the Philippines, have ratified the SUA Convention but have not implemented the Convention in their national legislation.[94]

The problems relating to the failure of ASEAN countries to ratify and implement the 1988 SUA Convention are illustrated by the hijacking of the tugboat *ASTA* on 5 February 2010.[95] The *ASTA* was flying a Singaporean flag and was on route from Singapore to Cambodia towing an empty barge when it was hijacked by seven Indonesians in Malaysian territorial waters. Eleven of the 12 crew members were set adrift in a life raft on 10 February, and were rescued by the Malaysian Navy on 17 February. The barge was also set adrift and was recovered in Malaysian waters on 17 February. While underway to the desired destination, the hijackers re-painted and re-named the vessel to 'mask' its identity. On 26 February the hijacked tugboat was found by the Philippine coast guard on a beach in the southern Philippines. One person, a Filipino, was aboard the tugboat when it was found. The seven Indonesian 'pirates' were arrested by the Philippines police.[96]

The seven Indonesians were charged with immigration offences by the Philippines. The Philippines was not able to charge them with a SUA offence because it had not passed legislation implementing the SUA Convention, even though it had ratified the Convention in 2004. If all the states concerned had been parties to the SUA Convention and had incorporated the Convention in their national legislation, the Philippines would have been able to either prosecute the hijackers for a SUA offence (ship-hijacking) or extradite them to the flag state (Singapore), to the state in whose territorial sea the attack took place (Malaysia), or to the state of nationality of the offenders (Indonesia).

---

[93]   UNTC, 'Penal Matters: International Convention Against the Taking of Hostages' <http://treaties.un.org/pages/ViewDetails.aspx?src=TREATY&mtdsg_no=XVIII-5&chapter=18&lang=en> accessed 21 December 2011.

[94]   M. Ibañez, 'The Philippines Country Report' (*Centre for International Law Research Project on International Maritime Crimes*, 2011) <http://cil.nus.edu.sg/wp/wp-content/uploads/2010/10/Country-Report-Philippines.pdf> accessed 22 December 2011.

[95]   ReCAAP Information Sharing Centre, Incident Report 02/2010 <http://www.recaap.org/DesktopModules/Bring2mind/DMX/Download.aspx?Command=Core_Download&EntryId=169&PortalId=0&TabId=78> accessed 22 December 2011.

[96]   ReCAAP Information Sharing Centre, 'Piracy and Armed Robbery against Ships in Asia: Half-yearly report, January–June 2011', 49 <http://www.recaap.org/Portals/0/docs/Reports/Half%20Yearly%202011%20Report.pdf> accessed 21 December 2011.

In light of the above, the CIL Workshop Report recommended that all ASEAN member states should ratify and implement the SUA Convention and the Hostages Convention to enable them to prosecute cases of hijacking of ships and hostage-taking of crew members.[97]

2.6.3   Need for Review of National Legislation

Another problem identified by the CIL Workshop Report was the definition of piracy in the national legislation of the ASEAN states.[98] The CIL Workshop Report found that the ASEAN states had not reviewed their national piracy legislation after becoming parties to UNCLOS.[99] Domestic legislation on piracy in ASEAN states ranges from piracy legislation that does not conform to UNCLOS, to the total absence of piracy as an offence under national laws. In addition, instead of giving courts universal jurisdiction over acts of piracy committed outside the territorial sovereignty of any state, the domestic legislation of some states limits jurisdiction on the basis of flag state, nationality or passive personality principles.[100] In some ASEAN member states it is not clear whether government agencies have the legal authority to arrest pirates outside the territorial sea of any state. In addition, some ASEAN member states do not have domestic legislation enabling them to prosecute persons who have been arrested for piracy.

The lack of national legislation on piracy has created problems for Malaysia in dealing with Somali pirates captured by the Malaysian Navy in the Gulf of Aden in January 2011. As Malaysia has no provision in its Penal Code making piracy an offence it could not charge the offenders with piracy. Consequently, the pirates have been charged for offences relating to the use of firearms against the Malaysian armed forces.[101]

The CIL Workshop Report recommended that ASEAN member states should review their national legislation on piracy and, if necessary, amend their legislation to ensure that (a) the offence of piracy under their

---

[97]   Workshop Report, *supra* note 85.

[98]   *Ibid.*

[99]   *Ibid.*

[100]   On the accepted principles governing the exercise of criminal jurisdiction over extra-territorial events in public international law, see: M. Shaw, *International Law* (6th edn, CUP 2008), 652–686.

[101]   'Somali "pirates" charged in Malaysia' (*BBC News*, 11 February 2011) <http://www.bbc.co.uk/news/world-asia-pacific-12430671> accessed 21 December 2011.

national laws is consistent with that of UNCLOS and that (b) their courts are afforded jurisdiction to prosecute acts of piracy committed by anyone on the high seas or outside the territorial sea of any state.[102]

2.7 CONCLUSION

Attacks on ships in Southeast Asia became a serious problem from 1998 to 2003. The attacks were primarily conducted against ships within maritime zones under the sovereignty and jurisdiction of coastal states. As piracy generally only applies on the high seas and in the EEZ, these attacks constitute 'armed robbery against ships' rather than 'piracy' and the UNCLOS piracy regime and the SUA Convention cooperative regime were inapplicable. Nevertheless, the states in Southeast Asia, with some assistance from outside powers, took effective measures to address the problem and substantially reduce the number of incidents. The measures were taken as a result of pressure from the international community, especially from the Secretary-General of the IMO. As a result, the three littoral states of Indonesia, Malaysia and Singapore agreed on new cooperative measures and on the common principles which would guide them in cooperating with other states. The measures taken were effective in part because they were consistent with international law and did not threaten the sovereignty of the coastal states. In particular, the measures were consistent with UNCLOS and with the sovereignty of coastal states in their territorial sea and archipelagic waters.

There is little likelihood that the Somali business model will be transferred to Southeast Asia. Because the governments in this region are generally able to control their own maritime space, it would not be possible for criminal syndicates to hijack large ships and hold them for ransom with the support of coastal communities.

However, incidents in 2010 and 2011 have raised concern that criminal syndicates are operating in Southeast Asia to engage in cluster piracy and to hijack tugboats. Some of these incidents are offences under the UNCLOS piracy regime and the 1988 SUA Convention. In addition, the prospect of syndicates holding crew members hostage for ransom cannot be ruled out. Therefore, it is in the common interests of the states in Southeast Asia to review their national legislation on piracy in order to bring it into conformity with UNCLOS. It is also in their interests to ratify and implement the SUA Convention and the Hostages Convention

---

[102]   Workshop Report, *supra* note 85.

so that the cooperative regime in those conventions can be utilized to combat transnational attacks on ships which involve offences under those conventions.

3. Piracy off Somalia and counter-piracy efforts

Douglas Guilfoyle

3.1 INTRODUCTION

Somali piracy is a highly adaptive business activity that can only be understood in context. The present chapter aims to provide an analysis of the phenomenon and in particular its impact on international law-making and organization. The relevant developments have moved fast enough that there is already a significant history of international cooperation in response to Somali piracy. The contention of this chapter is that the most important impact of Somali pirates as agents of change has *not* been on the substantive law of piracy but through generating new models of cooperation and soft law. This has been evident in a range of shifts: the move from a military approach to law enforcement operations; from unilateral enforcement to international authorization and then to transnational coordination; a shift from reliance on formal organizations to informal coordinating bodies; and from maritime operations in the Gulf of Aden to various land-based operations, most notably including law and prison reform. The use of soft law in particular is most evident in the shipping industry's response to piracy.

The present chapter thus proceeds by first offering an extended account of the history of Somali piracy and its context. This is important for two reasons: first, one must appreciate that Somali piracy is not a static phenomenon; and second, understanding how Somali piracy is shaped by its context cautions us against concluding that Somali-style piracy may 'spread' to other regions. The chapter then turns to the rise of international counter-piracy operations and counter-piracy cooperation. Here we see a rapid shift from a largely 'military paradigm' response (unilateral actions and Security Council authorized missions) to a 'law enforcement response'. The latter in particular requires transnational coordination, which has rapidly moved out of formal international organizations to a range of informal coordinating bodies. Finally, we can see how a response that commenced as, in effect, containment of piracy through maritime patrols is becoming increasingly engaged in operations ashore, though usually in the form of engagement with criminal justice sector reform rather than military strikes on pirate bases.[1] Some tentative conclusions are then offered about the effectiveness of current efforts.

3.2 ORIGINS AND PRESENT FORM OF SOMALI PIRACY: UNDERSTANDING THE BUSINESS MODEL

Somali piracy is often presented, typically by pirates themselves, as being a justified response to illegal fishing and toxic waste dumping in Somali waters by foreign vessels.[2] In truth, 'there were pirate attacks as early as in 1991, which targeted cargo ships, vessels not related to illegal fishing'.[3] From the very onset of Somali governmental collapse in 1991, local piracy had an element of opportunism unrelated to whether the vessels seized were engaged in illegal activity. There may have been an early period of piracy in the mid-1990s to early 2000s which encompassed self-styled volunteer coast guards 'targeting fishing vessels accused of fishing illegally in Somali territorial waters' and holding them to ransom[4] (or simply 'fining' them[5]); but in this early and sporadic phase the vessels taken included 'an equal representation of fishing vessels, commercial traders or private yachts'.[6] There is, therefore, little evidence of a clear-cut transition from 'coast guard' to 'criminal' forms

---

[1] Though these occur: Y. Bayoumy, 'EU helicopters strike Somali pirate base on land' (*Reuters*, 15 May 2012) <http://www.reuters.com/article/2012/05/15/us-somalia-piracy-idUSBRE84E0LA20120515> accessed 22 August 2012.

[2] United Nations International Expert Group on Piracy off the Somali Coast, 'Piracy off the Somali Coast: Final Report' (2008) ('UN Expert Report') 27 <http://www.asil.org/files/SomaliaPiracyIntlExpertsreportconsolidated1.pdf> accessed 21 August 2012. Cf. L Ploch *et al.*, 'Piracy off the Horn of Africa', Congressional Research Service (27 April 2011) ('CRS Report') 9 <http://www.fas.org/sgp/crs/row/R40528.pdf> accessed 21 August 2012.

[3] Stig Jarle Hansen, 'Piracy in the greater Gulf of Aden: Myths, Misconception and Remedies', Norwegian Institute for Urban and Regional Research (2009) ('NIBR Report') 20, 29.

[4] UN Expert Report, *supra* note 2, 19.

[5] Roland Marchal, 'Somali Piracy: The Local Contexts of an International Obsession' (2011) 2 *Humanity* 31, 37, 39–40 <http://humanityjournal.org/> accessed 27 February 2012. Compare CRS Report, *supra* note 2, 5.

[6] UN Expert Report, *supra* note 2, 18.

of piracy. Further, most pirates are not displaced fishermen but members of 'nomadic, land based clans' who 'generally have little or no knowledge of the sea'.[7] Certainly, illegal fishing has occurred and represents a vast potential loss of value and earnings to Somalia.[8] However, fishing has never been a large part of the Somali economy,[9] and the most demonstrable economic damage to local communities dependent on fishing resulted from the destruction caused by the 2004 tsunami.[10] Maritime toxic waste dumping is, as one would expect of such a crime, hard to prove. It certainly seems documented that various Somali warlords entered contracts with European companies to allow the latter to bury dangerous waste on land or coastal sites within Somalia.[11] UN missions in 1992, 1997, 1998 and 2004, however, found no evidence of the widely reported barrels of toxic waste allegedly dumped at sea and subsequently washed up along the Somali shore.[12] Indeed, the 2004 UN mission 'investigated three populated coastal locations' where 'toxic waste hazards' were allegedly freshly uncovered by the 2004 tsunami; no such waste was found.[13] Evidence of illegal oily waste discharge by passing vessels is, however, firmly established.[14] Ultimately, the truth or falsehood of these claims is irrelevant. 'Pirates are seen [by many Somalis] as genuine nationalists who fight the looting of national assets

---

[7]   *Ibid.*, 17–18.

[8]   'Report of the Secretary-General on the protection of Somali natural resources and waters', UN Doc. S/2011/661 (25 October 2011) ('UNSG Natural Resources Report'), paras 19–20.

[9]   The UN Food and Agriculture Organisation estimates that fishing represented, pre-war, no more than 2–3% of GDP: UN FAO, 'Country Profile: The Somali Republic' (2005) <http://www.fao.org/fi/oldsite/FCP/en/SOM/profile.htm> accessed 21 August 2012.

[10]   Gonzalo Tello, 'Fisheries Tsunami Emergency Programme: Somalia, End of Mission Report' (UNFAO, 2005) 10 <ftp://ftp.fao.org/FI/DOCUMENT/tsunamis_05/somalia/cons_miss_rep/Tello_oct_05.pdf> accessed 21 August 2012.

[11]   Debora MacKenzie, 'Toxic Waste Adds to Somalia's Woes' (19 September 1992) *New Scientist* 5; Tom Kington, 'From cocaine to plutonium: mafia clan accused of trafficking nuclear waste' (9 October 2007) *The Guardian* <http://www.guardian.co.uk/world/2007/oct/09/italy.nuclearpower> accessed 21 August 2012. Compare UNSG Natural Resources Report, *supra* note 8, paras 46–47 (dumping in Africa generally).

[12]   UNSG Natural Resources Report, *supra* note 8, paras 51–54.

[13]   See United Nations Environment Programme, *The State of the Environment in Somalia: A Desk Study* (2005) 33 <http://postconflict.unep.ch/publications/dmb_somalia.pdf> accessed 21 August 2012.

[14]   UNSG Natural Resources Report, *supra* note 8, paras 46–48.

and fine foreign vessels *recurrently* accused of depriving Somalis of their national wealth' (emphasis added).[15] This fits a (generally entirely justifiable) local narrative in which Somalis see Somalia as the victim of successive waves of foreign intervention and exploitation.[16]

That said, we can discern a number of shifts over time in Somali piracy. First, Somali piracy dating from 1991 through to the early-2000s saw few vessels captured and ransomed each year. These 'relatively rare incidences...were viewed somewhat sensationally' by the media, but were not seen as a major international problem.[17] This conclusion is supported by the fact that Somali piracy was not seriously raised in the International Maritime Organization (IMO) and UN Security Council until 2006–2007, and even then the international response only really commenced with the *Le Ponant* episode in April 2008 (discussed below).[18]

The boom in Somali hostage-taking piracy from approximately 2003–2004 onwards resulted from a combination of factors: the rise of an efficient business model; a collapse in government and policing in Puntland, the region of Somalia where most piracy is based; and a shift towards the use of mother ships. One must also bear in mind the strategic geographic position of Somalia in relation to some of the world's busiest shipping routes and the significant financial incentives for front-line or foot-soldier pirates. Getting anything done in Somalia usually requires, in the absence of effective centralized authority, the support of clans.[19] Hansen identifies as an important factor in the piracy boom the emergence of a new piracy cartel in the Hobyo-Harardhere area. The Hobyo-Harardhere cartel was established by Mohamed Abdi Hassan 'Afweyne' who was able to assemble an efficient, profit-oriented piracy

---

[15]   Marchal, *supra* note 5, 38.

[16]   Hansen, *supra* note 3, 11–12. Hansen also notes frequent clashes between Somalis over rights to use certain local fishing grounds. Cf. Marchal, *supra* note 5, 39–40; House of Commons Foreign Affairs Committee, 'Piracy off the coast of Somalia', HC 1318 (5 January 2012) ('House of Commons Report'), Evidence Annexe, Ev 30 <http://www.parliament.uk/business/committees/committees-a-z/commons-select/foreign-affairs-committee/publications/> accessed 27 February 2012.

[17]   UN Expert Report, *supra* note 2, 18.

[18]   See generally: A. Panossian, 'L'Affaire du Ponant et le renouveau de la lute internationale contre la piraterie' (2008) 112 *Revue Générale de Droit International Public* 660–667; Douglas Guilfoyle, 'Counter-Piracy Law Enforcement and Human Rights' (2010) 59 *International and Comparative Law Quarterly* 141, 145–146.

[19]   Hansen, *supra* note 3, 26.

enterprise and who 'managed to transcend [ordinary] clan [allegiances], by actively recruiting the best pirates for his group'.[20] That said, the cartel still relied very much on the labour of Afweyne's Suleiman clan and the training and leadership provided by more experienced pirates of the Majerteen clan (though skilled individuals from other clans were involved).[21] The impact of this 'entrepreneurial' approach to piracy is returned to below. Another enabling condition for piracy was provided by the financial collapse of the regional government of Puntland, which stopped paying its police in April 2008.[22] The Puntland government had always had only a relatively weak capacity to repress piracy; now it effectively had none. Finally, the most successful adaptation of Somali piracy has been in the use of mother ships, a practice which has evolved over time. At least as late as May 2007, it was thought that any vessel sailing 200 nm or more from Somalia would be safe from attack.[23] Somali pirates, however, were able to extend their range considerably through first using skiffs to hijack local (often Yemeni) fishing dhows and then using these larger dhows to tow the skiffs much further out to sea in order to attack merchant shipping. Mother ships, often indistinguishable from genuine fishing vessels and often with hostages still aboard, were in use in this basic manner no later than 2007.[24]

At the time of writing, Somali piracy has increased its range still further. The basic tactic remains the same: hijack fishing vessels and redeploy these as 'mother ships, in order to capture larger merchant vessels'.[25] However, now these larger merchant vessels may, in turn, not only be held for ransom but also used as mother ships themselves. This provides pirates with not only the ability to attack multiple further merchant vessels but also new supplies and increased range and endurance (especially in terms of staying at sea in poor weather). This new ability to ride out bad weather and await days with a calmer sea state, means that pirates can now operate in the monsoon season, a time of year which has previously seen a decline in attacks.[26] This shift in tactics also means that pirates can now 'almost always deploy[] with hostages on

---

[20] *Ibid.*, 23–24. On clan structure, see *Ibid.*, 25.

[21] *Ibid.*, 25.

[22] *Ibid.*, 32–33.

[23] See: 'Call to arms to tackle Somalia piracy threat; International shipping community must act to end violent attacks' (16 January 2008) *Lloyd's List* 15.

[24] UN Expert Report, *supra* note 2, 19.

[25] Michiel Hijmans, 'Threats of the Sea' (2011) 67(11) *The World Today* 22, 22.

[26] *Ibid.*, 22.

board', making military intervention difficult.[27] Pirates have thus progressively refined and developed the use of mother ships to expand their capabilities significantly. Pirate attacks now range as far as 1800 nm out from the Somali coast.[28] This so-called 'balloon effect' is in large part a consequence of naval success in securing the Internationally Recommended Transit Corridor (IRTC), discussed below.

The range of pirates is yet further increased by the psychology of the front-line pirates themselves. For example, if one had a vessel capable of holding supplies for 30 days then:

> A prudent mariner would steam for nine days and have 10 days loiter time, at which point [as a pirate] he would hope to get lucky and catch a ship; he would give himself one day's fudge factor and 10 days to get back. Somalis do not do that: they steam for 30 days until they run out of everything, at which point, in desperation...they will go for anything.[29]

An enabling condition for these tactics is the culture of physical bravery among young Somali men. Having grown up in a strife-torn country the calculus of risks involved to them must look very different than it might to those of us sitting in the West. The share of the profits made by front-line pirates is not large,[30] but it represents enormous wealth compared to the other available opportunities. Somali pirates may thus be understood as 'irrational rational actors'. They are willing to take extraordinary risks, but once that willingness is taken into account their tactics represent an entirely sensible business strategy.

At the same time, the violence of pirate attacks on merchant vessels and their violence in the treatment of hostages increased noticeably over 2011.[31] The former may be partially attributed to ship-board defences: even the adoption of passive or non-lethal defences by merchant shipping may prompt pirates to use greater violence in an effort to force a vessel

---

[27]   *Ibid.*, 23.

[28]   *Ibid.*, 22.

[29]   See: House of Commons Report, *supra* note 16, Evidence Annexe, Ev 16–17, Question 94 (evidence of Major General Buster Howes).

[30]   Gettleman suggests that in one case involving a record US $10 million ransom payment, the front-line Somali 'gunmen' involved received a $150,000 share but after advances and expenses were deducted by pirate bosses earned only $20,000: Jeffrey Gettleman, 'Money in Piracy Attracts More Somalis' (9 November 2010) *New York Times* A10 <http://www.nytimes.com/2010/11/10/world/africa/10somalia.html?ref=piracyatsea> accessed 21 August 2012.

[31]   E.g., Will Ross, 'US deaths show growing pirate violence in hijackings' (*BBC News*, 23 February 2011) <http://www.bbc.co.uk/news/world-us-canada-12548045> accessed 21 August 2012.

to stop and allow boarding. Theories as to the cause of increased violence (there are even allegations of torture)[32] against captured hostages vary. Some consider it an effort to increase pressure in ransom negotiations; others suggest the 'outsourcing' by pirates of the physical care and custody of hostages to other gangs may result in their immediate captors having less concern for their welfare and more for keeping costs down.[33] Still others suggest a greater percentage of pirates are coming from having spent time fighting in Somalia and so are more accustomed to using violence.[34]

Despite its success to date, a new difficulty for the pirate business model may be emerging. It may be that piracy has become geared around expectations of a level of return the insurance market will no longer bear in practice. For example, if pirates assume on capturing a merchant vessel they face a ransom negotiation period of no more than 90 to 120 days, and a ransom payment of at least US $3 to 4 million, they will make arrangements accordingly.[35] This will inform how much is promised to investors, how many guards they are willing to hire to watch over hostages, and how much credit they are willing to take from local businesses (who effectively underwrite the costs of feeding hostages and guards). During the ransom negotiation the pirate business effectively runs on credit. If, however, the pirates are forced to settle for less than anticipated they may actually run into trouble meeting their commitments to investors or creditors. Indeed, pirates may themselves default on creditors in order to maintain a profit.[36] Why have pirates in some cases been forced to settle for radically lower sums? Arguably, as more vessels transiting the Gulf of Aden adopt recommended safety measures (see the discussion of Best Management Practices, below) and/or armed guards the result is that those vessels taking least precaution for their own safety are more likely to be taken by pirates. In turn, these 'low-cost' shipping operators who could not or would not bear the costs of implementing better security are also those least likely to have extensive insurance. Increasingly, perhaps, the vessels that make easiest prey for pirates are

---

[32] The term must be understood colloquially. Other than in the context of a war crime or crime against humanity torture as a legal term requires the involvement or acquiescence of a government agent.

[33] On outsourcing, see Hansen, *supra* note 3, 36.

[34] Ross, *supra* note 31.

[35] Robert Young Pelton, 'Pirates Fight over MV Blida Ransom' (*Somalia Report*, 7 November 2011) <http://www.somaliareport.com/index.php/post/1973/Pirates_Fight_Over_MV_Blida_Ransom> accessed 21 August 2012.

[36] *Ibid.*

those least likely to be profitable. This, however, remains speculation. To date, piracy has proved sufficiently lucrative to sustain a variety of business models.

There is no single universal structure or even single type of organization behind the present Somali piracy industry. Notably, '[t]he 2008 boom led to the fragmentation of piracy, and groups became smaller and more varied', although these seem typically recruited based on pre-existing 'family or village ties'.[37] Hansen outlines three basic models:

- 'the first one involves a responsible group structure within which an investor functions as leader, carrying all costs, but also taking most of the ransom';
- '[t]he second ... has a shareholder structure in which the pirates themselves invest to meet the current running expenses of the group'; and
- the third 'has a shareholder structure in which a leader gathers shares from local investors and hires a crew (often on commission)', commission in this context meaning 'no prey, no pay'.[38]

The latter model most notoriously resulted in the 'pirate stock exchange' of Haradheere.[39] Under this model, ordinary Somalis could make modest contributions of money or weapons to a particular pirate mission and would take a share in the ransom paid in the event of a successful hijacking. Despite this evident decentralization, there are still suggestions that a significant part of Somali piracy is ultimately controlled by a 'relatively small number' of bosses and financiers, whose, 'identities ..., locations [often within Somalia] and political connections are widely known'.[40] Thus:

> Naval forces estimate that there are about 50 main pirate leaders, around 300 leaders of pirate attack groups, and around 2,500 'foot soldiers'. It is believed that financing is provided by around 10 to 20 individuals. In addition, there is

---

[37]   Hansen, *supra* note 3, 34.

[38]   *Ibid.*, 35–36.

[39]   Mohammed Ahmed, 'Somali sea gangs lure investors at pirate lair' (*Reuters*, 1 December 2009) <http://www.reuters.com/article/2009/12/01/us-somalia-piracy-investors-idUSTRE5B01Z920091201> accessed 21 August 2012.

[40]   'Report of the Secretary-General on the Modalities for the Establishment of Specialized Somali Anti-piracy Courts', UN Doc S/2011/360 (21 June 2011) ('Modalities Report'), para. 64.

a large number of armed individuals guarding captured ships, and numerous [English-speaking] ransom negotiators.[41]

On any approach the basic Somali piracy business model has a number of enabling factors and constraints which are indigenous to Somalia. The role of an ample supply of potential recruits and a culture of physical bravery has already been noted. Most importantly, the Somali business model requires a kind of highly ordered lawlessness: the absence of effective central government repression is needed to undertake piracy, but a degree of relative stability is needed for it to be profitable.[42] That is, functioning markets are required to finance missions and supply hostages/pirates, and an effective informal banking sector is needed to deal with the large quantities of physical cash generated by ransoms. In this sense, the combination of clan networks and weak government in Puntland appear to provide the requisite degree of stability in the absence of effective policing.[43] In this context, the start-up costs to forming a 'pirate action group' are relatively low, though not negligible:

> a 15-foot pirate skiff costs between USD 1000 and 2000 and supplies have to be bought. Skiffs are seldom rented, many attacks involve more than two boats and the investor has to provide food and supplies for the expedition, perhaps some USD 100 a day for a sizable group.[44]

The risks, however, are higher than many realise. Physically, it seems likely that more pirates are lost at sea than killed in naval encounters.[45] Financially, returns are generally either nil or very high. If a pirate action group comes back empty-handed, or not at all, the investment is lost. A

---

[41]   *Ibid.*, Annexe I, para. 3. Estimates vary as to the number of translators/negotiators.

[42]   See, in particular: S. Percy and A. Shortland, 'The Business of Piracy in Somalia' (Deutches Institut für Wirtschaftsforschung (DIW), Discussion Paper 1033, Berlin, 2011), especially at 13–14 <http://www.diw.de/documents/publikationen/73/diw_01.c.358500.de/dp1033.pdf> accessed 8 August 2012.

[43]   There is a risk, however, of local economies becoming dependent upon pirate activity: 'Report of the Special Adviser to the Secretary-General on Legal Issues Related to Piracy off the Coast of Somalia', UN Doc. S/2011/30 (25 January 2011) ('Lang Report'), para. 16.

[44]   Hansen, *supra* note 3, 14.

[45]   On some estimates up to 30% of Somali pirates are lost at sea: Joseph Goldstein, 'F.B.I.'s Man on the Pirate Beat, Seeking Confessions' (21 August 2011) *New York Times* A16 <http://www.nytimes.com/2011/08/22/nyregion/fbis-man-on-the-pirate-beat-seeking-confessions.html?pagewanted=all> accessed 21 August 2012.

further enabling condition in Somalia is obviously the extraordinary length of its coastline, 3,300 kilometres,[46] facing onto a vital and busy route for world shipping. However, the collapse of the central government and general economy places a constraint on Somali piracy. Somali pirates can only ransom crews and cannot evolve to the early 2000s Southeast Asian model of piracy where crews might be set adrift so the vessel and its cargo could be sold,[47] due to the lack of functional ports in Somalia.

Overall, one major theme is discernible in the evolution of Somali piracy. A key driver of change has been improvements in security.[48] Indeed, the expansion of the area of pirate operations and the escalation in pirate violence off Somalia may be seen as perverse consequences of efforts to suppress or mitigate piracy. These efforts are discussed further below, but in essence improved security in the Gulf of Aden provided by naval forces has displaced piracy elsewhere in the Indian Ocean, while improved ship-board security (brought about largely by industry self-regulation) may have contributed to an escalation in pirate violence. The important point to capture is that Somali piracy is not a static model, but a moving target.

The threat to the shipping community remains low, however, in terms of absolute risk. Only about 1.5 ships in every thousand transits are hijacked;[49] further while the absolute number of Somali pirate attacks on vessels increased through most of 2011 (other than a sharp drop at year's end), the success rate of such attacks has been falling. In the first nine months of 2011 attempted hijackings were successful in 12 per cent of cases, down from 28 per cent the previous year.[50] This may, of course, simply encourage pirate gangs to make more attacks in an effort to secure

---

[46] Lang Report, *supra* note 43, para 40.

[47] Douglas Guilfoyle, *Shipping Interdiction and the Law of the Sea* (CUP, 2009), 52–53; P. Mukundan, 'Piracy and Armed Robbery against Ships Today' (2004) 10 *Journal of International Maritime Law* 305–315.

[48] N. Hopkins and C. Chonghaile, 'Somali pirates take more risks and rethink tactics' (21 February 2012) *The Guardian* <http://www.guardian.co.uk/world/2012/feb/21/somali-pirates-rethink-tactics> accessed 21 August 2012.

[49] Hijmans, *supra* note 25, 24.

[50] 'As world piracy hits a new high, more ships are escaping Somali pirates, says IMB report' (18 October 2011) *ICC Commercial Crime Services* <http://www.icc-ccs.org/news/710-as-world-piracy-hits-a-new-high-more-ships-are-escaping-somali-pirates-says-imb-report> accessed 21 August 2012.

a profitable vessel, but the operating costs of such a strategy (food, fuel, etc.) may drive smaller pirate operations out of business.[51]

3.3 INTERNATIONAL COUNTER-PIRACY IN THE GULF OF ADEN: THE SHIFT FROM MILITARY OPERATIONS TO TRANSNATIONAL COOPERATION

3.3.1 Introduction

Until late 2007, Somali piracy drew relatively little international concern. In 2007–2008, however, the *Le Ponant* episode prompted both a French military intervention in Somalia and soon after a – in some ways quite traditional – Security Council resolution authorizing the use of force. A wide range of naval deployments off Somalia followed.

A striking feature of subsequent developments has been the rapidity of change. Very quickly the limitations of a military strategy to contain or deter piracy became apparent and a shift from a 'military' to 'law enforcement' paradigm followed. Even more noteworthy is the range of cooperative mechanisms that followed, almost all of which have been informal, decentralized and located outside the major international institutions such as the IMO and the UN. The change has not exclusively occurred in the public realm, the shipping industry has also been a notable contributor to the growth of relevant soft law.

3.3.2 Early Concerns

IMO statistics show a leap in attempted and successful high-seas pirate attacks off East Africa after 2004. Taking the figures for attempted and successful attacks together shows that: in 2004 the East African region accounted for nine out of 97 reported incidents worldwide of violence, robbery or hijack against ships on the high seas; in 2005 the figure was 26 out of 65 incidents; in 2006, 18 out of 60 incidents; and, in 2007, East Africa accounted for 33 out of 88 incidents.[52] The real figures may well

---

[51] Young Pelton, *supra* note 35.

[52] Guilfoyle, *supra* note 47, 49–50. See also the IMO Annual Reports on Acts of Piracy and Armed Robbery against Ships (MSC.4 report series) <http://www.imo.org> accessed 13 September 2012.

be higher, given the historic under-reporting of attempted piracy.[53] In December 2007, the IMO requested that the Transitional Federal Government of Somalia (TFG) and the Security Council take urgent action regarding piracy.[54] The TFG gave consent to such measures on 27 February 2008. The only action taken to that date by the Security Council had been in protection of World Food Programme convoys.[55] The spur to wider action came when in April 2008 crew and passengers aboard the French yacht *Le Ponant*, including 22 French nationals, were taken hostage by pirates in international waters off Somalia.[56] The hostages were released within a week, following payment of a ransom; however, French commandoes (with TFG permission) captured the pirates on their return to shore and the pirates were taken to Paris for trial.[57] The same month France co-sponsored what became Security Council resolution 1816.[58]

3.3.3   The First 'Use of Force' UN Security Council Resolutions and 'Deter and Disrupt Patrols': June 2008

Resolution 1816, the first of the major counter-piracy resolutions, was a classic UN authorization of the use of force: it authorized entry into Somalia's territorial waters (by states cooperating with the TFG) and the use there of all 'necessary means to repress acts of piracy and armed robbery' (paragraph 7); while on the high seas it urged states 'to be vigilant to acts of piracy' and to 'render assistance to vessels threatened by or under attack by pirates or armed robbers, in accordance with relevant international law' (paragraphs 2 and 3). While certainly contemplating state cooperation in 'the investigation and prosecution of persons responsible for acts of piracy and armed robbery off the coast of Somalia' (in paragraph 11), it is fair to say that resolution 1816 was more

---

[53]   Guilfoyle, *supra* note 47, 46 and 51.
[54]   IMO Doc. A 25/Res 1002 (6 December 2007) para. 6.
[55]   See: UNSC Res. 1772 (20 August 2007), UN Doc. S/RES/1772, para. 18; and later UNSC Res 1801 (20 February 2008), UN Doc. S/RES/1801, para. 12. Cf. UNSC Res. 1814 (15 May 2008), UN Doc. S/RES/1814, para. 11.
[56]   Panossian, *supra* note 18.
[57]   *Ibid.*
[58]   'UN urged to tackle Somali pirates' (*BBC News*, 28 April 2008) <http://news.bbc.co.uk/go/pr/fr/-/1/hi/world/europe/7372390.stm> accessed 21 August 2012; UNSC Res. 1816 (2 June 2008), UN Doc. S/RES/1816.

a general mandate to conduct 'deter and disrupt' patrols[59] than a clarion call for pirate prosecutions. Though it clearly did not invoke the laws of war, resolution 1816 was phrased more in terms of UN-authorized military intervention within a state's territorial jurisdiction (here, the territorial sea) rather than law enforcement cooperation. It was also presented on its face as being a measure which was exceptional, temporary and (to some states) worrying. This is most clearly expressed in paragraph 9, the rather dramatic savings clause in which the Security Council:

Affirms that the authorization provided in this resolution applies only with respect to the situation in Somalia and shall not affect the rights or obligations or responsibilities of member states under international law, including any rights or obligations under [UNCLOS], with respect to any other situation, and underscores in particular that it shall not be considered as establishing customary international law, and affirms further that this authorization has been provided only following receipt of ... the consent of the TFG.

The point was thus clearly made that piracy was not itself a threat to international peace and security warranting Security Council action; rather Somali piracy was presented as an extension of the situation in Somalia itself.[60] States like Indonesia (which has long suffered piracy problems of its own) clearly had a number of concerns about the potential impact of the resolution including: its potential to serve as a precedent justifying similar action in other regions in the future; its potential to destabilize the balance of rights and interests underlying the UNCLOS regime; and (somewhat bizarrely) a fear that it had the potential to create customary international law.[61] Perhaps in response to such concerns, the measures adopted in resolution 1816 involved both TFG consent and were initially authorized only for a period of six months (paragraph 7). Nothing, of course, is as permanent as a temporary

---

[59]   On 'deter and disrupt' or 'catch and release' as a counter-piracy tactic see: Chapter 7.4.1; and Guilfoyle, *supra* note 18, 141.

[60]   United Nations Department of Public Information, 'Security Council Condemns Acts of Piracy, Armed Robbery Off Somalia's Coast', Press Release (2 June 2008), comments of South Africa <http://www.un.org/News/Press/docs/2008/sc9344.doc.htm> accessed 21 August 2012.

[61]   *Ibid.*, comments of Indonesia.

solution, and this temporary measure has been renewed for a series of 12-month spans without being allowed to lapse ever since.[62]

Nonetheless, the resolution was clearly part of the spur to a variety of counter-piracy missions, in particular the Combined Task Force 151 (CTF-151), NATO and European Union Naval Force (EU NAVFOR) operations. CTF-151 is an offshoot of military operations in Afghanistan, as part of which 'US Naval Forces Central Command (NAVCENT) commands ... [a group of] Combined Maritime Forces ... operating in the ... [region]'.[63] In January 2009, the Combined Maritime Forces (CMF) command 'established Combined Task Force 151 (CTF-151), with the sole mission of conducting anti-piracy operations in the Gulf of Aden and the waters off the Somali coast in the Indian Ocean ... The list of countries participating in CTF-151 [at any time] is fluid and consists of personnel and approximately two dozen ships from 25 countries.'[64] This had been preceded in the period August 2008 to January 2009 by a different CMF taskforce (CTF-150), which had had a maritime opera- tions mandate including, but not limited to, counter-piracy. NATO has also conducted a series of counter-piracy missions in the region, giving it a more-or-less continuous presence in the Gulf of Aden since October 2008.[65] The present and longest-running operation, Operation Ocean Shield, commenced in August 2009 and involved five vessels as at April 2011.[66] The EU NAVFOR mission, Operation Atalanta, was established last, in December 2008. One should note that the EU NAVFOR is not a permanent body and has no wider mission than Operation Atalanta.[67] While '[m]ore than twenty vessels and aircraft take part in Atalanta'[68] the actual number of assets deployed at any one time may be closer to eight to ten.[69] Numerous individual states, most notably Russia, India, China

---

[62]   See: UNSC Res. 1846 (2 December 2008), UN Doc. S/RES/1846, para. 10; UNSC Res 1897 (30 November 2009), UN Doc. S/RES/1897, para. 7; UNSC Res. 2020 (22 November 2011), UN Doc. S/RES/2020, para. 9.

[63]   CRS Report, *supra* note 2, 25.

[64]   *Ibid.*

[65]   *Ibid.*, 15 on Operations Allied Provider (October–December 2008) and Allied Protector (March and June 2009).

[66]   *Ibid.*, 26–27.

[67]   F. Naert, *International Law Aspects of the EU's Security and Defence Policy* (Intersentia, 2009), chapter 3.

[68]   The House of Lords European Union Committee, 'Combating Somali Piracy: the EU's Naval Operation Atalanta', 6 April 2010 ('House of Lords Report') 7 http://www.publications.parliament.uk/pa/ld200910/ldselect/ldeucom/ 103/103.pdf> accessed 21 August 2012.

[69]   House of Commons Report, *supra* note 16, Evidence Annexe, Ev 13.

and South Korea, have also deployed independent naval missions to conduct counter-piracy missions off the coast of Somalia. These missions are further discussed in Chapter 5.

3.3.4   Cooperative Mechanisms and Their Evolution

This proliferation of missions required some efforts at coordination. As I have noted elsewhere:

> [I]n August 2008 ... [the US-led CMF] established 'a maritime security patrol area [MPSA] in international waters off the Somali coast'. The MPSA is a defined area within the Gulf of Aden, providing a common system of reference which allows naval forces in the Gulf to 'de-conflict' their activities. Running through the MPSA is an internationally [recommended] transit corridor (the 'IRTC'), [also] established in August 2008 by the United Kingdom Maritime Trade Organization. As of 1 February 2009, information for mariners using the IRTC is available through a secure website adminis- tered by the Maritime Security Centre (Horn of Africa), itself part of the EU counter-piracy mission Operation Atalanta.[70]

Deconfliction is the military term for a process aiming at creating mutual awareness among the various missions of each other's activities with the aim of avoiding duplication of effort; it is a term deliberately used to avoid any suggestion that there is some unitary command or central authoritative coordinator. It has since been given a more substantive dimension in the Shared Awareness and Deconfliction meetings discussed below. These early efforts have been highly successful. Ships that register with the Maritime Security Centre (Horn of Africa) (MSC-HOA)[71] and which use the IRTC are made much easier to protect. This is in part because the IRTC is 'picketed' with vessels such that any vessel attacked should be capable of being reached within half an hour.[72] Perhaps more effective is the potential to direct vessels registered with MSC-HOA to adjust speed and heading such that they may transit in groups. The group transit system is based on the observation that pirate attacks at night are rare and have a zero success rate.[73] Vessels are thus grouped to transit the

---

[70]   Guilfoyle, *supra* note 18, 151.

[71]   Similar registration/information services are provided by the UK Mari- time Trade Organization and the US Navy's Maritime Liaison Office, irrespective of a vessel's nationality.

[72]   House of Commons Report, *supra* note 16, Evidence Annexe, Ev 14–15.

[73]   See, e.g., EU NAVFOR, 'Gulf of Aden Internationally Recommended Transit Corridor and Group Transit Explanation' (March 2009) <http://www.

most vulnerable areas at night and to depart at dusk from and arrive at dawn in areas with a military presence. The net result is that there have been no merchant vessels captured in the IRTC since September 2010.[74]

Overall, the flavour of early efforts in counter-piracy off Somalia to late 2008 was that of a military response. While there was no suggestion that pirates were combatants, little thought or priority was given to the idea that navies would actively seek to arrest pirates for trial. Indeed, in some cases even thinking about the possibility at the level of national governments seems to have prompted a sense that the issues involved were too complicated, or cut across too many national agencies, or would raise awkward questions about the applicable legal regime aboard warships (e.g., the extent of extra-territorial human rights obligations and how to implement them).[75] Events, however, soon proved the problem could not be contained within an exclusively military mandate.

3.3.5   The Shift Towards Law Enforcement

One well-reported example, discussed further in Chapter 7, occurred on 11 November 2008, when boarding craft from the HMS *Cumberland* subdued a suspect pirate vessel. On-board Royal Marines discovered Yemeni fisherman being held by Somali pirates: the mother ship they had boarded was a hijacked vessel with its crew held hostage aboard. If the fishermen were set free with their craft, then something would have to be done with the pirates. The answer initially hit upon was transfer to regional states for trial, Kenya in particular. This was not without precedent. In 2006 a group of ten pirates intercepted by the USS *Churchill* had been transferred to Kenya for trial.[76]

By the end of 2008 a shift towards a law enforcement paradigm was underway. The shift was most decisively apparent in UN Security Council resolution (UNSCR) 1851 of 16 December 2008, in which the

---

intertanko.com/upload/IRTC%20%20GT%20Explanation%20-%20March%2020 09%20(2).pdf> accessed 21 August 2012.

[74]   House of Commons Report, *supra* note 16, Evidence Annexe, Ev 14–15, Question 87 and n. 1 (evidence of Major General Buster Howes).

[75]   See, e.g., 'World Scrambles to Deal with Pirate Threat' (*Spiegel Online*, 24 November 2008) <http://www.spiegel.de/international/world/0,1518,592433, 00.html> accessed 21 August 2012. Compare Westcott, 'Pirates in the Dock' (*BBC News*, 21 May 2009) <http://news.bbc.co.uk/1/hi/world/africa/8059345. stm> accessed 21 August 2012.

[76]   James Kraska, *Contemporary Maritime Piracy: International Law, Strategy, and Diplomacy at Sea* (Prager, 2011) 179.

emphasis on investigation and prosecution and the strengthening of criminal justice mechanisms is readily apparent. The resolution:

- called on all states with the capacity to do so to cooperate in combating Somali piracy through 'deploying naval vessels and military aircraft';
- granted a power of summary 'seizure and disposition of boats, vessels, arms and other related equipment used in the commission of piracy and armed robbery at sea off the coast of Somalia, or for which there are reasonable grounds for suspecting such use';
- invited 'all States and regional organizations fighting piracy off the coast of Somalia to conclude special agreements or arrangements with countries willing to take custody of pirates in order to embark law enforcement officials ("shipriders") from the latter countries, in particular countries in the region, to facilitate the investigation and prosecution of persons detained as a result of operations conducted under this resolution';
- encouraged 'all states and regional organizations fighting piracy ... off the coast of Somalia ... to [act to] increase regional capacity ... to effectively investigate and prosecute piracy and armed robbery at sea offences' with the assistance of the United Nations Office for Drugs and Crime (UNODC); and
- encouraged 'all States and regional organizations fighting piracy and armed robbery at sea off the coast of Somalia to establish an international cooperation mechanism to act as a common point of contact between and among states, regional and international organizations on all aspects of combating [Somali] piracy'.[77]

Each of these points is worth further consideration. As to the first point, as noted above, a significant expansion in navy deployments was already underway by this time. The grant of a power of summary disposal of suspected pirate equipment plugged a possible gap in the UNCLOS regime (which refers only to the power of *courts* to dispose of property in piracy cases).[78] The use of ship-riders is a potentially useful idea, but one which has not been implemented to date.[79] (The principal difficulties

---

[77] UNSC Res. 1851 (16 December 2008), UN Doc. S/RES/1851, paras 2–5.
[78] United Nations Convention on the Law of the Sea (adopted 10 December 1982, entered into force 16 November 1994) 1833 UNTS 397 (UNCLOS), Art. 105; see further Chapter 8.7.
[79] See further: Chapters 6.9 and 8.8.3; Douglas Guilfoyle, 'Combating Piracy: Executive Measures on High Seas' (2010) 53 *Japanese Yearbook of*

being whether the regional partner states are willing, have legislation allowing their police to operate outside their territory and have the personnel to spare.) Regional capacity building has occurred in a number of ways. In a relatively early development a number of regional coastal states, in an IMO-sponsored process, began negotiating a memorandum of understanding (MOU) on counter-piracy resulting in a draft MOU in April 2008.[80] This was then adopted as the so-called Djibouti Code of Conduct in January 2009.[81] The Djibouti Code aims at promoting cooperation, information sharing and capacity development to better allow regional states to combat piracy themselves. Its achievements to date have included support for reform of national piracy laws.[82] Djibouti Code information sharing centres in Tanzania, Kenya and Yemen became active in 2011[83] and an agreement on their use was concluded in November 2011.[84] This is a potentially significant step towards institutional arrangements along the lines of the Regional Cooperation Agreement on Combating Piracy and Armed Robbery against Ships in Asia 2004 (ReCAAP) (as discussed in Chapter 2). More significantly, perhaps, the UNODC has proven highly effective in criminal justice capacity building in the region. It has provided translators, judicial and prosecutorial training, refurbished prisons and court-houses, assisted with legislative reform and drafting prisoner transfers and evidence collection guidance, as well as undertaking various projects within Somalia itself.[85]

International Law 149–177, 170–172. On ship-riders more generally, see Guilfoyle, *supra* note 47, 72–73, 89–94, 119–120, 196–197, 209–211.

[80]   Douglas Guilfoyle, 'Piracy Off Somalia: UN Security Council Resolution 1816 and IMO Regional Counter-Piracy Efforts' (2008) 57 *International and Comparative Law Quarterly* 690–699, 697–699.

[81]   Code of Conduct concerning the Repression of Piracy and Armed Robbery against Ships in the western Indian Ocean and the Gulf of Aden (9 January 2009) <http://www.fco.gov.uk/en/global-issues/piracy/> accessed 21 August 2012.

[82]   J. Ashley Roach, 'Countering Piracy off Somalia: International Law and International Institutions' (2011) 104 *American Journal of International Law* 397, 410–411; CRS Report, *supra* note 2, 23–24.

[83]   International Maritime Organization, 'Status of the Implementation of the Djibouti Code of Conduct' (December 2011) 2 <http://www.imo.org/OurWork/Security/PIU/Documents/Update_paper_Dec_11.pdf> accessed 21 August 2012.

[84]   International Maritime Organization, 'Piracy centres expand information network' (IMO Media Briefing, 11 November 2011) 56 <http://www.imo.org/MediaCentre/PressBriefings/Pages/56-piracy-ISCS.aspx> accessed 21 August 2012.

[85]   Alan Cole, 'Prosecuting Piracy: Challenges for the Police and the Courts' in *Global Challenge, Regional Responses: Forging a Common Approach to*

The final measure highlighted above is the call to establish an 'international cooperation mechanism'. This took the form of the Contact Group on Piracy off the Coast of Somalia (CGPCS), discussed below.

3.3.6   Cooperative Mechanisms: A Second Phase

Two cooperative mechanisms in particular are worth brief discussion here: the CGPCS set up in response to UNSCR 1851 and the Shared Awareness and Deconfliction (SHADE) process established around the various Gulf of Aden counter-piracy missions. It is convenient to begin with SHADE. At its simplest, SHADE is a series of meetings held in Bahrain since December 2008:[86]

> It is a staff-level group of officers who meet regularly (approximately once every six weeks) to ensure that the naval forces conducting counterpiracy operations are effectively coordinating their efforts ... At these meetings tactical and operational coordination is discussed and agreements are made for a certain period of time with regard to the division of tasks, optimizing the use of available assets and coordination of the geographic presence.[87]

It is not an organization *per se* and has no formal decision-making authority; nonetheless it has been highly effective. The plethora of multinational and national missions involved in counter-piracy may appear inefficient absent some unified command structure. Nonetheless, the SHADE process has allowed 'the forces engaged in the counter-piracy effort ... [to] work and co-operate very closely' on a pragmatic, 'tactical, day-by-day level'.[88] Industry representatives also attend SHADE

Maritime Piracy – Selected Briefing Papers (Dubai: Dubai School of Government, 2011) 107–110 <http://counterpiracy.ae/briefing_papers/Forging%20a%20Common%20Approach%20to%20Maritime%20Piracy.pdf> accessed 21 August 2012. See also <http://www.unodc.org/piracy> accessed 21 August 2012.

[86]   Robin Geiß and Anna Petrig, *Piracy and Armed Robbery at Sea: The Legal Framework for Counter-Piracy Operations in Somalia and the Gulf of Aden* (OUP, 2011) 27–28. See further Chapter 5.3.3.

[87]   Kees Homan and Susanne Kamerling, 'Operational Challenges to Counterpiracy Operations off the Coast of Somalia', in B. van Ginkel and F. van der Putten (eds), *The International Response to Somali Piracy: Challenges and Opportunities* (Martinus Nijhoff, 2010) 85.

[88]   House of Commons Report, *supra* note 16, Evidence Annexe, Ev 13, Question 79 (evidence of Major General Buster Howes).

meetings and it has been credited with improving communications between industry and the military.[89]

The CGPCS was established on 14 January 2009. The need for some new forum to coordinate counter-piracy outside UN or IMO auspices may not be readily apparent. However, all existing organizations had, in effect, over- or under-inclusive mandates or expertise in only pieces of the problem. The IMO, for example, has a great deal of relevant expertise as regards the commercial shipping industry but no experience of military deployments. Thus the CGPCS is:

> not a UN or an IMO body. It is voluntary cooperation among states and organizations engaged in or with an interest in countering piracy off the coast of Somalia. The participants thus share a clear common goal and the work of the CGPCS has therefore been characterized with much specific and practical progress in a very short period of time. At its first meeting the CGPCS established four working groups on[:] operational matters and capacity building (WG1 – chaired by the United Kingdom), legal issues (WG2 – chaired by Denmark), cooperation with industry (WG3 – chaired by the USA) and communication (WG4 – chaired by Egypt).[90]

A fifth working group has since been established to examine financial flows. The working groups meet several times a year and consist of participants representing governments, international organizations and industry groups. Like SHADE, they serve principally as a forum for sharing information and experience and, to a certain extent, for coordinating efforts. That said, like SHADE they also lack formal decision-making authority. Their secretariat is provided by the government chairing the group and the make-up of the meetings can change significantly over time. SHADE and the CGPCS working groups are more a cooperative forum than a standard-setting body.

Nonetheless, both are clearly 'institutions' in the broader sense of looking beyond formal organizations to other '"rules, norms, and decision-making procedures" that shape expectations, interests and behaviour'.[91] Both mechanisms therefore fall within Scott and Trubek's

---

[89]   Geiß and Petrig, *supra* note 86, 28; Homan and Kamerling, *supra* note 87, 85.

[90]   Thomas Winkler, 'Foreword', in van Ginkel and van der Putten, *supra* note 87, viii. (Ambassador Winkler is the Chairman of WG2.) See further Chapter 5.3.1.

[91]   M. Finnemore and S. J. Toope, 'Alternatives to "Legalization": Richer Views of Law and Politics', in B.A. Simmons and R.H. Steinberg (eds), *International Law and International Relations* (CUP, 2006) 188, 191.

concept of 'new governance' institutions which: 'accept[] the possibility of coordinated diversity' among legal systems; use 'machinery that brings together actors from various levels of government' and industry to generate 'open-ended standards, flexible and revisable guidelines, and other forms of soft law'; all of which may be 'designed more to support and coordinate' policy rather 'than to create uniformity'.[92] Essentially, new governance eschews top down 'command and control' regulation and favours instead experimentation and sharing of best practice, the informal alignment of expectations, and loose horizontal cooperation. Such transnational governance networks have certain advantages. They can act and adapt quickly and can be a valuable way of sharing experience and promoting open-ended deliberation regarding a common problem.[93] They may allow a range of possible solutions to be explored at the national level before identifying and disseminating best practice. They may even bring national authorities or capabilities together in a manner that delivers unexpected efficiencies. Some of these experiments are discussed below and elsewhere in this book. They have certainly helped focus available political will to explore the possible options, and assisted different states and agencies to coordinate their efforts. This has had successes in terms of facilitating efficient cooperation in piracy prosecutions (see Chapter 8), and some impact in terms of assisting judicial and prosecutorial capacity building in the region (as discussed above and further below). One of the most effective examples, however, of such cooperative action through a loose network of international actors is provided by the shipping industry and IMO collaboration on 'Best Management Practices' for securing individual vessels from pirate attack (discussed below).

3.3.7 The Industry Response to Somali Piracy: A Move to Self-protection

The initial position of much of the shipping industry to Somali piracy was that this was a governmental problem requiring a 'robust' military measures to suppress it.[94] Further, while trust funds have been established under the CGPCS and the Djibouti Code to support counter-piracy

---

[92] Joanne Scott and David M. Trubek, 'Mind the Gap: Law and New Approaches to Governance in the European Union' (2002) 8 *European Law Journal* 1, 6.

[93] *Ibid.*

[94] In the present author's opinion, 'robust' has become a code-phrase for those who would like to see an extreme degree of force used against pirates

projects, industry has been slow to contribute to them. The usual explanation is that one does not ordinarily expect victims of crime to bear the costs of policing when they are already taxpayers. There was even initial reluctance in some quarters to using the IRTC. While responsible elements of the industry now do use the IRTC, anything up to 25 per cent of vessel transits through the Gulf of Aden still do not.[95]

The shipping industry as a whole, however, appears to have rapidly accepted that the most effective way to secure vessels from pirate attack is to secure the vessels themselves. In collaboration with the IMO, a series of Best Management Practice (BMP) documents have been issued.[96] These specify the range of (largely passive or non-lethal) measures vessels should take to protect themselves from pirate attack if they are transiting the 'high risk area' off Somalia and compliance demonstrably improves an attacked vessel's chances of eluding capture.[97] Further, being BMP-compliant attracts lower insurance premiums,[98] effectively making it a kind of industry-policed soft law. Nonetheless, there are still reports of a significant fraction of vessels not complying with BMP – and, unsurprisingly, such vessels appear more likely to be taken by pirates (as discussed above).[99]

In this context, there has been significant discussion about whether individual vessels should have *armed* protection. The two basic possible models are, obviously, private or state-sponsored provision. The former is now commonly referred to as privately contracted armed security personnel (PCASP)[100] and the latter as Vessel Protection Detachments (VPDs). In 2009, some shipping industry figures described the attitude of their

---

summarily and with minimal warning, but who wish to avoid appearing to call for measures which would be unacceptable under the rule of law and human rights.

[95] House of Lords Report, *supra* note 68, Evidence Annexe 45, Q177 (testimony of Dr Lee Willett, Royal United Services Institute for Defence and Security Studies).

[96] At time of writing, the most current version was BMP4. See: <http://www.gard.no/webdocs/BMP4.pdf> accessed 13 September 2012.

[97] House of Commons Report, *supra* note 16, paras 23–24, 29.

[98] *Ibid.*, Evidence Annexe 3–4, Q11 and Q15 (testimony of Andrew Volke, Lloyd's Market Association).

[99] House of Commons Report, *supra* note 16, Evidence Annexe 15, Q90 (testimony of Major General Buster Howes) and Evidence Annexe 63 (written evidence of the Chamber of Shipping).

[100] See IMO Docs MSC.1/Circ.1405 and 1406 (23 May 2011).

sector as 'resolutely oppose[d]'[101] to the use of PCASP due to the risk of violence escalating and legal liability. As the IMO has put it:

> It should also be borne in mind that shooting at suspected pirates may impose a legal risk for the master, shipowner or company, such as collateral damages. In some jurisdictions, killing a national may have unforeseen consequences even for a person who believes he or she has acted in self defence. Also the differing customs or security requirements for the carriage and importation of firearms should be considered, as taking a small handgun into the territory of some countries may be considered an offence.[102]

The clear preference of industry was for VPDs, typically paid for by the flag state.[103] Other than questions of cost, VPDs also benefit from sovereign immunity. Sovereign immunity, it is presumed, would greatly simplify the potential legal situation arising in the event of fatal shootings of foreign nationals.[104] However, only a handful of governments have been willing to bear these costs.[105] There thus appears to have been a cautious shift in government, industry, military and IMO opinion in favour of ships being allowed to take greater 'responsibility for their own protection by hiring' PCASP.[106] In particular, those in industry who once opposed PCASP have now taken a lead in drafting contracts for their

---

[101] See, e.g., 'Statement on International Piracy by Giles Noakes Chief Maritime Security Officer of BIMCO before the United States House of Representatives Committee on Transportation and Infrastructure Subcommittee on Coast Guard and Maritime Transportation' (February 2009) <http://www.marad.dot.gov/documents/HOA_Testimony-Giles%20Noakes-BIMCO.pdf> accessed 21 August 2012.

[102] IMO Doc. MSC.1/Circ.1334 (23 June 2009), para. 61.

[103] House of Commons Report, *supra* note 16, para. 25 (noting France, Spain, Israel and Italy already provide VPDs and other States are contemplating it); see also Recommendation 3 ('the Government should engage with the shipping industry to explore options for the industry to pay for vessel protection detachments of British naval or military personnel on board commercial shipping').

[104] Whether this is clearly the case may be open to a degree of doubt. On the case-law, see Guilfoyle, *supra* note 47, 299–323.

[105] Though the number may be increasing: House of Commons Report, *supra* note 16, para. 25.

[106] House of Commons Report, *supra* note 16, para. 30.

use.[107] Irrespective of whether PCASP are considered desirable, they are clearly here to stay. The topic is discussed further in Chapter 10.

3.4 ASSESSMENT

3.4.1   The Challenges of Asymmetric Organized Crime

Any assessment of the effectiveness of the international response to Somali piracy has to take into account a number of constraints and challenges. First, Somali piracy has proven itself to be agile and adaptive. As it is highly decentralized, physically dangerous and very profitable, it is a criminal activity with excellent incentives to experiment, adapt and learn. Its low start-up costs, multiple business structures and large potential labour pool also make it more flexible than state agencies and ordinary commercial organizations. State action to counter Somali piracy, by contrast, is limited by factors including: limited resources to support regional prosecution efforts or economic development in Somalia;[108] finite military resources; necessary adherence to the rule of law; and the lack of any 'kinetic solution' to Somali piracy (that is, it is not a problem that can be solved with firepower).[109] In this context the key issues to consider are: the rate of prosecution for Somali pirates, and the factors that may inhibit prosecution (a theme taken up in Chapter 8); the role and effectiveness of international organizations and networks (as discussed in Chapter 5); and whether the international community is making the best use of the finite resources available to tackle the problem. Only the latter point will be addressed briefly here.

3.4.2   The Reality of Scarce Resources

The international community has finite resources with which to combat Somali piracy, despite its very high costs to the international economy as

---

[107] E.g., 'BIMCO Creates Standard Contract for Armed Guards' (22 November 2011) *Naval Today* <http://navaltoday.com/2011/11/22/denmark-bimco-creates-standard-contract-for-armed-guards/> accessed 21 August 2012 (quoting Giles Noakes, *supra* note 101).

[108] House of Commons Report, *supra* note 16, para. 132 and the figures at paras 135–136.

[109] 'Navy head cool on Somalia strikes' (*BBC News*, 13 December 2008) <http://news.bbc.co.uk/1/hi/7780981.stm> accessed 21 August 2012.

a whole.[110] Coordination is clearly required to make the most of available resources. This truism extends beyond military patrolling. Sometimes, however, modest resources can be used or leveraged to create a disproportionate impact. For example, one early concern in prosecuting piracy cases in Kenya was severe prison overcrowding. This created human rights concerns for states transferring suspects to Kenya and problems for Kenya in terms of its capacity to receive suspects. An expensive solution would have been to embark on a prison-building scheme. Instead, the UNODC looked at a series of measures targeted at one prison (Shimo La Tewa). For example, a UNODC supported review of those being held on remand identified 517 prisoners for immediate release who had already served time equivalent to the maximum sentence they might receive at trial.[111] This process obviously required resources, but fewer resources than a new building. Similarly, the IMO Djibouti Code implementation unit is trying less to create complete new infrastructure systems to support maritime situational awareness (e.g., chains of radar and radio stations) than to plug gaps in existing networks and, where they exist, to integrate parallel infrastructure controlled by different state agencies.[112] Finally, there is also the capacity for win-win solutions. Funding regional prosecutions of piracy trials may also *de facto* be a form of rule of law development assistance.[113] Court and prison facilities improved to deal with piracy cases have lasting benefits beyond piracy trials; for example, local prosecutors may receive training and mentoring from internationally seconded staff funded by donor states. These are all causes for optimism. That said, coordination, leverage and looking for win-wins, of course, will only take us so far.

Obviously, the best solution to Somali piracy is a functional Somali state, justice system and economy. The resources the international community stands prepared to put into Somali reconstruction are, however, 'extremely limited'.[114] The reality of counter-piracy operations has

---

[110]   'The Economic Cost of Maritime Piracy' (One Earth Future Working Paper, December 2010) <http://oceansbeyondpiracy.org/sites/default/files/documents_old/The_Economic_Cost_of_Piracy_Full_Report.pdf> accessed 21 August 2012.

[111]   UN Office on Drugs and Crime, 'Counter Piracy Programme: Support to the trial and related treatment of Piracy Suspect' (February 2011) 5 <http://www.unodc.org/documents/easternafrica/piracy/20110209.UNODC_Counter_Piracy_February_Issue.pdf> accessed 21 August 2012.

[112]   International Maritime Organization, *supra* note 83.

[113]   See further Chapter 5.3.4.

[114]   House of Commons Report, *supra* note 16, para. 32.

been that states have had to deal – in the absence of the TFG having any effective authority – with the relatively stable territorial entities of Somaliland and Puntland. There is significant interest in seeing prisons constructed in these territories under UN oversight so pirates convicted in other states in the region could be transferred home to serve their sentences.[115] (Thus relieving a burden on other prison systems which may translate to a greater willingness to prosecute.[116]) There are dangers, perhaps, of international support becoming 'captured' by local partners and propping up governments with possible links to pirates. However, grass-roots engagement with Somaliland, Puntland and especially clan networks, is likely the only way of gaining any traction in Somalia. Realistically, the clans are the (competing) seat(s) of effective power in Somalia and engagement with them is the thing most likely to pay dividends. The UNODC is beginning to attempt such community out-reach,[117] but these are all experiments in untested waters.

Everyone acknowledges that Somali piracy is a maritime problem with its roots ashore and that the international response must address both aspects. The real risk, of course, is that while talking about the need for a 'two track' response all the available resources and political will is diverted into dealing with the immediate high-seas problem. If this occurs, we can only hope to reach a kind of equilibrium: using available resources to cobble together a series of measures that reduces piracy to an 'acceptable' level (in the eyes of markets and politicians, if not seafarers). What we have to hope is that the present series of greater and smaller experiments can identify the components of a successful wider counter-piracy strategy with both short and long term goals that can be meaningfully coordinated.

---

[115] Modalities Report, *supra* note 40, paras 28–31. The Seychelles has entered a series of such agreements with the TFG and the regional governments of Somalia.

[116] *Ibid.*, para. 28.

[117] See, e.g., Wayne Miller, 'UNODC Counter-Piracy Programme: Somalia Beyond Piracy' (2011) <http://piracy-europe.com/uploads/files/1169/Wayne_Miller.pdf> accessed 21 August 2012.

4. Petro-piracy: predation and counter-predation in Nigerian waters

Martin N. Murphy*

4.1 INTRODUCTION

The world's attention has been so focused on piracy off Somali that it is sometimes hard to believe piracy is occurring elsewhere. In the case of the Gulf of Guinea that is unwise. On the inland and coastal waters of Nigeria particularly, and on the waters over a hundred miles off its coast, acts of depredation against ships and fixed oil installation have been taking place which have resulted in far greater financial losses and had a far wider economic impact than anything seen so far anywhere else in the world.[1] The effects of that disorder are spreading to its neighbors.

Observers are divided as to whether these acts are criminally or politically inspired. Whatever the motivation they are a reaction to the rapacity of international oil companies (IOCs) over decades in the Delta region and the greed of Nigerian politicians who have colluded in the destruction of local habitat and the livelihoods it supported. Local inhabitants believe they have gained little or nothing from the billions of dollars paid for the oil extracted from beneath their feet.

The main grievances are poverty, high youth unemployment, hiring practices that discriminate against locals and between local tribes, and the manipulation of government power by powerful ethnic groups outside the oil-rich Delta region to seize its oil wealth for themselves.[2] The oil

* The author would like to thank Daniel Whiteneck and Arild Nodland in particular for their help.

[1] S. Baldauf, 'Pirates take new territory: West African Gulf of Guinea' (*Christian Science Monitor*, 15 January 2010) <http://www.csmonitor.com/World/Africa/2010/0115/Pirates-take-new-territory-West-African-Gulf-of-Guinea> accessed 26 May 2012.

[2] C. Obi, 'Nigeria's Niger Delta: Understanding the Complex Drivers of Violent Oil-related Conflict' (2009) XXXIV(2) *Africa Development* 106–107

industry and particularly the unsafe practices used to steal from it have resulted in endemic pollution.[3] Over the past 50 years 1.5 million tons of oil have been spilt, which equates to an Exxon Valdez catastrophe every year.[4] In 2006 many in the Delta felt it was on the verge of an ecological disaster.[5]

The sense of injustice and exploitation that pervades the region has roots in a long struggle by local people for autonomy stretching back over generations.[6] Drawing a Manichean distinction between politically and criminally motivated actions in this conflict is wrong-headed. In practice they are inseparable on land, on the water-courses that are such a distinctive feature of the region's geography, and on the coastal seas, where militants have made victims out of seafarers, fishermen, foreign oil workers and the inhabitants of neighboring states.

<http://www.ajol.info/index.php/ad/article/viewFile/57373/45753> accessed 26 May 2012; S. Joab-Peterside, 'On the Militarization of Nigeria's Niger Delta: The Genesis of Ethnic Militia in Rivers State, Nigeria', Working Paper No 21, *Niger Delta Economies of Violence Working Papers* (UC Berkeley, Institute of International Studies, 2007) 3 <http://geogweb.berkeley.edu/ProjectsResources/ND%20Website/NigerDelta/WP/21-Joab-Peterside.pdf> accessed 26 May 2012. On 'youth' and inter-generational tensions see: R. Soares de Oliveira, *Oil and Politics in the Gulf of Guinea* (Hurst 2007) 132 (note 31).

[3] P. Francis *et al.*, *Securing Development and Peace in the Niger Delta: A Social and Conflict Analysis for Change* (Woodrow Wilson International Center for Scholars 2011), 38–43; I. S. Ibaba, 'Alienation and Militancy in the Niger Delta: Hostage Taking and the Dilemma of the Nigerian State' (2008) 8(2) *African Journal on Conflict Resolution* 11, 16 <http://www.ajol.info/index.php/ajcr/article/viewFile/39424/59588> accessed 26 May 2012; M. Watts, 'Crude Politics: Life and Death on the Nigerian Oil Fields', Working Paper No. 25, *Niger Delta Economies of Violence Working Papers* (Institute of International Studies, 2009) 17 <http://oldweb.geog.berkeley.edu/ProjectsResources/ND%20Website/NigerDelta/WP/Watts_25.pdf> accessed 26 May 2012; A. Odoemene, 'Social Consequences of Environmental Change in the Niger Delta of Nigeria' (2011) 4(2) *Journal of Sustainable Development* 123, 125.

[4] A. Nodland, 'Guns, Oil, and "Cake": Maritime Security in the Gulf of Guinea', in B.A. Elleman *et al.*, *Piracy and Maritime Crime: Historical and Modern Case Studies* (Naval War College Press 2010) 193.

[5] United National Development Programme (UNDP), 'Niger Delta Human Development Report 2006' 74 <http://hdr.undp.org/en/reports/nationalreports/africa/nigeria/nigeria_hdr_report.pdf> accessed 26 May 2012.

[6] Obi, *supra* note 2, 114.

4.2 NIGERIA'S PRESENT AND ITS FUTURE: TWO INTERPRETATIONS[7]

Nigeria, granted independence from Britain in 1960, was expected to be Africa's success story. There are now two divergent interpretations of Nigeria's prospects. The first suggests the country is beginning to realize its promise. Between 2001 and 2010 its economy grew at an average rate of 8.9 percent[8] including in many sectors outside the oil industry.[9] Nigeria is also Africa's most populous country with 162 million people, including an emerging middle-class that is attracting the interest of international investors.[10] Politically, Nigeria is evolving towards a stable democracy with increasingly free and fair elections and the continent's most diverse and outspoken media.[11] An amnesty in the Niger Delta region has curbed the violent insurgency that threatened the country's oil industry. The only shadow is terrorism in the north of the country perpetrated by a militant Islamic group suspected of links to al Qaeda, Boko Haram.[12]

The alternative explanation is darker. It sees government at all levels as corrupt. Fingers, for example, are pointed at the Joint Task Force (JTF), a military unit first deployed against the Niger Delta militants and then redeployed against Boko Haram, which Amnesty International has

---

[7] The author would like to thank Ambassador John Campbell, US envoy to Nigeria 2004–2007, and now Ralph Bunche Senior Fellow for Africa Policy Studies at the Council on Foreign Relations, for his helpful contributions to this section.

[8] 'Africa's impressive growth' *The Economist* (6 January 2011) <http://www.economist.com/blogs/dailychart/2011/01/daily_chart> accessed 26 May 2012.

[9] F. Rintoul, 'Nigeria's poverty and corruption still bar way to promising future' *Financial Times* (20 January 2012) <http://www.ft.com/intl/cms/s/0/06f85bc0–4341–11e1–9f28–00144feab49a.html>#axzz1nWV4Eq4s> accessed 26 May 2012.

[10] See, e.g.: J. O'Neill, 'Down with "Emerging Markets"' (*Project Syndicate*, 7 February 2011) <http://www.project-syndicate.org/commentary/oneill2/English> accessed 26 May 2012; Rintoul, *supra* note 9.

[11] J.P. Pham, 'Goodluck's Win – and Nigeria's' *The New Atlanticist* (19 April 2011) <http://www.acus.org/new_atlanticist/goodluck%E2%80%99s-win%E2%80%94and-nigeria%E2%80%99s> accessed 18 February 2012; Francis *et al.*, *supra* note 3, 60–61.

[12] D. Hinshaw, 'New attacks threaten Nigeria's future' *Wall Street Journal* (17 February 2012) <http://online.wsj.com/article/SB1000142405297020464260457721496421409 0958.html> accessed 18 February 2012.

accused of rape, theft, torture and 'extrajudicial executions'.[13] While the 2011 presidential election was procedurally fair, the victor, Goodluck Jonathon, was widely seen in the north as flouting the convention that southern and northern candidates should hold the presidency alternately.[14] As a result the election was marred by considerable violence. Boko Haram has grabbed this opportunity and exploited long-existing inter-communal tensions to extend its campaign to the country's middle belt. This is now scarred by conflict amounting in some cases to ethnic cleansing. Southern Ibo migrants to the north have been driven from their homes and Christian churches burnt. The government has offered talks but its heavy-handed tactics have made the northern situation worse.

Meanwhile the situation in the Niger Delta is no nearer a solution. The Delta region, rich in oil, remains rich in resentment. Almost from the time oil was first discovered in 1956, its wealth has been appropriated by the central government with little returned. Billions of dollars have disappeared into the overseas bank accounts of corrupt politicians and officials. This combination triggered an insurgency on land, at sea and on the Delta's multitudinous water-courses. Unable to contain the violence, the government declared an amnesty which in 2009 induced some 26,000 militants to lay down their arms. However, government inaction on fundamental grievances has led to the formation of so-called 'third phase' militant groups. The worsening security situation in the north means that the federal government is spending over 20 percent of its budget on security. Money that has for some time flown to the south will undoubtedly be redirected northwards. In the Delta disaffection is likely to spark a return to violence.

Undoubtedly there is truth in both interpretations. How much exactly is hard to tell because so much of what is known about Nigeria is shaped by outsiders' experience of Lagos and Abuja. The violence that occurs in both cities is criminal; generally neither has experienced the ethnic violence found elsewhere. Crime, however, is a national epidemic: one that the police – lacking adequate pay, training or numbers – seemingly

---

[13]   Amnesty International, 'Conflict in the Niger Delta' (*Eyes on Nigeria*, ND) <http://www.eyesonnigeria.org/EON_Delta.aspx> accessed 26 May 2012; Hinshaw, *supra* note 12.

[14]   J.P. Pham, 'Nigeria at the Crossroads – Again' (*World Defense Review*, 16 September 2010) <http://worlddefensereview.com/pham091610.shtml> accessed 29 October 2010; 'Goodluck Jonathan: new president upsets Nigeria's delicate Muslim-Christian balance of power' *Los Angeles Times* (6 March 2010) <http://www.cleveland.com/world/index.ssf/2010/05/goodluck_johnson_as_new_presid.html> accessed 23 March 2012.

aid and abet through their own predatory behavior. The general lack of trust in government feeds vigilantism. In areas of particular stress, such as the Niger Delta, repressive security measures are seen as actively making such problems worse.

4.3 INGRAINED CHALLENGES

Four deeply-ingrained challenges do not auger well for the future: an exploding population (Nigeria could add 70 million people to its 162 million population by 2025);[15] wealth inequalities (while it is the continent's second largest economy, Nigeria had a poverty rate of 70 percent in 2007);[16] corruption and urban expansion. The latter two problems are discussed further below.

Income inequalities feed corruption, the country's over-riding curse[17] and primary cause of its poverty.[18] Eighty-five percent of the country's oil revenue flows to 1 percent of the population and 40 percent of that is stolen and sent abroad.[19] Nigerian society, it seems, applauds flamboyant affluence and seldom condemns ill-gotten wealth.[20] Nigeria is also a country where civil servants go for months without salaries and things can only happen if money is exchanged illegally.[21] At a political level it

---

[15] United Nations Department of Economic & Social Affairs/Population Division, *World Population Prospects: The 2010 Revision: Vol. 1, Comprehensive Tables* (2011) 88 (Table S2) <http://esa.un.org/unpd/wpp/Documentation/pdf/WPP2010_Volume-I_Comprehensive-Tables.pdf> accessed 26 February 2012.

[16] All figures from CIA *World Fact Book* <https://www.cia.gov/library/publications/the-world-factbook/> accessed 27 February 2012.

[17] O. Fagbadedo, 'Corruption, Governance and Political Instability in Nigeria' (2007) 1(2) *African Journal of Political Science and International Relations* 28, 30, citing V. E. Dike, <http://www.academicjournals.org/ajpsir/pdf/Pdf2007/Nov/Fagbadebo.pdf> accessed 26 May 2012.

[18] Cited in H. H. Werlin, 'Corruption and Foreign Aid in Africa' *Orbis* (Summer 2005) 524. For the 2011 ranking see: O. Yishau, 'Transparency International ranks Nigeria 143rd on corruption index' *The Nation* (2 December 2011) <http://www.thenationonlineng.net/2011/index.php/news/28348-transparency-international-ranks-nigeria-143th-on-corruption-index.html> accessed 4 March 2012.

[19] Obi, *supra* note 2, 123–124; Watts, *supra* note 3, 3.

[20] V. E. Dike, 'Corruption in Nigeria: A New Paradigm for Effective Control' *Africa Economic Analysis* (23 January 2008) <http://www.africaeconomicanalysis.org/articles/gen/corruptiondikehtm.html> accessed 4 March 2012.

[21] Werlin, *supra* note 18, 525.

is a country where advancement is open to those who can pay. Since 1999, politics have been dominated by the People's Democratic Party (PDP) which now wields enormous patronage. Some see most Nigerians as rooted in an almost fatalistic acceptance that corruption and dependence on government largesse is now a way of life,[22] making an entrepreneurial career an almost 'unfathomable' concept in Nigeria.[23]

The sheer scale of Nigerian corruption indicates how difficult it will be to eradicate. Corruption costs the country between US $4 and $8 billion per annum.[24] While politicians are corruption's principal beneficiaries, the police and judiciary are its most visible faces. Police in Nigeria have a history of corruption going back to colonial times. Methods used now include release fees following arbitrary arrest, demands for protection money, charges to investigate cases, and simple extortion at the country's multiple road blocks set up originally to curb rampant crime.[25]

Lagos, the country's principal port and commercial capital, has grown to be a mega-city of between 12 and 17 million. If current census figures are correct, then Lagos is the largest city in Africa and one of the four largest in the world. This growth has placed immense strain on the region's ecology. Lagos is part of Nigeria's coastal belt, which comprises inshore waters, coastal lagoons, estuaries and, in the Niger Delta especially, mangrove. Thirty-five percent of Lagos state consists of wetlands. The demand for human habitation has left expansion into these areas vulnerable to subsidence and flooding.[26]

The coastal belt as a whole stretches 530 miles (850 km) through nine of the federation's 36 states. Its width varies between about nine miles (15 km) in Lagos state in the west, to over 90 miles (150 km) in the Niger Delta, before narrowing again to around 15 miles (25 km) between

---

[22]   Nodland, *supra* note 4, 204.

[23]   Soares de Oliveira, *supra* note 2, 146 (note 85).

[24]   Human Rights Watch, 'Everyone's in on the Game: Corruption and Human Rights Abuses by the Nigerian Police Force' (August 2010) 20 <http://www.hrw.org/node/92390> accessed 29 October 2010.

[25]   Human Rights Watch, *supra* note 24; US Department of State, '2010 Human Rights Report: Nigeria' (8 April 2011) 19 <http://www.state.gov/j/drl/rls/hrrpt/2010/af/154363.htm> accessed 4 March 2012; O. N. I. Ebbe, 'Slicing Nigeria's "National Cake"' in R. Godson (ed.), *Menace to Society: Political-Criminal Collaboration around the World* (Transaction Publishers 2003) 148.

[26]   Y. Ojo and Mayowa, 'Lagos: Battling Surging Flood and Population' *Business Eye* (9 November 2011) <http://www.businesseyenigeria.com/business-news/environment/lagos-battling-surging-flood-and-population?print=1&tmpl=component> accessed 27 February 2012.

the Delta and the Cameroon border in the east.[27] The geography of the Delta heartland is challenging: its 27,000 square miles – roughly the size of Scotland – is a maze of swamps, creeks and rivers, where constructing roads costs four times more than on dry land and mobility by water is time-consuming.[28] It is home to 32 million people, 62 percent of them under 30. Across the region, communities have been subjected to unregulated development, pollution, inadequate sewage disposal, poor fisheries management, loss of mangrove habitat and coastal erosion. People have drifted to the cities in search of a better life but often find only a slum existence.[29] That pressure is likely only to increase as the country's explosive population growth, felt keenly in Lagos, imposes similar strains all along the coast.

4.4 DELTA DIVISIONS

Nigeria emerged from British colonial rule in 1960 as a federal state divided into Northern, Western and Eastern Regions. However, tensions rooted in ethnic differences – which underlie much of the post-independence turmoil – remained unresolved.[30] In 1967 they exploded into civil war. This was triggered by an attempted coup in 1966, blamed on members of the Ibo ethnic group, and followed by a counter-coup led by northern army officers during which 30,000 Ibo living in the north were killed and a further million were forced to flee. Within months the Ibo-dominated Eastern Region announced it would secede as the Republic of Biafra. The 1967–1970 war with the northern-dominated federal government that followed left at least three million more dead across the Niger Delta region, mostly from disease and starvation. The peace imposed by the victorious northerners was designed to leave the Ibo subjugated.

---

[27]   UNEP, 'The Status of the Nigerian Coastal Zones' <http://www.unep.org/AbidjanConvention/docs/THE%20STATUS%20OF%20THE%20NIGERIAN%20COASTAL%20ZONES%20version%202.pdf> accessed 27 February 2012.

[28]   T. O'Neill, 'Curse of the Black Gold: Hope and Betrayal in the Niger Delta' (February 2007) 211(2) *National Geographic*; M. Peel, 'Crisis in the Niger Delta: How Failures of Transparency and Accountability are Destroying the Region' Chatham House Briefing Paper AFP BP 05/02 (July 2005), 2 <http://www.chathamhouse.org/sites/default/files/public/Research/Africa/bpnigerdelta.pdf> accessed 27 February 2012.

[29]   Joab-Peterside, *supra* note 2, 11–12.

[30]   Soares de Oliveira, *supra* note 2, 130.

The effect of British rule in the Delta had been to marginalize the region's other (non-Ibo) inhabitants. These are divided between 40 distinct groups – the Ijaw being the largest – speaking 120 different languages and dialects.[31] They became, effectively, ethnic minorities. Naturally enough they protested, campaigning before and after the British left to have the three federal regions replaced by smaller states. In 1967 their ambition was realized: the regions were abolished and the country divided between 12 states, three of which were controlled by Delta minorities. However, the Ibo interpreted this as a device to exclude them from access to oil revenues. The Biafran War which followed was therefore partly a war over oil. Once the war was over, however, the northerners cast their allies among the minorities aside. Income from oil was collected and disbursed centrally, largely to the northerners' advantage. The political struggle between the oil producing states and the minority tribes on one side, and the non-oil producing states and the majority groups on the other, had begun.[32]

4.5 EARLY PIRACY

Piracy is a product of economic dislocation. The groups that practice it are, in the main, those who have been marginalized by changes in the economic order. The winners often brand the losers as 'pirates' if they retaliate using predation. This is the fate that befell the Western Ijaw. In the nineteenth century they were excluded from the developing trade between other tribes and Europeans.[33] The violent response (labeled 'piracy') continued until 1870 when they were finally defeated by the Itsekiri tribe. By the 1890s the Itsekiri were using a force of 20,000 'war boys' deployed on 100 war canoes to defend their market dominance.[34]

In the years between the Ijaw's defeat and the 1970s, piracy was practically unheard of in Nigerian waters. Corruption, on the other hand, was by the 1970s driven increasingly by Niger Delta oil production revenues. Shell made the first oil discovery in 1956. Other companies

---

[31] Francis *et al.*, *supra* note 3, 5.

[32] Obi, *supra* note 2, 114–116.

[33] U. Ukiwo, 'From "Pirates" to "Militants": A Historical Perspective on Anti-State and Anti-Oil Company Mobilization among the Ijaw of Warri, Western Niger Delta' (2007) 106(425) *African Affairs* 587, 592.

[34] P. C. Lloyd, 'The Itsekiri in the Nineteenth Century: An Outline Social History' (1963) 4(2) *The Journal of African History* 207, 225–226.

were granted concessions from 1959 onwards.[35] The 1973 oil price hike imposed by the newly created Organization of Oil Producing Countries (OPEC) was crucial. The price rocketed up and stayed high throughout the 1970s before collapsing in the early 1980s. Flush with revenue and the capacity to borrow even more, Nigeria embarked on extravagant industrialization, prestige projects and wasteful social expenditure.[36] One consequence was enormous cement imports to feed a construction boom.

Lagos harbor could not cope and at times over 400 ships lay anchored, many for months, waiting to unload. Pirate attacks on the 'cement armada' coupled to the wholesale theft of goods from wharves began.[37] Stolen goods quickly reached Lagos shops and markets.[38] This activity rapidly became organized. Pirates exchanged small boats for ones that could carry 20 to 30 men driven by outboard motors. Ships' captains soon became convinced that the gangs were being guided with inside information from port authority and customs officials.[39] The larger the gangs became the greater the level of actual or threatened violence; there were reports of ships being boarded by 40 to 50 pirates and attacks involving 12 boats.[40] In 1979 the master of the *Lindinga Ivory* was killed and all 14 crew injured. Despite promises by the Nigerian authorities, the crews of ships waiting offshore were largely left to fend for themselves.[41] During the first quarter of 1981, the Lagos roadstead was experiencing between three and 12 attacks *a day*.[42] Shortly afterwards, however, the problem declined, largely in response to the steep decline in oil prices, resulting in fewer ships calling at Lagos.

4.6 THE OIL PRIZE

Oil revenues in 1979 accounted for 82 percent of the federal government's income. As of 2000 little had changed: 40 percent of gross domestic product (GDP), 83 percent of federal government revenues and

---

[35] See generally: Soares de Oliveira, *supra* note 2, 172, 204–206.

[36] Soares de Oliveira, *supra* note 2, 70–71; Fagbadedo, *supra* note 17, 33.

[37] On the cement ships, see 'The cement block' *TIME* (27 October 1975); J. Darnton, 'Pirates plying Nigerian Seas' *New York Times* (9 January 1977).

[38] Darnton, *supra* note 37.

[39] R. Villar, *Piracy Today: Robbery and Violence at Sea since 1980* (Conway Maritime Press 1985) 16; Darnton, *supra* note 37.

[40] See Villar, *supra* note 39, 101–102.

[41] *Ibid.*, 16–17.

[42] *Ibid.*, 102.

98 percent of export earnings came from oil. In 2010 oil still accounted for 80 percent of government revenue and 95 percent of foreign earnings.[43]

The political process of sharing this revenue between Nigeria's 'haves' and 'have-nots' is called 'derivation'. Immediately following the Biafran War, the military government made itself the recipient of all revenue from IOCs operating in Nigeria, placing all the revenues – and the formula for their disbursement – under federal control. Federally created non-oil states lacking viable fiscal bases became federal clients and political counterweights to oil producing areas. The revenue allocation process became mired in secrecy and controlled by elites close to the president.[44]

Although the formula laid down for dividing oil revenue has been amended several times it remains a major political issue.[45] In 1980 75 percent of the federal allocation went to non-oil producing states; in the decade following, the proportion of federal monies going to oil producing areas fell further still, in the case of Rivers State to less than 3 percent.[46] From this low point it climbed to 13 percent in 1999.[47]

4.7   DELTA MILITANCY: RIGHTEOUS REBELLION OR CRUDE CRIMINALITY?

The money flowing to the Delta might have increased but local people saw little of it. As far as they were concerned the federal government, in

---

[43]   E. Bala-Gbogbo, 'Nigeria's oil revenue rose 46% to $89 billion on improved security' (*Bloomberg*, 14 April 2011) <http://www.bloomberg.com/news/2011–04–14/nigeria-s-oil-revenue-rose-46-to-59-billion-in-2010-on-improved-security.html> accessed 4 March 2012.

[44]   Soares de Oliveira, *supra* note 2, 67–68; I. Okonta, 'Behind the Mask: Explaining the Emergence of MEND in Nigeria's Oil-bearing Niger Delta', *Niger Delta Economies of Violence Working Papers*, Working Paper No. 11 (UC Berkeley, Institute of International Studies, 2006) 7 <http://oldweb.geog.berkeley.edu/ProjectsResources/ND%20Website/NigerDelta/WP/11-Okonta.pdf> accessed 28 May 2012.

[45]   Obi, *supra* note 2, 115–116.

[46]   M. Watts, 'Petro-Insurgency or Criminal Syndicate? Conflict, Violence and Political Disorder in the Niger Delta', *Niger Delta Economies of Violence Working Papers*, Working Paper No. 16 (UC Berkeley, Institute of International Studies, 2006) 11–12 <http://oldweb.geog.berkeley.edu/ProjectsResources/ND%20Website/NigerDelta/WP/16-Watts.pdf> accessed 28 May 2012.

[47]   *Ibid.*, 12.

partnership with the IOCs, was cheating them of what was rightfully theirs.[48] What they saw in their everyday lives was 'oil pollution, extreme poverty, high ... youth unemployment, perceived discriminatory employment practices against locals by oil companies ... neglect by successive administrations'.[49]

The first act of defiance took place in February 1966 when Isaac Adaka Boro and the 159 youths who made up the Niger Delta Volunteer Force (NDVF) launched the (quickly crushed) '12 Day Revolution', an attempt to secede and establish an independent Niger Delta republic.[50] It did, however, spur leaders from other ethnic groups to form other political organizations dedicated to raising awareness of the oil industry's operations in the Delta and the almost complete lack of interest in the region's inhabitants displayed by successive governments. The objective of each group was greater local autonomy. Ken Sara Wiwa formed the unarmed Movement for the Survival of the Ogoni People (MOSOP) in 1990, demanding local autonomy and control of Shell's operations in Ogoniland. His arrest and execution along with nine of his colleagues by the Abacha regime in 1995 outraged local feeling and first drew international attention to the Delta's problems.[51] The longer term consequence of his death was to confirm the view held by many in the Delta that the government saw any protest as economic sabotage and a challenge to its power that was indistinguishable from criminality to which its only response would be repression.[52] The number of armed groups consequently exploded. By the time an amnesty was announced in 2009 there were estimated to be 50,000 militants in the region, equivalent to more than 50 percent of Nigeria's armed forces.[53]

Increased derivation payments to Delta states were part of the federal government's response to regional protest movements, and were intended

---

[48] *Ibid.*, 13.

[49] Obi, *supra* note 2, 106–107.

[50] J. B. Asuni, *Understanding the Armed Groups of the Niger Delta*, Council for Foreign Relations Working Paper (September 2009) 5 <http://www.cfr.org/nigeria/understanding-armed-groups-niger-delta/p20146> accessed 28 May 2012; Francis *et al.*, *supra* note 3, 128; Obi, *supra* note 2, 128–129; Watts, *supra* note 3, 14; Okonta, *supra* note 44, 6.

[51] Asuni, *supra* note 50, 5; Francis *et al.*, *supra* note 3, 124; Obi, *supra* note 2, 119.

[52] Obi, *supra* note 2, 107, 120; Joab-Peterside, *supra* note 2, 4.

[53] V. Ojakoroto and L. D. Gilbert, 'Checkmating the Resurgence of Oil Violence in the Niger Delta of Nigeria' (18 May 2010) *Journal of Energy Security* 6 <http://www.ensec.org/index.php?option=com_content&view=article&id=246:checkmating-the-resurgence-of-oil-violence-in-the-niger-delta-of-nigeria&

to provide local political leaders with sufficient funds to co-opt such movements' leaders. By 2005 more money was going to Delta states than Lagos.[54] In 2009 the income of Rivers State alone was, at $2.9 billion, greater than that of several African countries.[55] The results were depressingly predictable: a portion of the region's elite diverted the funds for their own interests.[56] Decentralization of revenue, evident in an enormous increase in the wealth and patronage of state governors, meant the decentralization of corruption and with it the means to fund violence.[57] The Niger Delta gangs thus 'originated as politically sponsored thugs to intimidate opponents'.[58] This highlights an important truth: militants and members of the PDP have worked together to mutual advantage; the theft of oil has been a joint effort between militant-criminals and the political/ military class.[59]

Judith Asuni, perhaps the clearest historian of this gang phenomenon, traces it back to university student associations which arose in the 1950s.[60] Ironically the first such group, set up at the University of Ibadan in 1952, was called the Pyrates Association before renaming itself the National Association of Sea Dogs (NAS). Though initially little more than drinking clubs, by the mid-1970s they had become political and by the 1980s overtly threatening. This violence spread off campus, forcing the leaders to hire younger boys for protection. These in turn morphed into violent street gangs and then organized criminals who, by the 1990s, were actively involved in drug trafficking. Inevitably the profitability of this trade increased inter-gang violence. When that became too much the gangs turned to illegal oil bunkering, stealing oil from onshore pipelines and selling it to Lebanese and Russian interests amongst others who disposed of it on the international market.[61]

Two notorious gang leaders made millions from this trade. One, Mujahid Dokubo-Asari, claimed he was merely righting a wrong perpetrated against the Delta people. His first political venture was the Ijaw

---

catid=106:energysecuritycontent0510&Itemid=361> accessed 28 May 2012; PDF available at <http://www.iags.org/Niger_Delta_book.pdf>; Watts, *supra* note 3, 13–14.

54   Peel, *supra* note 28, 4.
55   Francis *et al.*, *supra* note 3, 44.
56   Ibaba, *supra* note 3, 29; Obi, *supra* note 2, 116, 123.
57   Watts, *supra* note 46, 12.
58   US Department of State, *supra* note 25, 23.
59   Watts, *supra* note 46, 25–26.
60   Asuni, *supra* note 50.
61   *Ibid.*, 8–10.

Youth Council formed in the late 1990s, followed by the Niger Delta People's Volunteer Force (NDPVF) formed in 2004, both ostensibly aiming to ensure greater local control over natural resources. His even more cynical rival, Ateke Tom, formed the Niger Delta Vigilantes (NDV) in response.[62]

From the beginning, the extraordinary profits in oil bunkering attracted the interest of military and political figures who demanded a share in return for their acquiescence and protection. As early as 1995 Ijaws involved in the trade were taken to Abuja where they struck deals with leading security officials. When these officials subsequently thought they were being underpaid, the Ijaws asked their foreign customers for arms heavy enough to take on the Nigerian military.[63]

Politicians quickly recognized the advantages of associating with such well-funded, and well-armed, gangs. Peter Odili, PDP candidate for the Rivers State governorship in 1999, supplied Ateke and Dokubo-Asari with arms to ensure his election. Both groups retained their weapons afterwards, although neither remained constant in their political allegiance, and eventually clashed violently over oil bunkering. In 2004 Dokubo-Asari's NDPVF threatened all-out attacks on the oil industry. President Obasanjo intervened, offering to address the groups' public grievances provided they disbanded and disarmed. Neither side honored the bargain and the accord fell apart. Group members, disillusioned by their leaders' performance, accused them of literally selling out in exchange for government gold and began forming break-away factions.[64]

In late 2005 representatives of the Federation of Niger Delta Ijaw Communities (FNDIC), NDPVF and various cult groups met to discuss a unified response to the arrest of several prominent leaders. They agreed to form MEND, the Movement for the Emancipation of the Niger Delta, under whose umbrella bunkering syndicates were merged and attacks mounted against oil installations. A few weeks later, on 11 January 2006, the group kidnapped its first foreign oil workers.[65] Yet MEND was never a unified entity nor, in Asuni's judgement, did it really work to advance the interests of the Delta people: its primary focus was making money from kidnapping oil workers and thieving oil.[66]

---

[62] *Ibid.*, 15–16; Watts, *supra* note 46, 22.
[63] Asuni, *supra* note 50, 14.
[64] *Ibid.*, 13, 15–16.
[65] *Ibid.*, 17–18.
[66] *Ibid.*, 19–20. MEND stated that it was 'not an organization "in the formal sense" but "an idea" underlying various, mainly Ijaw, movements': Okonta, *supra* note 44, 10.

Other commentators are less sure. No-one denies that criminality has been an element in the conflict from the late-1980s and many would concede that it is now arguably its defining characteristic.[67] Groups such as MEND have links to various suspect criminal enterprises[68] and may 'navigate between' the goals of personal reward or resisting the IOCs and corrupt local elites 'based on calculations of expediency'.[69] Joab-Peterside traces the genealogy differently from Asuni. He points first to the state's reluctance to provide security in situations that were not directly oil-related. He couples this to the tensions between the traditional gerontocracy and the upstart youth movements that clashed over IOC compensation for the land used and who should have a say in how that compensation was distributed. Each tribe formed armed groups to defend its interests but by the early 2000s these groups had begun to drift into criminality (as discussed above) or into associations with political figures who used the threat of ethnic violence to advance their own interests.[70]

A one-sided emphasis on criminality therefore ignores the economic and ethnic motivations for Niger Delta militancy that have given it wide popular support.[71] Okonta recounts villagers speaking of MEND fighters killed in a JTF ambush as 'heroes who had fallen in the battle of "Ijaw liberation"'.[72] The region's 'waterborne crimes', Samuel Menefee has written, 'resist easy interpretation. This is more than a question of government claim and tribal counterclaim: the number of "players" … makes assigning responsibility for any particular action tricky … Additionally, the sources available cannot exactly be called impartial.'[73]

---

[67] Soares de Oliveira, *supra* note 2, 250–251.

[68] Watts, *supra* note 46, 21.

[69] Obi, *supra* note 2, 114.

[70] Joab-Peterside, *supra* note 2, 5, 6–15; Asuni, *supra* note 50, 11.

[71] Obi, *supra* note 2, 121; Watts, *supra* note 3, 3, 14.

[72] Okonta, *supra* note 44, 1.

[73] S. P. Menefee, 'Delta Blues: Maritime and Riverine Crime in the Nigerian Delta' in M. Q. Meija and Jingjing Xu, *Coastal Zone Piracy and Other Unlawful Acts at Sea* (WMU Publications 2007) 211.

4.8 NIGERIA'S WATER WORLD

International law defines piracy as an act of private depredation commit-ted on the high seas.[74] Many of the acts of maritime depredation along Nigeria's coast take place within territorial and internal waters. Difficul-ties in ascribing private or political motivation to the various Niger Delta groups has added further confusion as to whether or not what has taken place off the coast should be called piracy.[75] The Governor of Rivers State, Chibuike Rotimi Amaechi, put it well in 2008 when he explained that there was a:

> thin, often overlapping, line between these groups. An attacker may one day kidnap an oil worker in order to buy a flashy car; the next day he may join a raid by a militant group and, on the third day, hijack a rig to generate cash for his chief or to get jobs, a new hospital or generator for his village.[76]

Strictly speaking most attacks fail the legal tests of place and motive in order to qualify unambiguously as piracy.

This, however, is not unusual. Somali and Malacca Strait piracy are rare in being relatively unambiguous. In many conflicts, drawing a clear line between privately motivated piracy and politically motivated mari-time depredation has proved difficult: the separatist movements in Sri Lanka and the southern Philippines both attacked shipping for profit. The closest historical parallel is arguably with banditry; the participants are clearly inspired by private gain but where their action is also inspired by a sense of alienation from the governing order, which is shared by sufficient numbers of people in the wider population, they can also exploit significant local support.

---

[74] See Chapter 6; United Nations Convention on the Law of the Sea (adopted 10 December 1982, entered into force 16 November 1994) 1833 UNTS 397, Art. 101.

[75] Arguing the relevant distinction is not, as widely held, between private and political violence but between private and *public* violence (i.e., all non-State violence is piracy) see: D. Guilfoyle, *Shipping Interdiction and the Law of Sea* (Cambridge University Press 2009) 32–42.

[76] C. R. Amaechi, 'Fundamental Causes of Maritime Insecurity' A lecture organized by the Nigerian Maritime Administration and Safety Agency and the Nigerian Navy, published by *The Tide Online* (6 May 2008). The Governor in fact lifted his remarks largely from a 2007 Bergen Risk Solutions analysis: 'BRS analysis gets "endorsement" of sorts from governor of Nigeria's hydrocarbon state' *Tradewinds* (11 July 2008) 20–21.

The importance of Nigeria's ports and offshore oil industry, and the difficulty of securing such vulnerable and widely dispersed facilities, was exploited dramatically by MEND, which announced itself with a major attack on the Opobo pipeline in December 2005. On 18 February 2006 it captured Willbros barge 318, a crude loading platform, an oil manifold and a gas pipeline in Chanomi Creek. This was in retaliation for a JTF assault on Ijaw villages by the Nigerian army (itself justified as an attack on illegal oil barges). The attacks cut Nigeria's oil output by 20 percent in one day.[77] By 2008 MEND's maritime capability had improved dramatically: it struck the Bonga floating production and oil storage platform 62 nm (100 km) offshore cutting production by 220,000 barrels per day throughout its shut-down.[78] According to Arild Nodland, Chief Executive of Bergen Risk Solutions, the attack changed the offshore security regime completely.[79]

4.9 ILLEGAL OIL BUNKERING

Oil theft – known as 'illegal bunkering' regardless of whether it takes place on land or at sea – is enormously profitable. Income from kidnapping is also lucrative but cannot rival oil theft. The scale of the losses is staggering. Leaving aside income lost to the Nigerian state and to oil companies because production has been 'shut in' following sabotage – which in reality is income deferred – more than $100 billion worth of oil has gone missing since 1960.[80] More oil is stolen in the Delta than some African countries produce.[81] Even though the problem

---

[77] Watts, *supra* note 46, 17.

[78] C. Mortished, 'Shell deepwater platform attacked as Nigerian separatists step up protests' *The Times* (20 June 2008) <http://business.timesonline.co.uk/tol/business/industry_sectors/natural_resources/article4175357.ece> accessed 28 May 2012; 'Nigeria – The Significance of the Bonga Offshore Oil Platform Attack' (*The Oil Drum*, 24 June 2008) <http://www.theoildrum.com/pdf/theoildrum_4196.pdf> accessed 28 May 2012.

[79] E-mail correspondence with the author, May 2012.

[80] Watts, *supra* note 3, 15–16. On 'shut-in-losses' see Watts, *supra* note 46, 4.

[81] S. Davis, D. Von Kemedi and M. Drennan, 'Illegal Oil Bunkering in the Niger Delta', in *Niger Delta Peace and Security Secretariat: Background Papers for PoS Working Group* (Niger Delta International Centre for Reconciliation, Academic Associates Peace Works, February 2006) 7–8 <http://www.legaloil.com/Documents/Library/Pas%20Paper%20Illegal%20Oil%20Bunkering%20210406.pdf> accessed 28 May 2012.

has long existed, the amounts lost have increased steeply over the past decade: losses in 2000 were estimated at 140,000 barrels per day. In 2001 the reported figure peaked at an astonishing 724,171 barrels daily before dropping to a fairly steady daily average of 100,000 to 300,000 barrels.[82] Rising oil prices have fueled enthusiasm for the practice. In July 2012 the head of Shell in Nigeria described illegal bunkering as 'out of control' and suggested that some of the operations appeared to have the support of foreign countries.[83]

What proportion of this oil theft takes place at sea is hard to quantify; indeed the assumption is that oil theft generally is under-reported. What is taken at sea is almost certainly far less than results from either 'hot tapping' into land pipelines or fraud in 'legal bunkering'. However, given the scale of losses overall it is safe to assume that the value of oil stolen at sea makes Nigerian 'piracy' the most lucrative in the world.

Illegal bunkering is widespread in the major export terminals such as Port Harcourt, Warri and Bonny. It also takes place in more remote locations such as Jonas Creek and Cawthorne Channel, often quite openly.[84] 'Hot tapping', the dangerous practice of cutting into pipelines where they emerge from swamps or cross rivers, occurs throughout the Delta. Pipes have to be tapped continuously during the operation to avoid pressure fluctuations giving them away. Gaining access to pipelines and making sure that other groups do not seize them involves paying off local communities, the navy and local law enforcement. The oil is loaded either directly into tankers moored on Delta waterways or transported to sea by barge for trans-shipment to ocean-going vessels and is then absorbed into the global market.[85] Much is believed to go directly to refineries in local states such as Ivory Coast, Senegal and The Gambia;

---

[82]   Davis *et al.*, *supra* note 81, 1; Watts, *supra* note 3, 16; Y. Adeoye, 'Of oil thieves and clueless governance' *The Vanguard* (6 March 2012) <http://www.vanguardngr.com/2012/03/of-oil-thieves-and-clueless-governance/> accessed 28 May 2012.

[83]   Onwuka Nzeshi. 'Shell: Nigeria loses $5bn to crude oil theft annually'. *This Day* (27 June 2012) <http://www.thisdaylive.com/articles/shell-nigeria-loses-5bn-to-crude-oil-theft-annually/118825/> accessed 14 August 2012.

[84]   Davis *et al.*, *supra* note 81, 2; Peel, *supra* note 28, 11.

[85]   Davis *et al.*, *supra* note 81, 2, 5–6; E. Chinwo and E. Alike, 'JTF arrests vessels carrying 1.3m barrels of stolen crude' *This Day* (9 May 2012) <http://www.thisdaylive.com/articles/jtf-arrests-vessels-carrying-1-3m-barrels-of-stolen-crude/115454/> accessed 28 May 2012.

some has been traded on the Rotterdam spot market.[86] Payments are usually in cash but weapons and drugs have also been traded.[87]

Not all oil is stolen from pipes. Authorized dealers may 'lift' more than their allocation from legal terminals. Despite the fact that this form of fraud is considered widespread it attracts little attention.[88] Neither does all the oil leave Nigeria: some is fed (or refined in incredibly dangerous illegal refineries and then fed) into the domestic market.[89]

None of this would happen without the complicity of many in Nigeria's political elites, the national oil company (NNOC) and military.[90] Illegal bunkering was common under the military governments but escalated sharply with return to civilian rule. Ships were seized and suspects arrested but even impounded ships were able to slip away: the *African Pride* loaded with 80,000 barrels of crude sailed away from a navy-secured wharf in 2004. Three Nigerian admirals were court-martialed as a consequence.[91]

4.10 PIRACY: TYPES, TACTICS AND CONSEQUENCES

The number of piracy attacks is also unknown. Under-reporting of piracy incidents is commonplace around the world, although its extent varies.[92] Off Somalia under-reporting is generally thought limited whereas off Nigeria it may be considerable; some observers suggest that between 50 and 80 percent of cases may go unreported with the numbers for those killed and injured similarly distorted.[93] Just as importantly, the baseline

---

[86] Davis *et al.*, *supra* note 81, 7.

[87] *Ibid.*, 6.

[88] *Ibid.*, 3.

[89] C. Purefoy, 'Death and oil in the Niger Delta's illegal refineries' (*CNN*, 10 August 2010) <http://articles.cnn.com/2010–08–03/world/nigeria.oil.niger. delta_1_heating-oil-oil-industry-crude?_s=PM:WORLD> accessed 28 May 2012.

[90] Soares de Oliveira, *supra* note 2, 93, 119; Francis *et al.*, *supra* note 3, 59; Nodland, *supra* note 4, 201.

[91] Davis *et al.*, *supra* note 81, 11–12.

[92] For a discussion of this issue see M. N. Murphy, *Small Boats, Weak States, Dirty Money: Piracy and Maritime Terrorism in the Modern World* (Hurst 2009), 65–72.

[93] ICC International Maritime Bureau, 'Piracy and Armed Robbery against Ships' Report for the Period 1 January–31 December 2011, 24; B. Komolafe, 'Nigeria: 50 percent of pirate attacks in country unreported – ICC' *The Vanguard* (22 October 2009) <http://allafrica.com/stories/200910221228.html> accessed 28 May 2012; R. Hawkes. 'Securing the Offshore Oil Industry in the Gulf of

of Nigerian piracy has remained consistently high: as recently as 2002–2003 there were many more *recorded* cases in Nigerian waters than there were off Somalia, where the upswing only started between 2004 and 2005.

Six types of piracy are identifiable around the world today (see Table 4.1). All except Type Five have occurred in the waters of Nigeria or its immediate neighbors.

Table 4.1 Modern piracy typology

Type	Category	Description	Example
1	Inland water assault	Small bands in harbors, etc. akin to petty thieving; rarely violent	Chittagong, Santos, Indonesian ports; Lagos
2	Local vessel assault	Can be violent; fishing common cause; often persistent	Ganges Delta; Malacca Strait, Nigeria
3	Coastal shipping/ installation assault	Perpetrators can use or threaten violence; primary objective is theft of crew valuables or ship's equipment; kidnap-and ransom (K&R) in some locations	Malacca & Singapore Straits; South China Sea; Nigeria & parts of Gulf of Guinea
4	Major ship assaults	Theft of ship and cargo; selective K&R; highly organized	SE Asia, Nigeria & parts of Gulf of Guinea
5	Major hostage-taking	K&R overriding objective; highly organized	Somalia
6	Coastal raiding	Currently rare; historically common	Philippines; Sabah; Gulf of Guinea

Guinea' in C. Berube and P. Cullen (eds), *Maritime Private Security: Market Responses to Piracy, Terrorism and Waterborne Security Risks in the 21st Century* (Routledge 2012) 138, 140.

The fact that the threat to shipping and offshore infrastructure is distributed so broadly makes Nigeria the most challenging maritime security environment on Earth. Most incidents occur in Nigeria's inland or territorial waters, although this is changing as gangs venture further out to sea. That this means they are not legally piracy but armed robbery at sea and, consequently, Nigeria's sole responsibility might go some way to explaining high under-reporting rates. As with any crime, reporting is discouraged if victims have little confidence that an attempt will be made to investigate or prosecute perpetrators.[94] Inadequate capacity at Lagos means that ships still have to drift offshore sometimes for weeks waiting for a berth.[95] At the same time the Nigerian navy lacks sufficient patrol craft to enforce national jurisdiction over the country's territorial waters let alone its exclusive economic zone (EEZ).[96] While it is taking steps to rectify this, training the personnel needed to man these vessels effectively takes time and needs to occur in parallel with action to reduce pervasive corruption in the armed forces. Confronting these two challenges simultaneously will not be easy and improvements may be slow to materialize.[97] Other Gulf of Guinea navies are even more debilitated.

Piracy is organized predation. In Nigerian waters, Type One, Two and Three attacks are perpetrated by loosely organized gangs that seek out opportunities based on perceived weakness: ships and platforms that have taken sufficient self-protection measures are ignored and weaker prey sought instead. These criminals look to get on-board quickly and quietly – often at night – and aim to leave quickly after taking the main portable

---

[94] J. Saul and M. John, 'Pirates eye share of Gulf of Guinea riches' (*Reuters*, 29 July 2011) <http://af.reuters.com/article/nigeriaNews/idAFL6E7IS1K9201 10729?sp=true> accessed 28 May 2012.

[95] Mike Schuler, 'West African Waters Receive "High Piracy Risk" Designation' (*gCaptain*, 30 March 2012) <http://gcaptain.com/west-africa-waters-receive-high/?43346&utm_source=feedburner&utm_medium=feed&utm_campaign=Feed%3A+Gcaptain+%28gCaptain.com%29> accessed 28 May 2012.

[96] D. J. Whiteneck, 'Piracy Enterprise in Africa' (Center for Naval Analyses, June 2011) 34 <http://www.cna.org/sites/default/files/OTA%20Piracy%20 Enterprises%20in%20Africa%20D0023394%20A2.pdf> accessed 28 May 2012.

[97] 'Nigeria takes delivery of security vessels' (*defenceWeb*, 2 May 2012) <http://www.defenceweb.co.za/index.php?option=com_content&view=article& id=25288:nigeria-takes-delivery-of-security-vessels&catid=51:Sea&Itemid=106> accessed 28 May 2012; 'Nigerian maritime police receive patrol craft as piracy, illegal bunkering increase' (*defenceWeb*, 9 May 2012) <http://www.defence web.co.za/index.php?option=com_content&view=article&id=25428:nigerian-marine-police-receive-patrol-craft-as-piracy-illegal-bunkering-increases&catid=108: maritime-security&Itemid=233> accessed 28 May 2012.

valuables amongst the crew's possessions and the ship's equipment. They will, however, readily use or threaten violence to enforce compliance.[98] These raids generally happen so rapidly that navies, even if they have resources available, have too little time to respond before the pirates have escaped. Those involved have knowledge of the local waters and also appear to have inside information about cargoes, ship movements and naval dispositions; they can undertake pre-attack reconnaissance easily by mixing with hundreds of similar small craft populating Nigeria's coastal waters.[99]

These craft include offshore support and supply boats which are perfect for opportunistic robbery because of their slow speed and low freeboards. Oil workers are equally easy to abduct for ransom from small, isolated offshore platforms.[100] Fishing vessels appear to be particularly vulnerable.[101] According to official figures, pirates attacked Nigerian fishing vessels 293 times between 2003 and 2008, losing the industry around $600 million annually in exports.[102] They succeeded in 'ravaging Nigeria's fisheries sector' and in response 'most of the boats were tied down at jetties' during 2008 in protest at the government's inaction.[103] Fishermen's leaders stated the problem extended from the Niger Delta as far west as Lagos.[104]

Of greater concern are the highly organized Type Four attacks mounted by militant groups such as MEND to disable oil installations and also by criminal gangs focused on oil theft. Their modus operandi is now closer to that of Somali pirates: a high speed approach culminating in automatic gunfire directed at the ship's bridge and accommodation block backed up

---

[98]   Hawkes, *supra* note 93, 143; Whiteneck, *supra* note 96, 32; Nodland, *supra* note 4, 196.

[99]   Whiteneck, *supra* note 96, 35–38.

[100]   Nodland, *supra* note 4, 197. See also, for example J. Gambrell, 'Oil supply ship workers kidnapped near Nigeria' *Associated Press* (19 November 2011)   <http://www.sfgate.com/cgi-bin/article.cgi?f=/c/a/2011/11/18/MNG81M 162M.DTL> accessed 28 May 2012.

[101]   'Militancy is responsible for piracy in the Niger Delta' *Nigeria News* (6 July   2010)   <http://news2.onlinenigeria.com/index.php?news=43932&output_ type=rss> accessed 28 May 2012.

[102]   Nodland, *supra* note 4, 195–196.

[103]   ONI, 'Worldwide Threat to Shipping Report' (14 July 2006). See also I. Obi, 'Fish on the run: How pirates attacks on fishing trawlers hike price of fish' *The Vanguard* (2 March 2008).

[104]   B. Olatunji, 'Operators withdraw trawlers over pirates' attacks' *This Day* (4 February 2008); S. Simpson, 'A rise in pirate attacks off Nigeria's coast' *Christian Science Monitor* (20 March 2008).

by the threat or use of rocket-propelled grenades (RPGs) to force the ship to accept boarders.[105] These groups appear to have substantial political and financial backing in Nigeria. Since 2010 there has been a rise in attacks off Benin and Togo, whose navies are even less capable than Nigeria's; more recently Nigerian pirates have begun using mother ships to extend their range.[106] Small product tankers are used to transfer oil stolen from larger ships to the same countries that have been known to accept Nigerian crude.[107] Attacks include those on a diesel carrier, the RBD *Anema e Core*, 23 nm off the coast of Benin in 2011 and the BW *Rhine* seized from an anchorage off Togo in April 2012, which was released minus an unspecified quantity of its $60 million cargo of gasoline.[108] Had all of it been taken it would have made Somali seizures look paltry; the highest ransom ever received by Somali pirates was believed to be $13.5 million in 2011 for the *Irene SL*, a Very Large Crude Carrier (VLCC) carrying a cargo worth $200 million.[109] Evidence suggests that the Gulf of Guinea gangs are becoming bolder and that the jump in attacks in the first quarter of 2012 – to as many as for the whole of 2011 – may be sustained.[110]

---

[105] Whiteneck, *supra* note 96, 40.

[106] 'Nigerian pirates expected to increase use of hijacked vessels as motherships' *Insurance Day* (12 April 2012) <http://www.insuranceday.com/insday/viewArticle.htm?id=282806&rss=true> accessed 28 May 2012.

[107] M.W. Bockman and R. Sheridan, 'Pirates double Gulf of Guinea attacks, lured by tanker cargoes' (*Bloomberg*, 8 March 2012) <http://www.bloomberg.com/news/2012–03–08/west-african-oil-tanker-hijackings-double-as-pirates-lured-by-ship-cargoes.html> accessed 28 May 2012; 'Nigeria MEND militants claim attack, threaten oil ships' (*Reuters*, 2 March 2012) <http://uk.reuters.com/article/2012/03/02/nigeria-militants-idUKL5E8E21HI20120302> accessed 28 May 2012.

[108] 'IMB issues piracy warning for Benin' (*ICC Commercial Crime Services*, 14 June 2011) <http://www.icc-ccs.org/news/297-imb-issues-piracy-warning-for-benin> accessed 28 May 2012; 'Italian tanker Anema e Core seized by pirates off Benin' (*BBC News*, 24 July 2011) <http://www.bbc.co.uk/news/world-africa-14270010> accessed 28 May 2012; 'Pirates release tanker after stealing gasoline cargo' (*The Maritime Executive*, 4 May 2012) <http://www.maritime-executive.com/article/pirates-release-tanker-after-stealing-gasoline-cargo> accessed 28 May 2012.

[109] A. Mwangura, 'VLCC Irene SL freed by pirates' (*Somalia Report*, 8 April 2011) <http://www.somaliareport.com/index.php/post/477/VLCC_Irene_SL_Freed_By_Pirates> accessed 28 May 2012.

[110] P. T. Leach, 'West Africa seen growing piracy hot spot' *The Journal of Commerce* (23 April 2012) <http://www.joc.com/trade-lanes/west-africa-seen-growing-piracy-hot-spot> accessed 28 May 2012.

The economic consequences are already apparent: the Joint War Committee of Lloyd's has extended the Perceived Enhanced Risk (PER) area for Nigeria to cover Benin and up to 200 nm miles off both coasts.[111] Because of the heightened risks to shipping, necessary investments in ships and port infrastructure will be deferred. Without investment in more efficient cargo handling systems, shipping companies will not introduce the large, fast ships that can avoid pirates onto African routes. The smaller, slower freighters that can use the Gulf of Guinea's under-developed ports will remain in operation and vulnerable to attack.[112]

The United Nations Security Council, having stated its disquiet about piracy in the Gulf of Guinea in August 2011, passed resolution 2018 in October in which it expressed its deepening concern about the problem and urged states to reinforce their domestic legislation, develop a comprehensive regional counter-piracy framework, issue appropriate guidance to shipping and cooperate in prosecuting pirates, their backers and financiers.[113] However, no measures under Chapter VII of the UN Charter were adopted.[114] In a follow-on briefing session held in February 2012 piracy was identified as a 'clear threat' to the region's stability and economic development. Benin explained that 'fees raised from the Port of Cotonou generated 80 per cent of the income for the national budget' but piracy attacks had seen 'the number of vessels entering the port-…[drop] by 70 per cent'. Looking at piracy's wider affects, the Economic Community of West African States (ECOWAS) and the Gulf of Guinea Commission (GGC) reported that piracy was 'rapidly spreading around the region and increasingly dovetailing into oil bunkering, robbery at sea, hostage-taking, human and drug trafficking, terrorism and corruption', while resource shortfalls and inadequate legal frameworks meant that pirate suspects were being released.[115] In an effort to overcome these

---

[111]   M. W. Bockman, 'Piracy spurs insurers to extend Nigeria war-risk zone, add Benin' (*Bloomberg*, 4 August 2011) <http://www.businessweek.com/news/2011-08-04/piracy-spurs-insurers-to-extend-nigeria-war-risk-zone-add-benin.html> accessed 28 May 2012.

[112]   M. L. Baker, 'Swapping Pirates for Commerce: An African Maritime Growth Initiative' *Foreign Affairs* (4 October 2010) <http://www.foreignaffairs.com/articles/66762/michael-lyon-baker/swapping-pirates-for-commerce> accessed 28 May 2012.

[113]   UNSC Res. 2018 (31 October 2011), UN Doc. S/RES/2018.

[114]   See, e.g., Chapters 6.3, 7.3, 8.3, 8.4 and 8.7.

[115]   UN Security Council, 'Gulf of Guinea piracy "clear threat" to security, economic development of region' (27 February 2012) <http://www.un.org/News/Press/docs/2012/sc10558.doc.htm> accessed 28 May 2012.

weaknesses the International Maritime Organization (IMO) began working with the Maritime Organization of West and Central Africa
(MOWCA) to develop a coast guard network and improve regional
maritime security cooperation.[116]

4.11 THINGS FALL APART

Nigeria's problems remain at the heart of this regional challenge. The
country's social structures may not differ substantially from those of its
neighbors but the comparative size of its population, the scale of its
economy and the overwhelming preponderance of its oil sector mean its
problems can affect them, particularly at sea where movement is easy and
security is lacking.

   With coercive response appearing to make little headway against Niger
Delta militants, the late president Yar'Adua wisely initiated the amnesty
program which continued under his successor Goodluck Jonathan. Most
of the MEND commanders, including, eventually, Henry Okah, the arms
dealer who might not have been MEND's leader as was suggested but
certainly had standing amongst its membership, accepted what was
offered although some who were more quickly disillusioned than others
picked up their arms again, most prominently John Togo, the leader of a
group named the Niger Delta Liberation Force (NDLF), who was
subsequently killed by the JTF.[117] However, this disillusionment appears
to be spreading and the amnesty looks as if it is beginning to unravel
fueled by a belief, similar to the one that drove the generational shift that
occurred in 2004, that the existing leadership had been bought off and
was now abandoning them.[118] During February 2012 an oil pipeline was

---

[116] C. Trelawny, 'The Naval Contribution to Sustainable Development in
West and Central Africa' (2007) 152(5) *RUSI Journal* 70–74.

[117] 'Nigerian rebel "accepts amnesty"' (*BBC News*, 10 July 2009) <http://
news.bbc.co.uk/2/hi/africa/8143195.stm> accessed 14 August 2012; Emma
Amaize, 'How the JTF bombed John Togo to death' *The Vanguard* (22 May
2012)   <http://www.vanguardngr.com/2011/05/how-jtf-bombed-john-togo-to-
death/> accessed 14 August 2012; Emma Amaize, 'Nigeria: John Togo – JTF
denies extra-judicial killing' *The Vanguard* (14 June 2012) <http://allafrica.com/
stories/201206140383.html> accessed 14 August 2012.

[118] Bisi Olaniyi, 'Niger Delta amnesty: Two years after' *The Nation* (16
October   2011)   <http://www.thenationonlineng.net/2011/index.php/politics/
22969-niger-delta-amnesty-two-years-after.html> accessed 14 August 2012;
Emmanuel Addeh, 'FG's amnesty and renewed insurgency in Niger Delta' *Punch*

sabotaged and a group of four police officers shot dead.[119] The renegades have styled themselves 'third phase militants'; they appear to be using MEND-style tactics in pursuit of more limited objectives. They are present in all the major oil producing areas and the security situation is likely to turn critical unless the financial and employment benefits of the amnesty are extended.[120]

Although Nigerian governments have tried amnesties before, notably the Obasanjo regime in 2004, the Yar'Adua initiative was a bold move. Under Obasanjo some 5,000 weapons were handed in and militancy declined sharply, but no attempt was made to reintegrate the youths involved or to address the wider sources of discontent. The 2009 amnesty was designed to overcome this shortcoming by not only inducing militants to hand in their weapons for cash payments but also to enroll them in rehabilitation and training programs.[121] Suspicion of the government's sincerity was strong initially but around 26,000 militants from various organizations eventually surrendered.[122] Nonetheless, if estimates placing the total militant population at 50,000 were correct, then many remained resistant to government entreaties.

(18 March 2012) <http://www.punchng.com/politics/fgs-amnesty-and-renewed-insurgency-in-niger-delta/> accessed 14 August 2012; 'Emeka Mamah and Emma Amaize, 'MEND resumes hostilities' *The Vanguard* (6 February 2012) <http://www.vanguardngr.com/2012/02/mend-resumes-hostilities-2/> accessed 14 August 2012.

[119] 'Nigeria's MEND claims fatal attack on police' (*AlJazeera*, 2 March 2012) <http://www.aljazeera.com/news/africa/2012/03/201232171741677448.html> accessed 14 August 2012; 'MEND attack Agip facility in Bayelsa' *The Vanguard* (14 April 2012) <http://www.vanguardngr.com/2012/04/mend-attack-agip-oil-facility-in-bayelsa/> accessed 14 August 2012; Elisha Bala-Gbogbo, 'Nigerian Delta unrest cuts oil output by 1 million barrels' (*Bloomberg*, 5 March 2012) <http://www.bloomberg.com/news/2012–03–04/nigeria-s-nnpc-says-unrest-cuts-oil-output-by-1-million-barrels.html> accessed 14 August 2012.

[120] Bergen Risk Solutions, *Niger Delta Security Briefing*, 3 May 2012, Slide 20; Osa Okhomina, 'Nigeria: JTF arrest militant leader, General Cairo over attacks on Agip, Shell facilities' (29 June 2012) *Leadership* (Abuja) <http://allafrica.com/stories/201206300163.html> accessed 14 August 2012.

[121] 'Nigeria offers militants amnesty' (*BBC News*, 26 June 2009) <http://news.bbc.co.uk/2/hi/8118314.stm> accessed 28 May 2012.

[122] Victor Ojakoroto and Lysias Dodd Gilbert, 'Checkmating the Resurgence of Oil Violence in the Niger Delta of Nigeria' (18 May 2010) *Journal of Energy Security* SPECIAL REPORT, pdf available at <http://www.iags.org/Niger_Delta_book.pdf > accessed 8 November 2012.

The amnesty's terms were generous: militants who turned themselves in were paid a monthly stipend worth three times the minimum wage.[123] This has naturally led to critics pointing out that the program was fiscally unsustainable with more money going to ex-militants than to the health service; on the other side of the debate the ex-leader of the NDPVF, Dokubo-Asari, argued the program cost no more than two days of oil revenue, which was nothing compared to the damage inflicted on the Delta over many years.[124] The amnesty's flaw, however, was the assumption that the militancy was simply an outbreak of 'large-scale organized crime' in which 'once legitimate grievances [had] been abandoned to outright predation'. It consequently failed to address the fact that Delta tribal groups felt they were supporting a corrupt political class and had not benefitted from the half a trillion dollars the oil industry has paid Nigeria since 1970. Whatever success the amnesty may have achieved has been further circumscribed by the government's failure to follow through with more substantial reform, infrastructure development and jobs.[125] Peace was bought not built. The risk was always that some would return to the region's creeks and begin the cycle of violence all over again.[126] This seems to be what is happening.[127] One expression of that has been the growth of piracy: militancy has moved offshore.[128]

---

[123] Francis *et al.*, *supra* note 3, 17.

[124] 'Jonathan's budget shocker: Ex-militant's get more money than health sector' (*PM News*, 16 March 2012) <http://pmnewsnigeria.com/2012/03/16/jonathans-budget-shocker-ex-militants-get-more-money-than-health-sector/> accessed 28 May 2012; 'Asari Dokubo says N74 billion not enough for amnesty programme' (*Channels*, 20 March 2012) <http://www.channelstv.com/home/2012/03/20/asari-dokubo-says-n74billion-is-not-enough-for-amnesty-programme/> accessed 28 May 2012.

[125] Watts, *supra* note 46, 29; M. N. Murphy, 'The Troubled Waters of Africa' (2011) 2(1) *The Journal of the Middle East and Africa* 82.

[126] T. Strouse, 'Will Nigeria's Amnesty Campaign Have a Lasting Impact on the Delta Insurgency?' (2009) VII(32) The Jamestown Foundation *Terrorism Monitor*, 5–8 <http://www.jamestown.org/uploads/media/TM_007_6193ae.pdf> accessed 28 May 2012.

[127] Addeh, *supra* note 118.

[128] 'Analysis: Niger Delta still unstable despite amnesty' (*IRIN*, 25 November 2011) <http://ww.irinnews.org/report.aspx?reportid=94306> accessed 28 May 2012.

4.12 CONCLUSIONS: PIRACY BY LAND AND SEA

In 2005 the US National Intelligence Council (NIC) predicted that Nigeria would be a failed state by 2020.[129] Arguably it had already failed when the prediction was made. Various criteria for state failure have been advanced but all center on the idea that states which are unable to control all their territory, cannot deliver public goods effectively to the majority of inhabitants and are no longer recognized by them as legitimate. On such criteria Nigeria was ranked 14th in the 2011 *Failed States Index*.[130] But elite attitudes are as good a guide as broken roads and rampant criminality. By encouraging corruption and criminality to flourish, elites can benefit economically to the point where a form of partial or controlled collapse serves their interests. From this perspective only one factor separates Nigeria from Somalia and that is oil.

Oil states in the developing world are shielded from the domestic and international pressures that can bring down their non-oil neighbors.[131] The current international system which makes international recognition, not internal legitimacy or functionality, the key to state authority works to the benefit of oil states. It encourages those parts which are valuable to industrialized powers – and to the domestic elites who facilitate and benefit from international legitimization – to function well enough for resource extraction to continue. The security of the state generally matters less than the security of key enclaves which support elite interests. These include the oil and gas fields and the necessary export infrastructure. As Soares de Oliveira has pointed out, these enclaves bear an uncanny resemblance to the trading and slaving factories established around the Gulf of Guinea in pre-colonial times.[132]

---

[129] *Mapping Sub-Saharan Africa's Future: Conference Summary* (National Intelligence Council, March 2006) 16 <http://www.dni.gov/nic/PDF_GIF_confreports/africa_future.pdf> accessed 28 May 2012. See also J. P. Pham: 'Nigeria Teeters Back from the Brink – For Now' (*World Defense Review*, 3 May 2007) <http://worlddefensereview.com/pham050307.shtml> accessed 28 May 2012; and 'Nigeria at the Crossroads – Again' (*World Defense Review*, 16 September 2010) <http://worlddefensereview.com/pham091610.shtml> accessed 28 May 2012. For a Nigerian commentary see, for example, 'Nigeria as a failing state' *Punch* (30 June 2011) <http://odili.net/news/source/2011/jun/30/834.html> accessed 28 May 2012.

[130] Foreign Policy and The Fund for Peace *Failed States Index 2011* <http://www.foreignpolicy.com/articles/2011/06/17/2011_failed_states_index_interactive_map_and_rankings> accessed 28 May 2012.

[131] Soares de Oliveira, *supra* note 2, 20–21, 39–40, 57.

[132] *Ibid.*, 54, 105–107.

Because oil emancipates the state from society, defensive perimeters are drawn around the enclaves leaving the space in between them relatively unprotected.[133] In Nigeria the response to insecurity has been further militarization rather than political engagement; disruptive actors are categorized as criminals and pirates.[134] These labels are applied indiscriminately.[135] As one senior company manager put it, the amnesty reduced onshore militancy but replaced it with 'staggering levels of theft and criminality'.[136] The term 'blood oil' has, moreover, entered the debate, seemingly designed to invoke comparisons with the 'blood diamonds' trade; a trade, it is worth recalling, that was controlled by failed state elites as much if not more than insurgents.[137]

The militants angrily reject the criminal label.[138] From their perspective the principal act of engagement, the amnesty, 'should not be an end in itself. Today, the devastation in the area remains the same ... there's no blueprint for development.'[139] Over 70 percent of Delta inhabitants continue to lack access to electricity, clean water, medical care and other services. Extraordinarily, since oil was discovered Nigerian GDP per capita and life expectancy have both declined.[140] The time that paying the militants should have bought to bring about change has not been used to advance a more broadly based political settlement. To do that would mean confronting the over-riding problem of elite corruption.

---

[133]   *Ibid.*, 36–37, 109; A. Hirsch and J. Vidal, 'Shell spending millions of dollars on security in Nigeria, leaked data shows' *The Guardian* (19 August 2012) <http://www.guardian.co.uk/business/2012/aug/19/shell-spending-security-nigeria-leak> accessed 20 August 2012.

[134]   E.g., Addeh, *supra* note 118.

[135]   'Resurgence of criminal militancy in the Niger Delta' *Punch* (12 February 2012)   <http://www.punchng.com/editorial/resurgence-of-criminal-militancy-in-niger-delta/> accessed 28 May 2012.

[136]   Adeoye, *supra* note 82.

[137]   J. B. Asuni, 'Blood Oil in the Niger Delta' (August 2009) US Institute of Peace,   *Special   Report   229*   <http://www.usip.org/files/resources/blood_oil_nigerdelta.pdf> accessed 28 May 2012.

[138]   D. Francis, 'Move over Boka Haram, Nigeria's MEND rebels set to restart oil war in Niger Delta' *Christian Science Monitor* (30 October 2011) <http://www.csmonitor.com/World/Africa/2011/1030/Move-over-Boko-Haram-Nigeria-s-MEND-rebels-set-to-restart-oil-war-in-Niger-Delta> accessed 28 May 2012.

[139]   Addeh, *supra* note 118.

[140]   Watts, *supra* note 3, 16.

The Delta's problems will not, however, be addressed with the urgency they demand because the militancy to which they give rise is perceived as manageable. At sea this requires that the major oil carriers must be able to come and go, and the major offshore platforms allowed to operate in relative safety. Ensuring that this remains the case will become the Nigerian navy's primary purpose; ships and platforms will become the equivalent of on-shore enclaves. It is likely, however, that private security companies (PSCs) will play an increasing role, as they have on land and off the coast of Somalia.[141]

Much will have to change if the fundamental social issues are to be addressed. Instead the amnesty has bought time to re-balance and reinforce the state's coercive power; including the purchase of new vessels for the Nigerian navy and army, the establishment of Operation Pulo Shield, a JTF campaign to hit illegal oil bunkerers and refiners, and closer cooperation with foreign navies.[142] The IOCs are complicit in this but so, ultimately, are their customers. The interests of the domestic elites and industrialized societies are aligned. Recommendations for reform are plentiful.[143] The bottom line, however, is that industrialized societies need oil. The US may import around one quarter of its oil requirement from the Gulf of Guinea – largely Nigeria – by 2015. External pressure for change will therefore never be applied beyond the point where supply is jeopardized; in any clash of interests, the language and methods of

---

[141] Hawkes, supra note 93, 139–140, 148. On the ex-MEND leader who won an anti-piracy security contract see: J. Gambrell. 'Nigerian ex-militant forges security contract' (*Associated Press*, 4 April 2012) <http://www.washingtontimes.com/news/2012/apr/4/nigerian-ex-militant-forges-security-contract/print/> accessed 28 May 2012.

[142] S. Oyadongha, 'FG approves new operational status for JTF' *The Vanguard* (11 January 2012) <http://www.vanguardngr.com/2012/01/fg-approves-new-operational-status-for-jtf/> accessed 28 May 2012; D. Axe, 'Allies copy US Navy smart-power strategy' (*World Politics Review*, 24 April 2009) <http://www.worldpoliticsreview.com/articles/3646/allies-copy-u-s-navy-smart-power-strategy> accessed 28 May 2012.

[143] See, e.g., Francis *et al.*, *supra* note 3, 101–121. For a summary of domestic recommendations see J. Shola Omotola, 'Niger Delta Technical Committee (NDTC) and the Niger Delta Question' in Victor Ojakorotu (ed.) *Anatomy of the Niger Delta Crisis: Causes, Consequences and Opportunities for Peace* (LIT Verlag 2010) 99–119.

security will prevail.[144] In this context there is perhaps little point in discussing the disinterested application of law at sea when it is applied so selectively on land.

---

[144] C. J. Kinnon, *et al. Failed State 2030: Nigeria – A Case Study* (Air War College, Center for Strategy and Technology Occasional Paper No. 67, February 2011) <http://www.hsdl.org/?view&did=697456> accessed 28 May 2012; M. N. Murphy, *Littoral Combat Ship: An Examination of its Possible Concepts of Operation* (Center for Strategic and Budgetary Assessments 2010) 54–60 <http://www.csbaonline.org/publications/2010/03/littoral-combat-ship-concepts-of-operations/> accessed 28 May 2012; Peel, *supra* note 28, 6.

5. Responses to contemporary piracy: disentangling the organizational field

Christian Bueger*

5.1 INTRODUCTION: COUNTER-PIRACY PRACTICE AND ITS ORGANIZATIONAL FIELD

The problem of contemporary piracy has led to the rise of a complex organizational field. A myriad of governmental and non-governmental actors, UN agencies and international organizations have become active in counter-piracy. This chapter sets out to disentangle the field of counter-piracy. The objective is to present a systematic overview of the different actors engaged in counter-piracy and the forums in which activities are organized and coordinated. The question that this chapter seeks to answer is hence straightforward: which actors do what and where in counter-piracy? I address this question by providing a mapping of counter-piracy practice. The mapping is organized along a functional axis: counter-piracy activities can be captured in the way they contribute to different functional streams or categories of practice. These streams include governance, epistemic, military, law enforcement, development and humanitarian practices. While attempting to be comprehensive, my focus is on the main actors and I do not consider unilateral or bilateral initiatives unless they have significantly shaped the international counter-piracy field.

Such a mapping is useful in several regards. It has become very difficult to navigate through the increasingly complex and rapidly developing organizational jungle of counter-piracy. This is especially the case for practitioners new to the field. Coordinating the diverse counter-piracy actors is an ongoing challenge not the least to avoid contradictory projects, and duplication. It is also important to guarantee a better

* I am grateful to Douglas Guilfoyle for comments which have considerably improved the manuscript and to Mohanvir Singh Saran for research assistance.

management of knowledge about piracy and counter-piracy and to ensure that lessons learned by one agency are recognized and considered by another. Mapping the field is moreover a means to identify where and how actors compete over resources and symbolic capital in the field. Since many, if not all of the agencies have been acronymized, I also provide a guide for encoding these acronyms.

The chapter is organized as follows. In the first section I briefly discuss the notion of an *organizational field* that underlies my mapping. I provide a succinct contemporary history of the field of counter-piracy and suggest that since 2008 it has significantly expanded, if not exploded, in size and complexity. As I demonstrate, the complex and networked character of the field is productive for addressing piracy. But the field is also not free of tensions, since some agencies compete, and practical approaches conflict with each other. Next, I give a brief overview of the categories of counter-piracy practices which organize my following mapping. The subsequent sections discuss each set of counter-piracy practices in more detail and show how different actors participate in them. I end in suggesting that one of the future challenges of counter-piracy will be to organize activities more coherently, without, however, loosing flexibility and problem-orientation.

5.2 COUNTER-PIRACY AS ORGANIZATIONAL FIELD

Piracy is an old problem, yet until recently it was not considered to be a politically relevant problem. It was an issue of interest for historians or political and legal theorists. A re-evaluation of maritime piracy can be observed since the late 1980s, when the first publications on maritime piracy as a contemporary problem appeared and piracy became an issue discussed in international organizations such as the International Maritime Organization (IMO) or the International Chamber of Commerce (ICC).[1]

In response to the piracy incidents in East Asia and later Somalia and West Africa (as discussed in Chapters 2 to 4) a growing number of

---

[1] Roger Villar, *Piracy Today: Robbery and Violence at Sea since 1980* (Conway Maritime Press 1985); Malvina Halberstam, 'Terrorism on the High Seas: the Achilla Lauro, Piracy and the IMO Convention on Maritime Safety' (1988) 82 *American Journal of International Law* 269; Samuel Pyeatt Menefee, 'The New "Jamaica Discipline": Problems with Piracy, Maritime Terrorism and the 1982 Convention on the Law of the Sea' (1990) 6 *Connecticut Journal of International Law* 127.

organizations have become active in counter-piracy. These include various types of organizations, such as governments, navies and coast guards, inter-governmental organizations, international administrative services and international implementation agencies, non-governmental organizations (NGOs), industry associations or private security companies (PSCs). Counter-piracy has become a nascent 'organizational field'.

The concept of 'organizational fields', as developed in sociology, refers to a set of organizations which are active in what Di Maggio and Powell call 'a recognized area of institutional life'.[2] An organizational field is a sphere of activity constituted by organizations which are committed to act within it. The organizational field of counter-piracy is constituted by the relations of organizations which recognize piracy as a major problem and are committed to act against it.

The notion of organizational fields is particularly useful to describe counter-piracy activities for at least three reasons. It is firstly increasingly employed in international relations analysis[3] since it transcends the boundary between the levels of private and public organizations, and the levels of sub-state, inter-state and supra-state organizations. Such a perspective allows disaggregating the state as a unified actor and paying attention to the various sub-, inter- and supra-state actors as they play in the international arena. Moreover, rather than taking boundaries, such as the public-private distinction or state sovereignty, for granted it enables the analysis to explore how various types of organizations interact and form through their relations a common sphere of activity. Hence, the notion invites exploration of how a broad array of organizations aims at addressing a distinct problem such as piracy.

Secondly, the perspective encourages studying the practice of organizations in the field.[4] Rather than studying the formal mandates and rules

---

[2] Paul J. DiMaggio and Walter W. Powell, 'The Iron Cage Revisited: Institutional Isomorphism and Collective Rationality in Organizational Fields' (1983) *American Sociological Review* 147, 148.

[3] See, among others, Klaus Dingwerth and Philipp Pattberg, 'World Politics and Organizational Fields: The Case of Transnational Sustainability Governance' (2009) 15 *European Journal of International Relations* 707; Julian Go, 'Global Fields and Imperial Forms: Field Theory and the British and American Empires' (2008) 26 *Sociological Theory* 201; Nicolas Guilhot, *The Democracy Makers. Human Rights and the Politics of Global Order* (Columbia University Press 2005).

[4] For the notion of a 'practice' as it is used here see Andreas Reckwitz, 'Toward a Theory of Social Practices' (2002) 5 *European Journal of Social Theory* 243; Emanuel Adler and Vincent Pouliot, 'International Practices' (2011) 3 *International Theory* 1; Christian Bueger and Frank Gadinger, 'Praktisch

informing organizational behaviour, the focus is on the (often informal) *activities* of organizations. Such a perspective is particularly useful for the case of counter-piracy, which is characterized by a more fluid, less orderly form of governance and informal decision making in settings such as contact and working groups.[5]

Thirdly, the notion of organizational fields highlights the importance of conflicts and struggles between organizations. While organizations in a field are committed to act within the field, they compete over resources and symbolic capital. Such resources not only include money, but also the power to define, to set the agenda, to prioritize activities or to position other actors in the field in providing roles for them. Phrased otherwise, an organizational field is always also a field of power relations characterized by a struggle for domination.[6] Paying attention to such struggles is important to understand the lack of cooperation, the overlap of activities, competition, and what happens when new organizations enter the field.

The organizational field of counter-piracy has become considerably extended since the mid-1980s. While the boundaries of the field are difficult to draw, since they constitute part of the struggle in the field,[7] it is useful to see the extension of the field along two dimensions: a geographical one and a functional one. Along the geographical dimension, counter-piracy was initially treated as an issue that referred to distinct coastlines or harbours. It was a 'local' problem to be dealt with by local authorities as well as through self-regulative means of the shipping industry. With the growing number of incidents in Southeast Asia, piracy was increasingly recognized as an inter-state and regional problem demanding governmental action from regional states throughout the 1990s. Finally, with the rise of Somali piracy, the problem of piracy,

---

Gedacht! Praxistheoretischer Konstruktivismus in den Internationalen Beziehungen' (2008) 15 *Zeitschrift für Internationale Beziehungen* 273.

[5] See, for instance, Douglas Guilfoyle, 'The Contact Group on Piracy off the Coast of Somalia: Piracy, Governance and International Law' (2013) *Global Policy* (forthcoming) and James Kraska, *Contemporary Maritime Piracy: International Law, Strategy, and Diplomacy at Sea* (Praeger 2011).

[6] Compare Mustafa Emirbayer and Victoria Johnson, 'Bourdieu and Organizational Analysis' (2008) 37 *Theory and Society* 1.

[7] These boundaries concern the relation between counter-piracy and counter-terrorism, the boundary towards the larger maritime security agenda and, if the root cause dimension is considered, the boundary to the statebuilding and failed states agenda.

and with it the organizational field, has become increasingly international. It was recognized that the problem demands action by international actors to complement the work of regional or national ones. Seen from a functional perspective, piracy was initially treated as a specialized problem of 'maritime safety' on a level with other crimes such as fraud in shipping.[8] Hence, counter-piracy was mainly an issue in the hands of specialized agencies such as the IMO, shipping associations or maritime insurers. Such a narrow understanding of the problem of piracy was significantly extended throughout the 1990s and 2000s, with piracy being linked to other issues of concern. Traditional international security actors, such as NATO, entered the field, and piracy was evaluated as having significant effects in terms of supply chain security, energy security or environmental security, and growing concerns over the link between piracy and terrorism were expressed. Yet it was also recognized that piracy relates to political and developmental issues such as poverty, official corruption, weak governance and state failure.[9] Piracy came to be acknowledged as a multi-dimensional problem that required a response by different functionally specialized actors; and the creation of new governance arrangements was considered to be necessary. As the result of these extensions, the organizational field of counter-piracy today is global in its reach and composed of various agencies including maritime, development and security organizations as well as a range of newly founded organizations and arrangements.

In what follows I disaggregate the organizational field of counter-piracy by providing a mapping of the practices that prevail in the organizational field. Since an organizational field is a sphere of activity, giving centre stage to practices is a useful way to organize a mapping. I detail what the practices are and the major organizations contributing to them.[10] My main focus is on the response to piracy originating in Somali

---

[8]   See for instance Villar, *supra* note 1.

[9]   See Jon Vagg, 'Rough Seas? Contemporary Piracy in South East Asia' (1995) 35 *British Journal of Criminology* 63; or Martin N. Murphy, *Somalia, The New Barbary?: Piracy and Islam in the Horn of Africa* (C Hurst & Co 2011).

[10]   Since my main objective is to provide an overview, I do not provide extensive references for the activities of each organization. For further details on the organizations the reader is advised to consult their homepages. An extensive list of links to such homepages is available at <http://piracy-studies.org>. I shall provide references only in so far as specific secondary literature is available on an activity. Related overviews of the counter-piracy field can be found in: Kraska, *supra* note 5; Christian Bueger and Jan Stockbruegger, 'Security Communities, Alliances and Macro-Securitization: The Practices of Counter-Piracy Governance', in Michael J. Struett, Mark T. Nance and Jon D. Carlson

piracy, since this has spurred the most extensive set of responses. I also attempt, however, to cover parts of the responses to piracy in East Asia and West Africa.

5.3   MAPPING COUNTER-PIRACY PRACTICE

My following discussion is structured through six broader categories of practices. These categories provide a working taxonomy for mapping counter-piracy practice. Firstly, *governance practices* are activities that attempt to give coherence to the overall field, to foster the interaction between organizations, to coordinate the other types of practices between organizations and to develop norms, rules and standards for the counter-piracy field. Secondly, *epistemic practices* are activities which render the phenomenon of piracy knowable and provide the backdrop from which to develop counter-piracy strategies and responses. Thirdly, *security practices* are activities that attempt to address piracy by exceptional measures, such as the use of military force. The underlying understanding of piracy is that of an existential threat and the main organizations are traditional security organizations. Fourthly, *law enforcement practices* treat piracy as a form of crime and attempt to address it by a range of law enforcement measures, such as arrest, prosecution and imprisonment. Fifthly, *developmental practices* are attempts to address piracy through its root causes. Piracy is framed as a problem of (under-)development and weak governance. The main organizations come from the field of development and aid. Sixthly, *humanitarian practices* highlight the consequences piracy has on individuals and communities and attempt to address piracy through measures such as assistance to seafarers. Below I discuss each of these practices in greater detail and show which organizations participate in them.

5.3.1   Governance Practices

Governance practices are activities that are attempts to give coherence to the overall field of counter-piracy. In such practices the relation and sharing of labour between organizations is negotiated and norms, rules and standards for the counter-piracy field are developed.

(eds), *Maritime Piracy and the Construction of Global Governance* (Routledge 2012) as well as Oceans Beyond Piracy, 'Counter Piracy Activity Matrix' (2012) <http://oceansbeyondpiracy.org/matrix/counter-piracy-activities-dynamic> accessed 9 August 2012.

Governance practices are carried out against the backdrop of existing norms and rules, such as the United Nations Convention of the Law of the Sea (UNCLOS). These norms and rules are re-interpreted in the frame of counter-piracy practice. Long-established organizations such as the IMO – the United Nations sub-organization dealing with maritime matters – and the United Nations Security Council (UNSC) – the main international body responsible for international peace and security – are pivotal organizations for governance practice. Yet also, recently established organizations explicitly founded to govern counter-piracy are crucial.

For the case of Somali piracy, the most important organization is the United Nations Contact Group on Piracy off the Coast of Somalia (CGPCS, hereafter: 'the Contact Group'). The Contact Group is not formally a UN body, but an informal consultation and negotiation mechanism without a standing secretariat. There are, moreover, increasing attempts to develop regional responses to East African piracy in the frame of existing organizations, such as the African Union (AU), the Southern African Development Community (SADC) and the East African Intergovernmental Authority on Development (IGAD). In addition, the IMO leads with support of the EU the development of a new organizational structure in the frame of the Djibouti Code of Conduct (DCoC) process that mainly includes Eastern African coastal states.

Counter-piracy concerning Somalia was initially an issue on the agenda of the IMO. Seeing itself not as having the mandate necessary to deal with the problem, the IMO forwarded the problem to the UNSC for the first time in 2005 and, in a second attempt, in 2007. The UNSC started to discuss the problem of piracy with reference to the Somali situation. In 2006 a first statement was issued, resolution 1801 on Somalia from February 2008 devoted a paragraph to piracy, and the subsequent resolution 1814 on Somalia equally referred to the piracy problem.[11] Resolution 1816 adopted in June 2008 was the first resolution dealing exclusively with piracy. A range of further statements and resolutions followed.[12]

The main governance vehicle for dealing with Somali piracy is the Contact Group.[13] The organization was established in January 2009 and was an outgrowth of Security Council resolution 1851, which called upon

---

[11]   See: UN Doc. S/PRST/2006/11; UNSC Res. 1801 (20 February 2008), UN Doc. S/RES/1801; UNSC Res. 1814 (15 May 2008), UN Doc. S/RES/1814.

[12]   See Chapter 3 and Kraska, supra note 5, 159 for an overview.

[13]   For an initial analyses of the work of the Contact Group see: Guilfoyle, *supra* note 5; Kraska, *supra* note 5; and Christian Bueger, 'The New Public Face

states to coordinate their counter-piracy activities. Upon its establishment it organized itself into a plenary and four working groups and, in 2011, a fifth working group was added. The Contact Group was originally launched as an initiative of 24 states. Since then, membership has considerably expanded. Further states joined the group, as did international organizations and, as observers, a growing number of industry associations. Today the Contact Group formally comprises 70 member states, and 19 international organizations (both inter-governmental and private). In addition, academic experts or representatives from entities such as the government of Somaliland and Puntland also participate in the meetings of the Contact Group. As James Kraska has remarked, the Contact Group is 'the broadest coalition of nations ever gathered to develop and coordinate practical solutions to the scourge of maritime piracy'.[14]

The Contact Group is an ad hoc, weakly institutionalized organization that has neither formalized working principles (in the form of a charter or terms of references) nor a secretariat beyond an internet presence and website. Since its establishment, the group has primarily served as a deliberative forum for strategy development and as a place to exchange information about the activities of the participating organizations. In its working groups it has facilitated military coordination in the Western Indian Ocean (further discussed in 5.3.3). It has elaborated and clarified a legal tool kit to address piracy, and provided a background arena for the preparation of several UN Security Council statements and resolutions. Moreover, it has assisted in the establishment of the IMO Djibouti Code of Conduct Trust Fund (a fund supporting the DCoC process), as well as the International Trust Fund to Support Initiatives of States Countering Piracy off the Coast of Somalia, which is a major funding vehicle for counter-piracy projects managed by the United Nations Office on Drugs and Crime (UNODC). It has moreover contributed to the development of the Best Management Practices (BMPs) for the self-protection of the industry by providing a forum for discussion, as well as formally endorsing the BMP. The main function of the Contact Group is firstly to be seen in providing a forum for exchange, and hence building trust and confidence among participating states and international organizations. Yet the Contact Group is also a form of accountability mechanism. In its format participating actors have to report on a frequent (bi-annual) basis

of the Contact Group' Piracy Studies Blog, 10 October 2011 <http://piracy-studies.org/2011/the-new-public-face-of-the-contact-group/> accessed 18 August 2012.

[14]   Kraska, *supra* note 5, 160.

on their activities. Hence, actors have to justify in front of a larger audience what they have (and have not) done in counter-piracy.

While the Contact Group is the main governance vehicle in Somali counter-piracy, the issue is also handled in other more formalized arenas, as well as in a range of informal deliberative processes. Formalized arenas include firstly the IMO governing bodies, that is, mainly the IMO Council and the IMO Maritime Safety Committee (IMO-MSC). Although the IMO initially hesitated to address piracy, its bodies have remained an important site for deliberating counter-piracy strategy and have been instrumental in legitimizing components of counter-piracy, such as the BMP or the DCoC process. The role of the IMO has notably changed with the launch of the 'Piracy: Orchestrating the Response' campaign in 2011, which was an attempt to move the IMO into the centre of counter-piracy governance activities. Also, with a new Secretary-General arriving in 2012 and a Special Representative on piracy being appointed in the same year, the IMO aims to strengthen its role in counter-piracy governance. Other more specialized formal bodies with a role in counter-piracy governance are the governing bodies of organizations including the management boards of the two international counter-piracy trust funds,[15] INTERPOL's Executive Committee, as well as the UN Political Office for Somalia (UNPOS), which has appointed a special counter-piracy advisor.

Regional and sub-regional inter-governmental organizations provide another major site for governance. Africa's sub-regional organization, the Southern African Development Community (SADC), as well as the Eastern African Intergovernmental Authority on Development have outlined strategies for coping with piracy, which so far, however, have not led to tangible implementation. Also the pan-African organization, the AU, has become a major site for deliberation, notably within the frame of its January 2012 summit. In addition, the Indian Ocean Commission (IOC) as well as the Gulf Cooperation Council (GCC) are active in addressing piracy. Notably the GCC has adopted a proposal to implement a joint maritime security strategy which includes counter-piracy elements.

A significant number of governance practices take place outside formal structures and often remain invisible. Such informal forums include the

---

[15]   Established under the Contact Group and the DCoC, as noted in Chapter 3.3.7.

working group meetings organized by the Oceans Beyond Piracy programme (OBP) of the One Earth Future Foundation (OEF), which
assembles experts and practitioners from counter-piracy agencies. A
monthly informal meeting held in Nairobi brings together counter-piracy
practitioners from resident embassies and local international organizations' offices. East African experts meet in the frame of the Project
Implementation Unit (PIU) of the DCoC process (discussed in more
detailed in the following sections), and military officials deliberate on a
monthly basis in the frame of the Shared Awareness and Deconfliction
Mechanism (SHADE, discussed in 5.3.3). Other informal mechanisms
are international piracy conferences in which counter-piracy experts and
organizational representatives meet to discuss strategy. These include the
annual conferences organized by Saudi Arabia, as well as industry-
oriented conferences, such as those organized by the conference service
company Hanson Wade. Finally, the major industry associations (including, for instance, Intertanko or Bimco) also meet on a frequent basis. One
of the core outcomes of these informal industry meetings was the
development of a draft of the fourth version of the BMP which were later
embraced by the IMO and the Contact Group.

In contrast to East African piracy, the issue has seen quite a different
trajectory in Asia. The Security Council did not engage in addressing
East Asian piracy, and there is less global activity to tackle the issue.
Rather than being dealt with within international forums or with the
assistance of international actors, piracy is dealt with in the frame of
regional structures. Governance has been mainly carried out in multilateral negotiations initiated by the oceanic powers, Japan and Australia.
Part of the reason for this different trajectory is that piracy has been
recognized as a regional problem since the 1990s,[16] and that the region
has a different level of naval capabilities and financial resources.

Two cooperation agreements provide the main structures for counter-
piracy action. Firstly, the Malacca Straits Patrols (MSP) is a coordinated
response based on a trilateral agreement between Indonesia, Malaysia
and Singapore.[17] The countries started to coordinate maritime patrols
from 2004, extended in 2005 by coordinated maritime air patrols (Eyes in
the Sky initiative (EiS)), and Combined Military Patrol Teams (CMPT).

---

[16] See, e.g., Vagg, *supra* note 9.

[17] See also Chapter 2.3.3. Detailed reconstructions of the MSP are also
provided in Ian Storey, 'Securing Southeast Asia's Sea Lanes: A Work in
Progress' (2008) 6 *Asia Policy* 95 and Nazery Khalid, 'With a Little Help from
My Friends: Maritime Capacity-Building Measures in the Straits of Malacca'
(2009) 31 *Contemporary Southeast Asia* 424.

Part of the agreement is a coordinating committee made up of officials from the three countries, which meets bi-annually, and three working groups focused on patrols, the EiS and information-sharing. While MSP is designed as a trilateral cooperation, the other arrangement, The Regional Cooperation Agreement on Combating Piracy and Armed Robbery against Ships in Asia 2004 (ReCAAP) is set up as a new regional organization which is open to every interested state. ReCAAP is a regional government-to-government agreement to promote and enhance cooperation against piracy and armed robbery in Asia.[18] It was initially proposed by Japan in 2001 in the frame of a summit of the Association of Southeast Asian Nations (ASEAN), the main regional integration mechanism in Southeast Asia. The negotiations of the agreement were concluded in spring 2005 and ReCAAP has been operational ever since. The institutional centrepiece of the agreement is the ReCAAP Information Sharing Centre (ReCAAP-ISC). The centre, based in Singapore, comprises a small Secretariat and a Governing Council. The ISC serves as an infrastructure for information exchange and coordinates a system of national focal points.[19] ReCAAP partners with organizations, including the IMO, which formally endorsed it, and the Asian Shipowners Forum (ASF). In addition, the bodies of ASEAN continue to be an important site for deliberating counter-piracy. In collaboration with other actors, ReCAAP-ISC has also arranged a number of conferences attended by practitioners and experts for deliberating counter-piracy strategy.

West African piracy is a problem which only from 2011 onwards has attracted international actors. The UNSC started to consider the situation on the West African coast and in the Gulf of Guinea from summer 2011. While the problem has not reached Somali proportions, international actors are attempting to keep the solution of the problem on a regional level. In contrast to the East African situation, international actors, including the IMO, work within an existing regional infrastructure which provides sites for deliberation and strategizing. Hence, much of the international activities concern the improvement of these structures. The major framework is the Maritime Organization for West and Central Africa (MOWCA) originally founded in 1975. To address piracy, the organization established a Subregional Integrated Coastguard Network (ICGN) in collaboration with the IMO in summer 2008. Also the Economic Community of Central African States (ECCAS) and the

---

[18] See for an overview and analysis, Joshua Ho, 'Combating Piracy and Armed Robbery in Asia: The ReCAAP Information Sharing Centre (ISC)' (2009) 33 *Marine Policy* 432.

[19] *Ibid.*

Economic Community of West African States (ECOWAS) have become active in the matter and, in the frame of a maritime safety and security conference held in spring 2012, agreed to develop a memorandum of understanding on the issue. Piracy is also one of the issues dealt with in the frame of the West African Coast Initiative (WACI). WACI is centred on countering transnational crime. In cooperation with UNODC, as well as the UN Secretariat, INTERPOL and ECOWAS, it strives to create a system of Transnational Crime Units (TCU) to enhance national and international coordination, as well as to enable intelligence-based investigations.

To summarize, what are the main practices of these organizations and in what way do they govern? The first practice is strategy development, counter-piracy strategies are developed and different organizations are given a role in the field. The discussed forums provide a site to deliberate about strategy as well as a mechanism of responsibility. Secondly, standardization: standards for counter-piracy behaviour are developed, including legal standards (e.g., the Contact Group's legal tool kit) and best practices which prescribe the optimal behaviour of actors (e.g., the BMP). The third main practice is funding, which are activities to identify resources and distribute them. As briefly introduced, many of the organizations also have a function in the sharing and distribution of information about piracy. This is part of epistemic practices, which shall be discussed next.

5.3.2 Epistemic Practices (Information, Research and Analysis)

Epistemic practices are activities which render the phenomenon of piracy knowable. To know about a problem is the crucial precondition to cope with it. Hence, epistemic practices by which knowledge about piracy is developed and disseminated are an essential precondition for counter-piracy. Starting from the mid-1980s, data about contemporary piracy has been systematically collected and prepared for publication in reports.[20] With the growing interest in piracy by several academic disciplines, generic knowledge of piracy has also become more and more advanced.[21]

---

[20] Villar, *supra* note 1, provided the first systematic collection of data on piracy.
[21] For an overview of piracy studies see the review in Samuel Pyeatt Menefee and Maximo Q. Mejia Jr. 'A "Rutter for Piracy" in 2012' (2012) 11 *WMU Journal of Maritime Affairs* 1; and Christian Bueger, 'Piracy Studies – Academic Responses to the Return of an Ancient Menace' (2013) *Cooperation & Conflict* (forthcoming) as well as the bibliography on contemporary piracy

Knowledge about piracy takes the form of incident reports, statistical trend analysis, daily information on (suspected) piracy activity, the analysis of piracy behaviour, the tracing of the root causes of piracy as well as strategic research on the impacts of counter-piracy. Such type of information gathering, research and analysis is firstly provided by (private and state) intelligence services and the maritime security industry. These organizations, however, keep their information classified. Public knowledge is provided secondly by a range of international organizations, by news media, and by think tanks and academics.

In response to increasing reports of piracy in Southeast Asia the International Maritime Board (IMB), a sub-body of the industry association, the International Chamber of Commerce (ICC), founded a Piracy Reporting Centre (PRC) in 1992, which was tasked to collect data on incidents of piracy. While the IMB started to record piracy incidents from 1984, the newly created centre provided a 24 hour live service and the recorded data was used to issue statistical analyses of trends in counter-piracy. The data collected and analysed by IMB remains up to today the most complete and important data on piracy incidents and trends. Besides trend analyses, the centre also offers a piracy map with the most recent incidents. Also the IMO systematically collects data on incidents. While the IMB bases the data on direct reports from shipping companies and maritime personnel, the IMO relies on official reports from flag state authorities. IMO started to compile reports from 1983, and since 1995 it issues monthly and quarterly reports. In 2002 a more complex classification system was introduced and since then individual incident data is available. Since IMO and IMB draw on different data sources, adopt different definitions of piracy and classify incidents differently, their data and statistics differ sometimes considerably.[22]

Today many more organizations provide incident data. These include the two regional mechanisms, which have the dissemination of incident reports as one of their crucial functions. ReCAAP's ISC provides incident data on its internet based knowledge exchange platform for Eastern Asia as well as offering analytical reports. The IMO led DCoC process has initiated a similar project with three information-sharing centres established in the Eastern African region tasked to share and publish incident data. Up-to-date incident reports for the Western Indian

provided by piracy-studies.org <http://piracy-studies.org/literature/> accessed 21 August 2012.
[22] See, e.g., M. Bruyneel, 'Current Reports on Piracy by the IMO and the IMB – A Comparison' (People and the Sea II Conference, Amsterdam, September 2003).

Ocean (in addition to the IMB and IMO sources) are provided by the NATO Shipping Centre (NSC) as well as the EU-led Maritime Security Centre Horn of Africa (MSC-HOA). While MSC-HOA restricts its data to shipping companies, the NSC data is publicly accessible. Both organizations also provide early warning information in the form of piracy alerts and data on the activities of suspected piracy vessels in the region.

These sources are authoritative for maritime developments, in terms of incidents, statistical trends, as well as alerts and preventive information, and are largely on a tactical level. In regards to land-based piracy-related developments, knowledge is primarily provided through UN agencies as well as media services. Several UN reports have become influential for understanding the developments in Somalia. These include the so-called Nairobi Report. Based on an expert conference held in 2008, it investigated the root causes of Somali piracy.[23] The so-called Lang Report, written by UN special advisor Jack Lang, investigated recent developments and evaluated legal options for prosecuting piracy; and the 2011 report by the UN Secretary-General on recent developments together with the report on the protection of Somali natural resources and waters have likewise become major sources of piracy knowledge.[24] An instrumental source is, moreover, the reports by the UN Monitoring Group on Somalia pursuant to Security Council resolution 1853, which, since 2008, reports regularly on piracy developments based on interviews in Somalia and the region.

In regards to news media, piracy has received broad news coverage, with the *New York Times*, *BBC* and *Al-Jazeera*, operating with correspondents in the region, regularly reporting on developments. Also the Nairobi based web source Somalia Report, which produces a weekly piracy report based on reporting from within Somalia, has become a major source of information about piracy. Media summaries are provided by the Public International Law & Policy Group (PILPG), which offers a bi-weekly newsletter of the piracy media coverage, and NATO's Civil-Military Fusion Centre (CFC), which produces an analytical summary of media reports and other internet sources on a regular basis.

---

[23] United Nations International Expert Group on Piracy off the Somali Coast, 'Piracy off the Somali Coast: Final Report' (2008) (UN Expert Report) 27 <http://www.asil.org/files/SomaliaPiracyIntlExpertsreportconsolidated1.pdf> accessed 21 August 2012.

[24] See UN Doc. S/2011/30 (25 January 2011), UN Doc. S/2011/662 (25 October 2011), UN Doc. S/2011/661 (25 October 2011), respectively.

In addition to the growing field of academic piracy studies, reviews of counter-piracy strategy have been conducted by a number of think tanks. The Oceans Beyond Piracy project has become a core think tank commissioning a number of influential reports on the costs of piracy, as well as reviewing the governance structure and investigating coordination problems. In addition, the UN Interregional Crime and Justice Research Institute (UNICRI) maintains a database on court decisions regarding piracy and the IMO Maritime Knowledge Centre systematically collects information resources including official documents on maritime piracy.

In summary, epistemic practices include the recording and dissemination of live incident reports and information on suspected piracy activities. Moreover, they include the analysis of trends based on incident data, investigations of land-based developments and reviews of counter-piracy strategy.

5.3.3   Security Practice

Security practices are activities that attempt to address piracy by means of military force. The underlying understanding of piracy is that of an existential threat and the main organizations are traditional security organizations. Counter-piracy security practices are primarily carried out by navies and special forces, as well as a range of private security companies.

An estimated number of 30 states participate in naval operations in the Gulf of Aden and the wider Western Indian Ocean. Navies are engaged in different tasks: firstly, surveillance (relying on assets such as planes, helicopters, satellites, drones or patrolling vessels); secondly, protection (through escorting vessels, providing a safe transit corridor and onboard armed guards); thirdly, early disruption (through the show of force or pre-emptive strikes on piracy logistics); fourthly, the disruption of attacks (e.g., through firing warning shots); and, fifthly, the recapture of vessels (e.g., by boarding and special forces operations).

Military contributions are organized in three multilateral naval missions and by a range of coordination and planning devices.[25] The multilateral missions are the Operation Atalanta by the EU Naval Force (EU NAVFOR), the Operation Ocean Shield by NATO and the Combined Maritime Task Forces (CMF), a US led, looser multilateral campaign that grew out of the war on terror operations. Both NATO as well as the EU NAVFOR mission have their headquarters in Northwood near London.

---

[25]   See also Chapters 3.3, 7.1.2 and 8.4.

NATO coordinates its relation to shipping companies through the NSC while EU NAVFOR relies on MSC-HOA. Operation Atalanta was established at the end of 2008. Operation Ocean Shield became active in summer 2009 and replaced the earlier NATO Operation Allied Protector.

Naval operations were initially coordinated through a Maritime Security Patrol Area (MSPA), a narrow, rectangular corridor between Somalia and Yemen, which was established by the CMF in August 2008. The area was used to focus efforts. Patrols were set up in the area in which participating ships were given a sector for which they were responsible. The MSPA was extended in spring 2009, responding to the geographical extension of pirate activities. In addition to the MSPA, in summer 2009 the Internationally Recognized Transit Corridor (IRTC) was initiated jointly by the CMF and EU NAVFOR to deploy naval assets strategically. The IRTC is a high protection area in the Gulf of Aden in which group transits are organized frequently. International group transits are coordinated by MSC-HOA in correspondence to the needs of the shipping industry. In addition, there are also group transits coordinated by navies operating under independent mandates.

Operations in the IRTC as well as the wider Western Indian Ocean are coordinated by the Shared Awareness and Deconfliction Mechanism (SHADE). SHADE was established in December 2008 to conduct informal discussions and deconflict the activities of nations and organizations involved in military counter-piracy operations in the region. Initially, SHADE involved only CMF, EU NAVFOR and NATO but it grew quickly. It now includes many navies operating under independent mandates, for instance China, India, Japan, Russia, South Korea and Ukraine. By 2012, 20 organizations and 27 countries were participating in the meeting comprising more than 100 participants. SHADE meetings are conducted on a monthly basis on the level of military officials and the chairmanship of the meeting rotates. One of the greatest successes of SHADE was the introduction of an innovative military communications system called MERCURY to which all SHADE participants have access, and which allows 'chat room-type' coordination in real time. The system allows ships to request information and cooperation from other ships or assets such as surveillance planes and helicopters. As a tactical communication system, its usage is largely depoliticized, allowing speedy communication beyond diplomatic channels.

Part of security practices is also the attempt to develop the coast guard capacities of regional states. This is mainly carried out as part of the DCoC process which includes the East African coastal states as well as the Gulf states. While DCoC does not provide assets, it aims at improving cooperation and information sharing among the participating states, trains coast guards and has contributed to the instalment of surveillance equipment. In summer 2012 the EU approved an additional civilian mission called EUCAP NESTOR, which, in collaboration with DCoC, aims at strengthening the sea-going maritime capacities of Djibouti, Kenya, the Seychelles, Tanzania and Somalia. As an expert-based mission it seeks to advise on legal, policy and operational matters concerning maritime security, deliver coast guard training and help to procure maritime equipment.

A further core component of security practice relates to the work of private maritime security companies (PMSC).[26] Initially PMSC supported shipping companies mainly in the training of crews, in the ransom negotiation process, the delivery of ransoms as well as in after-incident care. This was extended from 2009 onwards to the provision of armed guards onboard vessels sailing through the high-risk area. By 2012 these so-called vessel protection detachments (VPD) have become common practice. Guards protect vessels through the show of force and by firing warning shots. An increasing number of PMSC provide these services and in response to the regulation of PMSC new industry associations have become formed, such as the UK-based Security Association for the Maritime Industry (SAMI).

In summary, security practices entail surveillance operations, protection through armed guards, escorts and group transits, early disruption of piracy through the show of force and firing warning shots, interruption, through boarding, and, more rarely, the recapturing of vessels. A considerable number of multilateral missions and independently acting navies as well as PMSC are involved in these activities. In addition, there is a growing range of training and capacity building programmes as given in the frame of DCoC and EUCAP NESTOR.

5.3.4 Law Enforcement Practices

Legal practices treat piracy in correspondence with international and national laws as a form of crime.[27] They comprise attempts to address piracy by the enforcement of law and in using the legal apparatus of arrest, prosecution and punishment. Since legal practices are discussed in greater detail in the following chapters of this volume they shall be discussed here only very briefly.

---

[26] See further Chapter 10.
[27] See, in particular, Chapter 8.

In the realm of legal practices are, firstly, the practices of arresting piracy suspects. For the case of Somalia, suspects of piracy are primarily arrested by the security organizations discussed above, hence security and law enforcement practices overlap. Navies from Ocean Shields, the CMF, or Atalanta, as well as those from independent states, have arrested suspects. Upon arrest, evidence is collected. Suspects are then either transferred to a regional state with which the navy's government has signed a transfer protocol (including Kenya and the Seychelles) or, in rarer instances, to the respective legal system of the arrest state. After transfer, suspects are prosecuted and put on trial and, if convicted, imprisoned. The Shimo La Tewa prison in Mombasa has become the main prison facility and has the largest number of convicted pirates and suspects. In addition, a considerable number of pirates are imprisoned in Somaliland, Puntland and the Seychelles. By 2012, according to UNODC data, 1,054 piracy suspects had been prosecuted or were awaiting trials worldwide.[28]

Piracy trials are primarily the domain of national legislations and legal systems, of which a good summary is provided in the report on national legislation compiled by the UN Secretary-General's office.[29] Yet, a number of international actors play a role in the organization of legal practices in supporting national systems.

At the forefront of legal activities is the work of the UNODC in the frame of its Nairobi based Counter Piracy Programme (CPP). Funded mainly by the Contact Group's trust fund (International Trust Fund to Support Initiatives of States Countering Piracy off the Coast of Somalia), the organization has provided significant support to East African countries since 2008. The CPP assists Kenya, Seychelles, Mauritius, Tanzania and the Maldives with judicial, prosecutorial and police capacity building programmes as well as office equipment, law books and specialist coast guard equipment. A centre of activity of the CPP has been assistance to criminal justice professionals in Kenya and the Seychelles to assure standards of fairness as well as efficiency in transfers, trials and imprisonment. In addition, the programme also assists the governments of Somaliland and Puntland in constructing and refurbishing courts and prisons. The United Nations Development Programme for Somalia (UNDP Somalia) collaborates with UNODC and provides legal training in Somalia, and has also contributed to and assisted the building of

---

[28]　United Nations Office on Drugs and Crime, 'Counter-Piracy Programme. Support to the Trial and Related Treatment of piracy suspects. Issue nine: July 2012' (UNODC, 2012) 12.

[29]　UN Doc. S/2012/177 (23 March 2012).

facilities such as court rooms and prisons. Both of the regional capacity building programmes DCoC and EUCAP NESTOR have legal training components. DCoC primarily trains coast guards, while EUCAP NESTOR also aims at training judges and prosecutors.

Assistance to prosecutions is also provided by INTERPOL, which, in the frame of its project BADA, assists with forensic support and, since 2011, also collects evidence on transnational piracy networks and financial flows. Collecting and sharing evidence on transnational financial flows is also supported by the Working Group 5 of the Contact Group as well as EUROPOL. Assistance to prosecutions is also provided by the PILPG, which has provided legal advice, for instance, to judges in the Seychelles.

In summary, law enforcement counter-piracy practices are characterized by the classical criminal justice repertoire, including arrests, evidence collection, prosecution and trials, and imprisonment. There are a significant number of organizations which provide legal assistance to trials, to the development of counter-piracy legislation and the development of capacities in the Eastern African region.

5.3.5 Development Practice

Developmental practices are attempts to counter piracy by addressing what is understood as the 'root causes' of piracy. In counter-piracy discourse these root causes have been identified in weak state governance, corruption, the lack of law enforcement capacities, poverty, unemployment and the cultural acceptability of piracy.[30] In the range of development practices piracy is framed as a secondary problem that originates in these deeper, underlying root problems. Hence the counter-piracy challenge is interpreted as an (under-)development challenge. The main organizations active in these practices are international development and humanitarian aid organizations.

Organizations addressing Somali piracy do so largely in the frame of two different types of projects. Firstly, capacity building projects, including the DCoC projects, the work of UNODC and UNDP or the EU's NESTOR mission in the region and within Somalia. These projects mainly aim at addressing the problem of weak security governance and

---

[30] For a discussion of this literature see among others: Vagg, *supra* note 9, Murphy, *supra* note 9, Bueger, *supra* note 21, as well as Justin V. Hastings, 'Geographies of State Failure and Sophistication in Maritime Piracy Hijackings' (2009) 28 *Political Geography* 213; and Sarah Percy and Anja Shortland, 'Obstacles of Countering Piracy' (2013) *Global Policy* (forthcoming).

the lack of law enforcement capacities, and have been discussed in the previous sections. Secondly, a range of projects engage in more genuine development work. They aim at developing infrastructures in Somalia, including the fishing sector, provide vocational training and employment opportunities, and also conduct counter-piracy awareness campaigns.[31]

In the second type, the boundaries to the broader development and statebuilding work in Somalia become blurred. The main agencies active in projects with a significant counter-piracy component include international agencies, such as the International Labor Organization (ILO), the International Organization for Migration (IOM), which primarily engages in vocational training programmes, and the UNDP Office Somalia, which conducts larger infrastructure projects in line with the more general work of UNPOS. The development organization Norwegian Church Aid (NCA) has conducted from 2009 to 2011 a larger counter-piracy project in Puntland. The project was made up of rehabilitation and training measures as well as an awareness campaign which collaborated with elders, religious leaders and Civil Society organizations, such as Somalia Women Vision (SWV), and aimed at raising awareness for the dangers of piracy and convincing local populations to stop supporting piracy organizations. Similar awareness projects have been initiated by the OBP project, which supports a local radio station to disseminate counter-piracy messages, as well as a larger awareness project which was carried out by UNODC in collaboration with the Government of Puntland in 2011 and is continued by UNPOS.

While further infrastructure projects, such as the development of the port infrastructure are in the planning stage, the recently started Danish-Somali NGO Somali Fair Fishing, supported by funds from OBP, aims at developing the Somali fishing sector. In 2012 OBP also launched a programme titled 'Investing in Somalia' which aims at identifying and supporting investment opportunities in Somalia that can provide alternatives to piracy.

In summary, development counter-piracy practices include firstly activities which address the weak (security) governance aspect of the root causes of piracy, that is, the legal and maritime security sector programmes which are also part of the other practices. Secondly, they concern work addressing economic factors or the cultural acceptability of

---

[31] A detailed review of land-based counter-piracy projects is provided in Christian Bueger, 'Drops in the Bucket: A Review of Onshore Responses to Somali Piracy', in Sam P. Menefee and Max Meija (eds), 'Piracy at Sea' (2012) 15 *WMU Journal of Maritime Affairs* 15.

piracy, through awareness campaigns, alternative livelihood projects, infrastructure projects or rehabilitation and reintegration programmes.

5.3.6   Humanitarian Practices

Humanitarian practices aim at assisting the victims of piracy and thereby aiming at the consequences piracy has for victim groups. Humanitarian practices include firstly, preparedness and awareness training for seafarers, secondly, after care and legal support to seafarers at risk or suffering from a hostage experience, thirdly support for vulnerable populations in piracy infested areas, and fourthly, support to arrested piracy suspects.

Support to seafarers is firstly provided by the general seafarer assistance organizations including the International Seafarer's Association (ISA), the International Seafarers Assistance Network (ISAN), regional Seafarer's Assistance Programs (SAP), for instance the East African Seafarer Assistant Program or the Philippine Seafarer Assistance Program (PSAP), the Mission to Seafarers (MTS), Seafarers' Rights International (SRI), the Seamen's Church Institute (SCI) or the International Transport Workers Federation (ITF). These organizations provide emergency assistance, after-incident support (notably MTS), legal assistance in piracy-related cases (notably SRI and ITF), and are campaign and lobby organizations for seafarers.

The ITF is a global federation for transport workers aiming at improving the working conditions of a wide range of maritime professions. Its main contribution to counter-piracy has been in negotiating with the shipping industry the conditions under which seafarers transit high risk areas. ITF successfully contributed to the introduction of hazard pay in 2005, and to giving seafarers the right to refuse transit (at the costs of ship owners) if vessels take a route outside the IRTC or do not comply with the BMP.

The ITF has also launched a major internal petition titled 'Piracy: Enough is Enough'. Together with the Safe Our Seafarers (SOS) campaign, which is funded by the shipping industry, the petition is one of the major public relation campaigns in counter-piracy and aims at raising public awareness of the dangers of piracy for seafarers.

SCI is one of the main organizations addressing the psychological impact on piracy for seafarers. It has launched an extended scientific study on the impact of piracy designed to develop recommendations for clinical assessment and intervention. It has also issued a guideline document which provides a general structure to care for seafarers, addressing the continuum from transiting high-risk areas without incident to prolonged captivity of seafarers. Part of the guideline project is also the provision of audiovisual material to be used in crew training. Parallel to the SCI's work, the Maritime Piracy Humanitarian Response Programme (MPHRP) conducts work on the psychological aspects of piracy. The programme is funded by a pan-industry alliance of ship owners, unions, managers, manning agents, insurers and welfare associations and was established in 2011. It has issued a range of good practice documents on the preparation for piracy incidents for crew members and shipping companies and, in collaboration with NSC, runs awareness and training workshops in major port cities, for instance in Pakistan and India.

While seafarers arguably are the main victim group of piracy, a different set of practices targets victims in piracy-infested areas. Organizations which are also active in development work such as the IOM, ILO and UNDP have increasingly documented the negative effects of piracy for the populations in villages that host piracy operations. Such effects include economical ones, such as inflation induced by the higher prices for everyday goods paid by participants in piracy operations, but also the growing consumption of alcohol and drugs, prostitution as well as the spread of HIV/Aids, which has been linked to piracy in a study by IOM. While not having explicitly initiated programmes addressing these problems, organizations such as the IOM, ILO and other development agencies, including the EU, aim at integrating this dimension into their projects. A further dimension has been raised by the Canadian NGO Child Soldier Initiative, which has drawn public attention to children as an especially vulnerable group in piracy which increasingly participate in piracy operations.

A further component includes the treatment and support for piracy suspects. Programmes aim at ensuring that the basic human rights conditions are met for piracy suspects. Human Rights NGOs, including Amnesty International or Human Rights Watch, have, in taking a watchdog function, expressed concerns over deportation, inhumane treatment on arresting naval vessels and in Eastern African prisons.[32] They aim at ensuring that human rights aspects are included in transfer agreements between arresting and prosecuting states. Prisoner assistance in Eastern Africa is part of the work of the Red Cross and the Red Crescent and a significant component of the UNODC's counter-piracy

---

[32]   See, for instance, Amnesty International, Netherlands: Government Must Stop Imminent Deportation of Somalis, AI Index EUR 35/002/2010 (27 July 2010). Amnesty International, Australia, Cruel conditions for pre-trial prisoners in US federal custody, Amnesty International, <http://www.amnesty.org.au/news/comments/25351/> accessed 21 August 2012; and Deborah Osiro, 'Somali pirates have rights too: Judicial consequences and human rights concerns' (Institute for Security Studies, ISS Paper 224, July 2011).

programme. While the Red Cross and the Red Crescent deal with matters such as reaching out to the family of suspects, UNODC monitors prison conditions and provides legal support for suspects.

In summary, humanitarian practices include awareness and preparedness training as well as legal and psychological assistance to seafarers, public campaigns, and assistance to villages and piracy suspects.

5.4 SUMMARY AND CONCLUSION

This chapter has attempted to provide an overview of the different practices that counter-piracy organizations engage in. A mapping of the organizational field of counter-piracy made visible the plethora of (state and non-state) organizations active in fighting piracy. Over 50 different organizations and arrangements are crucial in the field and have been introduced in this mapping. As the discussion has shown, there are a number of leading agencies and a range of centres and nodal points in the field (including, for instance, the Contact Group, the DCoC process or ReCAAP). Yet there is, firstly, no visible hierarchy in the field, in the sense that one or several organizations or arenas represent the points from which the field is controlled. Secondly, rather than in formal, highly institutionalized settings, the majority of actors work together in the form of ad hoc, flexible and informal working arrangements. The Contact Group, which has invented its own (non-codified) working procedures, and the SHADE mechanism are paradigmatic in this regard.

The mapping moreover revealed a significant organizational overlap in activities which indicate a struggle over resources and capital. This firstly includes attempts of actors such as the IMO, the United Arab Emirates (UAE) and even the NGO OEF to take the initiative and attempt to lead and 'orchestrate' the response to piracy. Further examples include the overlap in the military missions, in the frame of the CMFs, NATO and the EU, the competition in providing incident data and early warning information among IMB, IMO, NATO, and the EU, or the diffuse attempts to organize awareness campaigns in Puntland by NCA, UNODC, as well as UNPOS. These examples stress that the field should not necessarily be understood as harmonious. Problems of coordination to a considerable degree are an outcome of this struggle over resources and symbolic capital.

Part of the challenge of reducing complexity in the field by better coordination and avoiding overlap will be to pay attention to struggles and the sensitivities, diverging interests and organizational cultures of participating organizations. Finally, one should not forget the pragmatic argument that a fuzzy, networked, non-hierarchical form of organization can have its virtues, or even be functionally superior to better coordinated forms. Such a field can be more flexible and devote more resources to problem solving rather than regulation and coordination. Hence the future challenges of counter-piracy will be a paradoxical one: to organize activities more coherently without, however, losing flexibility and problem-orientation.

PART II

Piracy and public law

6. Piracy and the international law of the sea

Tullio Treves

6.1 THE REVIVAL OF PIRACY

Although never absent from the international scene – one may recall attacks on ships carrying 'boat people' off the coasts of Southeast Asia – pirates seemed to have ceased to be a general menace to the international community justifying the traditional qualification of *hostis humani generis*, until the massive development of their activities off the coasts of Somalia, which started around 2000 and are still continuing.[1] Contemporary piracy is not limited to Somalia. Recently, for instance, piracy in the

---

[1] Interesting legal and factual elements are discussed in the report of the International Expert Group on Piracy off the Somali Coast, *Piracy off the Somali Coast, Workshop commissioned by the Special Representative of the Secretary-General of the UN in Somalia Ambassador Ahmedou Ould-Abdallah,* Nairobi 10–21 November 2008, *Final Report, Assessment and Recommendations,* with an appendix of *Detailed Recommendations,* Nairobi, 21 November 2008; as well in the UN Secretary-General's Reports: S/2009/146, S/2009/590/ S/2010/394, S/2010/556, S/201130, S/2011/360, S/2011/661, S/2011/662. An accurate short general survey of international law concerning piracy is in I. Shearer, 'Piracy', in R. Wolfrum (ed.), *Max-Planck Encyclopedia of Public International Law* (OUP, 2009), while an older, but penetrating analysis is in M. Giuliano, *I diritti e gli obblighi degli Stati, I, L'ambiente dell'attività degli Stati* (Padova 1956), 393–401. Recent developments are examined in M. Voelckel, 'La piraterie entre Charte et Convention: à propos de la résolution 1816 du Conseil de Sécurité', XII *Annuaire du droit de la mer 2007* (2008), tome XII, 479–500; E. Kontorovich, 'International Legal Responses to Piracy off the Coast of Somalia' (2009) 13(2) *ASIL Insights*; D. Guilfoyle, 'Piracy off Somalia: UN Security Council Resolution 1816 and IMO regional counter-piracy efforts' (2008) 57 *International and Comparative Law Quarterly* 690–699; A. Tancredi, 'Di pirati e Stati "falliti": il Consiglio di Sicurezza autorizza il ricorso alla forza nelle acque territoriali della Somalia' (2008) *Rivista di diritto internazionale* 937–966; J. Kraska, 'Developing Piracy Policy for the National Strategy for Maritime

Gulf of Guinea has been the subject of the UN Security Council's attention (further discussed in Chapter 4).[2] Piracy in Southeast Asia has also been a source of international interest in recent years (as discussed in Chapter 2). However, during the last decade piracy in Somalia has been at the centre of international attention, originating legal development whose relevance may, in some cases, go beyond the specific situation off the coasts of Somalia. It therefore forms both an appropriate case study through which to examine the traditional law and also an example of the kind of specialized legal measures that may be taken to deal with specific instances of piracy.

As the history of Somali piracy is covered in more detail in Chapter 3, only a brief account is required here. Capturing ships off the coast of Somalia and holding them and their crews for ransom has occurred since the 1990s. It was originally carried out by armed groups acting mostly in the territorial sea and claiming to protect Somalia's fishing resources, which were pillaged by foreign fishermen, and its coastal waters, which were used as a dumping ground for waste in the absence of a government able to enforce the law.[3] Taking advantage of the continuing lack of an

---

Security and the International Maritime Organization', S. P. Menefee, 'An Overview of Piracy in the first Decade of the 21st Century' and A. S. Skaridov, 'Hostis Humani Generis', in M. H. Nordquist, R. Wolfrum, J. N. Moore, R. Long (eds), *Legal Challenges in Maritime Security* (Leiden 2008), respectively at 331, 441, 479; D. Guilfoyle, *Shipping Interdiction and the Law of the Sea* (CUP 2009), 26–74; *Piracy off Somalia: the Challenges for International Law,* Panel with interventions of D. Guifoyle, A. P. Rubin, M. Halberstam, J. A. Roach, K. Shepherd, R. Beckman, in (2009) *American Society of International Law, Proceedings of the 103rd Annual Meeting,* 89–99; A. Roach, 'Countering Piracy in Somalia: International Law and International Institutions' (2011) 104 *American Journal International Law* 397–416; F. Graziani, *Il contrasto alla pirateria marittima nel diritto internazionale* (Editoriale Scientifica 2011); F. Munari, 'La "nuova" pirateria e il diritto internazionale: spunti per una ricerca" (2009) *Rivista di diritto internazionale* 325–363; H. Tuerk, 'The Resurgence of Piracy: A Phenomenon of Modern Times' (2009) 17 *University of Miami Intl. & Comp. Law Review* 5; R. Geiss and A. Petrig, *Piracy and Armed Robbery at Sea, The Legal Framework for Counter-Piracy Operations in Somalia and the Gulf of Aden* (Oxford 2011); Y. Dienstein, 'Piracy *Jure Gentium'*, in *Coexistence, Cooperation and Solidarity, Liber Amicorum Rüdiger Wolfrum (*Brill 2012), 1125–1156; V. Golitsyn, 'Maritime Security (case of piracy)', *ibid.,* 1157–1176; H. Neuhold, 'The Return of Piracy: Problems, Parallels, Paradoxes', *ibid.,* 1239–1258.

2   UNSC Res. 2018 (31 October 2011), UN Doc. S/RES/2018.

3   This aspect was mentioned at the Security Council by South Africa on 16 December 2008 (UN Doc S/PV.6046, 15). The Security Council has reaffirmed

effective government, and not without some evidence of connections with terrorist groups and with the political and armed fights going on in Somalia,[4] pirate activity then absorbed a growing number of people – including fishermen expert in handling boats – and became ever bolder. It now represents a very serious menace to navigation coming from the Suez Canal and going through the Gulf of Aden to the narrow area between the Horn of Africa and the Arabian Peninsula. In the sea areas off the Somali coast, as well as in those south of the Horn of Africa, piracy has developed, attacking ships even at great distance from the coast. The success in capturing ships and crews and in obtaining substantial amounts of money as ransom, as well as their efficient way of dealing with money so obtained, have made again of pirates, *sub specie* of the Somali pirates, the *hostes humani generis.* The danger for navigation through a choke-point of international traffic, as well as the outrage aroused by pirate attacks on ships carrying humanitarian supplies to the Somali population, have been decisive in alarming states from all over the world.

6.2 THE LAW OF THE SEA RULES ON PIRACY IN GENERAL AND THEIR INADEQUACY TO COPE WITH THE VIOLENT ACTIVITIES OFF THE SOMALI COAST IN PARTICULAR

The international law of piracy is set out in articles 100 to 107 and 110 of the UN Convention on the Law of the Sea (UNCLOS).[5] The fact that

---

its respect for 'Somalia's rights with respect to its offshore natural resources, including fisheries, in accordance with international law' in UNSC Res. 1851 (16 December 2008), UN Doc. S/RES/1851 (preamble) and most other resolutions, most recently UNSC Res. 2020 (22 November 2011), UN Doc. S/RES/2020 (preamble). On concerns about alleged toxic waste dumping and illegal fishing off Somalia see the discussion in Chapter 3 of this volume, and: UN Doc. S/2011/661, para. 63; UNSC Res. 2020, para. 24.

[4]   Contrast UN Doc. S/2011/661 (25 October 2011), para. 81 (UN Secretary General expresses concern as to linkages); and House of Commons Foreign Affairs Committee, 'Piracy off the coast of Somalia', HC 1318 (5 January 2012) (House of Commons Report), Evidence Annexe, Ev 30 <http://www.parliament.uk/business/committees/committees-a-z/commons-select/foreign-affairs-committee/publications/> accessed 27 February 2012 (only limited linkages found).

[5]   United Nations Convention on the Law of the Sea (adopted 10 December 1982, entered into force 16 November 1994) 1833 UNTS 397 ('UNCLOS').

these articles repeat almost literally articles 14 to 22 of the Geneva Convention on the High Seas of 1958, and that some states, including the United States as well as Israel and Venezuela, while not bound by UNCLOS, are bound by the Geneva Convention, entails that, either as a matter of customary or of conventional law, these articles state the law as currently in force.

For the present purposes it seems necessary and sufficient to recall the provisions concerning the definition of piracy and action against pirates. As regards the definition, its essential aspect is that piracy, under UNCLOS article 101(a), consists of 'any illegal acts of violence or detention, committed for private ends by the crew or the passengers of a private ship or aircraft and directed on the high seas against another ship or aircraft, or against persons or property on board such ship or aircraft'.

As regards action that may be taken against a pirate ship, apart from the right of warships of all states to exercise the right of visit aiming at ascertaining whether a ship is engaged in piracy set out in UNCLOS article 110(a), the main provision is article 105, which states:

> On the high seas, or in any place outside the jurisdiction of any State, every State may seize a pirate ship or aircraft, or a ship or aircraft taken by piracy and under the control of pirates, and arrest the persons and seize the property on board. The courts of the State which carried out the seizure may decide upon the penalties to be imposed, and may also determine the action to be taken with regard to the ships, aircraft or property, subject to the rights of third parties acting in good faith.

The definition of piracy is rather narrow, as it includes only action on the high seas and only action undertaken by one ship against another ship. So forms of violence conducted in the territorial sea or without the involvement of two ships, such as, for instance, the violent taking of control of a ship by members of its crew or passengers, even when the follow-up consists in holding for ransom the ship and its crew and passengers, are not included. Correctly, the taking of control by hijackers embarked as passengers on the Portuguese ship *Santa Maria* in 1961 and on the Italian cruise ship *Achille Lauro* in 1985, which had extensive press coverage, were not considered as piracy. Violent activities against ships off the Somali coast sometimes take place in whole or in part in the territorial sea thus often remain outside the scope of the definition. More rarely they do not involve the presence of one or more other ships, as usually very quick skiffs coming from bases on the mainland or from 'mother ships' at sea are used. It may be underlined that other acts of violence that may occur not directly linked to piracy are not included in the definition. Acts preparatory to piracy are covered only to the extent that they fall within UNCLOS article 101(b) and (c) covering, respectively, 'voluntary participation in the operation of a [pirate] ship' and 'any act of inciting or of intentionally facilitating' piracy.

While under the Geneva Convention on the High Seas there could be no doubt that the requirement that piracy be committed 'on the high seas' referred to the waters beyond the limit of the territorial seas, under UNCLOS some doubts could be raised in light of the fact that repression of piracy is not explicitly mentioned among the freedoms of the high seas applicable to the economic zone under article 58, paragraph 1. These doubts should be dispelled, however, in light of article 56, paragraph 2, of UNCLOS which makes articles 88 to 115 of the same Convention applicable to the exclusive economic zone.[6] The right of every state to engage in the repression of piracy is an exception to the flag state's exclusive power on its ships, which is the essence of freedom of navigation.[7] It seems, consequently, reasonable that the rules providing for such right be included in the reference to 'freedom of navigation' in article 58 of UNCLOS.

As far as action to be taken is concerned, under article 105 the flag state of the seizing ship enjoys very broad powers. These consist in the right of arresting persons and seizing property, and, through the above-mentioned right to decide upon penalties and on action to be taken with

---

[6] See Dienstein, Piracy *Jure Gentium*, *supra* note 1, 1133. Guifoyle, *Interdiction*, *supra* note 1, 43–45, among other arguments, quotes the 2005 Protocol to the Convention for the Suppression of Unlawful Acts against the Safety of Maritime Navigation (adopted 14 October 2005, entered into force 28 July 2010), IMO Doc. LEG/CONF.15/21, Art. 8*bis* (5) referring to the boarding of a ship 'located seawards of any State's territorial sea'. He comments that this reference 'may indicate that States now generally accepted that law enforcement action taken by foreign States' law enforcement vessels within an EEZ but outside territorial waters is permissible so long as it does not interfere with the subject matters reserved to the coastal State's jurisdiction'. This argument can be read as going beyond the balance established in UNCLOS between exclusive rights of the coastal State, set out in article 56, high seas freedoms mentioned in article 58 and matters attributed neither to the coastal state nor to other states mentioned in article 59. This is why it seems to me preferable to rely on the explanation set out in the text. On the Convention, see *infra* note 53, and accompanying text.

[7] The European Court of Human Rights Grand Chamber's judgment of 29 March 2009 in *Medvedyev v France* (Application No 3394/03), para. 85, comparing the 'minimal rules' of UNCLOS on drug trafficking to the eight articles on piracy, observes, incidentally, that the rules concerning piracy 'lay down, *inter alia*, the principle of universal jurisdiction as an exception to the rule of the exclusive jurisdiction of the flag State'.

regard to the ship, aircraft and property, the right to submit to judicial proceedings the persons arrested and the property seized. Thus universal jurisdiction[8] of the seizing state's courts is supported by international law. In other words, the exercise by these courts of criminal jurisdiction as regards pirates is compatible with international law independently from the presence of connecting factors with the forum state.

The language of article 105 (i.e., 'may') seems to indicate that the exercise of jurisdiction by the seizing state's courts is a possibility, not an obligation,[9] notwithstanding the 'duty' to cooperate in the repression of piracy stated in article 100.[10] The rule in article 105 does not establish, however, the exclusive jurisdiction to adjudicate of the seizing state's courts. Courts of other states are not precluded from exercising jurisdiction under conditions they establish.[11] Thus the international law rules on action to be taken against pirates permit action, but are far from

---

[8] UNSC Res. 1976 (11 April 2011), UN Doc. S/RES/1976, para. 14 recognizes that 'piracy is a crime subject to universal jurisdiction'. The Institut de Droit International gave the following definition: 'Universal jurisdiction in criminal matters, as an additional ground for jurisdiction, means the competence of a State to prosecute alleged offenders and to punish them if convicted, irrespective of the place of commission of the crime and regardless of any link of active or passive personality, or other grounds of jurisdiction recognized by international law': Resolution on Universal Criminal jurisdiction with Respect to the Crime of Genocide, Crimes against Humanity and War Crimes, Vol. 71-II *Annuaire de l'Institut de Droit International* (Session de Cracovie 2005) 297.

[9] This seems confirmed by UNSC Res. 1976, *supra* note 8, para. 14, which, in reiterating a call to all States 'to favourably consider the prosecution of suspected, and conviction of, pirates apprehended', seems to exclude that States have an obligation under international law to do so.

[10] Some consequences of Art. 100 are proposed by F. Munari, *supra* note 1, 355–357. According to S. Piedimonte Bodini, 'Fighting Maritime Piracy under the European Convention on Human Rights' (2011) 22 *European Journal of International Law* 829, 838, under the European Convention on Human Rights (especially Art. 2) it may be argued that in certain circumstances (knowledge about a real and imminent risk of a life threatening hostage taking) States parties are under 'a positive obligation ... to take preventive operational measures to protect an individual whose life is at risk'.

[11] The meaning of the second sentence of article 105 is discussed by scholars. Some consider that it limits to the seizing State the jurisdiction to prosecute pirates, while for others it must be read as a statement that the seizing state may decide on the penalties to be imposed. In my view the first opinion is too restrictive and would establish an unnecessary difference between enforcement and adjudicating jurisdiction, which could become problematic in light of the recent practice (discussed below) of surrendering for adjudication pirates captured by vessels operating off the costs of Somalia to coastal States on the

prescribing that such action is effectively taken. Domestic law rules are decisive to that effect. In light of this, and of the frequent insufficiency of such rules, the Security Council has called upon states 'to criminalize piracy under their domestic law and favourably consider the prosecution of suspected, and imprisonment of convicted, pirates apprehended off the coast of Somalia, consistent with applicable international human rights law'.[12] Domestic law may, however, rely on definitions of piracy that are different, and usually broader, than that of article 110 of UNCLOS.

6.3 THE SECURITY COUNCIL AND PIRACY OFF THE COASTS OF SOMALIA

The Security Council has linked the activities of pirates off the coast of Somalia with the notion of a threat to international peace and security. Since resolution 733, the Security Council has routinely invoked Chapter VII as regards the situation in Somalia,[13] and states that such situation constitutes or continues to constitute 'a threat to international peace and security'.[14] Since its first resolution on piracy off the coasts of Somalia, adopted in 2008, the Security Council has consistently 'determine[d]' that such piracy 'exacerbate[s] the situation in Somalia which continues to constitute a threat to international peace and security in the region'.[15] The declaration made on 16 December 2008 by the Chinese Minister of Foreign Affairs at the Security Council meeting approving resolution 1851 (held at the level of Foreign Ministers), clearly shows this approach: 'The long-term delay in the settlement of the Somali issue is posing a serious threat to international peace and security, while the

---

basis of specific agreements. For a summary of the scholarly discussion, Geiss and Petrig, *supra* note 1, 143–151.

[12] UNSC Res. 1918 (27 April 2010), UN Doc. S/RES/1918, para. 2, by UNSC Res. 1976, *supra* note 8, para. 13, also mentions criminalizing 'incitement, facilitation, conspiracy and attempts to commit acts of piracy', while UNSC Res. 2020, *supra* note 3, para. 15, calls upon States to favourably consider prosecution of the pirates' 'facilitators and financiers ashore'.

[13] UNSC Res. 733 (23 January 1992), UN Doc. S/RES/733, para. 5.

[14] UNSC Res. 1814 (15 May 2008), UN Doc. S/RES/1814, penultimate preambular paragraph. The determination has been repeated in most SC resolutions on piracy off the Somali coasts, most recently UNSC Res. 2020, *supra* note 3, penultimate preambular paragraph.

[15] UNSC Res. 1816 (2 June 2008), UN Doc. S/RES/1816, last preambular paragraph, and thereafter in all the Council's resolutions on piracy off the Somali coast.

rampant piracy off the Somali coast has worsened the security situation in Somalia.'[16] The link is made indirectly, avoiding the criticism which the Council often incurs when applying this notion to matters hitherto not considered to be covered by the notion of threat to international peace and security. It nonetheless reaches the objective that action against piracy off the Somali coasts be conducted within the framework of Chapter VII of the UN Charter.

Since 2008 and up to the end of 2011, acting in all cases under Chapter VII of the UN Charter, the Security Council has adopted ten resolutions on piracy off the coasts of Somalia.[17] The later resolutions repeat the main points made in the early ones. They have, however, become richer and more nuanced by taking into account the growing knowledge on the phenomenon brought to the attention of the Council by the increasingly sophisticated practice of pirates, of the states fighting them, and of the competent international organizations such as the International Maritime Organization (IMO). The reports of the Secretary-General have helped to collect and present such practice.

6.4 THE SECURITY COUNCIL RESOLUTIONS' BROADENING OF THE SCOPE OF INTERNATIONAL LAW RULES ON PIRACY

With resolution 1816 of 2 June 2008, and the others which followed it, the Security Council has endeavoured to cope with the growing alarm caused by pirate activities off the coast of Somalia. It has taken measures within the framework of Chapter VII which aim at remedying the limitations of the abovementioned rules of international law, as far as their application to the situation at hand is concerned.

These resolutions, while using the term 'piracy', do not define it. References to the provisions of UNCLOS and statements that these provisions set 'out the legal framework applicable to combating piracy and armed robbery at sea' and 'provide guiding principles for cooperation to the fullest possible extent in the repression of piracy' indicate that the starting point is the above-recalled definition in the Convention. These resolutions, however, always mention, together with piracy, 'armed robbery'. Armed robbery is not defined. It is a term routinely used within

---

[16] UN Doc S/PV.6046 (16 December 2008) 5.

[17] The relevant Security Council resolutions are: 1816 (2008), 1838 (2008), 1846 (2008), 1851 (2008), 1897 (2009), 1918 (2010), 1950 (2010), 1976 (2011), 2015 (2011), 2020 (2011).

the framework of the IMO, and may be understood to include all acts of violence whose purposes are identical or similar to those of piracy but are not covered by the conventional definition of it, in particular because they may be perpetrated without using a ship against the target ship.[18] More importantly, in IMO parlance 'armed robbery' refers only to activities in waters under the jurisdiction of a state, so that it does not include acts committed on the high seas without the presence of two ships. This is what the Security Council resolutions do, as they use the expression 'piracy and armed robbery against vessels in the territorial waters of Somalia and the high seas off the coast of Somalia'.[19] As in most of the Somali cases two or more ships are involved, the mention of 'armed robbery' would seem not strictly dictated by the needs of existing practice and rather inspired at the aim of including all acts connected with piracy (such as preparatory acts) and future possible acts involving only one ship.

The key element in the resolutions is set out in paragraph 7 of resolution 1816. It copes with the limitation of the definition of piracy to acts perpetrated on the high seas which, as mentioned, makes it inadequate to deal with acts that sometimes take place wholly in the territorial sea, and very often include an attack on the high seas followed by the pirated ship being brought by the pirates into the territorial sea and held for ransom in a port or near the coast, or by the retreat of the attacking skiffs into the territorial and internal waters of Somalia.

---

[18]   IMO Resolution A 922(22) of 29 November 2001 adopting the Code of Practice for the Investigation of the Crimes of Piracy and Armed Robbery against Ships: 'Armed robbery against ships means any unlawful act of violence or detention or any act of depredation, or threat thereof, other than an act of "piracy" directed against a ship or against persons or property on board such a ship within a State's jurisdiction over such offences'; the definition is almost literally repeated in the Regional Cooperation Agreement on Combating Piracy and Armed Robbery against Ships in Asia (adopted 11 November 2004, entered into force 4 September 2006), 44 ILM 829 (2005), Art. 1(2); and in the Code of Conduct concerning the Repression of Piracy and Armed Robbery Against Ships in the Western Indian Ocean and the Gulf of Aden, adopted in Djibouti (adopted 29 January 2009), IMO Doc. C 102/14 (3 April 2009), Art. 1(2) <http://www.imo.org/OurWork/Security/PIU/Documents/DCoC%20English.pdf> accessed 1 August 2012.

[19]   UNSC Res. 1816, *supra* note 15, penultimate preambular paragraph; UNSC Res. 1846 (2 December 2008), UN Doc. S/RES/1846, penultimate preambular paragraph; recently UNSC Res. 2020, *supra* note 3, penultimate preambular paragraph.

This key element of resolution 1816, paragraph 7, consists in that certain states (on which I will come to later) are authorized to:

(a) Enter the territorial waters of Somalia for the purpose of repressing acts of piracy and armed robbery at sea, in a manner consistent with such action permitted on the high seas with respect to piracy under relevant international law; and

(b) Use, within the territorial waters of Somalia, in a manner consistent with action permitted on the high seas with respect to piracy under relevant international law, all necessary means to repress acts of piracy and armed robbery.

The basic effect of these provisions is to make the rules of international law concerning piracy on the high seas applicable also to territorial waters, *inter alia* permitting pursuit from the high seas into these waters, and clarifying that states acting under these rules within the territorial waters of Somalia may use 'all necessary means'.

It may be added that – following an episode in which French troops pursued pirates onto the Somali mainland[20] – resolution 1851 added on 16 December 2008 an authorization to conduct 'all necessary measures that are appropriate *in Somalia* for the purpose of suppressing acts of piracy and armed robbery at sea' (paragraph 6, emphasis added). The expression 'in Somalia', while not explained in the preambular paragraphs, clearly alludes to action undertaken on the mainland.[21]

---

[20] This is the operation conducted on 11 April 2008 in Somali territory that succeeded in capturing six of the pirates, and part of the ransom collected in a piracy operation against the passengers of the French cruise ship *Le Ponant,* freed at sea by French forces. See facts and comments in *Sentinelle* No. 145 (20 April 2008) <http://www.sfdi.org> accessed 1 August 2012. On 20 April 2008, the Somali Prime Minister Nur Hassan Hussein, declared to international media: 'The French forces arrested six Somali pirates and took them to France to face justice. We encourage such steps by the French. The Somali government asks the international community to take action against piracy' (*ibid.*). The uncertainty as to the real meaning and scope of such declaration brought France to propose the draft of what became UNSC Res. 1851, *supra* note 3.

[21] See the interventions by the British Minister for Foreign Affairs and by the US Secretary of State upon approval of resolution 1851 in UN Doc S/PV.6046 (16 December 2008) 4 and 9.

6.5 THE LIMITATIONS OF THE NEW RULES: *RATIONE TEMPORIS, RATIONE LOCI*; THE CONCERN ABOUT CHANGING INTERNATIONAL CUSTOMARY LAW

Although the main effect of resolution 1816 and the following ones is to extend both *ratione loci* and *ratione materiae* the scope of the international law rules concerning piracy, the Security Council has framed the relevant resolutions very cautiously. It has introduced a number of limitations that make the provisions adopted less revolutionary than they might appear, and seem aimed, in particular, at fending off possible criticism against the Council acting as a 'legislator'.[22]

First, the authorization given is limited *ratione temporis*. Resolution 1816 limited to six months the validity of the authorization it introduces, while providing for a progress report and a more complete report on the application of the resolution to be submitted within, respectively, three and five months and stating the intention to review the situation and consider, 'if appropriate, renewing the authority provided in paragraph 7 for additional periods' (paragraphs 12, 13 and 15). The authority has in fact been renewed for periods of 12 months every year since resolution 1846 of 2 December 2008 (paragraph 10).[23] The authorization to undertake all necessary measures 'in Somalia' set out in resolution 1851 is also limited to the 12 months starting on the adoption of resolution 1846 and has been included in successive renewals.

Second, the scope of the resolutions is clearly limited *ratione loci* as it is stated that the authorization provided 'applies only with respect to the situation in Somalia' (resolution 1816, paragraph 9, resolution 1846, paragraph 11). This implies, in particular, that authorization to enter the territorial sea does not apply to the territorial sea of states different from Somalia (such as Yemen or Kenya).

Third, the resolutions request that activities undertaken pursuant to the authorizations they set out 'do not have the practical effect of denying or impairing the right of innocent passage to the ships of any third State'.[24]

---

[22] See with further references, T. Treves, 'The Security Council as Legislator' in A. Constantinides and N. Zaikos (eds), *The Diversity of International Law, Essays in Honour of Professor Kalliopi K. Koufa* (Nijhoff 2009) 61–70.

[23] Most recently, UNSC Res. 2020, *supra* note 3, para. 9.

[24] UNSC Res. 1816, *supra* note 15, para. 8; UNSC Res. 1846, *supra* note 19, para. 13; most recently, UNSC Res. 2020, *supra* note 3, para. 12.

This provision seems consistent with the idea that, while the authorizations set out in the resolutions introduce a limitation to the sovereignty of the Somali coastal state on its territorial sea, they should not have any consequence on the rights third states (states different from the coastal and from the authorized states) are entitled to exercise in the territorial sea, such as, especially, the right of innocent passage.

Fourth, the resolutions affirm that the authorization they contain 'shall not affect the rights or obligations or responsibilities of member states under international law, including any rights or obligations under the [Law of the Sea] Convention with respect to any other situation' and underscore in particular that they 'shall not be considered as establishing customary international law'.[25] These provisions correspond to concerns firmly stated in the Security Council by representatives of developing states keen to maintain the integrity of the UN Law of the Sea Convention.[26] Of course, it cannot be excluded that, if authorizations similar to those granted as regards the Somali situation where to be routinely granted in other situations, the possible formation of a customary rule could at least be discussed. The provisions just quoted would provide, however, a strong, although perhaps not insurmountable, argument against; as would the fact that Security Council resolution 2018 of 2011 on piracy in the Gulf of Guinea does not contain such authorizations. Apart from the aspect concerning repressive action in the territorial sea, the resolutions may, nonetheless, be seen as clear indication of the path that states, individually and in cooperation, should follow in general as regards the different aspects of piracy which have been brought to the Security Council's attention in connection with the situation off the coast of Somalia.

A comparison between the Security Council resolutions and the non-binding Code of Conduct adopted on 29 January 2009 concerning the Repression of Piracy and Armed Robbery against Ships in the Western Indian Ocean and the Gulf of Aden shows how keen many states are not to go beyond what is provided in UNCLOS and how dangerous

---

[25] UNSC Res. 1816, *supra* note 15, para. 9; UNSC Res. 1846, *supra* note 19, para. 11; UNSC Res. 2020, *supra* note 3, para. 9.

[26] Indonesia before the unanimous vote of the Council adopting Resolution 1816 stated: 'A burden of responsibility rests upon us all [parties to the LOS Convention] to maintain the Convention's integrity and sanctity … it is our duty to voice strong reservations if there are actions envisaged by the Council or any other forum that could lead to modifying, rewriting or redefining UNCLOS of 1982' (UN Doc S/PV.5902 (2 June 2008) 2) See also the declarations after the vote of Viet Nam, Libya, South Africa and China (*ibid.*, 4–5).

the provisions in the Security Council resolutions may appear to them.[27] The Code provides different rules for piracy in the high seas and for armed robbery in internal, archipelagic and territorial waters. On the high seas, the UNCLOS regime applies, while in the territorial sea, including pursuit from the high seas, the authorization of the coastal state is necessary. In the same vein, it is also worth noting that the Security Council does not include the authorization to act in the territorial sea in its resolution adopted in 2011 on piracy in the Gulf of Guinea.[28]

6.6 THE REQUIREMENT OF CONSENT OF THE TFG

The here considered resolutions of the Security Council are adopted on the basis of the consent of the Transitional Federal Government of Somalia (TFG). Paragraph 9 of resolution 1816 'affirms' that the authorization set out in paragraph 7 'has been provided only following receipt of the letter from the Permanent Representative of the Somali Republic to the United Nations to the President of the Security Council dated 27 February 2008 conveying the consent of the TFG'.[29] Similar formulations, referring to further letters conveying the consent of the TFG, are in the resolutions renewing the authorization first granted in resolution 1816.[30] From the tenor of a number of declarations made upon adoption of the resolutions, it would seem that, without such authorization, and notwithstanding the lack of control of the TFG on the waters off Somalia, unanimity in the Security Council would not have been reached.

---

[27] See references *supra* note 18. The non-binding character of the Code is explicitly indicated in Art. 15(a). The parties, however, intend to consult within two years 'with the aim of arriving at a binding agreement' (Art. 13).

[28] UNSC Res. 2018, *supra* note 2.

[29] This letter, not officially available, is quoted in the preamble to the resolution. It is also quoted in UN Doc. S/2008/323 (14 May 2008) containing a 12 May 2008 letter from the Permanent Representative of Somalia to the UN to the President of the Security Council stating that the Somali Government 'has granted a number of States authorizations to enter Somali territorial waters in order to deal with these threats' (i.e. threats posed by pirates/armed robbers: paragraphs 5 and 2), and supporting the adoption of a Resolution under Chapter VII 'to authorize States cooperating with the Transitional Federal Government to enter Somalia's territorial sea and use all necessary means within the territorial sea to identify, deter, prevent and repress acts of piracy and armed robbery at sea' (paragraph 6).

[30] Most recently UNSC Res. 2020, *supra* note 3, para. 10.

The reference to the authorization of the coastal state takes away all, or much of, the revolutionary content of the resolutions. Indeed, the activities purportedly 'authorized' by the Security Council, in light of the coastal state's authorization, could also be conducted in the absence of a Security Council resolution adopted within the framework of Chapter VII. Under international law, states are free to dispose of their rights in their territorial sea, for instance by allowing other states to conduct police activities in them. A precedent that may be quoted is the exchange of Notes of 25 March 1997 between Albania and Italy, in which Albania agreed that Italian naval forces could, in Albanian territorial waters, stop ships flying whatever flag and carrying Albanian citizens that had evaded controls exercised by the authorities of Albania in the latter's territory.[31]

The fact that no authorization of the Security Council under Chapter VII to exercise jurisdiction in the territorial sea of a state is needed if there is an authorization of the coastal state, is confirmed by the language used by the European Union Council's Joint Action concerning 'Operation Atalanta' in the waters off Somalia. The provision concerning transferral, for the purpose of prosecution, of arrested pirates or armed robbers is set out 'on the basis of Somalia's acceptance of the exercise of jurisdiction by Member states or by a third state, on the one hand [namely, as regards the territorial sea], or of article 105 of the United Nations Convention on the Law of the Sea, on the other [namely, as regards the high seas]'.[32] To invoke Security Council resolutions as basis has apparently (and correctly) been seen as superfluous.

The importance of the coastal state's consent seems highlighted by the fact that, contrary to the international law rules on piracy on the high seas which permit seizure of pirate ships by 'every State' (UNCLOS article 105), the Security Council resolutions limit the authorizations they provide to 'States cooperating with the TFG' for which 'advance notification has been provided by the TFG to the Secretary-General'.[33] Thus, the coastal state maintains (in fact, is allowed to maintain) control as regards which states are authorized to enter its territorial sea and, indeed, territory, for fighting pirates and armed robbers. At present, according to the most recent report of the UN Secretary-General, the flotilla patrolling

---

[31]   Gazzetta Ufficiale della Repubblica Italiana, No. 163, Suppl. of 15 July 1997.

[32]   EU Council Joint Action 2008/851/CFSP of 10 November 2008, OJEU L 301/33 (12 November 2008), Art. 13, para. 1, chapeau.

[33]   UNSC Res. 1816, *supra* note 15, para. 7; UNSC Res. 1846, *supra* note 19, para. 10; UNSC Res. 1851, *supra* note 3, para. 6; UNSC Res. 2020, *supra* note 3, para. 10.

the waters off the coast of Somalia (not necessarily its territorial sea) includes three multinational coalition naval forces (NATO, European Union and the Combined Maritime Forces led by the United States) and forces of nine states acting individually (China, India, the Islamic Republic of Iran, Japan, Kenya, Malaysia, Saudi Arabia, South Africa and Yemen).[34] For the first time China has deployed naval vessels outside the seas adjacent to it, and the European Union has formed and deployed a joint naval force within 'Operation Atalanta'.

The requirement of the coastal state's consent, unnecessary for action under Chapter VII, seems to pursue three objectives. The first is to pay homage to state sovereignty, meeting the abovementioned concerns that through these resolutions new customary international law rules could be 'established'. The second is to strengthen the TFG, which, while maintaining the Somali presence at the UN, exercises very limited effective power in Somalia, and especially lacks capacity to fight pirate activities off its coasts.[35] The third, through the designation by the TFG of the states whose vessels are authorized to act in its territorial sea, would seem to consist in limiting the foreign fleets' presence in Somali waters to the most involved states, and to states ready to cooperate with each other.

The overlap between the Security Council's authorization and that of the coastal state as represented by the TFG may, however, serve, additionally, or perhaps especially, another purpose. It must be recalled that, with a law of 1972, Somalia has adopted a territorial sea of 200 miles of width[36] and that, although Somalia ratified UNCLOS on 24 July 1989, there is no record (at least available to the present writer) that that law has been revoked. In the situation of possible conflict between a domestic statute and the international obligation assumed under UNCLOS to have 12 miles as the maximum width for the territorial sea,

---

[34] Report of the UN Secretary General, UN Doc. S/2011/662 (25 October 2011), paras 39–47.

[35] The letter of 12 May 2008 of the Somali Permanent Representative of Somalia to the UN (*supra* note 29) clearly states that 'the Transitional Government does not have the capacity to interdict the pirates or patrol and secure the waters off the coast of Somalia'. This aspect is analysed by Tancredi, *supra* note 1, 943–950.

[36] See: <http://www.un.org/Depts/los/LEGISLATIONANDTREATIES/ STATESFILES/S> accessed 1 August 2012. The same source is relied upon in A. Chircop, D. Dzidzornu, J Guerreiro, C. Grilo, 'The Maritime Zones of East African States in the Law of the Sea: Benefits Gained, Opportunities Missed' (2008) 16(2) *African Journal of International and Comparative Law* 121, note 32 and accompanying text.

compounded by the lack of effective authority in Somalia, the intent of the Security Council in ensuring the TFG's consent to action by other states against pirates and armed robbers within the territorial sea may be explained as that of granting a legal basis to such action whatever the width of the Somali territorial sea. From the behaviour of states patrolling the waters off the coast of Somalia it would seem clear that they assume that the external limit of the Somali territorial sea is 12 miles. Whether this is also the assumption of the TFG is uncertain, and the permission to act against pirates and armed robbers in its territorial sea has the beneficial result of avoiding discussion on this question. A contribution to the clarification of the situation is made by the 'Roadmap to end the transition in Somalia' adopted by competing Somali factions under UN auspices on 6 September 2011, by calling upon the TFG to declare an exclusive economic zone.[37] The need for such a declaration is seen in connection with the preservation of Somalia's natural resources and in particular with the prevention of illegal, undeclared and unregulated fishing by the Secretary-General's Report on such resources of 2011. In this report the Secretary-General calls upon the TFG to declare such a zone.[38]

6.7 WHAT TO DO WITH CAPTURED PIRATES AND ARMED ROBBERS?

As mentioned, international law recognizes universal jurisdiction to the courts of the seizing state. This jurisdiction, applicable under article 105 of UNCLOS for seizures and arrests of pirates on the high sea, applies also to seizures and arrests in the territorial sea of Somalia under the Security Council resolutions quoted above.

The seizing states – in other words: the states fighting pirates and armed robbers in the waters off Somalia and having arrested them – are,

---

[37] UNSC Res. 2020, *supra* note 3, antipenultimate preambular paragraph, welcomes the inclusion in the Roadmap of the declaration of an EEZ. The Roadmap can be found through a link in <http://unpos.unmissions.org/Default.aspx?tabid=1931&currentpage=3> accessed 1 August 2012. According to the Roadmap the EEZ was to be proclaimed by 19 December 2011. According to (unconfirmed) news in <http://www.shabelle.net/article.php?id=6255> accessed 2 January 2012 the EEZ was in fact proclaimed.

[38] UN Doc. S/2011/661 (25 October 2011), para. 65. See also the report by the Special Advisor to the UN Secretary General, Jack Lang, UN Doc. S/2011/30 (25 January 2011), addendum para. 89 ('Lang Report').

however, reluctant to exercise such broad powers by prosecuting and submitting to criminal proceedings in their courts the pirates and armed robbers arrested.[39] They seem concerned by the expense involved, by legal complexities, relating for instance to evidence,[40] inherent in criminal proceedings to be held far away from the place where the alleged crime has been committed, and, perhaps especially, by the human rights implications of exercising jurisdiction, as well as to the possibility of pirates requesting to be granted asylum.[41]

A recent, and not isolated,[42] case highlights these difficulties. The Danish navy ship *Absalon* captured on 17 September 2008 ten pirates in the waters off Somalia. After six days of detention and confiscation of their weapons, ladders and other implements used to board ships, the Danish government decided to free the pirates by putting them ashore on a Somali beach. The Danish authorities had come to the conclusion that the pirates risked torture and the death penalty if surrendered to (whatever) Somali authorities. This was unacceptable as Danish law prohibits extraditing criminals when they may face death penalty. Moreover, they were not ready to submit them to trial in Denmark as it would be difficult (in light of the possible abuses they would risk) to deport them back to

---

[39]   The US Secretary of State C. Rice observed in her declaration of 16 December 2008 before the Security Council: 'the international community already has sufficient legal authority and available mechanisms to apprehend and prosecute pirates, but sometimes the political will and the coordination have not been there to do so': UN Doc S/PV.6046 (16 December 2008) 10.

[40]   So, on 17 November 2010, a vessel of the European force Atalanta, after having captured pirates and seizing their weapons freed the pirates because the evidence collected was not deemed sufficient for prosecution: Lang Report, *supra* note 38, para. 59 of the Annex.

[41]   A vivid description of the problems encountered by a State whose vessel has captured pirates in made by Katherine Shepherd, of the UK Foreign and Commonwealth office, in *Am. Society of International Law Proceeding of the 103rd Meeting*, *supra* at note 1, 95–97. See also Y. M. Dutton, 'Pirates and Impunity: Is the Threat of Asylum Claims a Reason to Allow Pirates to Escape Justice?' (2011) 34 *Fordham Law Review* 236–295. According to Neuhold, *supra* note 1, 1254 note 48, one of the five pirates that were sentenced to five years' imprisonment by the District Court of Rotterdam (see: *The 'Cygnus' Case (Somali Pirates)* 145 International Law Reports 491) 'promptly applied for asylum'. See also Dienstein, *supra* note 1, 1143.

[42]   According to the Lang Report, *supra* note 38, Annex, para. 14, 'more than 90 per cent of the pirates apprehended by States patrolling the seas will be released without being prosecuted'. For further discussion see: D. Guilfoyle, 'Prosecuting Somali Pirates: A Critical Evaluation of the Options' (2012) 10 *Journal of International Criminal Justice* 767.

Somalia after their sentences were served.[43] It is clear that human rights considerations, or perhaps reasons of expediency presented as human rights concerns, prevailed on considerations concerning the fight against piracy. In the same vein, the British Foreign Office reportedly warned the Royal Navy against detaining pirates since this might violate their human rights and could lead to claims of asylum in the United Kingdom.[44] Similarly, in 2010 Russia, having captured the pirates which had hijacked the Russian tanker *Russian University*, released them on the very skiff they had used to board the tanker, alleging that 'in the absence of the necessary legal agreement it was impossible to bring these pirates' to justice.[45]

Capture and detention at sea of criminals, although not pirates, later brought to trial in faraway courts of the state of the arresting vessel, have been submitted by the captured persons to the judgment of the European Court of Human Rights (ECHR). This happened in the *Rigopoulos* and in the *Medvedyev* cases decided with judgments of 12 January 1999 and of 10 July 2008, the latter confirmed by the Grand Chamber in a judgment of 23 March 2010.[46] In these cases, persons were arrested on the high seas on a ship boarded, with the authorization of the flag state, under suspicion, proven well founded, of being engaged in smuggling narcotic drugs. The question submitted to the Court was whether detention on the arresting naval vessel for about two weeks was compatible with article 5(3) of the European Convention on Human Rights according to which, *inter alia*, arrested or detained persons 'shall be brought promptly before a judge or other officer authorized by law to exercise judicial power'. The Court, even though it decided, in both cases, that the circumstances were exceptional enough to justify an affirmative answer, stated clearly that the

---

[43] See reports at <http://www.lloydslist.com/ll/sector/piracy-and-security/article44917.ece> accessed 1 August 2012; US Office of Naval Intelligence, Civil Maritime Analysis Department, 'Worldwide Threat to Shipping, Mariner Warning Information' (17 October 2008) para. 10.

[44] See: D. B. Rivkin Jr. and L. A. Casey, 'Pirates Exploit Confusion about International Law', *The Wall Street Journal* (19 November 2008).

[45] See reports at <http://www.oldsaltblog.com/2010/05/06/russian-special-forces-capture-oil-tanker-moscow-university/> and <http://www.oldsaltblog.com/2010/05/10/mv-moscow-university-why-anti-piracy-efforts-in-somalia-are-doomed-to-fail> accessed 7 January 2012. Neuhold, *supra* note 1, 1253 note 46, qualifies the Russian solution as 'brutal' because, according to his information, the pirates were released without food and navigation devices 'so that they were in all probability sent to their deaths'.

[46] Respectively, European Court of Human Rights request Nos 37388/97 and 3394/03.

principle was that such a long detention was not compatible with the quoted provision.[47] Consequently, states parties to the European Convention might, in different circumstances, be confronted by a decision stating a violation of the human rights of the detained criminal (be it a drug trafficker or a pirate). Moreover, in the *Medvedyev* case the ECHR found a violation of article 5(1) of the European Convention, according to which *inter alia*: 'No one shall be deprived of his liberty save in the following cases and in accordance with a procedure prescribed by law' on the basis of a strict interpretation of the agreement authorizing the boarding and arrest, but which allegedly was not sufficiently clear as to the right to submit the arrested person to trial. The possibility of a similar decision seems highly unlikely in the case of piracy, in light of the broad powers recognized by general international law and the Security Council resolutions.[48] It shows, nevertheless, that a court such as the ECHR will tend to interpret the law of the sea and international law rules in such a way as to offer maximum protection to the individuals involved.

As a recent scholarly study has shown, the relevance, for its states parties, of the European Convention on Human Rights may go beyond the situations envisaged in the *Medvedyev* case.[49] Violations of the right to life (article 2) or the right to privacy (article 8) and others, concerning in particular, the right to a fair trial, may be envisaged. Moreover, difficult questions of attribution may arise if violations of the Human Rights Convention are committed by European states in the framework of Operation Atalanta, both before the European Union becomes a party to the Convention and afterward.[50]

---

[47] The Rotterdam District Court in the *'Cygnus' Case*, *supra* note 41, stressed that the time of 40 days elapsed before captured pirates were brought to justice constituted a breach of Art. 5 of the European Convention on Human Rights, although no consequences followed in the criminal proceedings before the Dutch Court.

[48] According to Piedimonte Bodini, *supra* note 10, the *obiter dictum* (quoted in the same footnote) set out in para. 85 of the *Medvedyev* judgment 'seems to imply that the anti-piracy provisions contained in the Convention [i.e. UNCLOS] would pass the "sufficient legal basis" test under article 5(1) when it comes to intercepting pirate vessels and detaining their crews'. See also for a broader analysis of the human rights implication of the fight against piracy: D. Guifoyle, 'Counter-piracy Law Enforcement and Human Rights' 59 (2010) *International and Comparative Law Quarterly* 141–169.

[49] Piedimonte Bodini, *supra* note 10, 834–842.

[50] Piedimonte Bodini, *supra* note 10, 845–846

6.8   THE ROLE OF THE SUA CONVENTION IN PROSECUTING PIRATES

The reluctance of the seizing states to prosecute and try pirates is implicitly taken into account in a paragraph repeated in various resolutions of the Security Council.[51] The latest version reads as follows:

> *Calls upon* all States, and in particular flag, port, and coastal States, States of the nationality of victims, and perpetrators of piracy and armed robbery, and other States with relevant jurisdiction under international law and national legislation, to cooperate in determining jurisdiction, and in the investigation and prosecution of all persons responsible for acts of piracy and armed robbery off the coast of Somalia, including anyone who incites or facilitates an act of piracy, consistent with applicable international law including international human rights law to ensure that all pirates handed over to judicial authorities are subject to a judicial process, and to render assistance by, among other actions, providing disposition and logistics assistance with respect to persons under their jurisdiction and control, such as victims and witnesses and persons detained as a result of operations conducted under this resolution[.][52]

This language is merely hortatory. However, most states involved as flag states of the ships that are victims of piracy or of the ships patrolling the waters off Somalia, or as neighbouring coastal states such as Djibouti, Kenya and Yemen, but not Somalia, are bound by the precise obligations set out for parties to the Rome Convention for the Suppression of Unlawful Acts against the Safety of Maritime Navigation of 10 March 1988 (the SUA Convention).[53] This Convention – adopted in the wake of the *Achille Lauro* affair – provides that states parties shall establish a

---

[51]   UNSC Res. 1816, *supra* note 15, para. 11; UNSC Res. 1846, *supra* note 19, para. 14.

[52]   UNSC Res. 2020, *supra* note 3, para. 14.

[53]   (Adopted 10 March 1988, entered into force 1 March 1992) 1678 UNTS 221. Under Art. 4, para. 1, the 'Convention applies if the ship is navigating or is scheduled to navigate into, through or from waters beyond the outer limit of the territorial sea of a single State, or the lateral limits of its territorial sea with adjacent States'. This means that only ships navigating between ports of the same state (cabotage) are excluded from the scope of the Convention. Even in this case, under Art. 4, para. 2 the Convention applies if 'the offender or alleged offender is found in the territory of a State party other than the State referred to in paragraph 1'. On the SUA Convention see, with further references, the present writer's essays: 'The Rome Convention for the Suppression of Unlawful Acts against the Safety of Maritime Navigation', in N. Ronzitti (ed.), *Maritime Terrorism and International Law* (Dordrecht 1990), 69–90; and 'The Convention

number of criminal offences, most of which correspond in whole or in part with actions committed by pirates or armed robbers including 'seiz[ing] or exercis[ing] control over a ship by force or threat thereof or any other form of intimidation' (notably, it does not require the presence of two ships and does not distinguish between maritime areas).[54] Especially, it makes it compulsory to 'take such measures as may be necessary to establish jurisdiction' over such offences for the flag state of the ship against or onboard of which the crime is committed, for the state in whose territory, including the territorial sea, the crime has been committed, and for the state whose national has committed the offence. It further authorizes other states to establish jurisdiction in additional cases, including the national state of a person seized, threatened, injured or killed and the state which the offence committed attempts to compel to do or to abstain from doing any act. In all cases, to establish jurisdiction is compulsory for the state in whose territory the alleged offender is present, unless it has extradited such offender to one of the states having established jurisdiction.[55]

While the SUA Convention is not mentioned in resolution 1816, resolutions adopted in later years, including the most recent one[56] recall the obligations set out in it and urge states parties 'to fully implement' these obligations.

6.9 TRANSFER OF CAPTURED PIRATE TO NEIGHBOURING STATES: 'SHIPRIDERS'

Reluctance of the seizing states is not the only cause of lack of efficiency in dealing with captured pirates and armed robbers. As said in a preambular paragraph of Security Council resolution 1846: 'the lack of capacity, domestic legislation, and clarity about how to dispose of pirates after their capture has hindered more robust international action against the pirates off the coast of Somalia and in some case led to the pirates being released without facing justice'.

A solution seen with great interest by capturing states consists of surrendering the captured pirates to a state near to the place of capture. This solution, however, raises difficulties as regards questions about the

---

for the Suppression of Unlawful Acts Against the Safety of Maritime Navigation' (1998) 2 *Singapore Journal of International and Comparative Law* 541.

[54] Art. 3.
[55] Art. 6.
[56] UNSC Res. 2020, *supra* note 3, para. 23.

ability and willingness of such states to exercise jurisdiction and to administer detention in full respect of human rights. In order to overcome these difficulties, bilateral agreements with Kenya have been concluded by the United Kingdom, the United States and the European Union,[57] and more recently by the European Union with the Seychelles and Mauritius. These allow for the transfer of suspect pirates captured by a patrolling navy into the custody of a regional state for prosecution.

These agreements sometimes provide for 'shipriders' as mentioned and encouraged by resolution 1846 and others (although such provisions are not used at all in practice). 'Shiprider' arrangements consist of agreements between the states whose ships are patrolling the waters off the coast of Somalia and 'countries willing to take custody of pirates' for embarking on these ships law enforcement officers (the 'shipriders') 'from the latter countries, in particular countries of the region, to facilitate the investigation and prosecution of persons detained'.[58] These arrangements require previous consent of the TFG 'for the exercise of third state jurisdiction by shipriders in Somali territorial waters' and provided they 'do not prejudice the effective implementation of the SUA Convention'.

In practice, states appear to ground their jurisdiction over pirates on one of several bases. Foremost is the assertion of universal jurisdiction, under national laws, by regional coastal states over suspects delivered to them by patrolling navies (discussed further below). Greater use of shipriders under the agreements discussed above would also permit to base the jurisdiction of Kenya (or of other states whose officers are onboard the seizing vessels) on the fiction that it is a seizing state under UNCLOS article 105. In other cases the connecting factor is the nationality of the victim ship or of the victims. So, reportedly, the Netherlands agreed with Denmark to extradite five Somali pirates who had attacked a Netherlands-Antilles cargo vessel in the Gulf of Aden which had been captured by Denmark.[59]

---

[57] R. Meade, 'US to sign Kenya deal to prosecute Somali pirates' *Lloyd's List* (16 January 2009) <http://www.lloydslistdcn.com.au/archive/2009/jan/21/us-to-sign-kenya-deal-to-prosecute-somali-pirates> accessed 1 August 2012.

[58] UNSC Res. 1846, *supra* note 19, para. 3. 'Shipriders' are used in some bilateral agreements concluded by the US regarding drug trafficking, see e.g., Guilfoyle, *Interdiction, supra* note 1, 91–94; they are mentioned also as 'Embarked Officers' in the 2009 Code of Conduct 2009 for the West Indian Ocean and the Gulf of Aden, supra note 18, Art. 7.

[59] Meade, *supra* note 57.

The European Union Joint Action 2008/851/CSFP[60] on the European Union military operation against piracy and armed robbery off the Somali coast envisages the situation now considered. It provides that the persons arrested during the operation with a view to their prosecution, if the competent authorities of the flag state of the ship 'which took them captive', 'cannot or does not wish to exercise its jurisdiction', shall be transferred to a 'Member State or any third State which wishes to exercise its jurisdiction over the aforementioned persons'.[61] This provision does not exclude the practice of 'shipriders', but adds possible transferral to other European Union member states or to other willing third states. In light of the abovementioned concerns, a provision of the same Joint Action seems relevant. The provision states that:

> no person ... may be transferred to a third State unless the conditions for the transfer have been agreed with that third State in a manner consistent with relevant international law, notably international law of human rights, in order to guarantee in particular that no one shall be subjected to the death penalty, to torture or to any cruel, inhuman or degrading treatment.[62]

Detailed provisions for the protection of human rights of pirates and armed robbers captured by the European Union naval force and transferred to Kenya are set out in articles 3 and 4 of the Exchange of Letters on such transfer concluded between the European Union and Kenya on 6 March 2009.[63] It is to be noted that this agreement, though not excluding their involvement, does not mention 'shipriders', further reinforcing the conclusion they are not greatly used in practice.

---

[60] *Supra* note 32.

[61] EU Council Joint Action 2008/851/CFSP, *supra* note 32, Art. 12, para. 1. This provision may be read as implying that in the view of the European Union article 105 UNCLOS does not rule out exercise of universal jurisdiction by a State different from that having seized the ship.

[62] *Ibid.*, para. 2.

[63] 'Exchange of letters for the conditions and modalities for the transfer of persons having committed acts of piracy and detained by the European Union-led Naval Force (EUNAVFOR), and seized property in the possession of EUNAVFOR, from EUNAVFOR to Kenya' OJ EU 2009 L79/49 as annexed to European Council Decision 2009/293/CFSP in OJ EU 2009 L79, 47.

6.10 THE INSUFFICIENCY OF THE TRANSFER AGREEMENTS. THE SEARCH FOR NEW SOLUTIONS TO OBTAIN THE TRIAL OF PIRATES

Transfer agreements, although attractive for capturing states, cannot be the only solution to the problem of what do with captured pirates. Notwithstanding substantial expenditure, especially by the European Union and the United States, for strengthening the judicial and penitentiary systems of the states accepting to receive captured pirates, the capacity of these states is rather limited. In March 2010 Kenya 'gave six months' notice of its withdrawal from the arrangements that it had entered into with Canada, China, Denmark, the European Union, the United Kingdom and United States, for the transfer of piracy suspects' while indicating its readiness to consider transfers on an ad hoc basis.[64] Even though it appears Kenya has subsequently received some new piracy cases for trial, the very announcement is an indication of unease and shows that other solutions must be sought.

Probably in light of the new Kenyan attitude, in the following months the Security Council focused on the link between prosecution of captured pirates and the efficacy of the fight against piracy. In resolution 1918 of 27 April 2010 the Security Council affirmed 'that the failure to prosecute persons responsible for acts of piracy and armed robbery at sea off the coast of Somalia undermines anti-piracy efforts of the international community'.[65] On 25 August 2010 the President of the Security Council stated that: 'The Security Council strongly believes that persons responsible for acts of piracy and armed robbery at sea off the coast of Somalia, including those who incite or intentionally facilitate such acts, should be brought to justice, and considers in this regard that the effective prosecution of suspected pirates and their supporters may deter future pirate attacks.'[66] In resolution 1976 of 2011 the Security Council expressed its concern 'over a large number of persons suspected of piracy having to be

---

[64] See the Report of the UN Secretary General, UN Doc. S/2011/360 (15 June 2011), Annex V, para. 3 and the statements by Kenya's Attorney General Amos Wako of 30 March 2010 in 'AG queried over Kenya's role on piracy cases', *The Nation (Kenya)* (30 March 2010) <http://www.nation.co.ke/News/ AG+queried+over+Kenya+role+in+piracy+cases/-/1056/889516/-/l25eie/-/index. html> accessed 1 August 2012 and further indications in Roach, *supra* note 1, 404 note 36 and in Lang Report, *supra* note 38, Annex, para. 72.

[65] UNSC Res. 1918, *supra* note 12, para. 1.

[66] UN Doc S/PRST/2010/16 (25 August 2010). See the discussion in UN Doc SC/PV/6374 (25 August 2010).

released without facing justice' and reaffirmed 'that the failure to prosecute persons responsible for acts of piracy and armed robbery at sea off the coast of Somalia undermines anti-piracy efforts of the international community'.[67]

Acting on the basis of the above-quoted resolutions, the UN Secretary-General on the 26 July 2010 presented a report on possible options for prosecuting captured pirates, in which seven such options were indicated.[68] On 26 August 2010 he appointed the French former Minister Jack Lang as a Special Advisor on Legal Issues Related to Piracy. In light of the drawbacks of some of the seven options indicated by the Secretary-General, Jack Lang's broad-ranging report favours the establishment of a court system comprising a specialized court in Puntland, a specialized court in Somaliland and a specialized extra-territorial Somali court that could be located in Arusha, United Republic of Tanzania.[69]

In its latest resolutions adopted at the end of 2011, the Security Council seems to orient itself in favour of at least some of these proposals. In resolution 2015 it decided 'to continue its consideration, as a matter of urgency, without prejudice to any further steps to ensure that pirates are held accountable, of the establishment of specialized anti-piracy courts in Somalia and other states in the region with substantial international participation and/or support'. This decision, reiterated in resolution 2020, included also a request that the Secretary-General undergo further consultations with Somalia and report within 90 days.

It must, nonetheless, be underscored that the establishment of a Somali extra-territorial court to be located out of Somalia is not explicitly mentioned, although it might be read as implied in the expression 'specialized anti-piracy courts in Somalia *and other States in the region with substantial international participation and/or support*'. As a matter of fact, the idea of establishing an extra-territorial Somali court out of Somalia had been unequivocally opposed during consultations held by representatives of the Secretary-General, by the TFG as well as by the regional governments of Puntland and Galmadug.[70]

Thus, it would seem that the centrepiece of Jack Lang's proposals to the Security Council, the establishment of an extra-territorial Somali

---

[67]   UNSC Res. 1976, *supra* note 8, 15th preambular paragraph.

[68]   Report of the UN Secretary General, UN Doc. S/2010/394 (26 July 2010). For further analysis see: Guilfoyle, *supra* note 42.

[69]   The Lang Report, *supra* note 38, Annex, paras 116–141 deal with the indicated 'jurisdictional component' of the proposals set out in it.

[70]   Report of the UN Secretary General, *supra* note 64, paras 52–55.

court with international involvement, meets with grave political difficulties. All that seems to remain unchallenged is the idea of establishing regional Somali specialized courts in Somalia with international help. This can hardly be seen as sufficient. Probably the strengthening of the current mix of trials of pirates in Somalia, in the neighbouring states and in the captors' courts will remain the only option. While it is true that the number of pirates and armed robbers submitted to trial and often sentenced in courts of about 20 states is (slowly) growing,[71] this does not go very far towards making the operation of criminal justice a serious disincentive to the activity of pirates and armed robbers in the waters off the coasts of Somalia.

6.11 USE OF FORCE IN OPERATIONS AT SEA AGAINST PIRATES AND ARMED ROBBERS

Seizing a pirate ship under the power granted to all states by UNCLOS implies the possibility of the use of force. This is even clearer under the quoted resolutions of the Security Council that mention the use of 'all necessary means for repressing acts of piracy and armed robbery'. It is well known that in the parlance of the Security Council 'all necessary means' means 'use of force'. The above quoted European Union Council Joint Action makes this explicit in defining the mandate of 'Operation Atalanta' when it says that Atalanta shall take 'all necessary measures, including use of force'.[72]

This is not 'use of force' against the enemy according to the law of armed conflict, because there is no armed conflict, international or internal. Pirates are not at war with the states whose flotillas protect merchant vessels in the waters off the coast of Somalia. It has been argued that pirates, not being combatants, are civilians which, under international humanitarian law, may not be specifically targeted except in immediate self-defence.[73] Whatever opinion one holds about the applicability of the law of armed conflict, it is a fact that practice in the waters off Somalia seems to indicate that warships patrolling these waters resort to the use of weapons only in response to the use of weapons against

---

[71] Report of the UN Secretary General, *supra* note 64, Annex I, para. 4.

[72] EU Council Joint Action 2008/851/CFSP, *supra* note 32, Art. 2(f).

[73] It must be noted that only in UNSC Res. 1851, *supra* note 3, authorizing action against pirates and armed robbers in the Somali mainland, does the Security Council specify that such action must be undertaken consistent not only with human rights but also 'with applicable humanitarian law'.

them. So, in an incident in the Gulf of Aden reported on 14 November 2008, a British naval vessel having positively recognized a Yemeni cargo ship that had participated in a hijacking attempt on a Danish cargo ship on the same day, tried to stop it by 'non forcible methods'. Only when these had failed, 'the Royal Navy launched small assault craft to encircle the vessel'. Once the pirates opened fire, 'the Navy fired back in self-defence'. In another episode reported on 21 November 2008, the Indian navy vessel *Tabar* patrolling the Gulf of Aden 285 miles off the coast of Oman requested to stop a vessel described as a pirate mother ship and whose crew was seen 'with a full complement of modern weapons'. When the pirate ship 'responded by threatening to "blow up the naval warship if it closed on her"' and fired at the Indian vessel, the *Tabar* responded and sank the vessel.[74]

Thus, self-defence against an armed attack or the threat thereof, either in the questionable framework of the law of armed conflict, or in the discussed framework of resort to it against non-state actors, or, more likely, as a self-imposed rule of engagement for police action, seems to be a guiding principle of states whose navies are engaged in fighting pirates off the coast of Somalia and neighbouring states.

The question must, however, be raised whether force may be used in action against pirates and armed robbers independently of self-defence, and whether, if an affirmative answer is given, international law pre-scribes limits to such use. Action against pirates may, in my view, be assimilated to the exercise of the power to engage in police action on the high seas on foreign vessels that is permitted to other states by exceptions to the rule stating the exclusive jurisdiction of the flag state. Such permissions are rarely and reluctantly given by flag states unless upon request on a case-by-case basis. There are, nonetheless, examples of permissions given in general terms in a few treaties on drug trafficking and on fisheries. Among these, the 1995 UN Fish Stocks Agreement is the main multilateral instrument that may be recalled.[75] This agreement permits certain non-flag states to board and inspect fishing vessels on the high seas. In principle such action should not involve use of force, as the

---

[74] These episodes are reported in bulletins of the (US) Office of naval intelligence, Civil Maritime Analysis Department, Worldwide Threat to Shipping, Mariner Warning Information, as posted online at <http://www.icc-ccs.org/>.

[75] Agreement for the Implementation of Provisions of the United Nations Convention on the Law of the Sea of 10 December 1982 Relating to the Conservation and Management of Straddling Fish Stocks and Highly Migratory Fish Stock, opened to signature in New York on (adopted 4 December 1995, entered into force 11 December 2001), 2167 UNTS 88.

flag state is, *inter alia*, bound to 'accept and facilitate prompt and safe boarding by the inspectors' and sanction the master in case he refuses to accept boarding (article 22, paragraphs 3 and 4). A possibility of use of force after the boarding is, nevertheless, envisaged in article 22, paragraph 1(f), stating that the inspecting state shall: 'avoid the use of force except when and to the degree necessary to ensure the safety of the inspectors and where the inspectors are obstructed in the execution of their duties'. General international law, in authorizing stopping and boarding for the purpose of exercising the right of visit under article 110 of UNCLOS or the seizure of a pirate ship under article 105, presupposes that force may be used to reach these objectives. In light of that they have accepted the relevant instruments and that they are bound by the relevant customary rules and by the relevant resolutions taken by the Security Council under Chapter VII, states can be considered as consenting to, or as being obliged to accept, the use of force undertaken in order to execute these police activities.

Limits to such use of force in the exercise of police action authorized by international law have been indicated in dispute-settlement and treaty practice. Repeating and developing points made in the *I'm Alone* arbitration Award and in the report of the Commission of enquiry on the *Red Crusader* case, the International Tribunal for the Law of the Sea, in its *M/V Saiga No. 2* judgment states: 'international law ... requires that the use of force must be avoided as far as possible and, where force is inevitable, it must not go beyond what is reasonable and necessary in the circumstances. Considerations of humanity must apply in the law of the sea, as they do in other areas of international law.'[76] The judgment further recalls the practice consisting in visual and auditory signals to stop, firing shots across the bow and a variety of other measures, normally followed before resorting to force.[77] In the same vein, the UN Fish Stocks Agreement concludes its above quoted article 22, paragraph 1(f), stating: 'The degree of force used shall not exceed that reasonably required in the circumstances.'

The *Saiga No. 2* case was quoted in the 2007 Arbitral Award deciding a maritime border dispute between Guyana and Suriname.[78] The question addressed was whether the order given by a Surinamese naval vessel to a Guyanese oil drilling platform situated on a disputed area of the continental shelf to leave the area with the statement that 'if they would

---

76   ITLOS Reports 1999, p. 10, at para. 155.
77   ITLOS Reports 1999, p. 10, at para. 156.
78   Award of 17 September 2007, 47 ILM 166 (2008).

not do so, the consequences would be theirs' constituted an illegal threat of use of force under article 2, paragraph 4, of the UN Charter and under customary law. The Arbitral Tribunal considered, *inter alia*, the remarks set out in the International Court of Justice (ICJ) *Military and Paramilitary Activities in and against Nicaragua* judgment of 1986 distinguishing the most grave forms of use of force, which constitute an armed attack, from 'other less grave forms'.[79] While not directly drawing consequences from this distinction, it 'accepts the argument that in international law force may be used in law enforcement activities provided that such force is unavoidable, reasonable and necessary' but concludes that: 'in the circumstances of the present case, ... the action mounted by Suriname on 3 June 2003 seemed more akin to a threat of military action rather than a mere law enforcement activity' and that it contravened the UN Charter and general international law (paragraph 445). The Tribunal does not specify whether this conclusion is based on the characteristics of the threatened use of force (the possible involvement of military means?) or that the use of force was illicit because it had taken place in an area the Award had determined to belong to Guyana and where, consequently, Suriname had no enforcement rights, and that it would have been considered a licit enforcement activity had the area been found to belong to Suriname. The latter seems to be the most reasonable explanation, but, admittedly, the Award is not clear on this key point.

As regards use of force against pirates, the *Guyana v Suriname* Award seems to confirm the trend emerging that activities permitted by international law for the enforcement of rights may include the use of force, provided such force be unavoidable, reasonable and necessary. The practice seen above clarifies these requirements by introducing the element of respect for the human rights of the persons involved that was implicit in the above-quoted mention of 'considerations of humanity' in the *M/V Saiga No. 2* judgment of the International Tribunal for the Law of the Sea.

6.12 CONCLUSIONS

As discussed above, the general definition of piracy at international law is narrow and the powers granted to suppress it are circumscribed. The central definition of piracy includes only violence or depredation on the high seas and only action undertaken by one ship against another ship.

---

[79] *Ibid.*, para. 445, referring to *Nicaragua v United States (Judgment)*, ICJ Reports, 1986, p. 14, para 191.

Therefore violence in the territorial sea or not involving two ships is excluded. Acts preparatory to piracy are covered only to the extent they fall within the curious UNCLOS provisions dealing with 'voluntary participation in the operation of a [pirate] ship' and 'any act of inciting or of intentionally facilitating' piracy. There is as yet relatively little case law on these concepts.[80] Further, states powers of enforcement are confined to the high seas, preventing the taking of direct action in another state's territorial sea or the pursuit of pirates onto land.

Some of these limitations in the case of Somalia have been addressed by the Security Council authorizing intervention in Somalia's territorial sea and even its land territory. While these aspects of the measures adopted by the Security Council may superficially appear quite radical, as noted above the authorization provided by Somalia takes away much of the revolutionary content of the resolutions. Nonetheless, in the context of Security Council concerns regarding piracy and maritime violence in relation to Nigeria, it is notable that such measures have not been adopted in respect of other situations.

Underlying the response to Somali piracy has been a degree of reluctance by flag states to prosecute captured pirates. This reflects a range of practical and legal challenges discussed in later chapters. The prosecution of Somali pirates has also involved extraordinary measures of cooperation between states regarding the transfer and prosecution of suspects. Other models of inter-state cooperation are discussed in Chapter 2, in relation to the Southeast Asian experience of piracy. A less obvious issue, explored in Chapter 9, is the need for inter-agency cooperation within governments to facilitate successful piracy prosecutions. The present chapter has also discussed the general law applicable to the use of force against pirates. Navies are faced with the more specific question of how these rules are to be applied in practice, a topic returned to in more detail in Chapter 7.

---

[80]   On 'inciting and facilitating', note the emerging US case law: Roger L. Phillips, 'Negotiator Sentenced to Multiple Life Terms – SCOTUS on the horizon', *Communis Hostis Omnium*, 15 August 2012 <http://piracy-law.com/2012/08/15/negotiator-sentenced-to-multiple-life-terms-scotus-on-the-horizon/> accessed 12 September 2012.

7. Capture and disruption operations: the use of force in counter-piracy off Somalia

Andrew Murdoch* and Douglas Guilfoyle

7.1 INTRODUCTION

7.1.1 Capture and Disruption Operations as Part of Counter-piracy

Warships, uniquely, have positive authorisation to intervene pro-actively against pirates. The purpose of this chapter is to discuss one of the most visible and discussed aspects of such counter-piracy operations off Somalia: what happens when a naval vessel encounters a suspect pirate craft which is either engaged in an attack on a merchant vessel or which uses (or threatens to use) force against a naval vessel or personnel? In such a situation, how much force can a naval vessel or personnel use either to deter or disrupt an attack, capture resisting suspects, or protect life and what law governs those events? This issue of the use of force against pirates by warships was touched on in Chapter 6.11 but is examined in more detail here. In particular, some further consideration is given to the legal reasons for concluding counter-piracy must be conducted under the law of law-enforcement, not the laws applicable to war. While the focus of this chapter will be on maritime capture and disruption operations, the law applicable to counter-piracy operations ashore is briefly noted.

Chapter 8 goes on to consider more generally the impact of (and rationale for) conducting counter-piracy operations within a law-enforcement paradigm, and explores some of the practical legal difficulties for navies at the moment they do capture pirates and have to consider

---

* The views expressed in this chapter are those of the author and do not necessarily represent those of the Foreign and Commonwealth Office or Her Majesty's Government.

the options for prosecuting them. This involves sometimes difficult questions of mutual legal assistance between states, a key question often being the delay between the capture of pirates and the decision either to transfer them for prosecution or release them. Chapter 9 will, in turn, suggest that maritime law-enforcement operations generally require the coordination of assets and expertise within states (i.e., between departments and agencies) if timely decisions are to be made.

In this context, the present chapter will begin by outlining the framework for cooperation between the various national and multi-national missions deployed off Somalia to combat piracy. It then discusses the general law governing the use of force in maritime law-enforcement operations before considering how that law has been modified by the relevant Security Council resolutions dealing with Somali piracy. Finally, it will consider how the law works in an operational context, particularly through the adoption of military Rules of Engagement (ROE). Two case studies will then be used to illustrate the practical situations navies may face and how the law may apply in such cases.

7.1.2   The Practical Framework for International Cooperation

In August 2008, as the threat from piracy activities increased, Combined Maritime Forces (CMF)[1] first established 'a maritime security patrol area (the MSPA) in international waters off the Somali coast'.[2] This MSPA is a defined area of operations providing a common system of reference that allows states with vessels in the Gulf to 'de-conflict' and/or coordinate their counter-piracy activities. Running through the MSPA is an internationally recommended (and military patrolled) shipping corridor in the Gulf of Aden, the Internationally Recognised Transit Corridor (IRTC), established in August 2008 by the United Kingdom Maritime Trade Organisation. Until 2008 the principal naval operation in this area was that providing an armed escort to World Food Program (WFP) vessels entering Somali ports. The more significant commitment of resources is now the military patrolling of the IRTC, and targeted deployments in the Somali basin to tackle pirate action groups. On average more than 20 vessels are now engaged in counter-piracy operations at any time off the coast of Somalia, under an array of mission and command structures. The

---

[1]   See: Combined Maritime Forces website: <http://combinedmaritime forces.com/> accessed 8 August 2012.

[2]   'Report of the Secretary-General on the situation in Somalia', UN Doc S/2008/709 (17 November 2008), para. 55.

level of military cooperation in the waters off the coast of Somalia has become increasingly sophisticated. A Shared Awareness and Deconfliction (SHADE) meeting is held regularly to improve the coordination and cooperation of maritime forces operating in the region and typically attracts in excess of 100 participants including representatives from the militaries of over 20 states, the EU and NATO.[3] The Contact Group on Piracy off the Coast of Somalia (CGPCS) serves as a forum for international cooperation and coordination to prevent piracy. It has established five working groups,[4] including one group tasked with military and operational coordination. A host of UN bodies[5] have also all been engaged in counter-piracy related work, with the UN Office on Drugs and Crime's (UNODC) Counter-Piracy Programme having a central role.

The US, UK, Denmark and the EU concluded memoranda of understanding or (in the EU case) exchanges of letters/agreements[6] with regional states for the transfer of captured pirates to their jurisdictions for trial. However, as of August 2012, only arrangements between the EU and Mauritius, the UK and Tanzania and Mauritius, and separate arrangements between the UK, US, Denmark, the EU and the Seychelles are still in force. Some pirates have also been taken to face trial in Puntland (Somalia), Yemen, European capitals and North America. The International Maritime Organization (IMO) has also worked to promote a regional response: a regional Code of Conduct Concerning the Repression of Piracy was concluded in Djibouti in January 2009.[7] Within this context there have been several notable cases in which force has been used against pirates at sea. Some of these are discussed in further detail below. First, however, it is relevant to examine the applicable international law standards governing such operations.

---

[3]   See: Combined Maritime Forces website, 'Combined Maritime Forces host 24th SHADE meeting', <http://combinedmaritimeforces.com/2012/06/17/combined-maritime-forces-host-24th-shade-meeting/> accessed 8 August 2012.

[4]   Group 1 is Military and Operational Coordination, Information Sharing, and Capacity Building, Group 2 is Legal Issues, Group 3 is Commercial Industry Coordination, Group 4 is Public Information, and Group 5 is Financial Flows.

[5]   UN Development Programme (UNDP), UN Political Office for Somalia (UNPOS), and UN Office on Drugs and Crime (UNODC).

[6]   See legal basis stated in Council Decision 2011/640/CFSP of 12 July 2011 on the signing of the Agreement between the EU and the Republic of Mauritius, satisfying the requirements of Joint Action 2008/851/CFSP for agreement on the conditions for such transfers.

[7]   See IMO Doc C 102/14 of 3 April 2009.

7.2 THE GENERAL LAW OF PIRACY AND AUTHORITY UNDER INTERNATIONAL LAW TO USE FORCE IN MARITIME LAW-ENFORCEMENT OPERATIONS

The general international law applicable to piracy was discussed in Chapter 6. As noted, the UN Convention on the Law of the Sea (UNCLOS)[8] says nothing directly about the use of force in its provisions on piracy. One must therefore turn to the general public international law governing the use of force in maritime law-enforcement operations. The critical case is *MV Saiga (No. 2)*,[9] where the International Tribunal for the Law of the Sea (ITLOS) found that in cases of 'boarding, stopping and arresting' a vessel international law:

> requires that the use of force must be avoided as far as possible and, where ... unavoidable, it must not go beyond what is reasonable and necessary in the circumstances. Considerations of humanity must apply ...

> The normal practice ... is first to give an auditory or visual signal to stop, ... [then to take other action], including the firing of shots across the bows of the ship. It is only after the appropriate actions fail that the pursuing vessel may, as a last resort, use force. Even then, appropriate warning must be issued ... and all efforts should be made to ensure that life is not endangered.

In reaching these conclusions ITLOS had only two cases to draw on: *Red Crusader* and *I'm Alone*.[10] The *I'm Alone* case concerned the deliberate sinking of a vessel to prevent its continued flight, while in *Red Crusader* 40mm solid shot was fired into a fleeing fishing vessel. The *MV Saiga* case itself involved the deliberate firing of large calibre live rounds without warning shots into a slow-moving vessel suspected only of customs offences. Such cases are potentially unhelpful because they deal with such clearly disproportionate uses of force. Perhaps as a result of this scant authority, the Tribunal went on to quote article 22(1)(f) of the

---

[8]   United Nations Convention on the Law of the Sea (adopted 10 December 1982, entered into force 16 November 1994) 1833 UNTS 397 (UNCLOS).

[9]   *M/V 'Saiga' (No. 2) (Saint Vincent and the Grenadines v Guinea)* ITLOS Case No. 2; (1999) 38 ILM 1323, 1355. See also Chapter 6.11 and *Guyana v Suriname* (2008) 47 International Legal Materials 164 at para. 443.

[10]   (1935) 3 Reports of International Arbitral Awards 1609 and (1962) 35 International Law Reports 485 respectively.

UN Fish Stocks Agreement (FSA)[11] as having further 'reaffirmed' the 'basic principle'.[12] The provision reads relevantly:

> The use of force shall be avoided except when and to the degree necessary to ensure the safety of the inspectors and where the inspectors are obstructed in the execution of their duties. The degree of force used shall not exceed that reasonably required in the circumstances.

The FSA is not an intuitive source of law for standards regarding the boarding and arrest of a vessel as it deals only with the use of force to carry out an authorised inspection *once already aboard*. It does not contemplate, for example, imminent threats to life as fisherman are not usually violent criminals. Nonetheless, the provision is consistent with ITLOS's broad conclusion that the key consideration is 'reasonableness'. A more useful standard is suggested by article 9 of the United Nations Basic Principles for the Use of Force and Firearms by Law Enforcement Officials[13] (UN Basic Principles) which provides that firearms shall only be used

> in self-defense or defense of others against the imminent threat of death or serious injury, to prevent the perpetration of a particularly serious crime…and only when less extreme means are insufficient…[I]ntentional lethal use of firearms may only be made when strictly unavoidable in order to protect life.

Similarly, article 8*bis*(9) of the 2005 Protocol to the Convention for the Suppression of Unlawful Acts against the Safety of Maritime Navigation provides:[14]

> When carrying out the authorized actions under this article, the use of force shall be avoided except when necessary to ensure the safety of its officials and

---

[11]   The United Nations Agreement for the Implementation of the Provisions of the United Nations Convention on the Law of the Sea of 10 December 1982 relating to the Conservation and Management of Straddling Fish Stocks and Highly Migratory Fish Stocks 1995, opened for signature 4 August 1995, 2167 UNTS 88 (entered into force 11 December 2001).

[12]   *M/V 'Saiga' (No. 2)*, *supra* note 9, 1355.

[13]   United Nations Basic Principles for the Use of Force and Firearms by Law Enforcement Officials, Adopted by the Eighth United Nations Congress on the Prevention of Crime and the Treatment of Offenders, Havana, Cuba, 27 August to 7 September 1990 <http://www2.ohchr.org/english/law/firearms.htm> accessed 8 August 2012 ('UN Basic Principles').

[14]   (Adopted 14 October 2005, entered into force 28 July 2010), IMO Doc. LEG/CONF.15/21.

persons on board, or where the officials are obstructed in the execution of the authorized actions. Any use of force pursuant to this article shall not exceed the minimum degree of force which is necessary and reasonable in the circumstances.

Taken together these instruments may tend to suggest the existence of a general principle of law recognised by states that their officials can use force when necessary to protect life, subject to the requirement that the degree of force used shall not exceed that reasonably required in the circumstances.

In maritime police actions, then, the use of force is a last resort – to be avoided where possible and in all cases must be strictly limited to what is reasonable and necessary. While an 'appropriate warning must be issued' in the case of attempting to board a vessel, no such warning need necessarily be given, for example, when there is an imminent and overwhelming danger to human life (as in the *Maersk Alabama* hostage-rescue incident).[15] True, these standards are far from a detailed code and might be thought to have more to say about the outer limits at which the use of force becomes impermissible, rather than providing clear guidance as to when force is permitted.

However, it is far from clear whether international law should do much more than set outer limits. As argued elsewhere, the circumstances in which a government vessel is entitled to use force against foreign merchant vessels on the high seas constitute a general exception to the prohibition on the use of force in international relations.[16] The *lex specialis* of the law of the sea grants a limited positive right to use force in certain cases – including the suppression of piracy – to warships and government vessels only.[17] Once a state is granted that exceptional right of extra-territorial law-enforcement jurisdiction, the matter will, within

---

[15]   See: 'In Rescue of Captain, Navy Kills 3 Pirates' *New York Times* (12 April 2009) <http://www.nytimes.com/2009/04/13/world/africa/13pirates.html> accessed 8 August 2012.

[16]   D. Guilfoyle, 'Interdicting Vessels to Enforce the Common Interest: Maritime Countermeasures and the Use of Force on the High Seas' (2007) 56 *International and Comparative Law Quarterly* 69; A. Murdoch, 'Forcible Interdiction of Ships Transporting Terrorists' (2009) 48 *Military Law and the Law of War Review* 287, at 297. The issue becomes confused in *Guyana v Suriname*, *supra* note 9, where the Arbitral Tribunal (at para. 445) suggests a dividing line between (non-prohibited) police uses of force and (prohibited) military uses of force without articulating relevant criteria. See further the discussion in Chapter 6.11.

[17]   This is necessarily implicit in UNCLOS Art. 105, see also Art. 107.

the limits set by international law, be regulated primarily by the national law of the enforcing state. Officers of the state conducting a counter-piracy operation should obviously, in the first instance, comply with their own national criminal law on questions of using force to prevent a crime, in defence of others or to relieve an immediate danger to human life. Attempts to suggest the laws of war might provide standards or guidance on the use of force against pirates are fundamentally unhelpful, for reasons discussed further below.

7.3 UN SECURITY COUNCIL RESOLUTIONS ON SOMALI PIRACY

7.3.1 The General Framework of the Counter-piracy Resolutions

As discussed in Chapters 3.3 and 6, a series of Security Council resolutions have been passed related to Somali piracy. The relevant Security Council resolutions for present purposes are 1816, 1846, 1851 (the 'territorial resolutions') as renewed, as well as resolutions 1814 (on protection of WFP convoys) and 1838 (on measures taken on the high seas).[18]

Resolutions 1816, 1846 and 1851 concern actions in Somalia's territorial waters or land territory, and each contains the talismanic Chapter VII authority to use 'all necessary means' to counter piracy, language usually associated with the use of force. Resolution 1816 has been discussed in detail elsewhere and requires only brief mention here.[19] Notably, it was only to operate for an initial period of six months. It was replaced by resolution 1846 on 2 December 2008, which has been renewed by resolution 1897 on 30 November 2009, resolution 1950 of 23 November 2010 and resolution 2020 of 22 November 2011.[20] The three 'territorial' resolutions contain a grant of power and a procedural limitation. In

---

[18] UNSC Res. 1814 (15 May 2008), UN Doc. S/RES/1814; UNSC Res. 1816 (2 June 2008), UN Doc. S/RES/1816; UNSC Res. 1838 (7 October 2008), UN Doc. S/RES/1838; 1846 (2 December 2008), UN Doc. S/RES/1846; and UNSC Res. 1851 (16 December 2008), UN Doc. S/RES/1851.

[19] Guilfoyle, 'Piracy Off Somalia: UN Security Council Resolution 1816 and IMO Regional Counter-Piracy Efforts' (2008) 57 *International and Comparative Law Quarterly* 690.

[20] The wording of operative paragraphs 7, 9 and 11 of resolution 1816 are repeated *mutatis mutandis* as paragraphs 10, 11 and 14 of resolution 1846. Subsequent resolutions refer back to the powers granted in UNSC Res. 1846 and 1851.

broad-brush terms resolutions 1816 and 1846 grant specific authority to 'cooperating States' to enter Somalia's territorial sea to repress piracy in a manner consistent with the international law applicable on the high seas. Resolution 1851 authorises 'cooperating States' to go further and engage in counter-piracy action on Somali soil.[21] To be a cooperating state under the resolutions a state must be operating with the consent of the Transitional Federal Government of Somalia (TFG) as notified in advance to the UN Secretary-General.[22]

7.3.2 Provisions on the Use of Force in the Counter-piracy Resolutions

Operation Atalanta invokes as the legal basis for its dual mission resolutions 1814, 1816 (as discussed above), 1838 and 1851.[23] Resolution 1814 '*calls upon* States and regional organizations, in close coordination with each other and as notified in advance to the Secretary-General, and at the request of the TFG, to take action to protect shipping involved with the transportation and delivery of humanitarian aid to Somalia'.[24] Resolution 1816 and its successor 1846 encourage states with an interest in nearby commercial maritime routes 'to increase and coordinate their efforts to deter…piracy…in cooperation with the TFG' and urge all states to 'render assistance to vessels threatened by or under attack by pirates or armed robbers, in accordance with relevant international law'.[25] Resolution 1838:

---

[21] See, Security Council Report, UN SCOR, 6046th mtg, UN Doc. S/PV.6046, 4 (United Kingdom), 9 (United States), 27 (Germany).

[22] The approach was first used in UNSC Res. 1814, para. 11, on protecting humanitarian shipments. On the reasons for the use of this mechanism, see Chapter 6.6.

[23] Council Decision 2008/918/CFSP, 8 December 2008, Official Journal of the EU, L 330/19-L 330/20; see also 'EU NAVFOR Somalia – Legal Basis' <http://www.consilium.europa.eu/eeas/security-defence/eu-operations/eunavfor-somalia/legal-basis?lang=en> accessed 8 August 2012. Council Decision 2012/174/CFSP of 23 March 2012 amended Joint Action 2008/851/CFSP and made express reference to conducting a military operation in support of resolutions 1814, 1816, 1838, 1846 and 1851.

[24] Para. 11. See also UNSC Res. 1838 para. 5.

[25] UNSC Res. 1838 paras 2, 3.

[c]alls upon States whose naval vessels ... operate on the high seas ... off the coast of Somalia to use ... the necessary means, in conformity with international law, as reflected in the [UNCLOS], for the repression of acts of piracy.[26]

None of these resolutions provides an independent legal basis for the use of force. Action under resolution 1814 is preconditioned on the 'request of the TFG', which could (as discussed in Chapter 6.6) be granted without a resolution. Resolution 1816 is merely hortatory and provides no novel legal powers. Resolution 1838 calls upon states to use 'necessary means' to combat piracy, but only where action is taken in conformity with UNCLOS (i.e., is already permissible). While much invoked, these resolutions add nothing to general international law. One must therefore turn to general international law for the applicable rule. However, a further question is whether humanitarian law is, in any sense, applicable.

Resolution 1851, paragraph 6 provides that states cooperating with Somalia (under the procedure described above):

[m]ay undertake all necessary measures that are appropriate in Somalia, for the purpose of suppressing acts of piracy and armed robbery at sea, pursuant to the request of the TFG, provided, however, that any measures undertaken pursuant to the authority of this paragraph shall be undertaken consistent with applicable international humanitarian and human rights law.

This authorisation to use force is subject to limitations: the invitation of the TFG; measures must be 'necessary', 'appropriate in Somalia' and for the 'purpose of suppressing acts of piracy and armed robbery at sea'; and compliance with 'applicable international humanitarian and human rights law'. The reference to international humanitarian law (IHL) has regrettably led to confusion. Some have interpreted it to suggest that the resolution per se makes all of IHL applicable to counter-piracy operations in Somalia's land territory.[27] This is clearly wrong: the resolution only refers to 'applicable' IHL; that is, law that would apply *irrespective* of the resolution. It would be a mistake to assume that the use of military

---

[26] UNSC Res. 1838 para. 3.

[27] See: E. Kontorovich, 'International Legal Responses to Piracy off the Coast of Somalia' (2009) 13/2 *ASIL Insights* <http://www.asil.org/insights 090206.cfm> accessed 6 August 2012. But see now: E. Kontorovich, '"A Guantanamo on the Sea": The Difficulty of Prosecuting Pirates and Terrorists' (2010) 98 *California Law Review* 243, at 270–272.

force necessarily implicates IHL. IHL is applicable only in an international or non-international armed conflict.

First, despite some classical writers' rhetoric suggesting that pirates are
at war with all humankind, it cannot be assumed that there exists *de jure*
such a war with pirates.[28] The existence of either an international or
non-international armed conflict is a determination of fact: 'an armed
conflict exists whenever there is a resort to armed force between states or
protracted armed violence between governmental authorities and organized armed groups or between such groups within a State'.[29] The term
'armed force' connotes a certain level or scale of violence required for an
international armed conflict, while the term 'protracted armed violence'
in relation to non-international armed conflicts excludes situations of
mere 'riots, isolated and sporadic acts of violence or other acts of a
similar nature'.[30] Both tests also require an element of 'identity' to be
satisfied: the actors in an international armed conflict must be states (or
their actions must be attributable to states); and in a non-international
armed conflict the relevant violence must be between armed bands or
between such bands and government forces. Somali pirates are at best
several different groups of armed bands acting without State sanction
who have mounted a series of individual attacks against vessels of
varying nationalities. These attacks have, on occasion, been seen off by
foreign naval vessels with (on even fewer occasions) shots being
exchanged occasioning loss of life. Neither the actors involved (disparate
private parties and disparate military forces), nor the level of violence
reached (small scale exchange of fire) could seriously justify the charac-
terisation of an international armed conflict. Nor do the pirates satisfy the
definition of those engaged in a non-international armed conflict: first,
their actions are not *within* a state; second, a series of violent attacks and
hostage takings committed against civilians satisfies neither the criterion

---

[28]   See generally: D. Guilfoyle, 'The Laws of War and the Fight against
Somali Piracy: Combatants or Criminals?' (2010) 11 *Melbourne Journal of
International Law* 141; compare Kontorovich, '"A Guantanamo on the Sea"',
supra note 27, 261–262.
[29]   *Prosecutor v Tadic* (*Decision on the Defence Motion for Interlocutory
Appeal on Jurisdiction*) (Case No IT-94–1-AR72, 2 October 1995) para. 70.
[30]   Rome Statute of the International Criminal Court (adopted 17 July 1998,
entered force 1 July 2002) 2187 UNTS 3, Art. 8(2)(d) and (f); compare Protocol
Additional to the Geneva Conventions of 12 August 1949, and relating to the
Protection of Victims of Non-International Armed Conflicts (Protocol II)
(adopted 8 June 1977, entered into force 7 December 1978) 1125 UNTS 609,
Art. 1(2) ('Additional Protocol II').

of identity nor that of 'protracted armed violence'.[31] On any evaluation, pirate activity seems closest to situations 'such as riots, [and] isolated and sporadic acts of violence' falling below the threshold for the existence of any armed conflict.[32]

Further, applying IHL would produce legal difficulties. Pirates should not be considered combatants. If so, they could legitimately be targeted with lethal force based on their status: participants in a conflict. The international law standards governing the use of force in policing actions would certainly not permit targeting pirates with lethal force simply on the basis of status. Thus, there is a risk that invoking IHL could justify using against criminals what would otherwise be excessive force. Alternatively, if one starts from the premise that there is a conflict and pirates are civilians, this may lead to the conclusion that they may not be deliberately targeted with lethal force at sea or on land.[33] Under IHL, civilian casualties are only acceptable where proportionate to achieving a legitimate military end, or where civilians have illegally taken up arms against enemy forces. The deliberate targeting of civilians *as such* is prohibited. Thus, if hostage-taking piracy is governed by IHL then either: (1) pirates are liable to be targeted with lethal force *at any time* as enemy combatants; or (2) pirates are civilians and any decision to target them directly would be illegal unless it was proportionate and incidental to securing some other legitimate military objective. Invoking IHL in counter-piracy actions ultimately only confuses the issues involved.

The resolution may be better construed as acknowledging either the possibility that 'some Somali pirates may also be civil war insurgents'[34] or that counter-piracy operations against those supplying or equipping pirates might result in military engagement with insurgents. In either case IHL would apply as 'any international counter-piracy forces on land ... [could then be] considered forces intervening in an otherwise internal conflict at the invitation of the government'.[35]

This construction is also consistent with a broad interpretation of resolution 1851. In interpreting the authorisation to use force in any Security Council resolution it is important to have particular regard to

---

[31] There is a separate issue of whether the pirates could satisfy the test of armed bands in control of territory found in Additional Protocol II, *supra* note 30, Art. 1(1).

[32] See references *supra* note 30.

[33] Kontorovich, 'International Legal Responses', *supra* note 27.

[34] D. Guilfoyle, *Shipping Interdiction and the Law of the Sea* (CUP 2009) 70.

[35] *Ibid.*

both the general and political context of the resolution, as well as related Council action.[36] In the case of resolution 1851 there is nothing in the text or background that supports a conclusion that the Council considered that the appropriate paradigm for tackling piracy was a war-fighting one. Rather, the text of the resolution consistently refers to a law-enforcement response to the problem: interdictions, seizure and disposition of pirate vessels, investigation and prosecution of suspects, and a clear statement that UNCLOS 'sets out the legal framework applicable for tackling piracy'.[37] Importantly, the request from the TFG of 9 December 2008 – on which the authorisation in resolution 1851 is expressly predicated – seeks assistance to interdict pirates that is consistent with a constabulary response.

In this context it is national criminal law and national military ROE that develop detailed rules as to when one has positive authority to use force, and in what manner, rather than public international law. International law sets much broader minimum standards. The starting premise is that states are dealing – in the maritime domain – with a parallel *lex specialis*: authority under customary international law to use reasonable force as a last resort to suppress piracy, capture pirates or preserve human life. Those questions will now be explored in respect of concrete cases.

7.4 THE OPERATIONAL CONTEXT

7.4.1 Military Response: Disrupt, Deter and Capture

Before the sharp spike in piratical activity in the Gulf of Aden in summer 2008, the majority of warships operating in these waters did so as part of the CMF[38] and, in particular, its longest standing Combined Task Force 150 (CTF 150).[39] At its inception at the beginning of Operation Enduring Freedom, CTF 150 had a purely counter-terrorism focus. This has gradually evolved to encompass 'Maritime Security Operations' (MSO),[40] a concept considered flexible enough to permit CMF to deploy

---

[36] See generally: M. Wood, 'The Interpretation of Security Council Resolutions' (1998) 2 *Max Planck Yearbook of United Nations Law* 73–95.

[37] UNSC Res. 1851, especially the fourth preambular para and paras 2 and 5.

[38] See *supra* n 1, and accompanying text.

[39] CTF 150's Area of Responsibility encompasses waters of the Gulf of Aden, Gulf of Oman, Red Sea and the North West quadrant of the Indian Ocean.

[40] See the US definition at: <http://www.cusnc.navy.mil/cmf/cmf_command.html> accessed 8 August 2012, and the UK description of what MSO

CTF 150 warships to respond to acts of piracy.[41] In January 2009 CMF created CTF 151 with a dedicated counter-piracy mission. Until this time, and prior to the NATO[42] counter-piracy mission and EU Operation Atalanta commencing in October and December 2008 respectively, CTF 150 was at the vanguard of the military maritime response to piracy.

CMF's immediate response to the piracy surge was to increase its military presence in the Gulf of Aden to deter attacks. However, with only a limited number of warships, the speed of pirate attacks, the difficulty in distinguishing pirate ships from innocent fishing vessels and the vast patrol area,[43] such a tactic was unlikely to succeed. With CTF 150's presence having only a localised deterrent effect, CMF examined alternative options. The powers reflected in UNCLOS appeared sufficient for warships to take enforcement action against suspected pirates and pirate vessels. However, even if international law grants certain powers, whether CMF warships could actually exercise them depended in practice upon the ROE in force.[44]

Generally, the ROE for an operation will have been drawn from a national compendium of Rules,[45] and issued to commanders by their higher authority. In some cases ROE are solely a matter for the military chain of command, but in many states (such as the UK) they require sign-off at a political level. ROE are shaped by many considerations, however, the principal factors are law (both national and international), operational, diplomatic and political. While ROE should never authorise conduct that is prohibited by applicable law, there is no requirement for

---

encompasses at: <http://www.royalnavy.mod.uk/operations/maritime-security> accessed 8 August 2012.

[41] NAVCENT (Fifth Fleet), 'Maritime Security Operations Key to Regional Stability, Security' (Combined Maritime Forces Press Release, 8 October 2007) <http://www.navy.mil/submit/display.asp?story_id=32468> accessed 8 August 2012.

[42] NATO efforts to deter and disrupt piracy Somalia and protect WFP shipping to Somalia commenced with Operation Allied Provider, continued under Operation Allied Protector, and is currently ongoing as Operation Ocean Shield.

[43] The Gulf of Aden is 205,000 square miles (530,000 square km) in area.

[44] For a useful discussion of Rules of Engagement see, R. McLaughlin, 'Protecting Civilians in Armed Conflict Through Rules of Engagement', in D. W. Lovell and I. Primoratz (eds), *Protecting Civilians During Violent Conflict: Theoretical and Practical Issues for the 21st Century* (Ashgate 2012) 119–140.

[45] For an example of an unclassified compendium see A. Cole *et al.*, 'SanRemo Handbook on Rules of Engagement' (International Institute of Humanitarian Law 2009) <http://www.iihl.org/Default.aspx?pageid=page12090> accessed 8 August 2012.

them to extend to the limit of what is legally permissible: often policy factors will determine that a more cautious approach is taken.

All ROE will contain details on the regulation of the use of force. They will normally also comprise prohibitions as well as authorisations for military elements, such as warships, to take certain actions when judged necessary to achieve a mission's aims.[46] Once approved, ROE will cascade down to military units on the frontline. Each level in the military chain of command can decide whether the units lower down will be able to act under all the authorisations in the ROE, or whether certain rules will be 'held' so that lower units will need to seek approval before they act under them (e.g., entering the territorial seas of X State is permitted with approval of the higher authority). Withholding ROE in this way allows commanders to exercise maximum control over frontline units, although it can result in operational delays while permission to act is requested and received. The interpretation and scope of what ROE will cover is not uniform, both doctrinally and in practice. Some states adopt a 'permissive' interpretative approach, and failing a prohibition in the ROE, an activity will be regarded as permitted. Other militaries adopt a 'restricted' approach to ROE and failing an express authorisation an activity is prohibited.

Owing to the different national approaches to ROE, agreeing ROE for a multi-national operation (such as those under NATO or EU Command) is complex and can be time consuming. Even once the ROE are agreed, different national positions may lead to some states entering 'caveats' against certain rules so that their forces will not operate beyond the boundaries of national law or policy. In certain multi-national operations partners do not seek to adopt a single set of ROE, but instead allow their units to operate under their national ROE. This was the ROE situation faced by CMF.

The national ROE regulating the conduct of every warship operating under CMF determined the limits of what tactics CMF commanders could *actually* employ against the pirates. In deciding whether to commence operations involving the arrest of suspected pirates for the purposes of criminal prosecution (so-called 'capture operations'), CMF had to determine whether warships under its command had appropriate ROE to do so. While states have different approaches to interpreting ROE, the arrest and detention of individuals would only be undertaken

---

[46] D. Fleck (ed.), *The Handbook of International Humanitarian Law* (OUP 2008) 655–656. An example for a maritime law enforcement mission would be to include Rules concerning seizure and detention in addition those concerning use of force.

with express authorisation from appropriate national authorities. Unfortunately, the patchwork of national ROE meant individual warships were subject to different permissions and constraints.[47] Despite the existence of universal jurisdiction over piracy, it therefore quickly became apparent that states were reluctant to permit their warships to commence widescale 'capture operations'.

Some states with warships in the region had, despite IMO recommendations to the contrary,[48] enacted only limited domestic law offences of piracy, requiring a national nexus to the crime (such as the nationality of the pirate or attacked vessel, or nationality of the pirates or victims). Others appear to require a national nexus as a matter of policy. The preference for many was, therefore, except in cases with the requisite national nexus, to transfer captured pirates to regional states for prosecution. However, in the summer of 2008 there were no formal arrangements in place to facilitate the transfer of suspected pirates from a CMF participating warship to another state willing to commence an investigation and prosecution. The resultant operational problems are well-illustrated by an incident in September 2008 involving the Danish warship *Absalon*, noted in Chapter 6.7.

As part of CTF 150 *Absalon* intervened during a piracy attack and arrested ten suspected pirates. The suspects were detained onboard the warship pending a decision by Danish authorities on their disposition. After being held for six days, the suspects were released on a Somali beach after Danish authorities concluded that they could not be prosecuted in Denmark owing to deficiencies in Danish law. The release of the pirates attracted some criticism and it was suggested that pirates would now regard themselves as able to operate with impunity.[49] The incident also highlighted the reluctance of some states to allow the transfer of suspected pirates from their warships to regional states for prosecution, if doing so would expose them to the death penalty, or

---

[47]   M. Houben, 'Making Waves and Building Bridges: Dutch Experiences in the Arabian Sea' (2007) 10 *RUSI Defence Systems* 82, <http://www.rusi.org/downloads/assets/Houben,_Making_Waves_and_Building_Bridges.pdf> accessed 8 August 2012.

[48]   *Code of Practice for the Investigation of the Crimes of Piracy and Armed Robbery Against Ships*, IMO, 22nd sess., Agenda Item 9, IMO Doc A 22/Res.922 (22 January 2002) para. 3(1).

[49]   M. Hand, 'Danish Navy Release 10 Somali pirates' *Lloyd's List*, 25 September 2008.

where there is a serious risk the suspected pirate would be subject to torture or cruel, inhuman or degrading treatment.[50]

On 2 January 2009 a second incident, also involving the *Absalon*, illustrated further legal and political complications involved in 'capture operations'. Five Somali pirates were detained following their attack on the *Samanyulo*, a Dutch-Antilles flagged cargo ship. During the attack the pirates' own vessel became unseaworthy and the pirates were rescued by the *Absalon*. The suspected pirates spent 40 days aboard the warship before agreement was reached with Dutch authorities for the suspects to be transferred to the Netherlands to stand trial. This prolonged detention attracted criticism from human rights organisations on the grounds that it was not subject to any judicial oversight.[51] Consideration of the extra-territorial application of human rights obligations during maritime law-enforcement operations, however, falls outside the scope of this chapter.[52]

The lack of a clear, reliable, disposition path to facilitate the investigation and, if there is sufficient evidence, prosecution of suspected pirates resulted in the CMF Commander directing that warships operating as part of CMF were not to arrest pirates until such criminal justice disposition arrangements were in place.[53] That the disposition problem was negatively affecting counter-piracy efforts was well-recognised by the international community.[54] Commanders of the NATO and EU operations faced the same disposition problem. While some states were prepared to detain pirates, this approach was very much the exception in 2008.[55]

---

[50]   *Ibid.*

[51]   'Amnesty demands Dutch and Danish take care of pirates' (*NRC International*, 4 February 2007) <http://www.nrc.nl/international/article2141530.ece/ Amnesty_demands_Dutch_and_Danish_take_care_of_pirates>   accessed   8 August 2012. At the subsequent trial the Dutch court found that the length of time it took to bring the suspects before a judge was in breach of Article 5 of the ECHR, although this infringement of rights was not considered sufficient to preclude a criminal prosecution: *Marine Log*, 'Netherlands court convicts Somali pirates',   17   June   2010   <http://www.marinelog.com/DOCS/NEWSMMIX/ 2010jun00172.html> accessed 8 August 2012.

[52]   See, e.g., *Medvedyev and Others v France*, Application No 3394/03 (ECHR, 10 July 2008) para. 50.

[53]   See: Vice Admiral W. Gortney, 'DoD News Briefing with Vice Adm, Gortney from the Pentagon' (News Transcript, 15 January 2009) <http:// www.defenselink.mil/transcripts/transcript.aspx?transcriptid=4341> accessed 8 August 2012.

[54]   See, e.g., UNSC Res. 1846, para. 14.

[55]   HMS *Cumberland*, which was operating off Somalia as part of NATO's Operation Allied Provider, reverted to national Command in order to transfer

Since then the conclusion of a number of transfer arrangements with regional states has led to a steady – if not large scale – number of capture operations. While efforts continue to increase the number of interdictions of suspected pirates that lead to an investigation and prosecution,[56] disruption operations remain the most common naval counter-piracy tactic for a variety of practical, operational and legal reasons.[57] Disruption operations can be divided into two broad categories: proactive and reactive. The first involves several stages: the identification of ships reasonably suspected of engaging in piracy; visiting such ships; seizing and disposing of unmanned pirate ships known as 'skiffs' (small, fast, open vessels used to commit the attack, launched from larger 'mother ships'); and seizing and disposing of arms and equipment used in committing piracy. Pirates are then released. The second type of operation involves warships or aircraft 'reacting' to merchant ships' distress calls. The aim is then to disrupt the attack, avert any threat to human life and prevent the pirates from boarding the merchant vessel. Both disruption and capture operations may result in the use of force as illustrated in the following case studies.

7.4.2   Case Studies: HMS *Cumberland* and INS *Tabar*

On 12 November 2008 HMS *Cumberland* was operating in the Gulf of Aden as part of NATO Operation Allied Provider when the master of the Panamanian registered MV *Powerful* reported he was being attacked by pirates in a 'skiff' using automatic weapons. After aggressive manoeuvring by the *Powerful* the pirates failed to board and returned to their mother ship, a nearby dhow (a small open decked wooden fishing vessel with an enclosed wheelhouse). Having received a description of and location for the mother ship the *Cumberland* identified the dhow and, with reasonable grounds to suspect it was engaged in piracy, decided to conduct an UNCLOS article 110 right of visit. At the time there was no indication the dhow contained anyone other than pirates. The boarding

---

pirates to Kenya in November 2008. See also Hand, *supra* note 49, involving HDMS *Absalon*.

[56]   See the 'Report of the Secretary-General on specialized anti-piracy courts in Somalia and other States in the region', UN Doc S/2012/50 dated 20 January 2012; House of Commons Foreign Affairs Committee, 'Piracy off the coast of Somalia', HC 1318, 5 January 2012, 48, <http://www.asil.org/files/SomaliaPiracyIntlExpertsreportconsolidated1.pdf> accessed 15 August 2012.

[57]   'HMS Portland intercepts pirates' *Defence News* (3 June 2009) archived at: <http://army-uk.info/news_detail.php?id=1182> accessed 8 August 2012.

was intended as part of a 'proactive' disruption operation to prevent the dhow and skiff from conducting further attacks. Despite being part of the NATO Operation, which at the time had its own ROE, *Cumberland* conducted this incident mission in accordance with UK ROE.[58]

The *Cumberland* approached the dhow and requested that it stop for boarding; the translated instructions were issued verbally and over VHF. The warship manoeuvred close to the dhow, which was being steered erratically, and used its siren and flashing lights to repeat the signal to stop. Flares and signal rockets were fired near, but not at, the dhow, but it continued to head towards Somali territorial waters. *Cumberland* then, rather inventively, went alongside the dhow and aimed a fire-hose at the dhow's wheelhouse to encourage its occupants to stop the vessel. This did not succeed. Royal Marine boarding teams were then launched in two Rigid Inflatable Boats (RIBs) with an armed helicopter overhead providing protection. Each RIB contained several Royal Marines armed with 5.56mm small arms and one manning a mounted 7.62mm General Purpose Machine Gun. The RIBs circled the dhow repeating instructions to stop and for the crew to move to the bow with their hands in the air. Fourteen individuals onboard congregated on the bow as instructed, leaving two pirates in the wheelhouse. These two then, without warning, each picked up an automatic rifle – later identified as AK47 variants – previously concealed out of sight, and aimed them at one of the RIBs 20–30m away. Six Royal Marines, in both the RIBs, opened fire at the two armed pirates at the same time as shots were fired by the pirates. Despite the difficulty in firing from a RIB on the high seas[59] the incident lasted only a few seconds, ceasing when the threat from the two individuals was no longer believed to exist. The two Somali pirates in the wheelhouse were shot dead as a result.[60] The Royal Marines then boarded the dhow discovering a third individual, later identified as a Yemeni national, injured. Despite receiving emergency treatment from *Cumberland*'s doctor he died shortly afterwards from an injury sustained during the firefight.

Only after the boarding was it discovered that the fishing dhow itself had been previously captured by the Somali pirates aboard. The Yemeni

---

[58] 'British Commandos kill two pirates in stand-off' *The Guardian* (13 November 2008) <http://www.guardian.co.uk/world/2008/nov/13/pirates-killed-gulf-aden> accessed 8 August 2012.

[59] I.e. in firing from an unstable platform at targets aboard another unstable platform.

[60] M. Evans, 'Navy goes to war against Somali pirates' *The Times* (13 November 2008) 3.

crew had been held, under the use and threat of violence, while the pirates looked for merchant vessels to attack using their own skiff. The crew was told they would be released once a large merchant vessel was successfully pirated. After an investigation into the incident by UK authorities, and following diplomatic discussions, the dhow and its crew were escorted to Yemeni territorial waters and released into the protection of the Yemeni coast guard. Although there was no plan at this time to capture pirates, arrangements were made for the eight Somali pirates to be transferred to Kenya for investigation and prosecution;[61] their trial started in January 2009. The two deceased Somali pirates were eventually, after consultation with Somali religious leaders, buried at sea.

Less than a week later, an Indian naval frigate, the INS *Tabar*, encountered the *Ekawat Nava 5*, a medium sized, steel-hulled, multi-deck fishing vessel which it believed was being used as a pirate mother ship.[62] An unspecified number of men were seen on deck openly displaying automatic weapons and rocket-propelled grenade (RPG) launchers, and the vessel was towing two skiffs. Unknown to the *Tabar*, most of the 16 crewmembers of the *Ekawat Nava 5* were tied up onboard and out of sight. The *Tabar* decided to stop and board the vessel as a suspected pirate ship. Over a period of approximately 90 minutes the *Ekawat Nava 5* failed to respond to repeated instructions to heave to for boarding. *Tabar* then fired several warning shots; the pirates responded by threatening to blow up the fishing vessel and warship.[63] At approximately 21.00 the pirates fired at the *Tabar*, although there are no reports of the nature and degree of force they used. The *Tabar* responded 'as per its ROE' by firing its medium range weapon system,[64] consisting of a single turret containing two 30mm six-barrel automatic weapons (which fire a thousand rounds a minute). This force resulted in a series of explosions on the *Ekawat Nava 5* and its sinking. While the pirates appear to have escaped in the skiffs, there was only one survivor of the fishing vessel's crew.

---

[61] 'Navy hands over pirate suspects' (*BBC News*, 18 November 2008) <http://news.bbc.co.uk/1/hi/uk/7735088.stm> accessed 8 August 2012.

[62] 'India navy defends piracy sinking' (*BBC News*, 26 November 2008) <http://news.bbc.co.uk/1/hi/world/south_asia/7749486.stm> accessed 8 August 2012.

[63] 'Ship shot down in self-defence: Navy', *The Times of India* (27 November 2008) <http://timesofindia.indiatimes.com/World/Middle-East/Ship-shot-down-in-self-defence-Navy/articleshow/3761244.cms> accessed 8 August 2012.

[64] *Ibid*.

7.4.3 Operational Use of Force – Analysis and Evaluation

The case studies are illustrative of incidents in which force has been used by the military during counter-piracy operations off the coast of Somalia; other incidents could also have been used.[65] What the HMS *Cumberland* and INS *Tabar* case*s* have in common is that they both demonstrate an escalatory approach to using force to stop and board suspected pirate ships. The UK warship very gradually escalated its measures, firing no shots to enforce a right to board. Similarly, the *Tabar* only used non-forcible measures to encourage the suspected pirate ship to stop, escalating eventually to the use of warning shots. Use of force to stop and board the pirate ships would have been justifiable as the next necessary measure, as envisaged in *MV Saiga (No.2)*. This use of force may also be escalated, starting with shots directed at non-critical areas, before aiming at critical areas that will disable the vessel (such as the rudder, engine-room or wheelhouse). Importantly, in using such force all efforts should be made to ensure life is not thereby endangered.

Neither warship, however, reached this stage, as the situation in both cases changed rapidly to become one of protecting life. In the *Cumberland* incident the two pirates presented an imminent threat to life. Six Royal Marines simultaneously and immediately used force either in defence of their own lives (those with weapons pointed at them) or the defence of those threatened. Giving warnings would have increased the likelihood of death or grave injury. The *Tabar* incident is more difficult to assess, given the paucity of information available; it is not known how many of the pirates fired, what weapons they used, and how far away the warship was at the time. Certainly, automatic or RPG fire presents a threat to life, even onboard a warship, and therefore a response by *Tabar* in self-defence, without warning, *may* have been necessary.

While the use of force to prevent loss of life was necessary in the *Cumberland* incident, and possibly the *Tabar* incident, the level of force used must also have been reasonable. There are no indications that the use of force by *Cumberland*'s marines was excessive, as lethal force was unavoidable given the threat, and the shots were only fired for a short period until the threat no longer existed. The *Cumberland* is armed *inter*

---

[65] See e.g.: 'South Korea rescues Samho Jewelry crew from pirates' (*BBC News*, 21 January 2011) <http://www.bbc.co.uk/news/world-africa-12248096> accessed 8 August 2012; 'EUNAVFOR disabling fire stops fleeing pirate skiff', EU NAVFOR Public Affairs Office (5 May 2010) <http://www.eunavfor.eu/2010/05/eu-navfor-disabling-fire-stops-fleeing-pirate-skiff/> accessed 8 August 2012.

alia with a 30mm multi-barrelled gun and an array of smaller calibre weapons for close-in force protection purposes. No doubt any of these weapons could have neutralised the threat on the dhow. However, only the smallest calibre weapons carried by individuals from the warship were used; weapons designed to be used with some precision against personnel. The *Tabar*'s use of its twin 30mm multi-barrelled weapon system poses more difficult questions. On the one hand it was highly effective at neutralising any threat to the *Tabar*, and it may have been the only weapon system immediately available at the time. However, such a weapon system is not designed to target individuals accurately; its purpose is to engage much larger and faster targets, such as incoming missiles, by presenting a cone of munitions. Its use inevitably led to considerable incidental damage to the *Ekawat Nava 5* in the process of responding to any threat from the pirates.

Principle 5 in the 1990 UN Basic Principles states that whenever the use of firearms is unavoidable, law-enforcement officials shall 'minimize damage and injury, and respect and preserve human life'. Principle 11 adds that rules and regulations on the use of firearms by law-enforcement officials should include guidelines ensuring firearms are used only 'in a manner likely to decrease the risk of unnecessary harm' and 'prohibit the use of those firearms and ammunition that cause unwarranted injury or present an unwarranted risk'. These Principles are intended to apply to military personnel when exercising police powers,[66] and to avoid a lacuna they should be a useful reference point when law-enforcement operations are conducted extra-territorially.

Warships, unlike police or coastguard vessels, are predominantly designed for armed conflict and not police actions against armed maritime criminals such as pirates. If they are to be used by states for such missions they should be equipped with suitable weapons and manned by trained personnel, if the limits on using force are to be respected. It is likely that warships will be called upon to use force, as a last resort, to stop pirate vessels to enforce a right of visit. As pirate vessels range from skiffs to steel-hulled mother ships, it will be necessary for warships to be able to choose from a range of weapons in order to deliver the level of force required to achieve the lawful aim, while minimising the risk of endangering life in the process. If a warship does not possess a weapon that can disable a ship without endangering life then it should not attempt such a task.

---

[66] See footnote 1 to the UN Basic Principles, *supra* note 13.

Suitable weapons, properly manned, should also be readily available such that, if force is necessary to protect life, whether one's own or others, during counter-piracy operations, then only a reasonable level of force is used. It is inappropriate to be too prescriptive about what weapons may be required. In some cases, owing to the number of pirates presenting an imminent threat, their weapons and lack of innocent bystanders, the use by the warship of an accurate large calibre weapon with a high rate of fire may be reasonable. However, as the *Maersk Alabama* and *Cumberland* incidents reveal, maritime law enforcement operations against pirates will more often require the use of a more precise response to a limited threat; small calibre, accurate, weapons capable of reducing the unnecessary risk of harm to others in the vicinity who present no threat. The use of snipers in the *Maersk Alabama* episode and the Royal Marines from *Cumberland* demonstrate how effective this capability can be.

Principle 22 of the UN Basic Principles states *inter alia* that when firearms are used in law enforcement operations:

> … Governments and law enforcement agencies shall ensure that effective review process is available and that independent administrative or prosecutorial authorities are in a position to exercise jurisdiction in appropriate circumstances. In cases of death and serious injury or other grave consequences, a detailed report shall be sent promptly to the competent authorities responsible for administrative review and judicial control.

This requirement to conduct a national review of an incident involving the use of firearms by law enforcement officials reinforces national authorities' primary role in ensuring that force has been used lawfully. Indeed, following the *Cumberland* incident, the UK Ministry of Defence emphasised that 'a post-shooting incident investigation' was being conducted.[67] Later the Royal Navy confirmed that a 'full inquiry into the circumstances around the incident has taken place' which found that 'personnel acted lawfully and in self defence'.[68] Investigating such incidents on board a warship that is required to remain in international

---

[67] Royal Navy, 'HMS Cumberland Fights Piracy' (13 December 2008) <http://webarchive.nationalarchives.gov.uk/20081120170436/http://www.royal navy.mod.uk/server/show/ConWebDoc.14222/changeNav/6568> accessed 8 August 2012.

[68] 'Pirate killings were lawful' *Western Morning News* (20 December 2008) <http://www.thisiswesternmorningnews.co.uk/news/PIRATE-KILLING-LAWFUL/ article-562319-detail/article.html> accessed 8 August 2012.

waters to continue its mission will pose significant logistical and practical challenges. However, there is no reason why military personnel should be subjected to a review process that is ineffective or lacks independence. While the exact review procedure is a matter for the state concerned, it should be in place before an incident occurs and require the compilation of a detailed report for scrutiny by competent authorities who can take appropriate action if there is evidence that national laws or procedures may have been breached. Such authorities should be independent and free from actual or perceived bias.

If military personnel use force during counter-piracy operations resulting in death or injury, they risk national criminal proceedings if force was used in a manner contrary to national law. Commanders can mitigate this risk by issuing well-drafted ROE and appropriate weapons, and train personnel in both. It must be recognised that ROE do have limitations if poorly drafted, because in most jurisdictions adherence to the Rules does not, in itself, provide a defence during criminal proceedings. In *Clegg*,[69] an appeal case involving a soldier convicted of murder as a result of using excessive force while on duty, the House of Lords considered ROE issued to soldiers on a 'yellow card' entitled 'instructions for opening fire in Northern Ireland'. On a literal reading, the ROE permitted firing at a car where a person had been injured, irrespective of the seriousness of the injury. In considering whether the ROE could assist Clegg, the Lords concluded that it had no legal force, because English law does not have a general defence of superior orders.

7.5 CONCLUSION

This chapter has principally discussed the rules applicable to the most usual form of naval counter-piracy operations, 'disruption', although the principles are equally applicable to the increasing number of 'capture' operations. Authority to conduct 'disruption' or 'capture' operations is grounded in the article 110 UNCLOS right of visit. This right of visit is subject to the general rules outlined in the *MV Saiga* and other case law. In essence, this is a law-enforcement operation requiring a ship to be stopped and boarded. The ordinary principles governing the measures that may be taken to get on board a suspect vessel apply. Force should only be used as a last resort, and the use of force to effect a boarding will be subject to over-riding constraints such as the requirement of giving

---

[69] *R v Clegg* [1995] WLR 80, 90.

warning, using force only as a last resort and taking measures to prevent risk to human life. However, if the vessel attempting to conduct the boarding is itself attacked or if suspect pirates threaten hostages aboard then the case becomes one of using lethal force to protect one's own life, or the lives of others. In such cases a warning should still be given unless do so would increase the risk of death or serious injury to anyone being threatened.

Serious questions as to the reasonableness of force used may arise, however, if a warship acts in self-defence (or to disrupt an actual pirate attack) with weapon-systems that are not designed to be used against individuals, as the INS *Tabar* incident illustrates. We have argued that naval vessels engaged in counter-piracy will need to be appropriately equipped and trained for their missions. This requirement extends further in the context of 'capture' operations designed to lead to subsequent prosecutions. Since the conclusion of regional transfer arrangements there has been an increased willingness to engage in 'capture' operations. Nonetheless, disruption operations remain the most commonly used tactic at present. Transferring suspect pirates to a regional state remains fraught with practical complexities (principally in relation to conducting evidence-gathering in a manner that will support prosecution in the receiving state and associated training) and prosecution by the capturing warship remains very much the exception.[70]

The importance of appropriate equipment, training and above all an acknowledgement that this is essentially a law-enforcement exercise is well illustrated by the reaction to the INS *Tabar* incident. Initially the sinking of the pirate ship was praised by the head of the International Maritime Bureau (IMB), Mr Choong, who stated: 'if all warships do this it will be a strong deterrent … it's about time that such forceful action is taken'.[71] However, once the deaths of the fishermen became known, Mr Choong described the incident as 'an unfortunate tragedy'.[72] The complexity of piracy off Somalia amply demonstrates the need for clear ROE setting out the limits on the use of force: failure to do so not only has the

---

[70]   In practice this usually only occurs where national interests are directly affected, typically where flag state nationals were taken hostage.
[71]   'India praised for sinking pirates' (*BBC News*, 20 November 2008) <http://news.bbc.co.uk/1/hi/world/south_asia/7739171.stm> accessed 8 August 2012.
[72]   'India navy defends piracy sinking' (*BBC News*, 26 November 2008) <http://news.bbc.co.uk/1/hi/world/south_asia/7749486.stm> accessed 8 August 2012.

potential to put innocent hostages in harm's way, but may also expose naval personnel to criminal prosecution under the law of their flag state.

8. Initiating criminal proceedings with military force: some legal aspects of policing Somali pirates by navies

Håkan Friman and Jens Lindborg

8.1 INTRODUCTION

On a national level criminals are dealt with by the police and prosecuting authorities, courts and perhaps prison authorities. This is done in accordance with *inter alia* national criminal procedural law. Procedural law now generally incorporates international human rights standards, among them the right to a fair trial. What about crimes under international law? The international community necessarily relies on national forces, including armed forces, to deal with criminals under international law. When this is done in an armed conflict humanitarian law is applicable. There may even be an international court set up to deal with the fallout afterwards. In the absence of armed conflict and an international court the international community, again, relies on national assets. These assets are, however, bound by national law and trained to function primarily in a national setting. National law differs from state to state. The differences are not least important in criminal procedural law, making cooperation between states pursuing criminal activity challenging. In almost all states, however, the armed forces are barred from prosecuting (domestic) crimes committed by civilians. It is in this context that collective operations by naval forces are conducting the deterrence, prevention and repression of acts of piracy and armed robbery off the Somali coast. We will examine some of the legal challenges operations of this sort give rise to.

8.2 PIRATES ARE CRIMINALS

Pirates are criminals under international law.[1] They are sometimes also regarded as enemies of mankind.[2] This difference in language is interesting because enemies would normally be treated differently from criminals and vice versa.[3] It would be quite normal for states to use military and naval force to kill or capture enemies, but not to issue warrants for their arrest. Conversely, it would not be normal to bomb the offices of a person suspected of insurance fraud, but it would be normal to bomb an enemy command centre.

Terrorists are also criminals under international law.[4] States differ in the way they pursue terrorists. Some few states claim to be at war with them, which makes the terrorists enemies, but choose to call them 'illegal combatants'.[5] As a result, they avoid having to treat them in accordance with international law setting out how to treat captured enemy personnel in war. When interrogating terrorists some states have legalized the use of 'enhanced interrogation techniques', which others view as torture, and which would be illegal to use against other criminals in those states' own jurisdictions and indeed against captured enemies.[6] Rendition instead of

---

[1]   See Chapter 6; R. Geiss and A. Petrig, *Piracy and Armed Robbery at Sea* (OUP 2011), 137–145; D. Guilfoyle, *Shipping Interdiction and the Law of the Sea* (CUP 2009), 27–32.

[2]   See Chapters 6.1 and 14.2 on the idea of *'hostis humani generis'*.

[3]   See: Eugene Kontorovich, '"A Guantanamo on the Sea": The Difficulty of Prosecuting Pirates and Terrorists' (2010) 98 *California Law Review* 243, 257–259; D. Guilfoyle, 'The Laws of War and the Fight against Somali Piracy: Combatants or Criminals' (2010) 11(1) *Melbourne Journal of International Law* 141–153.

[4]   E.g. International Convention for the Suppression of Terrorist Bombings (adopted 15 December 1997, entered into force 23 May 2001) 2149 UNTS 256; European Convention on the Suppression of Terrorism (adopted 27 January 1977, entered into force 4 April 1978) ETS 90; Arab Convention on the Suppression of Terrorism (adopted 22 April 1998, entered into force 7 May 1999) <http://www.unhcr.org/refworld/docid/3de5e4984.html> accessed 3 August 2012; and Convention of the Organization of the Islamic Conference on Combating International Terrorism (adopted 1 July 1999, entered into force 7 November 2002) reprinted in UN Pub Sales No. E.03.V.9 (2004).

[5]   E.g. Joseph P. Bialke, 'Al-Qaeda and Taliban – Unlawful Combatant Detainees, Unlawful Belligerency, and the International Laws of Armed Conflict' 55 *Air Force Law Review* (2004) 1–86; compare C. Gray, *International Law and the Use of Force* (CUP 2008) 53.

[6]   E.g. U.S. Military Commission, Yokohama, May 1–28, 1947, *United States of America v Yukio Asumo et al.*; and see generally E. Wallach, 'Drop by

extradition according to law is also something that some states view as acceptable to impose on illegal combatants, as well as detaining them for years without trial. This is not done to (other) suspected criminals in civilized societies. One assumes that the states so dealing with terrorists do not do so out of malice, but because they find it efficient as well as just. We would note, however, that it is a great mistake for any state to publicly fail its own standards on human rights, as this will only undermine the legitimacy of its actions.

In an armed conflict the acceptance of mistakes differs from what is required of criminal proceedings; in an armed conflict a level of civilian death and injury 'proportionate' to legitimate military objectives will be acceptable as 'collateral damage' if proper precautions were taken. Criminal justice is different. An innocent person being sent to prison (or even to execution) is never an acceptable outcome. Convicting the innocent usually also means that the legal system failed to find the real criminal, whose crime will go unpunished.

How should pirates be dealt with – as enemies, perhaps as illegal combatants, or as criminals? No state (in the twenty-first century) has, to our knowledge, claimed to be at war with piracy or stated that pirates should be viewed as illegal combatants. All states seem to view pirates as criminals. So they should be dealt with as such. Expecting the same tactical effect from criminal proceedings as from combat operations is unrealistic. If the international community chooses, as it has done, to pursue pirates as criminals, the effects of this difference in mind-set and legal paradigm should not be forgotten. Criminals of any kind are due their human rights. This implies that pirates, like all other criminals, are presumed innocent until proven guilty in a fair trial before a court of law. It also means that (persons suspected to be) pirates may not be killed as if they were the enemy nor may they be unlawfully renditioned, tortured or held for years without trial.

8.3 PIRACY AS A CRIME

All civilized states agree on the principle of legality, that there should be no crime without prior law (*nullum crimen sine lege* and *nulla poena sine*

Drop: Forgetting the History of Water Torture in U.S. Courts' 45 *Columbia Journal of Transnational Law* (2006–07) 468–506; and P. Sands, *Torture Team: Rumsfeld's Memo and the Betrayal of American Values* (Palgrave Macmillan 2008).

lege);[7] political, religious or moral reasons alone do not constitute a right for states to punish people under (international) criminal law.[8] In order to pursue those we believe to be pirates by legal means, we first need to know what the act of piracy is,[9] in particular under international law.[10] As noted in Chapter 6.2, piracy, as defined in UNCLOS Article 101(a), can only occur on the high seas or in waters that do not belong to any national jurisdiction.[11] The act of piracy is an attack on others involving any 'illegal acts of violence, or detention' or 'depredation'. The term 'illegal acts' risks being circular. We suggest however that the provision is understood to exclude violence in self-defence, lawful arrest and similarly lawful seizure and forfeiture. This would mean, *inter alia*, that private security company personnel using force to defend vessels under pirate attack are not themselves committing piracy.

Attacks carried out by state actors (unless they mutiny) are not piratical, as these do not act for private ends.[12] A pirate act is also defined as voluntary participation in the operation of a ship with knowledge of facts making it a pirate ship (discussed further below).[13] Not just the entire (knowing) crew of the pirate ship are pirates; those inciting or intentionally facilitating pirates are committing the act of piracy as well.[14] This means that financiers or providers of supplies (material or intellectual) for the pirates are themselves punishable as pirates. Usually, however, the financing and supplying takes place on shore and the shore is usually part of a jurisdiction, and one might therefore expect such acts

---

[7] A. Cassese, *International Criminal Law* (2nd edn, OUP 2008) 37.

[8] See: Kenneth S. Gallant, *The Principle of Legality in International and Comparative Criminal Law* (CUP 2009); Iulia Crisan, 'The Principles of Legality *nullum crimen nulla poene sine lege*: Its Role in the Progressive Positive Law' (June 2010) 5 *Effectius Newsletter* <http://www.Effectius_June_2010_Newsletter_Issue_5.16811333.pdf> accessed 1 May 2012.

[9] Though piracy is also a crime under customary law, we will use the definition of the act of piracy in the United Nations Convention on the Law of the Sea (adopted 10 December 1982, entered into force 16 November 1994) 1833 UNTS 397 ('UNCLOS').

[10] On national law approaches see: 18 USC § 1651 and s. 74(1), Criminal Code of Canada (R.S.C., 1985, c. C-46) (both referring to piracy as defined 'by the law of nations'); compare s. 26, Merchant Shipping and Maritime Security Act 1997 (UK) and ss. 51–56, Crimes Act 1914 (Commonwealth of Australia) as amended (both referring to, or incorporating language from, UNCLOS).

[11] But note the discussion of inciting or of intentionally facilitating piracy, below.

[12] UNCLOS Art. 102; Guilfoyle, *supra* note 1, 32–42.

[13] UNCLOS Art. 101(b).

[14] UNCLOS Art. 101(c).

to be excluded from the definition of piracy and the universal jurisdiction linked to it. However, there is an ambiguity in UNCLOS. The provisions criminalizing inciting and intentionally facilitating piracy 'do not explicitly set forth any particular geographic scope'.[15] Irrespective, in the instance of Somalia these provisions could be used to pursue on-shore inciters and facilitators since the UN resolutions regarding the suppression of piracy in Somalia permit operations on land.[16] Even so states seem somewhat reluctant to undertake land operations. From an enforcement perspective, this is unfortunate. Operations at sea only address the symptoms of the problem, not the problem as such. From a strictly legal perspective, however, land operations will give rise to a host of jurisdictional, possibly even constitutional, issues regarding the capture of alleged pirates and proceeds of crime and any subsequent criminal process. Nonetheless, things may be changing. In June 2012, the EU naval mission had its area of operations extended to Somali coastal territory (discussed further below).

An attempt to commit piracy is not expressly criminalized by UNCLOS, nor is planning for or making preparations for piracy beyond the specific provisions on incitement and facilitation (discussed above) and participation in pirate craft (discussed below).[17] This makes it harder to prevent acts of piracy with legal means before they happen. Ideally, national legal systems have provisions making planning, preparations for and attempting serious crimes an offence so as to make it possible to act before people are victimized. States implementing the piracy articles of UNCLOS should take due care in implementing it through (national) criminal legislation. Such legislation should include absolutely all the UNCLOS modes of participation in the offence.[18]

---

[15] United Nations Division for Ocean Affairs and the Law of the Sea, 'Piracy: elements of national legislation pursuant to the United Nations Convention on the Law of the Sea, 1982' IMO Doc LEG 98/8/1 (18 February 2011) 4 at note 15. On the controversy in US case law as to the scope of these provisions see: Roger L. Philips, 'Negotiator Sentenced to Multiple Life Terms: SCOTUS on the horizon' (15 August 2012) <http://piracy-law.com/2012/08/15/negotiator-sentenced-to-multiple-life-terms-scotus-on-the-horizon/> accessed 21 August 2012.

[16] United Nations Security Council resolution 1851 (2008) and subsequent resolutions at n. 19 below.

[17] See further J. Ashley Roach, 'Countering Piracy Off Somalia: International Law and International Institutions' (2010) 104 *American Journal of International Law* 397, 402–403.

[18] See: International Maritime Organizations Legal committee's findings in IMO Doc LEG 98/8/2 (18 February 2011).

8.4 EFFORTS TO COUNTER PIRACY OFF THE COAST OF SOMALIA

On the basis of relevant United Nations Security Council resolutions (UNSCR) on Somalia,[19] the international anti-piracy efforts off the coast of Somalia are conducted by naval forces of many nations. Collective operations have been set up by the European Union (the EU Naval Force (EU NAVFOR[20]) Operation Atalanta has been extended to the end of 2014) and NATO (its 'Operation Ocean Shield', replacing the previous 'Operation Allied Provider' and 'Operation Allied Protector', runs until the end of 2012).[21] The US-led Combined Maritime Forces (CMF) coalition also operates a counter-piracy force, Combined Task Force 151 (CTF 151).[22] In addition, naval forces from other countries, including China, Russia, India, Japan and South Korea, are or have been present.

A clear aim of the international operations off Somalia is law enforcement: to capture pirates and bring them to justice. Indeed, Security Council resolutions show a gradual change of emphasis from the authority to use force to closer law-enforcement cooperation and grounds for asserting criminal jurisdiction over the pirates.[23] Clearly, dealing with pirates as criminals rather than combatants may pose challenges for the military forces.

As noted, EU NAVFOR Operation Atalanta has been operational off the coast of Somalia since December 2008. Its mission is, among other things, to help *deter*, *prevent* and *repress* acts of piracy and armed robbery at sea.[24] *Deterrence* is, legally speaking, easy. In the presence of a warship or an armed helicopter people tend to behave rather well. No force need be used. In practice, deterrence is extremely demanding given the limited naval assets made available compared to the size of the

---

[19] See UN Security Council resolutions: UNSC Res. 1816 (2008), UNSC Res. 1838 (2008), UNSC Res. 1846 (2008), UNSC Res. 1851 (2008), UNSC Res. 1897 (2009), UNSC Res. 1918 (2010), UNSC Res. 1950 (2010), UNSC Res. 1976 (2011), UNSC Res. 2015 (2011) and UNSC Res. 2020 (2011).

[20] EU Council Joint Action 2008/851/CFSP of 10 November 2008, EU OJ L 301/33 (12 November 2008), 33–37.

[21] See further, Geiss and Petrig, *supra* note 1, 22–24.

[22] *Ibid.* at 24–25.

[23] See: D. Guilfoyle, 'Piracy off Somalia: a sketch of the legal framework' (*EJIL: Talk!*, 20 April 2009) <http://www.ejiltalk.org/piracy-off-somalia-a-sketch-of-the-legal-framework> accessed 13 September 2012.

[24] See Council Joint Action 2008/851/CFSP, *supra* note 20.

operational area and the number of potential pirates and victims. *Preventing* piracy with naval or military assets implies taking positive action before the pirates do. This usually means that some sort of repressive acts must be used. Naturally this demands a more complex legal framework than deterrence. *Repressing* acts of piracy involves having pirates convicted of their crimes. This is legally at least as demanding as any domestic criminal proceedings. In fact it is more demanding because it is in part carried out with armed forces operating abroad under their own national law as well as international law.

Originally the mandate for Operation Atalanta included the following passage:

> Atalanta shall ... in view of prosecutions potentially being brought by the relevant States ... , arrest, detain and transfer persons who have committed, or are suspected of having committed, acts of piracy or armed robbery ... and seize the vessels ... as well as the goods on board.[25]

The words limiting the mandate to acting against persons *having committed acts of piracy* may seem to conflict with the mission of preventing piracy,[26] that is, taking the initiative against the pirates. Since attempting and preparing piracy is not *expressly* outlawed by UNCLOS, the passage seems to suggest that EU NAVFOR has to wait for an attack to be launched before it can intervene. However, delay can be dangerous. If a target ship is successfully taken over by the pirates, there is little in practice that can be done, as any hostile action taken against the pirates would then endanger the safety of their hostages. The window of opportunity to act would therefore be narrow. In practice this would mean that EU NAVFOR units have less than 30 minutes to respond to distress calls. Very few ships are attacked at such close range to EU NAVFOR assets.

Hence, EU NAVFOR needed to find legal grounds to enlarge the window of opportunity for preventative action. The solution lay in the offence of voluntary participation in a pirate ship.[27] The definition of a

---

[25]   Council Decision 2012/174/CFSP of 23 March 2012 amending Joint Action 2008/851/CFSP on a European Union military operation to contribute to deterrence, prevention and repression of acts of piracy and armed robbery off the Somali coast, EU OJ L89/69 (27 March 2012), 69–71, Art. 2(e).

[26]   *Ibid.* Art. 2(d).

[27]   Art. 101 para. B UNCLOS ('any act of voluntary participation in the operation of a ship or of an aircraft with knowledge of facts making it a pirate ship [or aircraft]') and Art. 103 UNCLOS ('A ship or aircraft is considered a

pirate ship[28] does not only include ships that *have been* used in pirate acts but conveniently also ships that are *intended* (by those in dominant control) to be used for such purposes. If a person participating in the operation of a ship is aware of the facts making it a pirate ship, then that person commits piracy. The relevant *fact* may be the intention of the persons in dominant control. In practice the vessels used for the actual pirate attacks (usually skiffs) in the waters outside of Somalia are crewed by three or four persons. Often the skiffs work in pairs and, if they operate outside the Gulf of Aden, have a logistical vessel supporting them. One could safely assume that all of the crew members have the same intentions or at least know what the majority of the others intend.[29] If the intention is piracy, then they are committing a crime as soon as they start operating the vessel, that is, as soon as they pass the high water mark.

It is perhaps not the best legal drafting to define a fact, which is a requisite for a crime, to be the intention of someone (else). This makes this mode of piracy a pure Orwellian thought-crime. On the other hand, if a person knowingly takes part in a venture aimed at using illegal force for private ends against others he or she should not be shocked to find that this may result in legal consequences, with the provisions in UNCLOS discussed here as a first legal basis.

With this interpretation as a foundation, EU NAVFOR operations over time increasingly focused on trying to stop pirates before they attacked. It was easier finding them when leaving shore than when they hid among fishermen in busy fishing areas or in the vastness of the Indian Ocean. This proactive stance was subsequently formalized through a change in the Atalanta mandate by the EU Council.[30] The amended text now reads:

---

pirate ship or aircraft if it is intended by the persons in dominant control to be used for the purpose of committing one of the acts referred to in article 101 ...').

[28]   By *ship* we understand that UNCLOS in this article refers to any seaworthy vessel and not just floating vessels fulfilling the requirements of a certain size or build that are sometimes used.

[29]   Concerning the mother ship, however, this assumption is less straightforward; see, e.g., 'For Iranians Waylaid by Pirates, U.S. to the Rescue' *New York Times*, 6 January 2012.

[30]   Council Decision 2010/766/CFSP of 7 December 2010 amending Joint Action 2008/851/CFSP, OJ L 327/49, 11.12.2010, 49–50.

> Atalanta shall ... in view of prosecutions potentially being brought by the
> relevant States ..., arrest, detain and transfer persons *suspected of intending*,
> ... to commit, committing or having committed, acts of piracy or armed
> robbery ... and seize the vessels ... as well as the goods on board.[31]

The challenge then would be to avoid 'collateral damage', that is to avoid
using force or other repression against innocent fishermen (or perhaps
not so innocent smugglers of weapons and humans falling outside the
mandate).

As discussed, fighting crime with a view to prosecuting the suspects
involves less margin for error than fighting the enemy in an armed
conflict. In practice this means that the collection and assessing of
intelligence, which is a normal part of naval or military activity, must
shift focus. EU NAVFOR needs to know as much about smuggling,
fishing and other activity in the sea outside Somalia as about piracy.
Operating against suspected criminals, with a view to their prosecution,
requires intelligence that excludes the innocent from the process. In
practice intelligence is gathered until the Force Commander is certain
that the suspects indeed are pirates. The bottom line, however, should be
that the principle of presumption of innocence is respected and that
violence against innocents must be avoided.

8.5 PROSECUTION

Since Somalia has no effective, functioning government, law enforcement
or judiciary, the international community has taken on the task of
bringing captured pirate suspects to justice. The EU Joint Action for EU
NAVFOR Atalanta sets forth some options in case the capturing state
'cannot or do ... not wish to exercise jurisdiction', namely transfer of the
suspect to a 'Member State or any third State which wishes to exercise its
jurisdiction over the aforementioned persons'.[32]

Consequently, the EU NAVFOR mandate supposes that member states
are prepared to prosecute all suspected pirates. In reality this is rarely the
case.[33] For many reasons, patrolling nations have proved reluctant to

---

[31] *Ibid.* Art. 1(1)(e) (replacing Art. 2(e) of the previous decision) (emphasis
added).

[32] Council Joint Action 2008/851/CSFP, OJ L 301/33, 10.11.2008, Art.
12(1).

[33] However, within the EU five states have pursued piracy prosecutions
(Belgium, France, Germany, Netherlands and Spain); see UNODC, *Counter-
Piracy Programme: Support to the Trial and Related Treatment of Piracy*

shoulder the burden of transferring captured pirates to their home jurisdiction for prosecution. The transportation of suspects, witnesses and evidence may be difficult and costly. National law might be unclear, untested, or even inadequate concerning piracy, and the investigation and trial will be complex due to the transnational aspects. Formal rules on evidence may pose hurdles. The costs for transfers, translation, and for keeping suspects and witnesses may be high. Unless technology such as video conferencing can be used at trial, key personnel from the naval operation may have to spend considerable time on-shore for the proceedings. Finally, the situation in Somalia means that there is an obvious risk that the captured pirates cannot be repatriated to Somalia upon the completion of the criminal process and service of any sentence. In addition, a convicted pirate's incentives for seeking asylum may be strong[34] and some even argue a possible custodial stay in a Western state may reduce deterrence.[35] The expense associated with prosecution in the region is considerably lower than in most of the naval patrolling nations, hence there is a good business case to support regional prosecutions.[36]

The preferred option is prosecution in the region. The first country of choice was Kenya, with which the United Kingdom signed a Memorandum of Understanding in December 2008 allowing transfer of captured pirates to Kenya for prosecution.[37] In January 2009 the United States

---

Suspects, February 2012, <http://www.unodc.org/unodc/en/piracy/index.html? ref=menuside> accessed 21 April 2012.

[34] See, e.g., House of Lords, *Combating Somali Piracy: The EU's Naval Operation Atalanta: Evidence,* 19 March 2009, HL Paper 103; and Karl Sörensen, *Wrong Hands on Deck? Combating Piracy & Building Maritime Security in Eastern Africa,* Swedish Defence Research Agency (FOI, July 2011), 32. For a critical view, see Y. M. Dutton, 'Pirates and Impunity: Is the Threat of Asylum Claims a Reason to Allow Pirates to Escape Justice?' (2011) 34 *Fordham International Law Review* 236.

[35] E.g. B. Waterfield, 'Somali pirates embrace capture as route to Europe' *The Telegraph* (19 May 2009) <http://www.telegraph.co.uk/news/worldnews/ piracy/5350183/Somali-pirates-embrace-capture-as-route-to-Europe.html> accessed 13 September 2012.

[36] Anna Bowden and Shikha Basnet, *The Economic Costs of Maritime Piracy 2011* (One Earth Future Foundation, Working Paper, February 2012), 22–24.

[37] Signed on 11 December 2008, by Foreign Affairs Minister Moses Wetangula (Kenya) and Security Minister Lord West (UK). It formalized an ad hoc arrangement that the Kenyan government had entered into with the British in November 2008, leading to the prosecution of eight pirate suspects. The agreement is not public. See: J. Thuo Gathii, 'Kenya's Piracy Prosecutions' (2010) 104 *American Journal of International Law* 417, footnote 4.

concluded a similar agreement with Kenya,[38] and in February 2009 the EU followed suit.[39] Subsequently, the EU has entered into such agreements with Mauritius and the Seychelles.[40] Further such bilateral transfer agreements have been concluded, and the EU is seeking similar arrangements with Mozambique, South Africa, Tanzania and Uganda.[41]

In practice, if no regional state accepts to try the suspects, often there will be no prosecution,[42] and the suspects will be released.[43] Since Atalanta is an operation predicated on respecting the suspect's human rights, there is no legal alternative to prosecution. Hence, alleged pirates will continue to be released safely ashore in Somalia, having been looked after on-board EU NAVFOR vessels, unless there are sufficient arrangements in place for conducting piracy trials. Naturally, this result runs contrary to the aim of combating piracy and is of great concern.[44]

---

[38] E.g. L. Ploch *et al.*, 'Piracy Off the Horn of Africa' (Congressional Research Service Report No. R40528, 27 April 2011) 35. The agreement is not public.

[39] Annex to Council Decision 2009/293/CFSP of 26 February 2009 concerning the Exchange of Letters between the European Union and the Government of Kenya on the conditions and modalities for the transfer of persons suspected of having committed acts of piracy and detained by the European Union-led naval force (EU NAVFOR), and seized property in the possession of EU NAVFOR, from EU NAVFOR to Kenya and for their treatment after such transfer, OJ EU L79/49 (25 March 2009).

[40] Annex to Council Decision 2009/877/CFSP of 23 October 2009 on the signing and provisional application of the Exchange of Letters between the European Union and the Republic of Seychelles on the conditions and modalities for the transfer of suspected pirates and armed robbers from EU NAVFOR to the Republic of Seychelles and for their treatment after such transfer, OJ EU L315/37 (3 December 2009), 37–43; Annex to Council Decision 2011/640/CFSP of 12 July 2011 on the signing and conclusion of the Agreement between the European Union and the Republic of Mauritius on the conditions of transfer of suspected pirates and associated seized property from the European Union-led naval force to the Republic of Mauritius and on the conditions of suspected pirates after transfer, OJ EU L254/3 (30 September 2011), 3–6.

[41] EU Foreign Affairs Council meeting, 22 March 2010; see Press Release, 3005th Council Meeting, EU Doc. 7828/1/10 Rev 1 (Presse 73) 16.

[42] Especially if there has not been an actual attack, only suspicion of intent to commit piracy. It is not clear what evidence a court would accept as conclusive regarding such a charge e.g. by a Kenyan court. Therefore it is perhaps wise not to prosecute as a not guilty verdict would set an unnecessary precedent.

[43] Giving rise to jokes relating to the fly fishing practice of 'catch-and-release'.

[44] See, e.g., UNSC Res. 1918 (27 April 2010) UN Doc. S/RES/1918.

Increasingly piracy prosecutions do take place, and regardless of the venue they have particular challenges. These include ensuring Somali interpretation, admission of evidence and attendance of witnesses from other states.[45]

8.6 ARREST AND DETENTION

Successfully bringing suspected pirates to court and securing a conviction by naval forces belonging to states with different legal systems from the one where the trial will take place is challenging. A key question may be the lawfulness of detaining a person before trial. Pre-trial detention without a lawful basis may jeopardize subsequent prosecution. UNCLOS expressly permits states to arrest pirates,[46] but that is not the end of our enquiry.

Arrest is often the starting point for criminal proceedings under national criminal procedural law.[47] In the absence of national rules delegating powers of arrest to naval officers, any detention carried out by them might be viewed not as an arrest, but as some sort of pre-arrest detention; the suspected pirates are held in custody pending a decision regarding their (formal) arrest as suspected pirates. In practice they are held by EU NAVFOR until the question of whether an EU member state will prosecute or whether a regional or other state (e.g., the flag state of the attacked ship) will do so.[48] During this time, the flag state's human rights obligations are applicable regarding the detainees.[49]

8.7 SEIZURE AND FORFEITURE

If the persons believed to be pirates are set free, the question arises what happens to their tools of the trade: vessels, arms, boarding ladders,

---

[45] See Contact Group on Piracy off the Coast of Somalia, *9th Meeting of Working Group 2 on Legal Issues: Seychelles, 11–12 October 2011 – Chairman's Conclusions* (copy on file with authors).

[46] UNCLOS Art. 105.

[47] Arrest as a starting point for criminal process is a common law concept and does not generally apply in other legal systems.

[48] See House of Lords, *supra* note 34, 52.

[49] See e.g. European Court of Human Rights, *Medvedyev and Others v France,* Appl. No. 3394/03, Grand Chamber, Judgment 29 March 2010 and Chapter 6.7.

provisions (normally fuel, food and Khat), and navigational and communications equipment. Is it legal to deprive them of their possessions if they will not be tried as criminals? UNCLOS states in Article 105 that: '... every State may seize a pirate ship ... or a ship taken by piracy and under the control of the pirates, and ... seize the property on board ... '. Arguably, this includes not only cargo on the pirated ship, but also the property of the pirates. In resolution 1851 (2008), the Security Council, acting under Chapter VII:

> Calls upon States, regional and international organizations...to take part actively in the fight against piracy and armed robbery at sea off the coast of Somalia, ... consistent with ... international law, by deploying naval vessels and military aircraft and through *seizure and disposition of boats, vessels, arms and other related equipment used in the commission of piracy* and armed robbery at sea off the coast of Somalia, or for which there are *reasonable grounds for suspecting such use.*[50]

Interestingly the resolution sets out a level of proof needed for the lawful seizure and forfeiture ('disposition') of pirate paraphernalia: reasonable grounds for suspecting its use for piracy or armed robbery at sea off Somalia. As regards seizure, this is not very controversial. However, denying someone their property permanently without having to prove beyond reasonable doubt that it has been used for criminal purposes might appear rather harsh in many national criminal jurisdictions.

Elsewhere in the resolution the Security Council stresses that any action taken should conform with human rights.[51] One might assume, therefore, that the Council believes that the fairly low level of proof needed for forfeiture does not infringe human rights. However, the evidentiary standard set out in the resolution seems even lower than the standard for 'non-conviction based forfeiture' applied primarily in common law jurisdictions.[52] Hence, it is hard to avoid the feeling that this was perhaps written more with a view to the efficient conduct of military operations rather than effective proceedings against suspected criminals. Under resolution 1851 it is possible, perhaps as the result of 'bad intel', to burn an innocent person's boat and take away his satellite phone

---

[50] UNSC Res. 1851 (16 December 2008) UN Doc. S/RES/1851, para. 2 (emphasis added).

[51] E.g. *ibid.*, paras 6–7.

[52] On non-conviction based forfeiture see, e.g., Theodore S Greenberg *et al., Stolen Asset Recovery: A Good Practices Guide to Non-Conviction Based Asset Forfeiture* (The World Bank, Stolen Asset Recovery (StAR) Initiative, Washington D.C. 2009).

without convincing proof of piracy. The acceptance of such a result resembles the mind-set which accepts collateral damage in an armed conflict. It does not resemble the expectations of avoidance of error regarding criminal proceedings which respect human rights. However, this power of summary confiscation and forfeiture is undoubtedly a very useful tool in the fight against piracy. In practice it is used extensively.

Within EU NAVFOR the decision to forfeit property is taken at the Force Commander-level in every case. As the states participating in EU NAVFOR have all ratified the European Convention on Human Rights (ECHR) their national laws should include safeguards fulfilling their obligations to respect property rights and the right to a fair trial.[53] While the suspected pirates under certain circumstances have the right to claim protection under the ECHR, even when taken on the high seas,[54] this may be a right in theory only. In practice, they have little opportunity to have a forfeiture decision tried under the law in the state whose representatives ordered it or carried out the order. Nonetheless, the decision to forfeit is taken by naval officers with advice from lawyers, in a much less pressured environment than an armed conflict. These officials remain bound by their national laws even when they carry out international missions. In effect this means that the level of proof required by EU NAVFOR before suspected pirate goods are forfeited is set higher than it is by UNSCR, as participating national missions must respect the conditions for deprivation of property under the ECHR.[55]

8.8 INTERNATIONAL CRIMINAL COOPERATION

At some point in this process, the military operation will turn into a criminal process and thus the legal framework for criminal investigation and prosecution, and for cooperation in criminal matters, will apply. A full criminal investigation and prosecution of piracy will, in most cases,

---

[53] Convention for the Protection of Human Rights and Fundamental Freedoms (adopted 4 November 1950, entered into force 3 September 1953) ('ECHR') ETS 5, 213 UNTS 22, Art. 6; Protocol (No. 1) to the ECHR (adopted 20 March 1952, entered into force 18 May 1954), 213 UNTS 262, Art. 1.

[54] On the jurisdiction of the European Court of Human Rights, see e.g. *Medvedyev, supra* note 49, paras 62–67.

[55] Protocol (No. 1) to the ECHR Art. 1. One may note that it is not a question of post-conviction confiscation and therefore that the exception in the second para. of Article 1 arguably does not apply, cf. *Phillips v United Kingdom* (Appl. No. 41087/98), Judgment, 5 July 2001. Hence, the normal requirements for deprivation of property applies.

require international cooperation in criminal matters (often called 'mutual legal assistance' or 'MLA'). Cooperation in criminal matters is a voluntary undertaking: a state is not obliged to provide MLA unless it has agreed to do so. In practice, many states require a bilateral or multilateral agreement in order to cooperate (and thus a promise of reciprocity), although there are states willing and able to do so without an agreement. Irrespective, MLA is likely to occur through national procedures. However, extradition and MLA processes are often slow and sometimes difficult to obtain in practice. Hence, other forms of more or less unregulated cooperation may occur in practice, which in turn could jeopardize the human rights of suspects.

International criminal cooperation is a key element in combating piracy, perhaps even more important than the deployment of additional naval forces.[56] Various cooperation agreements that are, or could be, relevant to the prosecution of Somali pirates are discussed below. Apart from providing for criminal cooperation, some of these agreements also regulate criminalization (of certain crimes) and criminal jurisdiction. Quite apart from the pre-condition for prosecution that the state has a national criminal law covering piracy, issues of criminal jurisdiction may also create difficulties. Prosecutions in Kenya were suspended after a judge of the High Court ruled that Kenyan courts lacked jurisdiction over matters occurring outside its territorial waters. That decision is now the subject of a pending appeal.[57] Nonetheless, lower courts have continued to hand down verdicts and Kenya is accepting transfers from international naval forces on a case-by-case basis.

Bilateral and multilateral efforts are also being made to strengthen the capacity of regional states to handle piracy prosecutions and imprison convicted pirates in a human rights compliant manner. The UN Office on Drugs and Crime (UNODC) plays a pivotal role in this respect.[58] UNODC provides technical assistance in criminal justice sector capacity-building and implementation of relevant United Nations conventions. Its counter-piracy programme focuses on: '1. [f]air and efficient piracy trials

---

[56] See James Kraska and Brian Wilson, 'Fighting piracy' *Armed Forces Journal,* February 2009.

[57] E.g. 'Judge's absence halts against piracy trials judgment' (*MaritimeSecurity.Asia,* 1 March 2012) <http://maritimesecurity.asia/free-2/piracy-2/judge%E2%80%99s-absence-halts-appeal-against-piracy-trials-ruling/> accessed 20 April 2012.

[58] See Security Council resolutions: UNSC Res. 1918 (2010), UNSC Res. 1950 (2010), UNSC Res. 1976 (2011), UNSC Res. 2015 (2011), UNSC Res. 2020 (2011) and UNSC Res. 2036 (2012).

with humane and secure imprisonment in regional countries, and 2. [h]umane and secure imprisonment in Somalia for convicted pirates returned there to serve their sentences'.[59]

8.8.1 International Agreements

Article 100 UNCLOS requires states to cooperate to the fullest possible extent in the repression of piracy. However, the provision lacks specificity. For all practical purposes such cooperation depends upon other international and national rules.

Multilateral treaties of a general character
Organized piracy might qualify as a 'transnational organized crime' and thereby fall under the 2000 UN Convention against Transnational Organized Crime (UNTOC).[60] There are good reasons to consider Somali piracy organized crime.[61] Under UNTOC once the (somewhat complicated) basic requirement of an offence that is 'transnational in nature and involves an organized criminal group' is met,[62] the Convention offers a modern regime for cooperation on confiscation, extradition and MLA.[63] In addition, the Convention notes other forms of cooperation, such as transfer of prisoners, joint investigations, special investigative techniques, and transfer of criminal proceedings, but without placing any firm obligations on states parties.[64] The Convention is widely accepted and it has 166 states parties, including 26 of the EU member states (and the EU itself), regional states such as Djibouti, Kenya, Madagascar, Mauritius, Oman, Yemen, the Seychelles, and Tanzania, as well as India, the Russian

---

[59]   UNODC, *Counter-Piracy Programme: Support to the Trial and Related Treatment of Piracy Suspects*, February 2012 <http://www.unodc.org/unodc/en/piracy/index.html?ref=menuside> accessed 21 April 2012.

[60]   United Nations Convention against Transnational Organized Crime ('UNTOC') (adopted 15 November 2000, entered into force 29 September 2003) 2225 UNTS 209.

[61]   See: Chapter 3; and S. Percy and A. Shortland, 'The Business of Piracy in Somalia' Deutches Institut für Wirtschaftsforschung (DIW), Discussion Paper 1033, Berlin 2011, at 14–23 <http://www.diw.de/documents/publikationen/73/diw_01.c.358500.de/dp1033.pdf> accessed 20 April 2012.

[62]   UNTOC Art. 3(1).

[63]   UNTOC Arts 13–14, 16 and 18.

[64]   UNTOC Arts 17 and 19–21.

Federation, and the United States.[65] Somalia has not signed the Convention and neither have entities such as Somaliland and Puntland.

The 1988 Convention for the Suppression of Unlawful Acts against the Safety of Maritime Navigation (SUA Convention)[66] was a response to the *Achille Lauro* attack in 1985, and is designed to establish a legal basis for prosecuting maritime violence not falling within the UNCLOS piracy framework.[67] The Convention has 160 states parties.[68] Apart from criminalization provisions, it contains an 'extradite or prosecute' clause (also referred to as '*aut dedere aut judicare*')[69] and a few basic provisions on extradition and MLA.[70] A Protocol to the Convention from 2005[71] contains, *inter alia,* a scheme for temporary transfer of a person who is detained (or serving a sentence) to another state for the purposes of identification, testimony or otherwise obtaining evidence for the investigation or prosecution of a crime.[72] Other international conventions that could possibly apply in some cases are the 1979 International Convention against the Taking of Hostages,[73] and the 1999 International Convention for the Suppression of the Financing of Terrorism.[74] The former has 168

---

[65]   Status as of 16 March 2012 (UNTS). The only non-party EU-state is the Czech Republic.

[66]   Convention for the Suppression of Unlawful Acts against the Safety of Maritime Navigation ('SUA Convention') (adopted 10 March 1988, entered into force 1 March 1992) 1678 UNTS 221.

[67]   See M. Halberstam, 'Terrorism on the High Seas: The Achille Lauro, Piracy and the IMO Convention on Maritime Safety' (1988) 82 *American Journal of International Law* 269.

[68]   As of 30 April 2012 (covering, according to the IMO, 94.66% of the gross tonnage of the world's merchant fleet). The states parties include all EU Member States, India, Philippines, Russian Federation, United States, Djibouti, Kenya, Madagascar, Mauritius, Mozambique, Oman, Seychelles, Tanzania and Yemen.

[69]   SUA Convention Arts 6(4) and 10(1).

[70]   *Ibid.*, Arts 11–12.

[71]   Protocol of 2005 to the Convention for the Suppression of Unlawful Acts against the Safety of Maritime Navigation ('2005 SUA Protocol') (adopted 14 October 2005, entered into force 28 July 2010), IMO Doc. LEG/CONF.15/21. As of 30 April 2012, the Protocol has 22 states parties.

[72]   *Ibid.*, Art. 11 (introducing new Art. 12*bis* in the SUA Convention).

[73]   (Adopted 17 December 1979, entered into force 3 June 1983) 1316 UNTS 205.

[74]   (Adopted 9 December 1999, entered into force 10 April 2002) 2178 UNTS 197.

states parties and the latter 178, with membership similar to UNTOC.[75] However, in all cases, cooperation in practice requires additional agreements or arrangements to be entered into, or domestic legislation in the requested state that allows unilateral cooperation absent such agreements.

African regional and sub-regional instruments

There are also some regional instruments of interest, mainly adopted under the auspices of the African Union (AU). These include: the AU Maritime Transport Charter; and the Durban Resolution on Maritime Safety, Maritime Security and Protection of the Marine Environment in Africa.[76] These instruments include, *inter alia,* commitments to support the International Maritime Organization's (IMO's) efforts in coordinating an international response to piracy and its capacity-building activities, to enact national legislation, and to encourage implementation of the Djibouti Code (see below). However, cooperation concerning criminal investigations and prosecutions is not explicitly mentioned in the Durban Resolution, and is mentioned in the Maritime Transport Charter only by way of a general cooperation commitment and as an area for development.[77] As of 23 December 2011, the Charter had not yet entered into force.[78]

On criminal cooperation more generally, African sub-regional agreements on extradition and MLA have also been concluded. In 2002 the Southern African Development Community (SADC)[79] adopted a Protocol on Mutual Legal Assistance in Criminal Matters which sets forth a

---

[75] Status as of 16 March 2012 (UNTS). The Czech Republic, but not the EU as such, is party to the Conventions.

[76] Both instruments adopted at the Second African Union Conference of Ministers Responsible for Maritime Transport, Durban, South Africa, 16 October 2009, AU Docs. AU/MT/MIN/1(II) (Maritime Transport Charter) and AU/MT/MIN/Draft/Res.(II) (Durban Resolution). A revised version of the Maritime Transport Charter was adopted by the AU Assembly on 26 July 2011 in Kampala, Uganda.

[77] Maritime Transport Charter, Arts 3(9), 12(4) and 24.

[78] See AU Press Release N.199/2011 <http://au.int/pages/sites/default/files/PR%20COTE%20D'IVOIRE%20SIGNS%20CHARTER%20ON%20MARITIME%2027.12.11.pdf> accessed 16 March 2012. Entry into force requires 15 ratifications; Art. 49 of the Charter.

[79] *Ibid.* Arts 28–29. The SADC member states are: Angola, Botswana, Democratic Republic of the Congo, Lesotho, Madagascar, Malawi, Mauritius, Mozambique, Namibia, Seychelles, South Africa, Swaziland, Tanzania, Zambia and Zimbabwe.

modern scheme for cooperation.[80] Also in 2002, a SADC Protocol on Extradition was adopted.[81] Both Protocols are in operation.

For the many African states that belong to the Commonwealth, the Harare Scheme relating to Mutual Assistance in Criminal Matters within the Commonwealth[82] and the London Scheme on Extradition are also applicable. Another agreement is the 2002 Mutual Assistance Pact between the member states of the Economic Community of Central African States (ECCAS).[83]

Initiatives by inter-governmental organizations

The Eastern and Southern Africa–Indian Ocean (ESA–IO) Regional Strategy and rolling Regional Plan of Action, of 2010, is an EU-sponsored initiative with a threefold aim: (1) the development and implementation of a Somalia Inland Action Plan to counter and prevent piracy; (2) encouraging states in the region to prosecute pirates with the financial and technical support of the international community; and (3) strengthening regional states' capacities to secure their maritime zones.[84]

---

[80]   SADC Protocol on Mutual Legal Assistance in Criminal Matters, adopted on 3 October 2002 in Luanda, Angola <http://www.sadc.int/english/key-documents/protocols/protocol-on-mutual-legal-assistance-in-criminal-matters/> accessed 16 March 2012. The Protocol has entered into force within SADC on 1 March 2007 (source: SADC).

[81]   SADC Protocol on Extradition, adopted on 3 October 2002 in Luanda, Angola;   <http://www.sadc.int/english/key-documents/protocols/protocol-on-extradition/> accessed 16 March 2012. The Protocol entered into force within SADC on 1 September 2006 (source: SADC).

[82]   Scheme relating to Mutual Assistance in Criminal Matters, adopted in 1966, and amended in 1986, April 1990, November 2002 and October 2005 <http://www.thecommonwealth.org/shared_asp_files/uploadedfiles/2C167ECF-0FDE-481B-B552-E9BA23857CE3_HARARESCHEMERELATINGTOMUTU ALASSISTANCE2005.pdf> accessed 16 March 2012.

[83]   ECCAS Mutual Assistance Pact, adopted on 24 February 2002 in Malabo, Equatorial   Guinea   <http://www.ceeac-eccas.org/pdf/traites/ASSISTANCE_ MUTUELLE.pdf> (in French) accessed 16 March 2012. The member states are: Angola, Burundi, Cameroon, Central African Republic, Chad, Democratic Republic of the Congo, Gabon, Equatorial Guinea, Republic of the Congo and Sao Tome & Principe.

[84]   See Joint Communiqué from the Eastern and Southern Africa – Indian Ocean Ministers and European Union High Representative at the 2nd Regional Ministerial Meeting on Piracy and Maritime Security in the Eastern and Southern Africa and Indian Ocean Region, 7 October 2010, Mauritius <http://www. consilium.europa.eu/uedocs/cms_data/docs/pressdata/EN/foraff/116942.pdf> accessed 16 March 2012.

The IMO-sponsored, non-binding Djibouti Code of Conduct to Combat Acts of Piracy was concluded in 2009 as a forerunner to a treaty on preventing and suppressing piracy and armed robbery at sea in the western Indian Ocean and the Gulf of Aden.[85] Important elements include a commitment to review domestic legislation and consider joint operations in the form of so-called 'ship-riders' (see below). The Code also includes a commitment to cooperate 'to the fullest possible extent' in 'arresting, investigating, and prosecuting persons who have committed piracy or are reasonably suspected of committing piracy'.[86] However, the 13 signatory states (regional and observer states) do not seem to have made much use of the Code in practice and, in addition, the Code has not been adopted by the major 'victim states', that is, the major shipping and crew-providing nations.[87]

The most recent criminal cooperation regime, adopted in response to piracy (and terrorism), consists of two conventions adopted under the auspices of the East African Intergovernmental Authority on Development (IGAD): the 2009 Extradition and Mutual Legal Assistance Conventions.[88] The Conventions provide the Horn of Africa states with modern and comprehensive regulation of these matters, and only three ratifications are required for their entry into force. Reportedly, the Conventions are not yet in force,[89] but training sessions for practitioners are being held with international support.

---

[85] Code of Conduct concerning the Repression of Piracy and Armed Robbery against Ships in the Western Indian Ocean and the Gulf of Aden, signed on 29 January 2009 (in effect from date of signature), IMO Doc. C 102/14 <http://www.imo.org/OurWork/Security/PIU/Documents/DCoC%20English.pdf> accessed 16 March 2012. The signatories are: Comoros, Djibouti, Egypt, Eritrea, Ethiopia, Jordan, Kenya, Madagascar, Maldives, Mauritius, Oman, Saudi Arabia, Seychelles, Somalia, Tanzania, United Arab Emirates and Yemen. See also Geiss and Petrig, *supra* note 1, at 48–51.

[86] *Ibid.* Art. 4(3)(a).

[87] See Deborah Osiro, 'Somali pirates have rights too: Judicial consequences and human rights concerns' (Institute for Security Studies, ISS Paper 224, July 2011) 9.

[88] IGAD Extradition and Mutual Legal Assistance Conventions, adopted, 7–8 December 2009, <http://www.globalct.org/images/content/pdf/discussion/10March23–25_Nairobi_BackgroundPaper.pdf> accessed 13 September 2012. The earlier IGAD Convention on Judicial Help in Penal Matters, was adopted in Djibouti in June 2000, and entered force on 8 December 2009. IGAD Member States are: Djibouti, Ethiopia, Kenya, Somalia, South Sudan, Sudan and Uganda.

[89] M. Ewi and A. du Plessis, 'Criminal Justice Responses to Terrorism in Africa: The Role of the African Union and Regional Organizations', in: A. M.

8.8.2 Transfer of Suspects

As military forces operating in Somalia and the Indian Ocean come from
different countries and are often deployed in multinational missions, the
issue of formal criminal cooperation may already arise within an
international force. For example, transferring captured pirates from one
unit to another within a multinational force could, arguably, require a
formal inter-state mechanism. A preferable view, however, is to consider
the international force as one unit in this respect, operating under
common rules of engagement; that is, cooperation measures are not
conducted between different countries but instead within the joint military force as a separate entity. The opposite view would simply lead to an
unworkable situation, requiring the involvement of prosecutors, judges
and other authorities in each state involved. A pre-requisite for this
'one-force approach', however, is that the applicable operational rules
and regulations contain appropriate safeguards for affected individuals.
The Rules of Engagement (ROE) of Operation Atalanta are confiden-
tial.[90] But in line with general recommendations for the drafting of ROE
concerning maritime interdiction operations,[91] it is safe to assume that
provisions on detention and the treatment of detainees are included in the
Atalanta ROE.

The transfer of the suspected pirate outside the military force, for
example from the capturing vessel of one state to another state for
prosecution, is a different matter. Then normal extradition proceedings,
or surrender between EU member states under the European Arrest
Warrant (EAW), could be required. For example, the Netherlands has
concluded that extradition or the EAW is required if Dutch authorities
want to prosecute pirates captured by other naval forces or when another
state wants to prosecute a pirate captured by the Dutch navy.[92] Accordingly, in January 2009 the Netherlands requested Denmark to extradite

---

Salinas de Frias *et al.* (eds), *Counter-Terrorism: International Law and Practice*
(OUP 2012) 1020.

[90]   See Council Decision 2008/918/CFSP of 8 December 2008 on the launch
of the European Union military operation to contribute to the deterrence,
prevention and repression of acts of piracy and armed robbery off the Somali
coast (Atalanta), OJ L 330/19, 9.12.2008, 19–20, which includes a reference to
the Rules of Engagements but does not reveal their content.

[91]   See International Institute for Humanitarian Law, *Rules of Engagement
Handbook* (The Institute 2009) 21.

[92]   P. van Heuzen, 'Netherlands State Practice for the Parliamentary Year
2008–2009' (2010) *Netherlands Yearbook of International Law* 241, 285.

five pirates held on a Danish naval frigate after an unsuccessful attack against a Netherlands-Antilles cargo ship.[93]

As noted above, the preferred solution in most cases is to transfer suspects to regional states. Such transfers do not occur through extradition. Extradition normally involves a state *requesting* a suspect be transferred into its custody. Here, the initiative comes from the international force or state that has captured the suspect and wishes to find a venue willing to prosecute. Hence, special transfer schemes have been developed. Nevertheless, extradition could still be an option in some cases, as noted above.

Some commentators have questioned the legality of these transfer agreements, suggesting that the power conferred in Article 105 UNCLOS was intended to preclude transfers to third states.[94] However, it has been convincingly argued that even if UNCLOS only expressly confers adjudicative jurisdiction on the capturing state, public international law does not generally oppose transfers per se to third states which may then exercise universal jurisdiction under customary international law.[95]

In this context one should also note the special transfer mechanisms established in the SUA Convention, to which the Security Council has referred in various resolutions on Somalia. SUA Convention Article 8 provides that the 'master of a ship' of a state party may deliver a person suspected of an offence under the Convention to the authorities of any other state party. There is a debate, however, as to whether this provision may be used by a warship.[96] With the entry into force of the 2005 SUA Protocol, the delivery mechanism will clearly be applicable to such warships,[97] a fact that, in itself, can be held against the interpretation that the SUA Convention already authorizes this. While the SUA Convention

---

[93]   'Dutch seek Somali pirates' extradition from Denmark' (*AFP/Expatica*, 16 January 2009) <http://www.expatica.com/nl/news/dutch-news/-Dutch-seek-Somali-pirates_-extradition-from-Denmark-_48708.html> accessed 16 March 2012.

[94]   See E. Kontorovich, 'International Legal Responses to Piracy off the Coast of Somalia' (2009) 13/2 *ASIL Insights* <http://www.asil.org/insights 090206.cfm> accessed 6 August 2012. For a more moderate view see: Kontorovich, *supra* note 3, at 270–272.

[95]   Geiss and Petrig, *supra* note 1, at 148–152 and 197; Douglas Guilfoyle, 'Counter-Piracy Law Enforcement and Human Rights' (2010) 59 *International and Comparative Law Quarterly* 141, 144–145.

[96]   Compare Geiss and Petrig, *supra* note 1, at 188–191, and Guilfoyle, *supra* note 95, at 149.

[97]   Article 8*bis* (10)(d)–(e) of the 2005 SUA Protocol, *supra* note 71.

is relevant to Somali piracy due to its wide membership, the Protocol (with only 22 states parties) is not yet so.

A recurrent theme is concern for the human rights implications of transferring pirates to regional states for prosecution or otherwise. European states bound by the ECHR have duties towards those in their custody.[98] Regarding transfers to another country, these states must uphold prohibitions against returning certain persons to places of persecution (the obligation of non-refoulement) or where they may face torture or inhumane or degrading treatment or punishment;[99] and must also ensure that the transferred person does not risk a flagrant denial of justice in the receiving state.[100] Detention or prison conditions may also give rise to prohibited treatment preventing a transfer,[101] including questions of a prisoner's future treatment.[102] In fact, in November 2011 a German court ruled that the transfer of Somali piracy suspects to Kenya was illegal due to poor prison standards (it also noted, in passing, possible concerns regarding fair trial rights).[103] In coming to this conclusion, the court concluded that while EU organs command Atalanta, the participating national naval forces retain concrete authority with respect to the transfer of suspects and, thus, the responsibility to uphold the obligations under the ECHR.[104] Thus, surrender to Somalia has in some instances been ruled out as an option by ECHR states parties due to concerns that pirates could risk torture and capital punishment.[105] On the other hand, at least one state, France, has reportedly handed over suspected pirates to

---

[98]   See the European Court of Human Rights, *Medvedyev v France*, Appl. No. 3394/03, Judgment, 10 July 2009.

[99]   E.g. the European Court of Human Rights, *Saadi v Italy* [GC], Appl. No. 37201/06, Judgment, 28 February 2008, paras 125 and 138.

[100]   European Court of Justice, *Othman (Abu Qatada) v United Kingdom*, Appl. No. 8139/09, Judgment, 17 January 2012, paras 231–233 and 258–262.

[101]   E.g. the European Court of Human Rights, *Babar Ahmad and Others v United Kingdom*, Appl. Nos 24027/07, 11949/08, 36742/08, 66911/09 and 67354/09, Judgment, 10 April 2012, paras 200–215.

[102]   European Court of Human Rights, *Soering v United Kingdom*, Appl. No. 14038/88, Judgment, 7 July 1989, para. 111.

[103]   Court of Administrative Law in Cologne (Verwaltungsgericht Köln), Case No. 25 K 4280/09, Decision, 11 November 2011 <http://www.justiz.nrw.de/nrwe/ovgs/vg_koeln/j2011/25_K_4280_09urteil20111111.html> (in German) accessed 2 February 2012. However, the Court dismissed claims that the arrest and detention of the petitioner by a German frigate in the Gulf of Aden were unlawful.

[104]   *Ibid.*, paras 57–58.

[105]   See, e.g., the discussion of the *Absalon* episode in this volume, Chapter 6.7.

Somalia as a standard practice.[106] Such questions are not unique to ECHR parties; similar issues regarding torture, the death penalty and non-refoulment may also arise under the International Covenant on Civil and Political Rights, or the Convention Against Torture.[107]

Human rights concerns have been one important motivation for the conclusion of the memoranda of understanding with Kenya and other regional states. The EU Joint Action requires that third state transfers take place 'in a manner consistent with international law, notably international law of human rights',[108] and the subsequent memoranda include detailed provisions for the protection of the transferred persons' human rights.[109] Hence, the schemes established for transfer from EU NAVFOR to regional states are meant to satisfy (at least) the same human rights obligations that the European states have with respect to extradition. Whether the justice systems in the regional states, particularly in Kenya, meet the required standards is, nonetheless, a contested issue.[110]

8.8.3   Collecting Evidence (Mutual Legal Assistance)

Normally, military forces are not accustomed to gathering and preserving evidence for criminal proceedings. An additional challenge is that it is often not clear from the outset where proceedings will take place and thus which procedural rules should be followed. Since, typically, pirates throw their weapons overboard when approached by military forces, methods that secure evidence in spite of this practice must be employed. In addition, witness testimony from sailors of an attacked (or hijacked)

---

[106] See 'French Warship Thwarts Pirate Attack' (*NPR News*, 6 January 2009) <http://www.npr.org/templates/story/story.php?storyId=99036159> accessed 1 May 2012 (referring to an agreement between France and the Transitional Government of Somalia).

[107] International Covenant on Civil and Political Rights (adopted 16 December 1966, entered force 23 March 1976) 999 UNTS 171; Convention Against Torture and Other Cruel, Inhuman or Degrading Treatment or Punishment (adopted 10 December 1984, entered into force 26 June 1987) 1465 UNTS 85. See Guilfoyle, *supra* note 95, 153–168.

[108] Joint Action 2008/851/CFSP, *supra* note 20, Art. 12(2). See also Joint Decision 2012/174/CFSP, *supra* note 25, Art. 1(3) (replacing Art. 12 of the Joint Action).

[109] EU–Kenya Agreement, *supra* note 39, Arts 3–4; EU–Seychelles Agreement, *supra* note 40 ; EU–Mauritius Agreement, *supra* note 40, Arts 3–5.

[110] Compare, e.g., Geiss and Petrig, *supra* note 1, at 174–179, and the highly critical Osiro, *supra* note 87.

ship or from members of the capturing force may be difficult to secure. Efforts to overcome these problems vary.

Evidence by way of MLA can be obtained under the rather sophisticated provisions of UNTOC[111] and the various regional agreements noted above. For example, UNTOC creates possibilities for assistance in the form of video conferencing.[112] Nevertheless, in practice MLA is often slow and hampered by manifold grounds for refusal, such as strict double criminality conditions. Since the main rule is that the request shall be executed in accordance with the law of the requested state, such assistance does not always produce results that are useful in the criminal process of the requesting state. Hence, a preferable practice is the one employed by EU NAVFOR whereby an 'evidence pack' is produced by the international forces, when possible, before the transfer of the alleged pirate.[113]

In December 2009, the IMO Assembly adopted a resolution on a Code of Practice for the Investigation of Crimes of Piracy and Armed Robbery against Ships.[114] It includes guidance on training of investigators, investigation strategies, how to deal with initial reports (including protection of the crime scene and securing evidence) and how to conduct the investigation. Various instruments have also encouraged so-called 'ship rider agreements'. A ship-rider is a law-enforcement official from one state who is embarked aboard another state's vessel with a mandate to authorize various actions (in accordance with the law of his or her home jurisdiction).

Regardless of the quality of the evidence gathering at sea or availability of mutual legal cooperation, however, the laws of the prosecuting state may hamper such efforts. This is the case in Kenya, where the law on evidence has been described as 'archaic'.[115] For example, Kenyan law requires witnesses to provide evidence in person and does not provide for photographic or video-based evidence, although the Court of Appeal has begun to conduct sessions via video.[116] Apart from ill-equipped courts and other problems, these challenges may hamper prosecutions.

---

[111]   Art. 18 UNTOC.

[112]   *Ibid.*, Art. 18 (17)–(18).

[113]   See House of Lords, *supra* note 34, 52.

[114]   Annex to IMO resolution A.1025(26), adopted on 2 December 2009 (replacing an older Code of Practice).

[115]   See L. Otto, 'Kenya and the Pest of Piracy' (Institute for Security Studies Situation Report, 22 February 2012) 2 <http://www.issafrica.org/uploads/22Feb12Kenya.pdf> accessed 1 May 2012.

[116]   See Osiro, *supra* note 87, 13 (fn. 129).

8.8.4   Transfer of Prisoners

Transfer of prisoners, upon conviction, to serve their sentence elsewhere is usually a rather straightforward matter. However, generally both states involved must agree to the transfer in question and procedures under international instruments normally afford wide discretion to the states concerned. In addition, the consent of the prisoner is often required. Even in the rare instances of agreements allowing transfer without the person's consent, the lack of consent could be held against the transfer since the basic objective behind such transfers – 'social rehabilitation of sentenced persons'– is likely diminished when the person objects.[117] Moreover, the only multilateral convention of relevance to Somali pirates on point is UNTOC, which simply states that states parties 'may consider concluding bilateral or multilateral agreements or arrangements' regarding prisoner transfers.[118]

It has been claimed that 'one of the greatest challenges to prosecuting Somali pirates appears to be determining where to incarcerate them'.[119] Apart from problems of capacity, the standards of prisons in the region are such that states, particularly European states, are often unwilling to transfer suspects to the countries in question due to human rights concerns. Extensive case law of the European Court of Human Rights addresses detention conditions and the treatment of prisoners, including issues such as solitary confinement, overcrowding, health rights and ill-treatment. With respect to cross-border cases, the Court has unambiguously stated that the protection against torture and other forms of ill-treatment in contravention of Article 3 ECHR applies 'equally to extradition and other types of removal from the territory of a Contracting State'.[120] Hence, it applies also with respect to post-conviction transfer of prisoners.[121] The above-mentioned decision by a German Court in November 2011 found that (at least the detention facilities of) the Shimo

---

[117]   See, e.g., Additional Protocol to the European Convention on the Transfer of Sentenced Persons (adopted 18 December 1997, entered force 1 June 2000), ETS 167, Preamble.

[118]   UNTOC Art. 17.

[119]   Ploch *et al.*, *supra* note 38, 35.

[120]   *Babar Ahmad*, *supra* note 101, para. 176.

[121]   See also European Court of Human Rights, *Veermäe v Finland*, Appl. No 38704/03, Decision, 15 March 2005.

La Tewa prison in Mombasa, Kenya, did not meet the required standards.[122]

The issue of prison capacity is also high on the agenda for the regional states accepting transfers of piracy suspects. For example, the EU–Mauritius transfer agreement was accompanied by EU and UNODC agreements on financial support to Mauritius' courts and prison sectors.[123] Likewise, the Government of Seychelles has consistently expressed concern over transfers of pirates for prosecution unless the issue of onward transfer of prisoners is resolved.[124] Consequently, in at least one case the Seychelles have declined a transfer of piracy suspects under its agreement with the EU due to a lack of prison capacity.[125]

International efforts have been made to improve the prison capacity and standards in the region. UNODC is tasked with the consolidation of international assistance to increase prison capacity, the construction of prisons, the provision of training for prison staff in accordance with relevant international human rights standards and the monitoring of compliance with such standards. The results of the 'Piracy Prisoner Transfer System' include new prison facilities in Hargeisa, Somaliland, and soon in Bosasso, Puntland, and plans for a new 500-bed prison in Garowe, Puntland, with an associated court, a prison academy, a prison farm and a ministry of justice building.[126]

In February 2012, the Seychelles concluded an agreement with the Transitional Government of Somalia and memoranda of understanding with Somaliland and Puntland on the transfer of prisoners, in order to deal with Somali pirates captured by the Seychelles' coast guard or

---

[122]   Court of Administrative Law in Cologne, *supra* note 103, paras 70–74. On UNODC efforts to raise prison to international standards see references below note 126.

[123]   Statement by High Representative Catherine Ashton on the signature of the EU-Mauritius Transfer Agreement of Suspected Pirates, 16 July 2011, EU doc. A 285/11.

[124]   E.g. 'International cooperation between Seychelles, UK and Denmark takes tough stance on piracy' (*MaritimeSecurity.Asia*, 31 January 2012) <http://maritimesecurity.asia/free-2/piracy-2/international-cooperation-between-seychelles-uk-and-denmark-takes-tough-stance-on-piracy/> accessed 1 May 2012.

[125]   'Seychelles refuse to take Somali pirates held by Danes' (*Reuters*, 17 January 2012) <http://www.reuters.com/article/2012/01/17/denmark-somalia-pirates-idUSL6E8CH3XH20120117> accessed 20 April 2012.

[126]   UNODC, *Counter-Piracy Programme: Support to the Trial and Related Treatment of Piracy Suspects*, February 2012 <http://www.unodc.org/unodc/en/piracy/index.html?ref=menuside> accessed 21 April 2012.

transferred to the Seychelles by other states.[127] The relevant Somali authorities' acceptance is required in each individual case.[128] Under these agreements, the first convicted pirates were transferred from the Seychelles to Somaliland's Hargeisa prison in March 2012.[129]

The transfer of prisoner agreements should be seen as a step towards creating a system to enable Somali pirates to be prosecuted regionally. However, transferring prisoners to Somaliland and Puntland requires specific agreement with the local authorities and will not apply to all regional cases. Nonetheless, it would generally be a great relief to prosecuting regional states if convicted pirates could be transferred to Somalia to serve their sentences. With appropriate prison conditions in place, this would also serve the rehabilitation rationale behind prisoner transfer schemes in general. Hence, Mauritius is considering negotiating an agreement with Somali authorities and this would also be a reasonable move for Kenya, which has not taken steps in this direction.[130] Recently a Kenyan court reportedly declined to allow 11 convicted Somali pirates to serve their sentences in Somalia, and instead ordered deportation upon completion of their sentences.[131] This may, perhaps, be attributed to the absence of an appropriate prisoner transfer agreement. One should note, however, that the transfer for prosecution agreements that the EU and individual states have concluded with Kenya and other regional states generally require that the naval state gives its consent before any onward transfer either for trial or imprisonment in a third state.[132]

---

[127] E.g. 'Somali pirates to be returned from Seychelles' (*afrol News*, 11 February 2012) <http://www.afrol.com/articles/37299> accessed 20 April 2012.

[128] Report of the UN Secretary-General on specialized anti-piracy courts in Somalia and other States in the region ('Specialized Courts Report'), 20 January 2012, UN Doc. S/2012/50, para. 57.

[129] Foreign and Commonwealth Office (UK), 'Minister for Africa welcomes the transfer of pirates to Somaliland' (29 March 2012) <http://ukinsomalia.fco.gov.uk/en/news/?view=News&id=747517482> accessed 20 April 2012.

[130] Specialized Courts Report, *supra* note 128, paras 80 and 97.

[131] 'Piracy: Mombasa court hands 20-year jail term to 11 Somalis' (*Business Daily*, 20 April 2012) <http://www.businessdailyafrica.com/Corporate+News/Mombasa+court+hands+20+year+jail+term+to+11+Somali+pirates/-/539550/1389718/-/xokv1n/-/> accessed 21 April 2012.

[132] Regarding Kenya, see: Specialized Courts Report, *supra* note 128, para. 78.

8.8.5   Proceeds of Crime

In addition to more traditional forms of international criminal
cooperation – extradition, mutual legal assistance and transfer of prisoners – the search-light is increasingly put on proceeds of crime. This is a
general international trend as well as a trend in the context of Somali
piracy.[133] The aim would be to counter illicit financial flows linked to
piracy by seeking to establish a mechanism and procedures to identify,
freeze and seize illicit financial flows from piracy, leading to the
prosecution of the financiers and sponsors of piracy. Of course, neither
the culprits nor the proceeds are confined to Somalia.[134]

Efforts of this kind, however, fall outside the UNCLOS and SUA
regimes and would require the application of other cooperation arrangements, in particular those originally developed in the fight against money
laundering or terrorism financing.[135] Apart from legal difficulties with
respect to applying existing agreements or arrangements to piracy, it has
been noted that the countries in the region lack the necessary legislation
and capacity.[136] Although such moves might represent a move towards
addressing the leaders and not only the 'foot soldiers', the necessary
cooperation is still in its infancy.

8.9   CONCLUDING REMARKS

We would like again to emphasize the differences between using military
forces in a conflict scenario and conducting military operations with a
view to initiating criminal proceedings. Even if the latter can be done by
the same personnel as the former, it cannot be done in the same way or
under the same rules. If piracy is to be treated, as we suggest, as a
criminal problem, much more attention must be given to the resulting
legal challenges. States detailing military forces to collective operations
must ensure that they have the legal tools necessary to perform a

---

[133]   See, e.g., Financial Action Task Force (FATF-GAFI), *Organised Maritime
Piracy and Related Kidnapping for Ransom* (FATF Report, July 2011) <http://
www.fatf-gafi.org/media/fatf/documents/reports/organised%20maritime%20piracy%
20and%20related%20kidnapping%20for%20ransom.pdf> accessed 1 May 2012.
See also See House of Lords, *supra* note 34, at 55–59.

[134]   E.g. Osiro, *supra* note 87, at 16 (recommending that Kenya should
address alleged Kenyan sponsors of piracy).

[135]   UNTOC contains useful provisions on international cooperation concerning confiscation (Arts 13–14) and on law enforcement cooperation (Art. 27).

[136]   FATF Report, July 2011, *supra* note 133, at 22.

law-enforcement job efficiently. International organizations, for example, the UN, EU and NATO, should verify that troop contributing nations have implemented into national law all relevant international law, including MLA-instruments, before letting them join. Just hoping that naval officers will somehow find a way through the uncharted waters of international, intra-national and national legal challenges is not enough. Doing so risks either the operation collapsing into the sporting but inefficient catch-and-release approach to suspects, or that naval officers – yearning for tactical effect – may dump the 'legal niceties' as so much unneeded ballast and set course for the well-known waters of armed conflict instead.

9. Reshaping maritime security cooperation: the importance of interagency coordination at the national level

Brian Wilson

9.1 INTRODUCTION

Somali piracy takes place in a vast ocean operating space with overlapping national authorities, gaps in jurisdiction and the involvement of multiple states and organizations seeking to repress it. In this context, cooperation between states is crucial. Recent efforts to repress piracy also demonstrate that cooperation *within* each state is equally crucial. Maritime security operations may involve extensive cooperation and coordination between different governmental agencies if they are to succeed. As discussed in previous chapters, the response to Somali piracy has primarily been a law enforcement effort that brings with it particular challenges for the naval states involved.

While the onus of resolving maritime threats traditionally has rested with naval assets, the spectrum of responses now extends into diplomatic, investigative and judicial venues. The intersection of agencies with separate command structures, operating procedures and authorities poses considerable coordination challenges, such as resolving which agency is lead for investigation, where will evidence be stored, where will pirates be detained, which nation will prosecute and where will convicted pirates be confined. In response to these issues, collaborative constructs have emerged that facilitate information sharing and unity of effort.

In the United States, a Presidentially-approved plan creates a process for interagency coordination in the response to maritime threats. The Maritime Operational Threat Response (MOTR) Plan has guided US action following piratical attacks against the *Maersk Alabama, Magellan Star* and *Quest*, among others. This chapter will explore the MOTR Plan's origins, its implementation, specific cases and lessons learned.

9.2 HISTORIC CONTEXT

9.2.1 Introduction

A mishandled defection request in 1970 highlighted an arcane, but vitally important, aspect of governance: how to ensure the timely alignment of federal agency action. At that time, there was no national-level coordination process in the United States, nor any mechanism to ensure operational and policy issues were expeditiously raised to proper levels within, and across, relevant departments and agencies. The lessons learned from the attempted defection of Simas Kudirka have, perhaps surprisingly, relevance today in counter-piracy operations.

Forty years ago, a Lithuanian sailor desperate to defect to the United States leapt spectacularly from the deck of a Soviet ship onto a US Coast Guard cutter.[1] After discussions among numerous US Government departments failed to produce a coordinated response, the Commanding Officer of the Coast Guard cutter was ordered by his operational commander to return the 40-year old sailor to the Soviets. Kudirka did not go easily though; several Soviet 'seamen' had to beat him into submission; all while aboard a US military vessel off Martha's Vineyard, Massachusetts. When the Soviets finally departed the Coast Guard ship with their would-be defector wrapped in a blood-drenched blanket, it was widely believed Kudirka was dead.[2]

News of the event spread quickly. A *New York Times* editorial from 1970 asserted the forcible removal of Kudirka is 'surely one of the most disgraceful incidents ever to occur on a ship flying the American flag'. The *Washington Post* declared, 'No more sickening and humiliating an episode in international relations has taken place within memory … '

Presidential outrage and Congressional hearings soon followed.[3] Bad decisions certainly led to the outcome, but equally bad coordination among federal departments contributed as well. The details of the Kudirka story are well documented, as the subject of eight Congressional

---

[1] 'Attempted Defection by Lithuanian Seaman Simas Kudirka', Hearings before the Subcommittee on State Department Organization and Foreign Operations of the Committee on Foreign Affairs, House of Representatives, 91st Congress, Second Session (7, 8, 9, 14, 17, 18 and 29 December 1970) ('Kudirka Congressional Hearings'). See also Secretary of Transportation John A. Volpe, 'Attempted Defection by a Crew Member of the Sovetskaya Litva', Memorandum for the President (2 December 1970).

[2] Algis Ruksenas, *Day of Shame* (David McKay Company 1973) 247–248.

[3] *Ibid.*, 268–272.

hearings,[4] two books[5] and an Emmy-award winning TV movie starring Alan Arkin.[6]

In 1970, cell phones, instant messaging, e-mails and BlackBerries were still years away. There existed few 24-hour national-level federal agency command/operations centers and certainly no clear guidance regarding when departments should consult with one another. What emerged from the ashes of the Kudirka incident was a Presidential Directive mandating a stronger, more integrated interagency process charged with ensuring that critical operational decisions were made with input from all relevant government stakeholders.[7] The salience of the Kudirka incident lives on through a contemporary mechanism for interagency coordination, the MOTR Plan, discussed in detail below.[8]

9.2.2 Simas Kudirka

Kudirka found himself off Martha's Vineyard on 23 November 1970, because the Soviets had finally agreed to a bilateral meeting to discuss the volume of yellowtail flounder[9] being snagged by their fisherman off

---

[4] On 3 December 1970, at one of the eight Congressional hearings (Kudirka Congressional Hearings, *supra* note 1, 2) Representative Wayne Hays remarked: 'I concur with the cartoon in the Washington Evening Star of last night, which … showed a big blot on the Statute of Liberty, and the Statute of Liberty hiding its eyes and shedding tears … I repeat, this is a reprehensible incident, and I think that Congress and the American people have a right to know what happened, and I propose to find out one way or another.'

[5] Ruksenas, *supra* note 2. See also: S. Kudirka and L. Eichel, *For those Still at Sea: The Defection of a Lithuanian Sailor: Simas Kudirka's Own Story of His Four-Year Journey to Freedom* (Dial Press 1978).

[6] *The Defection of Simas Kudirka* premiered 23 January 1978 on CBS.

[7] The interagency is both a process and community that involves multiple federal agencies or departments. The interagency has also been referred to as the operating space below the President and above departments. Studies conducted by the Project on National Security Reform are at <http://www.pnsr.org/index.asp> accessed 28 February 2012.

[8] The Maritime Operational Threat Response (MOTR) Plan, approved by US President George W. Bush in 2006.

[9] As the United Nations Convention on the Law of the Sea (adopted 10 December 1982, entered into force 16 November 1994) 1833 UNTS 397 ('UNCLOS') did not yet exist, there was no Exclusive Economic Zone, a 200-mile area of water off a nation's coast where, among other things, fishing laws could apply and be enforced.

the US coast.[10] Bad weather changed the plans for an underway meeting, causing the US and Soviet vessels to proceed to US territorial waters where they anchored next to each other.

Despite speaking four languages and training as a radio technician, Kudirka's job on the ship was to clean heads and move garbage.[11] At one point in the day, Kudirka threw a crumpled note,[12] hidden in a pack of cigarettes, onto the US Coast Guard cutter *Vigilant* manifesting his intent to defect to the United States.

The *Vigilant*'s executive officer immediately, and correctly, notified and sought higher-level guidance to the possibility of Kudirka attempting to defect by jumping into the water and swimming towards *Vigilant*: should the Americans try to beat the Soviets to the rescue; would Kudirka be treated as a deserter or asylum-seeker; do other US agencies/ departments need to be notified? The senior intelligence officer in the Coast Guard headquarters in Washington DC initially was not allowed to see the *Vigilant* message because he was not on the 'cleared list'.[13]

Operating errors on ship transmissions further delayed the dissemination of critical information regarding the situation. Finding the appropriate State Department contact consumed several hours. After finally reaching him, the State official refused to provide definitive policy or guidance to the Coast Guard, characterizing the potential asylum situation as a 'sticky question'.[14] US policy on asylum was not clearly delineated at the time,[15] but the State official neglected to share basic guidance for handling such a request.[16]

---

[10] Smith, 'Coast Guard Officers Relieved of Duties in Defector Incident' *New York Times* (5 December 1970).

[11] Ruksenas, *supra* note 2, 54. Kudirka's Baltic heritage and previous refusal to testify against a relative contributed to his job assignment.

[12] Undated photograph, Coast Guard's Historian's Office. Copy on file with the author.

[13] Ruksenas, *supra* note 2, 80.

[14] *Ibid.*, 86, 108–111.

[15] C. R. Mann, 'Asylum Denied; The Vigilant Incident' (1971) 23 *Naval War College Review* 4. On 23 November 1970, there was no Coast Guard regulation regarding asylum.

[16] Smith, 'Coast Guard Officers Relieved of Duties in Defector Incident', *New York Times* (5 December 1970): 'The State Department has acknowledged that the guidance it provided the Coast Guard on the day of the incident was less specific than it should have been.' However, the State representative added: 'Department officials were never fully informed of the details of the incident until the decision to return the sailor had already been made.'

Then Kudirka did the unexpected: rather than jumping in the water, he leapt from the deck of the Soviet vessel onto the *Vigilant*. Kudirka's jump occurred at approximately the close of the business day. A senior Coast Guard officer in the cutter's immediate chain of command, based on both the time of day and the responses from earlier, believed it would not be productive to again seek guidance from Washington DC. He then provided decisive, but inaccurate, direction saying that Kudirka is a deserter who must be returned if the Soviets make a request.[17] Because the *Vigilant*'s secure communications systems were inoperable, the ship used unclassified transmissions, easily accessed by the Soviets. Within minutes of the cutter's radio transmissions, the Soviet's requested Kudirka's return.

The *Vigilant*'s commanding officer continued to raise concerns to his chain of command until he was blasted with the following, unambiguous edict, which he followed: 'You have no discretion! You have your orders! Use whatever force is necessary! Do not let an incident occur!'[18]

The *Vigilant*'s captain told the Soviets, 'He's all yours.'[19] Kudirka sought to evade capture, but was apprehended by Soviet seamen on board *Vigilant*, who took turns hitting and kicking Kudirka, at times in front of the cutter's officers and enlisted crew.[20] Because the two ships had now separated from each other and were underway, the Soviets required Coast Guard assistance to transport the Soviets, with a visibly injured Kudirka, to their vessel.[21]

President Nixon reportedly learned of the incident through a newspaper article.[22] Indignation and anger soon followed.[23] In New Bedford, some merchants declined service to Coast Guardsmen and subjected

---

[17] Admiral William B. Ellis was on convalescent leave, but was nevertheless contacted at home by the 'acting' Commander of the First Coast Guard District, Captain Fletcher W. Brown, Jr. Admiral Ellis was administratively disciplined for disobedience of an order or regulation, receiving a punitive letter of censure.

[18] Ruksenas, *supra* note 2, 212.

[19] Kudirka and Eichel, *supra* note 5, 41.

[20] *Ibid.*, 43–47.

[21] *Ibid.*, 47.

[22] *Ibid.*, 60.

[23] Representative Samuel S. Stratton in a House speech ('Lawmaker Assails Admiral for Order', *Hartford Courant* (15 December 1970)) declared: 'It is obvious that the person primarily responsible for this shocking, stupid, and probably very costly fiasco was the rear admiral in charge of the Boston district of the Coast Guard, who gave the order.'

them to jeers. Even the captain's son was not spared; his fourth grade teacher asked him why his father returned Kudirka.[24]

Kudirka may have been assaulted and ferried back to the Soviet Union, but he did not die. Four years later, US President Gerald Ford shocked his staff, including Henry Kissinger,[25] by disregarding their advice and requesting that Kudirka be released in his first meeting with the Soviets.[26] The Soviets unexpectedly complied with President Ford's request.[27]

9.2.3 The Presidential Directive 27 Process

In 1978, in addition to the premiere of the TV movie, *The Defection of Simas Kudirka*, a Presidential Directive was approved for handling non-military incidents, such as the one involving Kudirka. While the Coast Guard and State Department developed guidance following the Kudirka incident, and the State Department formalized their policy in 1972 for 'dealing with requests for asylum', the directive issued in 1978 covered a broader scope of issues and was promulgated by the Office of the President.

The PD 27 process was written to apply to all non-military incidents which could adversely impact US foreign relations, but in practice became an interagency mechanism that was employed primarily to address the US Government response to migrants and drug traffickers in the maritime domain. PD 27 issues included diplomatic engagements with foreign nations, investigative challenges, prosecution options and operational concerns. The PD 27 process was extensively used, aligning US Government courses of action in more than a thousand incidents from 1978 to 2005.

When US Coast Guard assets suspected ships of carrying drugs, for example, they turned to the PD 27 process to secure interagency agreement on requesting flag state consent to stop, board and search the

---

[24] Ruksenas, *supra* note 2, 275.

[25] 'Henry A. Kissinger's Eulogy for President Ford' *New York Times* (2 January 2007) <http://www.nytimes.com/2007/01/02/washington/02cnd-ford-kissinger.html> accessed 28 February 2012.

[26] B. Werth, *31 Days: Gerald Ford, the Nixon Pardon, and a Government in Crisis* (Anchor 2007) 68.

[27] 'A White House Memorandum of Conversation regarding a September 5, 1974, meeting in the Oval Office, the White House, with President Ford, Dr. Henry Kissinger, Lt. General Scowcroft and Jerrold Schecter' <http://geraldrfordfoundation.org/documents/memcons/1552773.pdf> accessed 28 February 2012.

vessel. Requests for foreign flag state consent to US jurisdiction to enable US prosecutions also occurred through the PD 27 process.

The PD 27 process proved to be a pioneering mechanism to ensure unity of effort, but, as with any decision-making process, it was reliant on timely and accurate information as well as training/awareness at the operational level.[28]

9.3 THE MARITIME OPERATIONAL THREAT RESPONSE (MOTR) PLAN

Following 9/11, interagency alignment expanded significantly with the creation of a process to coordinate the US Government response to drug trafficking, illegal migrants and fishing violations, as well as piracy, terrorism, and other unlawful acts in the maritime domain. The PD 27 process addressed *non-military incidents*, whereas the new plan covered *maritime threats*.

Efforts to draft the MOTR Plan spanned six months, with approximately a dozen representatives from multiple agencies meeting weekly. The working group developed a plan that supported a 'whole of government' response to the full spectrum of maritime threats. Importantly, the document created a construct that both mandated coordination and protected agency authorities.

The MOTR Plan, a process that is *used by all, owned by none*, brings together multiple departments for discussions and decisions through integrated national-level command/operations centers. The rank, grade or position of an agency representative to MOTR is within the prerogative of the agency, but generally includes Commanders and Captains (and their civilian equivalents, GS 14/15s[29]), with Lieutenants and Lieutenant Commanders as well as Senior Executive Service, Admirals, Generals, Departmental Deputy Assistants and Ambassadors at times participating. Because MOTR is a flexible process that is unique to each case, coordination activities can be either unclassified or classified and have included as few as four participants and as many as 50.

---

[28] Regarding challenges with obtaining accurate information, Chairman of the Joint Chiefs of Staff and Secretary of State Colin Powell once noted that the first reports of an incident are almost always wrong.

[29] GS (General Schedule) 14/15s refer to civilian pay bands for senior US civil service employees.

The Presidentially-approved MOTR Plan[30] has already been used more than 1,000 times to ensure alignment of the US Government's response to piracy, drug trafficking, migrant smuggling, fishing violations as well as terrorist and other threats.

The MOTR process is best described by the response to the attack on the M/V *Maersk Alabama*, a cargo ship transporting food aid for Somalia. The boarding by Somali pirates represented the first time an American-flagged vessel had been hijacked in more than 150 years. Three pirates departed the ship with *Maersk Alabama*'s master, Captain Richard Phillips. Within hours of the hijacking, MOTR coordination activities were occurring. Representatives from the Departments of State, Justice, Defense (which included the Office of the Secretary of Defense, the Joint Staff and Combatant Commands), Transportation and Homeland Security, as well as the intelligence community and other government agencies participated.

Secure video teleconferences were held twice daily over six days to connect senior US Government officials on three continents. The MOTR process facilitated expeditious and transparent information dissemination, interagency concurrence on desired national outcomes and alignment of courses of action. Issues discussed included the legal authority for the proposed courses of action, timing of a response, public affairs posture and guidance, and potential logistics limitations of response assets, such as fuel capacity and weather conditions. Following the rescue of Captain Phillips by US Special Forces, collaboration was again necessary to bring the surviving pirate to the United States for trial. The development of an evidence package and a prosecution decision shortly followed, along with responding to medical issues and other matters, such as organizing transport, determining which federal agency would pay for the flight to the United States, and securing diplomatic support from partner nations for transit logistics.

Aligning federal action and securing international cooperation in the maritime environment is especially critical as most threats, particularly piracy, involve multiple countries. The US President's 2010 National

---

[30] The MOTR process was first implemented in 2005 when President Bush approved an *interim* MOTR Plan that is substantially similar to the *final* MOTR plan of October 2006. The MOTR plan is one of eight maritime plans, along with the National Strategy on Maritime Security, directed by National Security Presidential Directive 41/Homeland Security Presidential Directive 13, Maritime Security Policy, 21 December 2004. The Presidential Directive provided, in part, that the Maritime Threat Response plan would ensure the 'seamless United States Government response to maritime threats against the United States'.

Security Strategy noted: 'To succeed, we must update, balance, and integrate all of the tools of American power and work with our allies and partners to do the same.'[31]

The oceans comprise approximately 140 million square miles of operating space. In the United States, there are more than 350 ports, 95,000 miles of coastline, 110,000 commercial fishing vessels and millions of recreational boats. Data from just one of the agencies that could be involved in maritime issues underscores the need for a national coordinating mechanism in the maritime domain: In its 2009 annual performance report, the United States Coast Guard, 'removed over 350,000 pounds of cocaine headed to the United States … interdicted nearly 3,700 undocumented migrants attempting to illegally enter the United States', and conducted more than 5,400 fisheries conservation boardings.[32] Any one of those boardings or interdictions could involve multiple agencies (such as the Departments of Defense, Homeland Security, Justice and State) and result in national-level coordination activities in accordance with the MOTR Plan and its protocols.[33]

One case that required interagency coordination involved a foreign-flagged tanker en route to the United States. There were reports of potential links between the vessel's owner and terrorist organizations, the vessel was in poor material condition, it had not made a port call in the United States in approximately 15 years and was carrying liquid urea, a fertilizer which could have a legitimate commercial purpose or potentially be used as an explosive.[34]

---

[31]   White House, 'National Security Strategy', in *Strengthening National Capacity – A Whole of Government Approach* (2010) 14 <http://www.white house.gov/sites/default/files/rss_viewer/national_security_strategy.pdf> accessed 28 February 2012. See also *Ibid.*, 47: 'Many of today's challenges cannot be solved by one nation or even a group of nations. The test of our international order, therefore, will be its ability to facilitate the broad and effective global cooperation necessary to meet 21st century challenges.'

[32]   Released by Admiral Thad W. Allen, Commandant, US Coast Guard in February 2010, 9 <http://www.uscg.mil/posturestatement/docs/USCG_FY09_Performance_Report.pdf> accessed 28 February 2012.

[33]   The MOTR Protocols contain, among other things, operational guidance and contact information for specific types of threats.

[34]   Gary L. Tomasulo, 'Evolution of Interagency Cooperation in the United States Government: The Maritime Operational Threat Response Plan' (MBA Thesis, Massachusetts Institute of Technology, June 2010) 52–55 <http://dspace.mit.edu/bitstream/handle/1721.1/59157/659552377.pdf?sequence=1> accessed 28 February 2012.

The possibility of a national security threat led to interagency discussions regarding the desired national outcome and courses of action.
Agencies discussed the need to identify and respond to the threat as far
from the US as possible. Some agencies raised concern over disrupting
commercial trade, others questioned whether an at-sea boarding, versus
waiting for the ship to arrive in port, would damage an ongoing
investigation into a transnational criminal network and yet another
discussion focused on the implications of the boarding in bilateral and
international fora.[35] Under appropriate circumstances, a boarding based
on master's consent can be conducted rapidly to identify and, as
necessary, nullify a threat, yet this approach has considerable law
enforcement limitations, whereas a request for flag state approval may be
provided for in a bilateral agreement with the flag state of a suspect
vessel, but could be time consuming or result in a negative reply.[36]

Interagency participants agreed to courses of action that included
requesting flag state confirmation of registry and consent to the boarding,
which was expeditiously granted.[37] A boarding, inspection and interview
with crewmembers occurred approximately 900 miles from the United
States coast, which, along with other actions, enabled the US Government to confirm the legitimacy of the shipment and authorize its port
entry.[38]

In another case, information was received that migrants were being
smuggled inside a container on a foreign-flagged ship with thousands of
containers en route to the United States. Immediate action was necessary,
but waiting for the ship to arrive in the United States would take several
days. The MOTR process facilitated expeditious US Government action
that included requesting flag state consent for the US (Coast Guard) to
contact the ship's master and implement a plan to ensure safety of life,
while protecting sensitive investigative information.

The successful response to the *Maersk Alabama* hijacking, discussed
above, sparked efforts to create an office dedicated to supporting the
MOTR process. The Global MOTR Coordination Center (GMCC), a
Department of Homeland Security entity within the US Coast Guard, was
established in February 2010 to support the United States' interagency
MOTR partners and to serve as a national MOTR coordinator and its
executive secretariat. While the MOTR process has existed since 2005,

---

[35]   *Ibid.*
[36]   James Kraska, 'Broken Taillight at Sea: The Peacetime International Law
of Visit, Board, Search and Seizure' (2010) 16 *Ocean & Coastal Law Journal* 1.
[37]   Tomasulo, *supra* note 34.
[38]   *Ibid.*

the GMCC, a small office of six (four civilians and two active duty military officers), provides a number of functions for the interagency including facilitating coordination activities, maintaining the MOTR protocols, organizing the MOTR war games, and capturing lessons learned and best practices.

Another piracy case resolved through the MOTR process occurred in September 2010 following the US Marines rescue of the hijacked M/V *Magellan Star*. Issues included which federal law enforcement agency would lead the investigation, which state would prosecute, what regional states should be approached for logistics support, and where the suspected pirates would be detained pending resolution of those decisions. When migrants in a distressed vessel that capsized in the Gulf of Aden were brought aboard a US Navy vessel, the MOTR process was again employed with the Departments of State, Homeland Security and Defense to facilitate the migrant's transfer to land.

The MOTR process has been effective because of several key enablers: clear national-level guidance; strong agency involvement and support (at all levels); frequent training and informational briefs;[39] development of detailed 'protocols' (operational guidance); familiarization: MOTR participants generally work together on a daily basis and thus have awareness of issues, authorities and concerns of their interagency colleagues even before they are raised in a MOTR call; and the involvement of policy officials and both operators and the intelligence community in the process.

Agency representatives to the MOTR process improve awareness and training through an annual 'war game' that has been held at the Naval War College in Newport, Rhode Island and at the Army War College in Carlisle, Pennsylvania.[40] This two-day exercise addresses current and emerging issues, agency roles and responsibilities, as well as gaps and seams. More than 60 representatives from the Departments of Defense,

---

[39]   Representatives from the GMCC have conducted more than 100 training and familiarization briefs to ensure senior-level, as well as operational (e.g., command watch centers) awareness and support. Details of the MOTR Plan, the MOTR Protocols and historical examples are discussed. MOTR training is also occurring at military service academies to familiarize the next generation of military leaders with details of the plan and how it is implemented. In addition, GMCC representatives have met with officials from partner nations to discuss interagency coordination.

[40]   See the Naval War College's website for more information on war gaming: <http://www.usnwc.edu/Research–Gaming/War-Gaming.aspx> accessed 28 February 2012.

State, Justice, Homeland Security and Transportation, among others, participated in the August 2012 war game. Scenarios have explored the full array of responding to a threat, including potential courses of action, national-level policy decisions, legal issues, public affairs considerations as well as authorities, capability and capacity. Scenarios have included fictitious maritime attacks, including piracy, terrorism and those involving biological weapons, and threats affecting multiple countries. In meetings with partner nations, scenarios are often discussed to explore the details of the MOTR process as well as communication and collaboration.

The MOTR Protocols is a separate document that complements the MOTR Plan, by providing, among other things, pre-planned responses to specific types of threats, a script for calls, subject matter experts in each agency and agency command/operations center contact information. Interagency review of the protocols occurs periodically. This review process, and the document it produces, enables MOTR calls to occur with a level of consistency, as hopefully most of the difficult policy questions have been addressed.

9.4 CONCLUSIONS

Though piracy tactics vary throughout the world, and each attack is factually unique, the MOTR process provides a consistent, uniform and repeatable national-level framework to ensure alignment. A range of factors contributes to effective MOTR coordination activities, but the timely flow of accurate information is vital. Guidance on some of the information that might be required is presented below in the form of checklists. This information may be relevant to, among other things, planning the logistics or practicalities of a response as well as assessing its legal consequences (see further the discussion in Chapter 8 for a European perspective on some of these issues).

First, information that is crucial for senior policy officials on MOTR coordination activities following a piracy attack includes, in part:

- the location of the interdiction/incident, including, if available, the latitude/longitude and closest point of approach to or from nearby coastal states;
- how the agency became aware of the suspected pirates;
- what actions, if any, were taken to contact suspected pirates;
- what actions did the suspected pirates take when observed (e.g., did they show weapons, dump items overboard, wave, etc.);

- what was the intent of the naval contact with the suspect vessel (e.g., identification query, right of visit boarding);
- were there any reported piracy events in the area within the past 48 hours; and
- whether the government vessel(s) had video capability/video equipment on board and whether it was employed.

Second, to preserve the possibility of a prosecution, critical information and steps to take regarding suspects include:

- the identity, including name, family (father's/mother's) name, age, race, nationality and language spoken, and place of birth (parish, village, settlement, landmark, etc.);
- copies of any identity documents;
- photographing the subject(s) when first contacted (e.g., in their skiff);
- photographing the subject(s) in their own clothing;
- taking an inventory of all the subject(s) clothing and personal items;
- creating a diagram or documentation identifying the location of subject(s) during the incident (who was in each skiff);
- an assessment of the general medical condition of each subject(s), and photographs of subject wounds, if any, with scale;
- ensuring that silence is maintained amongst subjects; and
- further ensuring, absent exigent circumstances, that law enforcement personnel will either conduct or authorize interrogations.

Third, in dealing with victims, critical information to gather includes:

- the name, family name (mother's and father's), age, place of birth (parish, village, settlement, landmark, etc.), race, nationality and language spoken;
- a copy of any identity documents;
- photographs of victim(s) at the point of naval contact with them;
- an individual photograph of each victim;
- photographs of any victim's wounds with scale; and
- the next port of call for the victim(s).

Without such information it will be difficult to trace victims later, or provide contemporaneous evidence of the injuries they suffered in the course of a pirate attack.

Fourth, given that government personnel may be potential witnesses, it is beneficial to maintain and provide, through their chain of command, lists of personnel: directly involved in the incident (as part of their assignment); who observed the incident, but may not be directly involved; and who detained the suspects as well as those who maintained custody of the suspected pirates. Again, without such lists tracing important witnesses may become difficult or time consuming.

Finally, maintenance of a log book helps keep track of contacts, medical treatment, and related information regarding an interdiction or incident. Regarding equipment or items possessed by suspected pirates, it is critical to document and maintain:

- a legally proper chain of custody, which documents the seizing party, location, date, and time of seizure;
- a list of any communication equipment found in the subject(s) possession;
- a list of any boarding equipment (e.g., ladders, hooks);
- a list of any fishing equipment or fish;
- a list of weapons; and
- photographs of weapons on subject vessel, if possible.

Overall, institutionalizing collaboration between agencies and departments is more than just a maritime security challenge: it is a governance challenge. Interagency constructs have recently emerged in several countries – Canada, Australia, Philippines and India, among others – highlighting the value of bridging civil and military agencies. Forty years after the Kudirka episode, an enduring lesson is that communication, coordination, training and leadership best position a nation to respond effectively to maritime threats and, particularly, to piratical attacks.

PART III

Piracy and private law

10. International and comparative regulation of private maritime security companies employed in counter-piracy

James Kraska[*]

10.1 INTRODUCTION

This chapter analyzes the legal issues surrounding the use of private security companies (PSC)/private maritime security companies (PMSC)[1] and their use of private contracted armed security personnel (PCASP)[2] to protect commercial vessels. In particular, standards and rules are emerging for employment of PCASP to guard ships transiting the High Risk Area (HRA) threatened by Somali pirates in the western Indian Ocean.[3] Flag states, the shipping industry and the International Maritime Organization (IMO) have developed recommendations to states and guidelines

---

[*] The views presented are those of the author and do not reflect the official policy or position of the Naval War College or the Department of Defense.

[1] PMSC, or private maritime security companies are defined as 'Private contractors employed to provide security personnel, both armed and unarmed, on board for protection against piracy'. Interim guidance to shipowners, ship operators and shipmasters on the use of PCASP on board ships in the High Risk Area, IMO Doc. MSC.1/Circ. 1405/Rev. 1 (16 September 2011), para. 1.1.

[2] PCASP are defined as 'armed employees of PMSC'. *Ibid.*

[3] The High Risk Area (HRA) is an area that includes the Gulf of Aden, the Arabian Sea, and the western Indian Ocean; it is bounded by Suez Canal and the Strait of Hormuz to the North, 10°S and 78°E. When piracy activity in the HRA declines due to the Monsoon cycle, it is likely to increase farther south, off the coasts of Kenya and Tanzania, the Mozambique Channel, and in the area of the Strait of Bab el Mandeb and the Gulf of Aden. Piracy attacks have occurred at the outermost extremities of the HRA. See also: Best Management Practices for Protection against Somali Based Piracy (Version 4 – August 2011) (BMP 4) in IMO Doc. MSC.1/Circ.1339 (14 September 2011), Annex, chapter 2.

for the shipping industry to standardize practice and regulate the use of PCASP. The regulations concern the command relationship between the master and the armed security contractors, appropriate rules for the use of force against threats to the vessel or its crew, questions of liability, and carriage of weapons in the ports of other countries. Most of these issues fall within the prerogative of the flag state. Questions arising from the use by PCASP of weapons against persons on board a foreign-flagged ship, the presence of weapons or use of force in foreign ports, or perhaps in some cases, use of PCASP in territorial seas, may require diplomatic negotiation.

Amidst the work to develop international standards, chief master Sergeant Massimiliano Latorre and Sergeant Salvatore Girone, guards on board the Italian-flagged oil tanker *Enrica Lexie* and active duty members of the elite San Marco Marine regiment, were involved in a 15 February 2012 incident off Alappuzha near Kerala, India. The two Marines allegedly shot and killed two Indian fishermen, Ajesh Binki (age 25) and Valentine Jalastein (age 45), apparently mistaking them for pirates.[4] The tanker was traveling from Singapore to Egypt when the incident occurred. Although the ship was sailing in international waters, within hours of the incident Indian authorities from Kerala brought it into port at Kochi. Kerala chief minister Oommen Chandy charged that the firing off the Kollam coast was 'cold blooded murder'. The guards claimed the Indian fishing boat was behaving aggressively, and had ignored repeated warnings before the officers fired warning shots and then engaged with deadly force. On 19 February, the two guards were removed from the ship and taken into judicial custody, and held at Thiruvananthapuram Central Prison in advance of standing trial.

On 2 June 2012, the Marines were released on bail of about US $220,000, but remained in the state and surrendered their passports to the Kollam Magistrate Court, as Italy launched a diplomatic offensive to transfer them out of the country.[5] The Kerala High Court ruled against a

---

[4] 'Killing of Fishermen Cold-Blooded Murder: Chandy' *Times of India* (18 February 2012); 'Shipping Minister Says Italian Ship Firing "Unfortunate, Unacceptable"' *Times of India* (18 February 2012); 'Italy Sends Top Envoy to India over Ship Firing Arrests' *Times of India* (21 February 2012); 'Fishermen's Killing: Kerala Had No Authority to Detain Italian Ship, Centre Says, Oommen Chandy Disagrees' *Times of India* (20 April 2012). All at: <http://articles.timesofindia.indiatimes.com/> accessed 14 August 2012.

[5] 'Fishermen's Killing: Kerala HC Grants Bail to Italian Naval Guards' *Times of India* (30 May 2012) <http://articles.timesofindia.indiatimes.com/> accessed 14 August 2012.

claim of sovereign immunity asserted by the Italians. Justice P.S. Gopinathan stated that the shooting was 'cruel and brutal', and therefore 'cannot be said to be an act of sovereign function and the naval guards are not entitled to sovereign immunity'.[6] On 20 July 2012, the Supreme Court in New Delhi declined to stay the trial of the Italian Marines, but issued notices on their plea for quashing proceedings against them based upon clarification from the government that the incident occurred outside Indian territorial waters (and beyond the territorial jurisdiction of Indian authorities).[7]

Although the case of the *Enrica Lexie* involves public officials – members of the Italian armed services – it nonetheless serves as a point of departure for thinking about development of standards and rules pertaining to PCASP. Since several high-profile hijackings by Somali pirates in 2008, there has been a flood of PMSC offering various protection and armed security services for ships transiting the area.[8] In 2011, the Baltic and International Maritime Council (BIMCO) estimated that 5 to 10 percent of ships transiting the high-risk waters off the Horn of Africa employed PMSC.[9] Still more shipping carriers were using private security forces for training, establishing passive defensive measures on ships and assisting as lookouts during transit.

But the major shipping industry associations, including BIMCO and the International Association of Independent Tanker Owners (INTERTANKO) had long discouraged the use of armed guards on civil shipping

---

[6] 'Fishermen's Killing: Kerala High Court Dismisses Italy's Plea, Says Indian Courts Can Try Naval Guards' *Times of India* (29 May 2012) <http://articles.timesofindia.indiatimes.com/> accessed 14 August 2012.

[7] 'Supreme Court Declines to Stay Enrica Trial' *Times of India* (20 July 2012) <http://articles.timesofindia.indiatimes.com/> accessed 14 August 2012. Lack of territorial jurisdiction in the international law of the sea, however, does not necessarily preclude other jurisdictional theories, such as Indian jurisdiction over the flagged vessel of Binki and Jalastein, or of a passive nationality principle that would allow India to try foreign nationals for offenses committed abroad against its citizens.

[8] K. Houreld, 'Security Firms Join Somali Piracy Fight' (*Associated Press*, 26 October 2008) <http://www.usatoday.com/news/world/2008–10–26–2583935117_x.htm> accessed 14 August 2012; and P. Apps, 'Special Report: As Pirate Attacks Grow, Shipowners Take Arms' (*Reuters*, 3 May 2011) <http://www.reuters.com/article/2011/05/03/us-special-report-pirates-idUSTRE7421RY 20110503> accessed 14 August 2012.

[9] Guidelines for Shipping Companies on the Use of Private Maritime Security Companies (PMSC), Submitted by BIMCO (Baltic and International Maritime Council), IMO Doc. MSC 89/18/10 (22 March 2011).

due to legal and commercial liability and the risk that armed contractors might lead to an escalation in violence that would place more seafarers at risk. The pirates are fierce and adaptable, and as naval forces have become more aggressive about taking down mother ships the pirates have changed tactics by keeping some hostages as an 'insurance policy', even after payment of ransom. These hostages could be punished if private security used deadly force against a related pirate gang attempting to hijack another vessel.

Industry organizations, however, have come to recognize that armed security may be appropriate for particularly vulnerable vessels, used on a case-by-case basis, and after a thorough risk assessment. In March 2011, the International Parcel Tankers Association (IPTA), for example, reluctantly began endorsing the use of private security contractors on its commercial ships, but only as a stopgap measure to be used when military vessel protection detachments (VPDs) were unavailable.[10] One industry insider in London stated in confidence in November 2011 that three to five new PMSC were entering the market to supply services to ships transiting the HRA off the Horn of Africa. By the spring of 2012, it was estimated that 35 to 40 percent of the ships transiting the HRA embarked PCASP.[11]

10.2 PRIVATE SECURITY CONTRACTORS ON THE BATTLEFIELD

The wars in Iraq and Afghanistan, combined with a constrained US military force structure, encouraged the Pentagon to turn toward private military and security companies to fill tertiary roles, such as protecting diplomats, guarding key facilities, conducting training and providing logistics and services to US forces. The presence of private contractors on or near the field of battle, some of whom were outfitted to be virtually indistinguishable from the active duty military component, raised new questions about the role of PSC and their relationship to governments during hostilities.

---

[10] Employment of Private Armed Security Providers, Submitted by IPTA (International Parcel Tankers Association), IMO Doc. MSC 89/18/11 (22 March 2011), para. 6.

[11] Security Association for the Maritime Industry (SAMI) Programme and Standards for Private Maritime Security Company (PMSC) Accreditation, Submitted by the Marshall Islands, IMO Doc. MSC 90/20/11 (14 March 2011), para. 1.

10.2.1 Montreux Document

A Personal Security Detail from private security company Blackwater USA shot and killed 17 Iraqi civilians in Nisour Square Baghdad on 16 September 2007, highlighting the question of whether contract security guards were performing inherently military duties – in effect, as mercenaries. The incident in Nisour Square led to numerous investigations and civil and criminal trials in the United States, but the major impact of the shooting was to illuminate the need for standardized approaches to the use of private security.

The Blackwater incident occurred in the middle of an effort launched by the Government of Switzerland and the International Committee of the Red Cross (the 'Swiss Initiative') to craft regulations for PSC. The initiative was supported by the governments of Afghanistan, Angola, Australia, Austria, Canada, China, France, Germany, Iraq, Poland, Sierra Leone, South Africa, Sweden, Switzerland, the United Kingdom, Ukraine and the United States, and included a series of meetings from 2006 to 2008. The result was the release on 17 September 2008 of the *Montreux Document on Pertinent International Legal Obligations and Good Practices for States related to Operations of Private Military and Security Companies during Armed Conflict* (Montreux Document). The Montreux Document is the most comprehensive instrument on the management and use of private military security companies during time of war.[12] By reaffirming that states have a duty to ensure that PSC operating in armed conflicts comply with international humanitarian law and human rights law, the Montreux Document helps dissolve some of the mystery surrounding such organizations.

The document set forth 70 recommendations based on responsible state practice. States using PSC during wartime, for example, should verify their track record and examine procedures used to vet personnel. States should also ensure that the companies' staff members are made available and subject to criminal prosecution if they commit serious breaches of the law. Toward this end, states should enact legislation necessary to provide effective penal sanctions for contractors committing, or ordering to be committed, grave breaches of the laws of war. States have an obligation to investigate, prosecute, or extradite persons suspected of having committed other crimes under international law, such as torture or

---

[12]   Montreux Document on Pertinent International Legal Obligations and Good Practices for States related to Operations of Private Military and Security Companies during Armed Conflict, IMO Doc. MSC 89/INF.20 (8 March 2011), Annex.

hostage taking. In such cases, the punishment imposed should be commensurate with the gravity of the crime.

Although the Montreux Document only reflected existing law and practices and the agreement was not legally binding, it served as a reminder that governments have responsibilities of oversight over the private military companies that they employ – dispelling the myth that the companies operate in a legal vacuum.

10.2.2   International Code of Conduct

The International Code of Conduct for Private Security Service Providers (ICoC) built upon the Montreux Document.[13] The ICoC emerged from a series of workshops which culminated in a Wilton Park Conference in June 2009, where substantial agreement among PMSC was reached on a general framework. Thereafter, a draft ICoC was developed by members of the private security industry in cooperation with the Swiss Department of Foreign Affairs, the Geneva Centre for the Democratic Control of Armed Forces and the Geneva Academy of International Humanitarian Law and Human Rights. Representatives of PSC, industry associations, and governments from the United States,[14] the United Kingdom, Canada, and other nations and nongovernmental organizations (NGOs), participated in the discussions. PSC and NGOs will continue to have a role in shaping the implementation of the Code.[15]

The final version of the ICoC was completed in September 2010, and the document was formally signed at a ceremony on 9 November 2010 that was attended by 58 PSC.[16] By 1 February 2011, 71 companies had signed the International Code of Conduct; as of 1 June 2012, 404 companies from 57 nations had signed the ICoC. The Code is accepted by the leading industry organizations as well, including the International

---

[13] The Code maintains an Internet website <http:www.icoc-psp.org> accessed 14 August 2012, which serves as a portal for sharing information.

[14] J. R. Cook, 'United States Supports Conclusion of Code of Conduct for Security Companies' (2011) 105 *American Journal of International Law* 156. See also, US Department of State Press Release No. 2010/1608, 'Legal Adviser Harold Hongju Koh to Attend the Signing of the International Code of Conduct for Private Security Service Providers' (8 November 2010) <http://www.state.gov/r/pa/prs/ps/2010/11/150669.htm> accessed 14 August 2012.

[15] Letter from Ambassador Claude Wild, Directorate of Political Affairs, Swiss Federal Ministry of Foreign Affairs, 8 October 2010.

[16] 'Private Security Companies Sign Code of Conduct' (*Associated Press*, 9 November 2010) <http://www.businessweek.com/ap/financialnews/D9JCHI100.htm> accessed 14 August 2012.

Association of Maritime Security Professionals (IAMSP) and the Security Association for the Maritime Industry (SAMI). Although the ICoC is only open for signature to PSC, some governments have committed to making adherence to the Code a precondition for award of service contracts with private security.

The ICoC captures principles for PMSC in accordance with international humanitarian law and international human rights law. By maintaining a high bar, the ICoC is designed to influence corporate practice, such as the exercise of due diligence in selecting personnel and in serving clients. The goal of the ICoC is to establish a means of independent oversight and effective accountability of member PMSC. Governments that are contracting with private security providers can include provisions in the contracts that require performance in accordance with the ICoC. The ICoC can fulfill a preventive function, but it will be effective only insofar as it can be independently and effectively enforced. Accordingly, signatory companies are working with other stakeholders to establish by 2012 external mechanisms for governance and oversight. Oversight will include mechanisms for company certification of compliance, auditing and monitoring in the field, and a system of reporting alleged violations of the Code.

A multi-stakeholder Steering Committee (StC) was tasked with developing the oversight mechanisms, which was unfolding in 2011. At the end of July 2011, the StC had developed bylaws and a charter, and an operational plan was due by the end of November 2011. Working in tandem, companies and stakeholders were crafting discrete and measurable standards for providing security services based upon the Code. This effort was facilitated by development of additional resources by the Swiss Department of Foreign Affairs, including an implementation guide, a human rights impact assessment tool and guidelines for reporting suspected violations.

Because the ICoC is a non-state mechanism, it complements or supplements measures taken by national governments. By offering an additional device through which companies may be held to account, potentially including redress for victims, the ICoC may serve as a stabilizing force in conflict areas that lack governmental authority or recourse to established courts. Thus, the Code could come to serve as a grievance method and venue through which compensation for injuries, payment for damages, or even solatia, may be offered to injured parties on the ground, thereby promoting social cohesion and political stability.

10.3 REGULATION OF PRIVATE MARITIME SECURITY COMPANIES

The Contact Group on Piracy off the Coast of Somalia (CGPCS) and the IMO are working in tandem as the most important venues for international anti-piracy collaboration. The CGPCS is an ad hoc group of more than 50 states and international organizations that first met in January 2009 to develop and coordinate more effective anti-piracy measures.[17] The Contact Group has five working groups. While the issue of armed security generally falls within the domain of CGPCS Working Group 3 on self-protection of commercial vessels (chaired by the United States), it has also been a topic of discussion at CGPCS Working Group 2, chaired by Denmark, which is focused on increasing cooperation in legal matters, and particularly the extradition and prosecution of suspected pirates.

10.3.1 The International Maritime Organization

The IMO is the UN specialized agency for maritime matters. The organization has taken up the matter of armed security as an issue, beginning as an agenda item within the scope of its 2011 World Maritime Day theme: 'Piracy: Orchestrating the Response'.[18] The issue of maritime piracy generally falls within the ambit of the Marine Safety Committee (MSC) of the IMO, and the MSC is exploring guidelines for maritime PSC.

The IMO generally has cautioned governments and industry that the use of privately contracted armed security personnel may lead to an escalation of violence. The 86th session of the MSC, which met from 27 May to 5 June 2009, adopted two key documents concerning piracy in the HRA: MSC.1/Circ.1334, Guidance to ship owners and ship operators, shipmasters and crews on preventing and suppressing acts of piracy and armed robbery against ships[19] and MSC.1/Circ.1333, Recommendation to Governments for preventing and suppressing piracy and armed robbery

---

[17]   See further Chapters 3.3.6 and 5.3.1.

[18]   World Maritime Day theme for 2011: 'Piracy: Orchestrating the Response'; Progress Report, Note by the Secretary-General, IMO Doc. MSC 89/INF.25 (28 April 2011).

[19]   Guidance to ship owners and ship operators, shipmasters and crews on preventing and suppressing acts of piracy and armed robbery against ships, IMO Doc. MSC.1/Circ.1334 (23 June 2009).

against ships.[20] The decision whether to employ PCASP, however, is a matter for flag states to determine in consultation with ship owners, operators and companies.[21] Furthermore, PCASP is just one element of shipboard security, complementing the shipping industry Best Management Practices (BMPs) and other measures for avoidance, evasion and defense.[22] The guidance to governments advises that:

> The use of privately contracted armed security personnel on board ships may lead to an escalation of violence. The carriage of such personnel and their weapons is subject to flag State legislation and policies and is a matter for flag States to determine in consultation with ship owners, companies, and ship operators, if and under which conditions this will be allowed. Flag States should take into account the possible escalation of violence, which could result from carriage of armed personnel on board merchant ships, when deciding on its policy.[23]

In any event, all legal requirements of flag, port, and coastal states concerning armed security and private security should be fulfilled.[24] The Guidance to ship owners and ship operators explains: 'guards employed in port or at anchorage on different ships should be in communication with each other and the port authorities during their watch. The responsibility for vetting such guards lies with the security personnel companies, which themselves should be vetted by the appropriate authorities.'[25]

---

[20] Recommendation to Governments for preventing and suppressing piracy and armed robbery against ships, IMO Doc. MSC.1/Circ.1333 (26 June 2009).

[21] *Ibid.*, at Annex, para. 7. See also: Guidance to ship owners and ship operators, shipmasters and crews on preventing and suppressing acts of piracy and armed robbery against ships, IMO Doc. MSC.1/Circ.1334 (23 June 2009), Annex, para. 63. 'Masters, ship owners, operators and companies should contact the flag State and seek clarity of the national policy with respect to the carriage of armed security personnel'. *Ibid.*

[22] Flag State Framework for Implementation of Avoidance, Evasion, and Defensive Best Practices to Prevent and Suppress Acts of Piracy against Ships, IMO Doc. 90/20/14 (13 March 2012), Annex, submitted by the United States. The US submission repeats much of the information already contained in IMO Doc. A.1044(27) (20 December 2011). See also: BMP 4, *supra* note 3.

[23] Recommendation to Governments for preventing and suppressing piracy and armed robbery against ships, IMO Doc. MSC.1/Circ.1333 (26 June 2009), Annex, para. 7.

[24] IMO Doc. MSC.1/Circ.1334 (23 June 2009), para. 63 and IMO Doc. MSC.1/Circ.1333 (26 June 2009), para. 7.

[25] IMO Doc. MSC.1/Circ.1334 (23 June 2009), Annex, para. 26.

The 86th session of the MSC also established the Working Group on Piracy and Armed Robbery against Ships, and instructed the group to harmonize and update guidance to the shipping industry and recommendations to governments.[26] The Working Group on Piracy and Armed Robbery against Ships met from 29 May to 3 June 2009 under the Chairmanship of Ms Birgit Sølling Olsen of Denmark and updated the comprehensive guidance and recommendations related to maritime piracy.[27]

During the 87th meeting of the MSC, the IMO established the Working Group on Maritime Security including Piracy and Armed Robbery against Ships (MSPWG) to develop guidance to shipowners, masters and crews with respect to investigation of piracy attacks and guidelines for the care of seafarers affected by piracy.[28] The 88th session of the MSC was held from 24 November to 3 December 2010. The MSPWG clarified the use of Ship Security Alerts and developed guidance for company security officers.[29] The MSPWG built upon the work of the 87th and 88th sessions of the MSC, and provided additional draft text for consideration at the 89th session, which met from 11 to 20 May 2011.[30]

In preparation for the 89th session of the MSC, the Cook Islands suggested that the MSC should develop standards for oversight and accountability for privately contracted armed security personnel engaged in the commercial maritime sector.[31] The Cook Islands forwarded the ICoC to serve as a basis for the IMO to develop formal guidelines and a Code of Conduct for the regulation of privately contracted armed security personnel in the maritime sector:

> While it is recognized that piracy and armed robbery against ships is a criminal activity and thus does not come under the ambit of the law of armed conflict; that the repression of piracy and armed robbery against ships was not

---

[26] Report of the Maritime Safety Committee on its Eighty-sixth Session, IMO Doc. MSC 16/26 (12 June 2009), para. 18.43.

[27] Report of the Working Group Part I, IMO Doc. MSC 86/WP.7 (3 June 2009) and Report of the Working Group Part II, IMO Doc. MSC 86/WP.7/Add.1 (4 June 2009).

[28] Report of the Maritime Safety Committee on its Eighty-seventh Session, IMO Doc. 87/26 (25 May 2010), paras 19.59–19.63.

[29] Report of the Maritime Safety Committee on its Eighty-eighth Session, IMO Doc. MSC 88/26 (15 December 2010), paras 18.52–18.54.

[30] Report of the Maritime Safety Committee on its Eighty-ninth Session, IMO Doc. MSC 89/25 (27 May 2011).

[31] International Code of Conduct for Private Security Providers, Submitted by the Cook Islands, IMO Doc. MSC 89/18/1 (7 May 2011).

considered in the development of the ICoC; and that measures relating to 'armed conflict' may not be appropriate for the civilian maritime sector, it is clear that there is an urgent need to regulate the privately contracted armed security personnel that are marketing their services to an increasingly desperate shipping community.

While the ICoC relates to the use and self-regulation of private military and security companies (PMSCs) in areas of land-based armed conflict and is a non-State mechanism, the Cook Islands believes that the ICoC could be used as the basis for the Organization to develop more formal Guidelines and a Code of Conduct through which Governments and the Shipping Industry could properly and effectively regulate the use of privately contracted armed security personnel in the maritime sector.[32]

Singapore, supported by the Philippines, from which many merchant mariners come, and, joined by BIMCO and the International Chamber of Shipping (ICS), also submitted a proposed framework based on the ICoC to guide discussions at MSC 89.[33] The Singapore proposal called for the MSC to discuss the need for development of guidance for shipowners and operators of the employment of private armed security service providers on board ships to deter and counter piracy in the Gulf of Aden, the western Indian Ocean and the Arabian Sea. Philippines and Singapore suggested that the first line of defense against piracy attack remains the industry's BMPs,[34] but that additional guidance should be developed concerning the employment of private armed security. In the view of these states such guidance should cover:

- the process and criteria for the selection of the service provider and the armed security personnel that would be embarked on the ship;
- the terms of the contract for the use of armed security services, including any application for licenses that may be required under domestic laws;
- the delineation of roles and responsibilities among guards, master and crew on board the ship and the command and control structure;
- the principles underlying the use of arms or the rules of engagement; and

---

[32] *Ibid.*, at para. 3–4.

[33] Development of Guidance for the Industry on the Employment of Private Armed Security Service Providers to Deter and Counter Piracy against Ships, Submitted by the Philippines, Singapore, BIMCO, and ICS, IMO Doc. MSC/89/18/5 (8 March 2011).

[34] *Ibid.*, para. 3.

- contingencies that may involve damage to the vessel, injury to persons on board the ship, or loss of life.[35]

The combined Philippines/Singaporean submission culled elements of proposed guidance from various sources, including the ICoC, and was not intended to be exhaustive.[36]

Similarly, Liberia also proposed establishment of guidelines on the use of armed security personnel, and submitted draft guidance in an Annex to its submission paper that reflects the experience of the country's approach to the issue.[37] The Liberian Maritime Regulation provides that the ship's master assumes full responsibility for the safety of the members of the crew and passengers and is authorized with taking 'all necessary and appropriate steps in connection therewith'.[38] On Liberian-flagged ships, the master has 'overriding authority and discretion' to take deemed necessary action to protect the ship and its passengers, officers, crew, and cargo, as well as the marine environment.[39] Furthermore, the master has complete discretion to 'permit the use of armed security personnel or allow armed personnel from an escorting military vessel to board the vessel' in HRA.[40]

Bahamas and the Marshall Islands recommended creation of an international maritime security service industry association to which flag states might choose to refer vessel operators seeking maritime security services and advice.[41] The two nations suggested that the association might abide by these ten basic requirements:

1. The association and its members must be resident in a state subject to the Montreux Document, which addresses substantive legal concerns, such as the status of private military and security companies' personnel under the 1949 Geneva Conventions, individual accountability for misconduct in different jurisdictions, and the authorities' duty to oversee and screen the actions of firms for potential misconduct.

---

[35] *Ibid.*, at Annex.

[36] *Ibid.*, para. 7.

[37] Use of Armed Security on Board Vessels, Submitted by Liberia, IMO Doc. MSC 89/18/6 (8 March 2011).

[38] *Ibid.*, at para. 8.

[39] *Ibid.*

[40] *Ibid.*

[41] The Need for More Proactive Protective Measures, IMO Doc. MSC 89/18/7 (8 March 2011), para. 9.

2. The association must be signatory to the ICoC.
3. The association should represent the collective interests of member providers of maritime security services; equipment, technology and hardware; maritime security training establishments and maritime security operatives as a professional body.
4. The association should promote close cooperation by interfacing with international and national bodies including government bodies (such as the military); shipping associations; oil and gas and other offshore operators; port authorities and legal and insurance bodies involved in maritime security.
5. The association should set and maintain clear minimum standards of acceptable maritime security service and professionalism and equipment, technology and hardware provision through an established Code of Conduct and appropriate Rules for the Use of Armed Force that are easily recognized by the maritime industry.
6. The association should vet each potential member and their operatives at least in accordance with compliance with the International Ship and Port Facility Security (ISPS) Code, the International Convention for the Safety of Life at Sea (SOLAS) 1974, the 1982 United Nations Convention on the Law of the Sea (UNCLOS), associated standards of the International Organization for Standardization (ISO) and Voluntary Human Rights Principles.
7. The association should provide the framework for training, certification, competence and recruitment.
8. The association should establish a 24/7 maritime security legal service center to provide legal advice to all parties.
9. The association should comply with all applicable competition law (competition, antitrust and similar laws) of all countries in which the association is active.
10. The association should have developed a formal, standardized maritime security company engagement agreement, which will provide flag states with a common contract that could be a prerequisite to the engagement of maritime security companies by vessel operators.[42]

The IPTA, which represents chemical and parcel tanker shipping industry at the IMO, has warmed to the idea of PMSC to protect its ships. The IPTA submitted a paper to MSC 89 that reflected a 'change of heart' constituting an 'almost total reversal of opinion' on the employment of

---

[42] *Ibid.*, para. 10.

armed guards on board its ships.[43] The chemical and parcel tankers operated by IPTA members are generally relatively smaller, slower ships with a low freeboard when fully laden.[44] The configuration of these ships makes them especially vulnerable to pirate attacks, and many IPTA member ships have been hijacked over the past few years. The IPTA had been opposed to the use of armed guards based on a desire to avoid escalation of violence, and the volatile cargoes of chemical tankers made the prospect of a firefight especially dangerous.[45]

Many IPTA members use PMSC to protect their ships, due to the changing nature of the threat in the Indian Ocean. First, Somali pirates are using 'mother ships' to extend their reach well beyond the Somali Basin.[46] Second, the pirates have increased the level of violence, negating the argument about avoiding a firefight. 'Pirates now fire indiscriminately upon vessels.'[47] Finally, unlike in past hostage negotiations, there currently is less assurance that the pirates will not harm the crew, and reports of torture or murder of seafarers are increasing.[48]

Similarly, although BIMCO appears even more reluctant than the IPTA to endorse the use of PMSC, the organization suggests that there is an urgent need for guidance on the employment of armed guards on board merchant ships. BIMCO produced a draft outline endorsed by the Working Group 3 of the CGPCS titled 'Guidelines for shipping companies on the use of private maritime security companies (PMSC)'.[49] The draft guidelines were presented at IMO and reflected a shift in attitude by industry toward PCASP, and provided text for development of the IMO guidelines that followed.[50]

---

[43] Employment of Private Armed Security Providers, Submitted by the International Tankers Parcel Association, IMO Doc. MSC/89/18/11 (22 March 2011), para. 4.

[44] *Ibid.*, para. 2.

[45] *Ibid.*, para. 3.

[46] *Ibid.*, para. 4.

[47] *Ibid.*

[48] *Ibid.*, para. 5.

[49] Guidelines for Shipping Companies on the Use of Private Maritime Security Companies (PMSC), Submitted by BIMCO (Baltic and International Maritime Council), IMO Doc. MSC 89/18/10 (22 March 2011), para. 5. Similar rules later were reflected in Flag State Framework for Implementation of Avoidance, Evasion, and Defensive Best Practices to Prevent and Suppress Acts of Piracy against Ships, submitted by the United States, IMO Doc. 90/20/14 (13 March 2011), Annex.

[50] *Ibid.*

In concluding the 89th session, the MSC reiterated the importance of current standards on the carriage of firearms on board merchant ships, provided in the *Recommendations to Governments for preventing and suppressing piracy and armed robbery against ships*[51] and in the *Guidance to shipowners and ship operators, shipmasters and crews on preventing and suppressing acts of piracy and armed robbery against ships.*[52] Next, the MSC considered four courses of action to proceed with regulation of PMSC: (1) developing guidance for flag states; (2) developing guidance to shipowners, ship operators and shipmasters; (3) developing guidance for both flag states and for shipowners, ship operators and shipmasters; or (4) regulation of security companies themselves, either in the form of a self-regulating security industry association (i.e., ICoC) or with IMO serving as the regulatory body.[53] Following extensive discussions in plenary, the MSC reaffirmed its position that it did not endorse the use of armed personnel on board merchant ships, a decision that is at odds with the prevailing trend in industry toward greater use of shipboard security personnel.[54] In the end, however, the MSC emphasized that the issue was one for the decision of flag states, and agreed that the priority at IMO would be to develop guidance for shipowners, as it was apparent that many flag states and their ships were indeed pursuing PCASP as a method of self-defense.[55]

The salient issues reflected in standing IMO guidance was affirmed, including:

- 'For legal and safety reasons, flag States should strongly discourage the carrying and use of firearms by seafarers for personal protection or for the protection of a ship';[56]
- 'The use of unarmed security personnel is a matter for individual shipowners, companies, and ship operators';[57]
- 'The use of privately contracted armed security personnel on board ships may lead to an escalation of violence ... Flag States should

---

[51]   IMO Doc. MSC.1/Circ.1333 (26 June 2009), paras 4–8.

[52]   IMO Doc. MSC.1/Circ.1334 (23 June 2009), paras 59–64 and Draft Report of the Maritime Safety Committee on its Eighty-Ninth Session, MSC 89/WP.1 (16 May 2011), para. 18.24.

[53]   IMO Doc. MSC 89/WP.1 (16 May 2011) Draft Report of the Maritime Safety Committee on its Eighty-Ninth Session, para. 18.36.

[54]   *Ibid.*, para. 18.37.

[55]   *Ibid.*, para. 18.39.

[56]   IMO Doc. MSC.1/Circ.1333 (26 June 2009), para. 5.

[57]   *Ibid.*, para. 6.

take into account the possible escalation of violence which could result from carriage of armed personnel on board merchant ships, when deciding on its policy';[58] and

- 'Flag States should provide clarity of their policy on the use of such teams on board vessels entitled to fly their flag.'[59]

In addition to the MSC, the IMO Working Group on Ensuring Security in and Facilitating International Trade of the Facilitation Committee (FAL) also addressed the issue of PMSC and PCASP. The 37th session of FAL was held from 5 to 9 September 2011. A joint MSC-FAL circular contained a questionnaire on port and coastal state requirements related to PCASP on board ships transiting near the state or entering port.[60] In particular, FAL recommended that coastal states bordering the Indian Ocean, Arabian Sea, Gulf of Aden and Red Sea, distribute information on their relevant national legislation, procedures and best practices relating to the carriage, embarkation and disembarkation of firearms and security-related equipment through their territory and, as appropriate, the move-ment of PCASP.[61] Specifically, the questionnaire requested the following information:

1.   Does the state require notification for vessels intending to enter or depart port?
2.   Does the state require information regarding notification regarding firearms and ammunition carried on board ships intending to enter or depart the port, and if so, when and to whom should that information be sent?
3.   Does the state require information regarding notification on other security-related equipment (i.e., all specialized PCASP equipment) carried on board ships both transiting and intending to enter the port?
4.   Does the state require information regarding notification for PCASP on board vessels intending to enter or departing the port?
5.   Does the state have a point of contact to which notification of security incidents in territorial seas should be sent? Does the state

---

    58   *Ibid.*, para. 7.
    59   *Ibid.*, para. 8.
    60   Development of Guidance on the Use of Privately Contracted Security Personnel on Board Ships, IMO Doc. MSC/MSPWG 1/4/3 (12 September 2011), Annex (IMO Doc. MSC-FAL/Circ.[2], Draft Questionnaire on Information on Port and Coastal State Requirements related to PCASP on Board Ships).
    61   *Ibid.*, Annex, para. 5.

require flag state documentation regarding the authorization for use of PCASP, and/or the possession of firearms, ammunition or other PCASP security equipment, when transiting the territorial seas or contiguous zone before arrival or after departure?

6. Does the state have any import or export requirements in place for firearms and ammunition and other PCASP security-related equipment?

7. Does the state have any specific requirements in place related to the storage of firearms and ammunition and any special security-related equipment while on board ships when the ship is in the port, anchorage or territorial waters?

8. Does the state have any specific requirements in place related to the storage of firearms and ammunition and any special security-related equipment prior to embarkation or after disembarkation?[62]

In a submission to FAL, Brazil noted that the management of weapons and ammunition used by security personnel should be consistent with the laws of the flag state as well as the laws of the destination country.[63] Brazilian law does not permit foreign merchant ships with armed guards embarked to moor at Brazilian ports.[64] Brazil also requested flag states that have vessels with armed guards on board be notified of Brazilian law when they are in Brazilian territorial waters, whether moored or conducting innocent passage. Once in Brazilian territorial seas, the shipmaster of a foreign-flagged vessel should inform Brazilian Federal Police about existing weapons on board before mooring at any Brazilian port.[65] The weapons should be registered properly in the flag state, and sealed in a safe compartment by the Federal Police once the ship is moored or anchored. The Federal Police will produce a transcript identifying the weapons, and a copy of the list will be given to the master of the ship.[66] At the last Brazilian port of call, the shipmaster should advise the Federal Police, who will inspect the secured compartment to ensure that it is intact.[67]

---

[62] *Ibid.*, Annex.

[63] Development of Guidance on the Use of Privately Contracted Armed Security Personnel on Board Ships, Submitted by Brazil, IMO Doc. FAL 37/4/8 (13 July 2011).

[64] *Ibid.*, para. 5.

[65] *Ibid.*, at para. 6.1.

[66] *Ibid.*, at para. 6.2–3.

[67] *Ibid.*, at para. 6.4.

Dominica released to the IMO member states guidance on the use of PCASP on board ships flying its flag.[68] The country has detailed directives and marine safety circulars issued by the Dominica Maritime Administration (DMA) concerning armed security. Shipowners must carry firearms in secure-safe storage aboard all vessels that may transit high-risk waters, and may transfer private security guards to those vessels prior to entering high-risk areas.[69] Personnel employed as armed security guards are required to undergo background checks and training in basic ship operation, basic shipboard safety, security procedures and use of firearms.

Once the requirements are met, the DMA issues a Marine Security Worker Identification Credential (MSIC) and a Standards of Training, Certification and Watchkeeping (STCW) credential.[70] Armaments are prescribed by DMA and should be stored in dedicated containers subject to a two-key access control. The weapons remain on board ships and the PCASP embark and disembark as needed by the navigation route. Consequently, PCASP are not entitled to carry weapons when they are not on board the ship.[71] Finally, Dominica is developing a bilateral agreement or memorandum of understanding to facilitate port entry of Dominica ships carrying arms into foreign ports, and to facilitate shore leave and joining Dominica ships for security purposes for DMA approved security personnel.[72]

The 89th session of the MSC approved revised interim guidance to shipowners, ship operators, and shipmaster on the use of PCASP on board ships in the HRA.[73] Shipowners should consult with the flag state for guidance on and statutory compliance of their decision to emplace PCASP on board ships. Generally, the risk assessment to make a decision about private armed security should involve analysis of seven elements:

---

[68] Development of Guidance on the Use of Privately Contracted Armed Security Personnel on Board Ships, Submitted by Dominica, IMO Doc. MSC/MSPWG 1/4 (17 August 2011).

[69] *Ibid.*, para. 5.

[70] *Ibid.*

[71] *Ibid.*

[72] *Ibid.*

[73] Interim guidance to shipowners, ship operators and shipmasters on the use of PCASP on board ships in the High Risk Area, IMO Doc. MSC.1/Circ. 1405/Rev. 1 (16 September 2011).

1. vessel and crew security, safety and protection;
2. whether all practical means of self-protection have been effectively implemented in advance;
3. the potential misuse of firearms resulting in bodily injury or death;
4. the potential for unforeseen accidents;
5. liability issues;
6. the potential for escalation of the situation at hand; and
7. compliance with international and national law.[74]

Companies seeking to hire PMSC are urged to exercise due diligence, including investigation of the company structure and registration, ownership, financial position and insurance coverage, experience of senior management and quality management indicators, such as compliance with ISO accreditation.[75] The PMSC should be able to document criminal and background checks of its employees; the history of the employee verification and checks; the experience of the employees (such as military and law enforcement experience); medical, physical, and mental fitness and alcohol and drug testing records of employees; the experience of the employees in the certification and use of firearms; and a system for provision of security identity documentation, travel documents, and visas for personnel embarking and disembarking ships.[76] Detailed training records should also be made available.[77]

The shipowner may incur liability, loss or expenses arising from the deployment or actions of PMSC on board his or her ships. The potential impact on the shipowner may be considerable, particularly as it relates to armed engagements. Consequently, the shipowner will want to ensure that the PMSC has adequate insurance coverage for the duration of the contract to cover liabilities relating to personal accident, medical care and hospitalization, and repatriation of injured persons. Clear rules for command and control, particularly involving the use of force, should be included in the contract. The IMO states that the master of the vessel remains in command and retains overriding authority on board the ship.[78] Duties or the division of labor between the PCASP and the master and crew of the ship should be set forth in the contract.

---

74 *Ibid.*, para. 1.2, Risk Assessment.
75 *Ibid.*, para. 2.1.
76 *Ibid.*, para. 2.3.
77 *Ibid.*, para. 2.4.
78 *Ibid.*, para. 3.3.

Firearms, ammunition and security equipment should be maintained in appropriate containers.[79] A complete inventory of all firearms, ammunition, and security equipment available upon arrival aboard the vessel (including make, model, caliber, serial number and company end-user certificates and proof of purchase of all firearms and accessories), and details concerning type and amount of ammunition, should be maintained on board the ship.[80] Specific control procedures should be in place for weapons and ammunition, such 'areas where firearms may or may not be carried, together with the weapon state (e.g. unloaded & magazine off, magazine on and safety catch on and no round chambered) and what will initiate a change in that state or status of the normal rules'.[81] Finally, rules for the use of force should be promulgated, with both the shipowner and the PMSC having a clear and shared understanding of the circumstances under which force may be used, the type of force to be applied, escalation ladders and pre-determined warnings and protocols.[82]

The MSC also approved recommendations for flag states regarding the use of PCASP on board ships in the HRA. The recommendations are applicable only if a flag state determines that PCASP are appropriate and lawful measures. In deciding whether to authorize PCASP, flag states 'should take into account the possible escalation of violence' resulting from the use of firearms and carriage of armed personnel on board ships.[83] If PCASP are determined to be appropriate and lawful, the flag state should establish a policy regarding their use, which may include:

1.   the minimum criteria or minimum requirements with which PCASP should comply, taking into account the relevant aspects of the guidance set out in MSC.1/Circ.1405/Rev.1 on Revised interim guidance to shipowners, ship operators, and shipmasters on the use of privately contracted armed security personnel on board ships in the High Risk Area;

2.   a process for authorizing the use of PCASP which has been found to meet minimum requirements for ships flying its flag;

---

[79]   *Ibid.*, para. 3.4.

[80]   *Ibid.*

[81]   *Ibid.*

[82]   *Ibid.*, para. 3.5.

[83]   Revised interim recommendations for flag States regarding the use of privately contracted armed security personnel (PCASP) on board ships in the High Risk Area, Annex, IMO Doc. MSC.1/Circ.1406/Rev. 1 (16 September 2011), para. 3.

3. a process by which shipowners, ship operators or shipping com-
    panies may be authorized to use PCASP;
4. the terms and conditions under which the authorization is granted
    and the accountability for compliance associated with that author-
    ization;
5. references to any directly applicable national legislation pertaining
    to the carriage and use of firearms by PCASP, the category assigned
    to PCASP, and the relationship of PCASP with the master while on
    board; and
6. reporting and record-keeping requirements.[84]

Meeting between the 89th and 90th sessions of the MSC, the MSPWG
gathered in London from 13 to 15 September 2011, to continue development of guidance to industry and recommendations to governments on
the use of PCASP.[85] The updated texts were adopted at the 27th session
of the IMO Assembly, which met from 21 to 30 November 2011.

The Assembly took stock of the effort, cataloging the major authorities
produced by the organization. First, the interim recommendations for flag
states regarding the use of PCASP on board ships in the HRA had been
revised and published as IMO Doc. MSC.1/Circ.1406/Rev. 1.[86] Second,
the revision of the interim guidance to shipowners, ship operators and
shipmasters on the use of PCASP on board ships in the HRA was
completed, and it was released as MSC.1/Circ. 1405/Rev. 1.[87] Third, the
development of new interim recommendations for port and coastal states
with respect to the use of PCASP was completed and promulgated as
MSC.1/Circ.1408. Finally, the IMO adopted MSC-FAL.1/Circ.2 for the
circulation of a questionnaire on port and coastal state requirements
related to PCASP. The IMO Assembly adopted Resolution 1044(27) on

---

[84] *Ibid.*, at Annex, para. 5.

[85] Provisional Agenda for the Intersessional Maritime Security and Piracy
Working Group to be held from 9.30 a.m. on Tuesday, 13 September to
Thursday, 15 September 2011, IMO Doc. MSC/MSPWG 1/1 (11 July 2011).

[86] Revised interim recommendations for flag States regarding the use of
privately contracted armed security personnel (PCASP) on board ships in the
High Risk Area, IMO Doc. MSC.1/Circ.1406/Rev. 1 (16 September 2011).

[87] Interim guidance to shipowners, ship operators and shipmasters on the
use of PCASP on board ships in the High Risk Area, IMO Doc. MSC.1/Circ.
1405/Rev. 1 (16 September 2011). The second revision was released thereafter as
MSC.1/Circ. 1405/Rev. 2 (25 May 2012). The second revised edition contains a
new paragraph 3.2.5 that addresses the size and type of weapons that may be
employed in accordance with applicable flag state national legislation regarding
carriage and use of firearms.

30 November 2011, which approved interim recommendation for flag states.[88] The Resolution also endorsed the MSC's position that seafarers should not carry firearms on board ships, and that the decisions on the carriage of armed personnel – either government VPDs or PCASP – should be left to the flag states, once a thorough risk assessment was completed.[89] Resolution 1044(27) urged governments that have not already done so to:

1. decide, as a matter of national policy, whether ships entitled to fly their flag should be authorized to carry PCASP and, if so, under what conditions; and
2. in their capacity as port or coastal states, to decide on their policy on the embarkation, disembarkation and carriage of PCASP and of the firearms, ammunition and security-related equipment, and to promulgate it widely to other member states, to industry, and to the Organization.[90]

10.3.2   Maritime Safety Committee 90

The 90th session of the MSC met from 16 to 25 May 2012. The MSC conducted a high-level segment that considered three issues – guidance for PMSC and provision of PCASP on board ships; additional issues related to PCASP and littoral states; and guidelines on the use of firearms.[91] On the latter issue, the MSC reaffirmed its view that seafarer's should not carry firearms on board ship, but that the decision of whether to enhance security by other means, such as government VPDs or PCASP, was a matter for flag states to decide.[92]

During 2011, there was a significant increase in the number of shipping companies utilizing PCASP that adopted the guidance in MSC.1/Circ.1405/Rev.1.[93] Similarly, the number of flag states observing

---

[88]   Piracy and Armed Robbery against Ships in Waters off the Coast of Somalia, IMO Doc. A.1044(27) (20 December 2011).

[89]   *Ibid.*

[90]   *Ibid.*, para. 8(c)–(d).

[91]   Report of the Maritime Safety Committee on its Ninetieth Session, IMO Doc. MSC 90 (31 May 2012), para. 20.4.

[92]   *Ibid.*, para. 20.2.

[93]   Security Association for the Maritime Industry (SAMI) Programme and Standards for Private Maritime Security Company (PMSC) Accreditation, Submitted by the Marshall Islands, IMO Doc. MSC/90/20/11 (14 March 2012), para. 1.

MSC.1/Circ.1406/Rev.1 also increased over the year.[94] By the spring of 2011, it was estimated the 34 to 40 percent of the ships transiting the HRA had embarked PCASP.[95] The increasing use of private security throughout the year continued to raise concern that there was no international framework in place to better define their role. In order to help to address this shortfall, SAMI, a private industry group, developed an Accreditation Programme to establish standards for the vetting and accreditation of privately contracted maritime security on board ships.[96]

The SAMI Accreditation Programme is based on IMO guidance, the ICoC, and Best Management Practices of industry. The three-stage process includes due diligence, systems checks and site visits. The first stage – due diligence – includes assessing the financial, legal and insurance posture or position of the company.[97] Once a company has passed stage one, it progresses through stage two, which involves an in-depth analysis of the company's infrastructure, physical verification of premises, systems and documentation.[98] The third stage involves an operational review and checks conducted by SAMI. Once the SAMI review is complete, the PMSC can be accredited through the National Security Inspectorate, an independent third party certification body.[99] The SAMI certification includes closer examination of the following areas:

- company structure – the PMSC must have a clearly defined management structure; transparent ownership, full disclosure of company principals, the ability and willingness to disclose bankruptcy filings and criminal convictions;
- quality management – the PMSC must operate under a quality management system, such as ISO 9001 to protect the marine environment;
- records and data must be stored and obtainable, and a system of internal audits in place;
- A PMSC must be a signatory to the ICoC, having accessible, written codes of business practices and ethics. The company must cultivate a culture of ethics;
- financial soundness;
- insurance commensurate with the operational risk;

---

[94]   *Ibid.*
[95]   *Ibid.*
[96]   *Ibid.*, para. 1.
[97]   *Ibid.*, para. 4.1.
[98]   *Ibid.*, para. 4.2.
[99]   *Ibid.*, paras 4.3–4.4.

- tactical planning and information on class size and composition, organization, operations and equipment;
- operational support to the team, including intelligence, logistics, command and control; pre-mission briefs and local liaison officers.

The recommendation by the Marshall Islands to adopt SAMI standards in governance and use of PCASP was accepted by IMO in order to avoid having a 'patchwork' of conflicting national standards spread around the world.[100]

BIMCO submitted an intervention to IMO concerning development of PCASP standards by the ISO for certification of PMSC.[101] BIMCO and ISO set forth the strategic direction of the standards, and coordinated with private maritime security contractor GUARDCON to develop standard contract provisions for security guards on ships.[102]

Although flag states always retain sovereign authority over whether to permit PCASP on ships that fly their flag, BIMCO and the shipping industry Protection and Indemnity (P&I) clubs offered a standard contract for the employment of private armed security on board ships that flag states may use as a reference point.[103] Because the P&I clubs participated in designing the standard contract, the contract provides shipowners with comfort that the use of private security will not prejudice their P&I cover. The standard contract requires PMSC to carry adequate liability insurance. Rules on the use of force are set forth in the contract based upon the IMO guidance in MSC.1/Circ.1405/Rev.1 and MSC.1/Circ.1406/Rev.1 and input by industry from Working Group 3 of the CGPCS.[104]

---

[100] *Ibid.*, para. 6.

[101] ISO Standards for Guidelines and the Certification of Private Maritime Security Companies Providing Contracted Armed Security Personnel on Board Ships and Pro Forma Contract, submitted by the International Organization for Standardization (ISO) and BIMCO, IMO Doc. MSC 90/20/9 (12 March 2012).

[102] ISO Standards for Guidelines and the Certification of Private Maritime Security Companies Providing for Contracted armed security personnel on board ships and pro forma contract, submitted by the IMO for ISO and BIMCO, IMO Doc. MSC 90/20/9 (12 March 2012). See also: 'GUARDCON', A Standard Contract for the Employment of Security Guards on Ships, submitted by BIMCO, IMO Doc. MSC 90/INF.5 (13 March 2012).

[103] 'GUARDCON', A Standard Contract for the Employment of Security Guards on Ships, submitted by BIMCO, IMO Doc. MSC 90/INF.5 (13 March 2012).

[104] *Ibid.*, para. 3. See also, Flag State Framework for Implementation of Avoidance, Evasion, and Defensive Best Practices to Prevent and Suppress Acts

The standard GUARDCON document contains coverage of the essential features of agreement between the shipowner and the contractor, including the scope of the contractor's obligations and responsibilities in undertaking to provide armed security. The GUARDCON paper also provides that contractors should provide general advice to the crew and advise or assist with implementation of industry practices, in accordance with BMP4, that make the vessel less vulnerable to attack. During transit, the guards should monitor suspicious vessels and advise the master on security-related issues, including routing, liaising with United Kingdom Maritime Trade Operations (UKMTO) and Maritime Security Center – Horn of Africa (MSC-HOA) and other authorities along the route to be traveled. The PCASP should be appropriately trained, armed, have relevant prior experience, and be able to communicate effectively in English.[105] The master of the ship retains 'ultimate responsibility for the safe navigation and overall command of the Vessel'.[106] Thus, any decision made by the master 'shall be binding and the contractors undertake to instruct the Security Personnel accordingly'.[107]

GUARDCON tracks the aforementioned MSC circulars on the use of force, and is also consistent with customary international law and UNCLOS[108] more specifically. First, rules on the use of force (RUF) for private maritime security personnel should be in accordance with flag state law. Second, RUF also must conform to the regulations of ports and coastal state laws governing the storage and use of weapons, equipment, and ammunition.[109] The provision concerning notification to the coastal state begs the question as to how far coastal state authority extends over such vessels, but the IMO has not entered into the political thicket. The issue of carriage of weapons by embarked private contract security on board ships in innocent passage was one of a handful of high-level issues addressed on the first day of MSC 90.[110]

---

of Piracy against Ships, submitted by the United States, IMO Doc. 90/20/14 (13 March 2012), Annex.

[105]   *Ibid.*, Annex 1, section 2.

[106]   *Ibid.*, Annex 1, section 4.

[107]   *Ibid.*

[108]   United Nations Convention on the Law of the Sea (adopted 10 December 1982, entered into force 16 November 1994) 1833 UNTS 397.

[109]   BIMCO, Guidance on Rules for the Use of Force (RUF) by Privately Contracted Armed Security Personnel (PCASP) in Defense of a Merchant Vessel (MV), IMO Doc. MSC 90/INF.5 (13 March 2012), Annex 2, para. 3.

[110]   High-level Segment on Arms on Board, Note by the Secretary-General, IMO Doc. MSC 90/27/7 (8 March 2012), para. 4.2.

The World Customs Organization (WCO) has been collecting data from IMO member states concerning customs regulations regarding PCASP weapons. By MSC 90, the WCO had received 36 replies to its questionnaire on the subject – including 'four or five' responses from nations situated along the HRA.[111]

The RUF set forth a fairly common model for the use of force, guided by three principles: that graduated force should be used in a manner that is necessary and proportional; human dignity and human rights of all persons should be respected; and attempts at defense that are non-violent should be applied first.[112] Concerning this latter point, non-violent means include visual warnings, such as lasers or flares, use of the long range acoustic device (LRAD) or hailers to project audio warnings, and demonstrations of intent or resolve, including the use of hoses, release of objects to hinder the approach of pirate skiffs (e.g., nets or logs), and display of weapons.[113]

> The RUF should reflect that each of the Security Personnel shall always have the sole responsibility for any decision taken by him for the use of lethal force, including targeting and weapon discharge, always in accordance with the Rules for the Use of Force and applicable national law. Under most national laws individuals have a right to use reasonable force to prevent a serious crime and the right to use force in their own personal self-defense, and the RUF should reflect these rights as appropriate.[114]

Lethal force is a last resort. Graduated escalation should be used, and it includes warning shots, followed by disabling fire. Deliberate direct fire should only be employed against persistent attacks that have failed to respond to less lethal methods.[115]

There was great support at MSC 90 for development of international standards along the lines of the GUARDCON submission. The delegation from the Republic of Korea, for example, submitted an intervention calling for in-depth discussion on the need for mandatory standards or international guidelines, either by IMO or another international

---

[111]   Measures to Enhance Maritime Security; Piracy and Armed Robbery against Ships, Report of the Working Group, IMO Doc. MSC 90/WP.6 (23 May 2012).

[112]   'GUARDCON', A Standard Contract for the Employment of Security Guards on Ships, submitted by BIMCO, IMO Doc. MSC 90/INF.5 (13 March 2012), Annex 2, para. 7.

[113]   *Ibid.*

[114]   *Ibid.*, para. 5.

[115]   *Ibid.*, para. 7.

organization, to control the activities of PMSC.[116] Korea also supported promulgation of clear and unambiguous roles and responsibilities of all persons on board ships carrying PCASP, including delineation of respective authorities of the ship's master and security personnel.

India submitted for consideration a proposal that both private maritime security contractors or members of the armed forces providing security or protection on board merchant ships transiting in a coastal state's exclusive economic zone (EEZ) should be required to report 'details' of their presence on the ship.[117] The Indian suggestion clearly derived from the unfortunate incident involving lethal force against two Indian fishermen by Italian Marines aboard the *Enrica Lexie* on 15 February 2012, as the ship transited India's EEZ, as related in the introduction to this chapter.[118] The Indian proposal was not supported, however, and the MSC did not adopt it.[119]

The United Kingdom submitted an Action document on the accreditation of PCASP in the United Kingdom, but then in a corrigendum withdrew and reissued the document as an Information Paper after the European Union decided that it had core competency in counter-piracy policy and that the United Kingdom could not submit an action paper unilaterally without coordination with the EU.[120] The paper informed the MSC of a proposal for an accreditation scheme for PSC in the maritime domain allowing for the use of PCASP on board

---

[116] Comments Related to the Use of Armed Security Personnel on Board Ships, Submitted by the Republic of Korea, IMO Doc. MSC 90/20/15 (27 March 2012), paras 5–7.

[117] Piracy and Armed Robbery against Ships: Armed Security Personnel on Board Ships, Submitted by India, IMO Doc. MSC 90/20/16 (27 March 2012).

[118] Report of the Maritime Safety Committee on its Ninetieth Session, IMO Doc. MSC 90 (31 May 2012), para. 20.7.

[119] *Ibid.*

[120] The use of privately contracted armed security personnel (PCASP) on board United Kingdom registered ships in exceptional circumstances for the purposes of defending against acts of piracy, Submitted by the United Kingdom, IMO Doc. MSC 90/20/4 and 90/20/4/Corr.1 (9 May 2012); and Accreditation of private security companies in the maritime domain allowing the deployment of privately contracted armed security personnel on board United Kingdom-registered ships in exceptional circumstances for the purposes of defending against acts of piracy, Submitted by the United Kingdom, IMO Doc. MSC 90/INF.13 (9 May 2012). See also, Appendix 1, Draft Standard for Maritime Private Security Companies, *Ibid.*

UK-registered ships. The United Kingdom proposed a single accredit-ation system for PSCs in the maritime domain.[121] The government of the United Kingdom and industry partners appointed a national Security in Complex Environments Group (SCEG) to develop standards and accreditation for PSC.[122]

The British standards recognize the use of PCASP in exceptional circumstances, which are defined as:

1. when the ship is transiting the high seas throughout the HRA (an area bounded by Suez and the Straits of Hormuz to the North, 10° S and 78° E);
2. the latest BMP is being followed fully but, on its own, is not deemed by the shipping company and the ship's master as sufficient to protect against acts of piracy; and
3. the use of armed guards is assessed to reduce the risk to the lives and well-being of those on board the ship.[123]

The SCEG seeks to develop PCASP standards that are based on quality management practices that demonstrate to clients that a company is well managed and has good personnel, risk management and continuous improvement practices in place. The group already contributed to the development of similar standards for land-based PSC (PSC1). PSC1 builds relevant specialist elements into ISO 9001-based quality manage-ment standards by turning the principles of the ICoC into auditable management and operational standards.[124] Similar standards that are relevant to the maritime security environment include: recruitment, vetting and screening of personnel sub-contractors; weapons carriage and transport in compliance with the relevant flag, coastal and port state regulations; command and control of the on board security team, taking account of the role of the ship's master; performance of security functions, including rules for the use of force and appropriate training thereof; incident monitoring and reporting protocols; and adequate insur-ance.[125] The UK draft standards take into account and are consistent with

---

[121]   IMO Doc. MSC 90/20/4, para. 1.
[122]   *Ibid.*, para. 2.
[123]   *Ibid.*, para. 6.
[124]   *Ibid.*, Annex, para. 1.
[125]   *Ibid.*, Annex.

MSC.1/Circ.1405/Rev.1[126] and MSC.1/Circ.1406/Rev.1 and complement the BIMCO draft industry standard contract for the employment of PCASP.[127]

MSC 90 reached two major conclusions pertaining to the use of PCASP and port states and coastal states. First, 'masters, shipowners and companies were alerted that ships entering the territorial sea and/or ports of a State are subject to that State's legislation'.[128] It is interesting that the IMO would stipulate that firearms on board foreign-flagged ships conducting innocent passage would be considered subject to coastal state regulations. The MSC further suggested that the differing customs or security regulations of coastal states concerning the carriage and importation of firearms while transiting in the territorial sea may give rise to a criminal offense in some countries.[129] Furthermore, contending perspectives on the right of self-defense may also raise even graver issues, since 'firing weapons at suspected pirates may impose a legal risk for the master, shipowners or company'.[130] 'In some jurisdictions,' for example, 'killing a national may have unforeseen consequences even for a person who believes he or she has acted in self-defense.'[131] Some coastal states are concerned that in order to avoid these legal issues, PSC were positioning PCASP on logistical platforms adjacent to the territorial sea of the state in order to quickly embark and disembark armed personnel and their firearms.[132]

Second, guidance for industry and recommendations for governments are evolving. Rather than crafting a detailed statute, the IMO has instead created a broad framework that accommodates the spectrum of different choices that shipowners and shipping companies and flag states and governments may make over the issue of private security. Although a framework exists that enables industry and governments to make informed decisions, the disparate guidance for privately contracted armed

---

[126] Subsequently updated and released as Interim guidance to shipowners, ship operators and shipmasters on the use of PCASP on board ships in the High Risk Area, MSC.1/Circ. 1405/Rev. 2 (25 May 2012).

[127] Revised interim recommendations for flag States regarding the use of privately contracted armed security personnel (PCASP) on board ships in the High Risk Area, IMO Doc. MSC.1/Circ.1406/Rev. 1 (16 September 2011).

[128] Report of the Maritime Safety Committee on its Ninetieth Session, IMO Doc. MSC 90/28 (31 May 2012), para. 20.11.

[129] *Ibid.*

[130] *Ibid.*

[131] *Ibid.*

[132] *Ibid.*, at para. 20.12.

security companies and their personnel has not been consolidated into a single source.[133]

On the first day, MSC 90 featured a high-level discussion on the major issues associated with PMSC and PCASP. The Committee agreed to develop guidance for PMSC to complement existing guidance, and to assist policy development by flag states.[134] Consequently, MSC appointed a working group on PCASP to develop interim guidance based upon the proposal contained in MSC 90/20/8, which was submitted to the session by a powerhouse collection of organizations representing the worldwide shipping industry.[135] The working group produced guidance on 23 May 2012, which will be considered by the MSC at its 91st session, and by the Assembly as a whole. The working group produced interim guidance to shipowners and recommendations to governments for vessels operating in the HRA. The guidance captures the basic framework of due diligence for industry in dealing with PMSC and recommendations to governments to fulfill their flag state responsibilities, and the guidance and recommendations are to be read in conjunction with the existing guidance contained in MSC.1/Circ.1405/Rev.2 for shipowners and ship operators, MSC.1/Circ.1406/Rev.1, on recommendations for governments, and MSC.1/Circ.1408 on recommendations for port and coastal states.

10.4 CONCLUSION

Over the past few years, the member states of the IMO and the representatives from industry have slowly shifted position on the use of PCASP. The rise of the threat of Somali pirate gangs to international shipping began in 2005–2006. Initially, attacks occurred within 50 nautical miles of shore along the Somali Basin, although the zone of danger expanded into the Gulf of Aden and out to sea as far as 200 nautical miles by late-2006 and 2007. By 2008, pirates were effectively using mother ships to extend their range 500 miles or farther into the

---

[133] *Ibid.*, at para. 10.1.

[134] Measures to Enhance Maritime Security; Piracy and Armed Robbery against Ships, Report of the Working Group, Annex 1, IMO Doc. MSC 90/WP.6 (23 May 2012), para. 3.

[135] *Ibid.*, at para. 9.1. See also, Guidance for flag States on measures to prevent Somalia-based piracy Submitted by ICS, ITF, BIMCO, INTERTANKO, INTERCARGO, Intermanager, International Group of P&I Clubs, ICC-IMB, IPTA, SIGTTO and WSC, IMO Doc. MSC 90/20/8 (12 March 2012).

Indian Ocean. Today virtually anywhere in the western Indian Ocean, Gulf of Aden and Arabian Sea is subject to a heightened risk of piracy, with a vast expanse from the Mozambique Channel in the south nearly to the coast of Sri Lanka in the east designated as the HRA.

The concerted naval response alone provided insufficient force to deter attacks. Despite surface and aviation forces from more than 20 states, the dispersed nature of the threat means that warships are not always able to protect merchant ships. The international shipping community adopted industry BMP in order to institutionalize passive security measures on board ships in the HRA. However, the combined deterrent effect of the BMP and naval forces still left an intolerably high number of ships and seafarers being captured and held for ransom. Consequently, the international shipping industry began reluctantly to accept that PCASP could provide an additional hedge against ship hijacking. The embrace has not been complete, and the issue is complicated by an array of flag, port, and coastal state rules that are often not compatible. Thus, the IMO has been an instrumental forum for ascertaining the practice of states, sharing experiences and regulations among member states, and developing guidance for shipowners and ship operators and recommendations to governments.

Private security is still considered a supplementary measure that is used in exceptional circumstances, yet the rapid spread of the practice belies the official expressions by IMO and the shipping industry, and even some flag states, that it is a rather exceptional option to be used sparingly. There has not been a successful hijacking of any ship carrying on board armed security. The weariness of dealing with the threat of piracy, escalating ransom demands and increased violence by pirates, combined with a realization that naval forces are unwilling or unable to defeat piracy decisively has driven industry toward greater acceptance of private security.

The social, political, and economic acceptance of private security means that states and industry demand greater predictability and standardization. Particularly for states that do not have a widespread culture or acceptance of firearms, the profusion of privately contracted armed security is, at a minimum, disquieting. The work at the IMO, and the associated effort through the ISO, to promulgate guidance, recommendations, and standards for PCASP serves to reduce transaction costs and broaden acceptance of private maritime security.

11. What is a pirate? A common law answer to an age-old question

Peter MacDonald Eggers QC

11.1 THE SEARCH FOR A DEFINITION

Everyone has his or her own conception of a pirate. Anyone who has read *Treasure Island* or *The Sea Hawk* will have an idealised notion of a pirate. However, it is not as obvious as that. As one judge has said, 'It is not necessary that the thieves must raise the pirate flag and fire a shot across the victim's bows before they can be called pirates.'[1] One might add that pirates need not have wooden legs and parrots on their shoulder. With such an engrained popular notion of piracy, it is important to distance oneself from such images and focus on the quintessence of piracy. The commercial and civil law requires such definitions, as much as public and international law. Legal rights and obligations, as well as offences and crimes, depend on a stable definition of piracy. It is far from satisfactory to leave such categorisations to impressionistic assessments.

Pirates have been an endemic feature of the seas, coasts and islands from the earliest times, recorded from the time of the Sea Peoples in the Mediterranean. Piracy came in different flavours. There was organised piracy conducted as an instrument of state (by privateers) and piracy by rogue elements. Those pirates who were free of the ties of a state are those who seem to have attracted the greatest hostility and yet the distinction was in reality quite thin. In *De Civitate Dei*, St Augustine refers to a meeting between Alexander the Great and a pirate chief, during which the pirate defended his actions in the following terms: 'How darest thou molest the whole world? But because I doe it with a

---

[1] *Athens Maritime Enterprises Corporation v Hellenic Mutual War Risks Association* [1983] 1 QB 647, 661 (Staughton, J). That is not to say that pirates do not raise piratical flags: see *Dean v Hornby* (1854) 3 E&B 180, 182.

little ship only; I am called a theefe: thou doing it with a great Navie, art called an Emperour.'[2]

Such distinctions are a critical feature in defining piracy and pirates. Laws dealing with piracy, both as criminal punishment and regulating the civil consequences of piratical attacks, apply to a defined conception of piracy. Although there will be a large measure of agreement amongst courts, lawyers and the general public as to whether a garden-variety pirate (whatever that means) is in fact a pirate, definition by impression is an inadequate means of legislating against piracy. Precisely worded definitions are an essential aspect of the law of piracy.

Laws concerning piracy have been around since piracy itself, such as the Lex Rhodia and the Lex Gabinia.[3] Pirates have, again since ancient times, been branded as *communes hostes gentium* or *hostes humani generis*, the enemies of mankind.[4] This phrase is oft-repeated by the English courts, and is used as the basis of the universal jurisdiction assumed by the Courts in respect of the trial of pirates irrespective of whether the pirates, the piratical attack or their victims are otherwise within the jurisdiction of the Courts.[5] Speaking in the US House of

---

[2]   Augustine, *Of the Citie of God* (Tr. J. Healey) (1620), Book 4, Chapter 4, 150.

[3]   H. A. Ormerod, *Piracy in the Ancient World* (Hodder & Stoughton, 1924), 55, 235.

[4]   Along with slave traders and torturers in more recent times: *Filartiga's case* 630 F 2d 876, 890 (Kaufman, J), cited by Mance, LJ in *Jones v Ministry of the Interior of the Kingdom of Saudi Arabia* [2005] 1 QB 699, para. 62.

[5]   *Charge to the Grand Jury* (1680) Burr 255, 256 (Sir Leolin Jenkins); *Drinkwater v The Royal Exchange Assurance Company* (1767) Wilm 282, 290 (Wilmot, CJ); *Le Louis* (1817) 2 Dods 210, 244 (Sir William Scott); *Dean v Hornby* (1854) 3 E&B 180, 190–192 (Lord Campbell, CJ); *In re Tivnan* (1864) 5 B&S 645, 677–678 (Cockburn, CJ); 688 (Blackburn, J); 690 (Shee, J); *Republic of Bolivia v Indemnity Mutual Marine Assurance Co Ltd* [1909] 1 KB 785, 804 (Kennedy, LJ); *R (Fawwaz) v Governor of Brixton Prison* [2002] 2 WLR 101, para. 142 (Lord Rodger); *Masefield AG v Amlin Corporate Member Ltd* [2011] 1 WLR 2012, para. 66 (Rix, LJ). See also Blackstone, *Commentaries on the Laws of England* (12th edn., 1793), Book IV, 71. In *R v Serva* (1845) 2 Car & K 53, 82, Baron Alderson suggested that this rule is necessary because otherwise piracy, being without a country, would not be justiciable anywhere. This, however, is unlikely to have been the true basis of the principle. In *R v McCleverty* (1871) LR 3 PC 673, 686, it was held that the Court of Admiralty has jurisdiction to order the restitution of goods piratically seized on the high seas (see also *Prinston v The Court of Admiralty* (1616) 3 Bulstrode 147). As to the desirability of universal jurisdiction over pirates, see J. Goodwin, 'Universal Jurisdiction and the Pirate: Time for an Old Couple to Part' (2006) 39 *Vanderbilt*

Representatives, John Marshall (later Chief Justice of the United States) said that:[6]

> A pirate, under the law of nations, is an enemy of the human race. Being the enemy of all, he is liable to be punished by all. Any act which denotes this universal hostility, is an act of piracy...But piracy under the law of nations, which alone is punishable by all nations, can only consist in an act which is an offence against all.

This description, however, denotes an essential characteristic of a pirate, namely that a pirate is a person who indiscriminately attacks ships without regard to their nationality, as opposed to ships belonging to a particular state.

Until relatively recently, there was during the development of the law – both as part of public international law and at the domestic or municipal level – uncertainty about the precise definition applied to piracy. Holdsworth declared that the lack of such precision in explaining the essence of piracy was attributable to 'the infrequency of the offence in modern times'.[7] It is obvious that today piracy is and perhaps remains anything other than a rare phenomenon, there having been some 445 actual or attempted piratical attacks during 2010 and 439 actual or attempted attacks during 2011.[8] Indeed, even in 1935, Lenoir could write that piracy was by no means obsolete and that its definition as a matter of substantive law was then open to argument.[9]

Journal of Transnational Law 973–1012. Goodwin states that Coke was the first to describe pirates as the enemies of mankind (Third Part of the Institutes). For a sceptical account of the law's development see: A. Rubin, *The Law of Piracy* (2nd edn, Naval War College Press 1998).

   [6]   Cited in *In re Tivnan* (1864) 5 B&S 645, 662.

   [7]   W. S. Holdsworth, *A History of English Law* (2nd edn, Methuen & Co Ltd, 1937) (Vol. VI), 401.

   [8]   International Maritime Bureau ('IMB'), Annual Report on Piracy and Armed Robbery against Ships (2011), 6 <http://www.icc-ccs.org/piracy-reporting-centre> accessed 4 September 2012. The IMB figures include both armed robberies with territorial jurisdiction and piracy as defined in United Nations Convention on the Law of the Sea (adopted 10 December 1982, entered into force 16 November 1994) 1833 UNTS 397 ('UNCLOS'), Art. 101.

   [9]   J. J. Lenoir, 'Piracy Cases in the Supreme Court' (1934) 25(4) *Journal of Criminal Law and Criminology* 532–553.

11.2 SEA ROBBERY

The definition of a pirate has developed as a matter of English law, often by reference to the meaning of piracy adopted by public international law. In *De Jure Maritimo et Navali*,[10] Molloy stated (with his emphasis) that:

> A Pirate is a Sea-Thief, or Hostis humani generis, who for to enrich himself, either by surprise or open force, sets upon Merchants and others trading by Sea, ever spoiling their Lading, if by any possibility they can get the mastery, sometimes bereaving them of their lives, and sinking of their Ships; the Actors wherein, Tully[11] calls Enemies to all, with *whom neither Faith nor Oath is to be kept.* Against Pyrates and such as live by Robbery at Sea, any Prince hath power to make War, tho' they are not subject to his Government.

The essence of a piracy was therefore traditionally regarded as robbery at sea. This is the touchstone of piracy in the minds of the judges and the opinions of the commentators. In *R v Dawson* (1696) 13 St Tr col. 451, upon an indictment concerning the taking of a vessel *Gunsway* in the East Indies, Sir Charles Hedges, the judge in the High Court of Admiralty, sitting with other eminent judges, said that:

> now piracy is only a sea-term for robbery, piracy being a robbery committed within the jurisdiction of the Admiralty. If any man be assaulted within that jurisdiction, and his ship or goods violently taken away without legal authority, this is robbery and piracy[.]

The law of nations and the common law were traditionally indistinguishable in this respect. Indeed, in *United States v Smith*, 18 US 5 Wheat 153 (1820),[12] the United States Supreme Court considered the jury's finding upon an indictment of the accused for piracy, who with a crew took control of the vessel *Irresistible* and robbed and plundered a Spanish vessel whilst on the high seas in 1819. The United States Supreme Court was constitutionally constrained to define piracy by reference to public international law (which it acknowledged formed part of the common law) and concluded (at page 162) that the common law, the maritime law and the law of nations 'universally treat of piracy as an offense against

---

[10] C. Molloy, *De Maritimo et Navali: or, a Treatise of Affairs Maritime and of Commerce* (6th edn, 1707), 55.

[11] Cicero, *De Officiis*, Book III, 107.

[12] See also *United States v Pirates* 5 Wheat 184 (1820); *United States v Holmes* 5 Wheat 412 (1820); Lenoir, note 9, *supra*.

the law of nations and that its true definition by that law is robbery upon the sea' and that the essence of piracy was 'robbery or forcible depredations upon the sea, *animo furandi*'.

Blackstone could describe piracy in the following terms by the eighteenth century: 'The offence of piracy, by common law, consists in committing those acts of robbery and depredation upon the high seas, which, if committed upon land, would have amounted to felony there.'[13]

In *The Attorney-General v Kwok-a-Sing* (1873) LR 5 PC 179, the Privy Council hearing an appeal concerning the taking of a vessel in Hong Kong adopted the definition laid down by Sir Charles Hedges and held (at page 200) that, for the purposes of defining piracy, there was no material difference between a taking by a mariner or a passenger.[14] The issue for the Court was whether there was a felonious intent. The absence of such an intention – in particular, the *animus furandi* – prevented a conviction on an indictment for piracy.[15]

In 1934 (*In re Piracy Jure Gentium* [1934] 1 AC 586), the Privy Council gave an advisory opinion on an issue referred to it by the King in Council in respect of a decision of the Full Court of Hong Kong acquitting Chinese nationals who had been apprehended in an attempt to seize a Chinese cargo junk, which the accused persons had pursued in armed junks and had further attacked by firing shots at the cargo junk. Before the accused persons could complete their design, two steamships intervened and through their agency the accused persons were taken into custody by the commander of HMS *Somme*. The Privy Council was asked to consider the question whether actual robbery is an essential element of the crime of piracy *jure gentium* or whether a frustrated attempt to commit a piratical robbery is not equally piracy *jure gentium*.

---

[13] Blackstone, *supra* note 5, Book IV, 72.

[14] See also *R v McGregor* (1844) 1 Car & K 429, 431 (Lord Abinger, CB); *Republic of Bolivia v Indemnity Mutual Marine Assurance Co Ltd* [1909] 1 KB 785, 802–803 (Kennedy, LJ); *China Navigation Co v Attorney-General* [1932] 2 KB 197, 246.

[15] In *Sivewright v Allen* [1906] 2 KB 81, 89–90, Darling J held that the Russian capture of a British ship during the Russo-Japanese War did not constitute an act of piracy because 'they had no felonious intent in so acting, their object probably being to prevent information as to the position of the Russian fleet from coming to the knowledge of the Japanese; but with the exception of the felonious intent all the other incidents essential to piracy were present'. See also *United States v Klintock* 5 Wheat 144 (1820).

The Privy Council concluded that a frustrated attempt to commit a piratical robbery was equally piracy *jure gentium*.[16]

11.3 PIRACY BEYOND ROBBERY

The purpose of plunder, or the *animus furandi*, has not always been regarded as an essential element of piracy. In *The Malek Adhel* 43 US 210 (1844), Mr Justice Story appears to have ignored his earlier decision in *United States v Smith* and said (at page 232):[17]

> We cannot adopt any such narrow and limited interpretation of the words of the act; and in our judgment it would manifestly defeat the objects and policy of the act, which seems designed to carry into effect the general law of nations on the same subject in a just and appropriate manner. Where the act uses the word 'piratical,' it does so in a general sense; importing that the aggression is unauthorized by the law of nations, hostile in its character, wanton and criminal in its commission, and utterly without any sanction from any public authority or sovereign power. In short, it means that the act belongs to the class of offences which pirates are in the habit of perpetrating, whether they do it for purposes of plunder, or for purposes of hatred, revenge, or wanton abuse of power. A pirate is deemed, and properly deemed, hostis humani generis. But why is he so deemed? Because he commits hostilities upon the subjects and property of any or all nations, without any regard to right or duty, or any pretence of public authority. If he wilfully sinks or destroys an innocent merchant ship, without any other object than to gratify his lawless appetite for mischief, it is just as much a piratical aggression, in the sense of the law of nations, and of the act of Congress, as if he did it solely and exclusively for the sake of plunder, lucri causa. The law looks to it as an act of hostility, and being committed by a vessel not commissioned and engaged in lawful warfare, it treats it as the act of a pirate, and of one who is emphatically hostis humani generis.

---

[16]   In *Athens Maritime Enterprises Corporation v Hellenic Mutual War Risks Association* [1983] 1 QB 647, 655, Staughton, J considered that the Privy Council resolved the meaning of piracy at common law by reference to principles of public international law. However, the Privy Council was plainly concerned with the definition of the 'crime of piracy *jure gentium*' and did not consider that the scope of that crime was a matter only of municipal law: [1934] AC 586, 588. Note the view of John Marshall, speaking in the US House of Representatives: 'Not only an actual robbery therefore, but cruizing on the high seas without commission, and with intent to rob, is piracy' (quoted in *In re Tivnan* (1864) 5 B&S 645, 662).

[17]   Lenoir, note 9, *supra*.

This judgment suggests that piracy may be constituted not only by acts of plunder but also acts of hatred, revenge or abuse of power, even without the involvement of robbery. It may well be, therefore, that viewing piracy as 'sea-robbery' is too limiting and that the real essence of piracy lies in its essentially private, as opposed to public, nature. In *The Magellan Pirates* (1853) 1 Sp Ecc & Ad 81, Dr Lushington sitting in the High Court of Admiralty said (at page 83) that it was common to all nations that 'piratical acts are murder and robbery upon the high seas'. This reinforces the view that it is not only acts of robbery, but also other acts of violence, which may be condemned as piracy.[18] Thus, Sir Hersch Lauterpacht could speak of piracy in the following terms (*Oppenheim's International Law* (1955), Vol. I, page 608, paragraph 272):[19]

> Piracy, in its original and strict meaning, is every unauthorised act of violence committed by a private vessel on the open sea against another vessel with intent to plunder (animo furandi). The majority of writers confine piracy to such acts, which indeed are the normal cases of piracy. But there are cases possible which are not covered by this narrow definition, and yet they are treated in practice as though they were cases of piracy. Thus, if the members of the crew revolt and convert the ship, and the goods thereon, to their own use, they are considered to be pirates, although they have not committed an act of violence against another ship. Again, if unauthorised acts of violence, such as murder of persons on board the attacked vessel, or the destruction of goods thereon, are committed on the open sea without intent to plunder, such acts are in practice considered to be piratical. Therefore several writers, correctly, it is believed, oppose the usual definition of piracy as an act of violence committed by a private vessel against another with intent to plunder.

---

[18]   See also *R v Townsend (The Illeanon Pirates)* (1849) 6 Moore 471, 483–484. In *Serhassan (Pirates)* (1845) 2 W Rob 354, 357, the Court said that 'it is sufficient, in my view of the question, to clothe their conduct with a piratical character if they were armed and prepared to commence a piratical attack upon any other persons'. In *In re Piracy Jure Gentium* [1934] 1 AC 586, 594 the Privy Council suggested the proposition that 'armed men, sailing the seas ... could attack and kill everybody on board another vessel ... without committing the crime of piracy unless they stole, say, an article worth sixpence' was contrary to common sense.

[19]   Cited by Macfarlan, J in the New South Wales Supreme Court in *The Cythera* [1965] 2 Lloyd's Rep 454, 464. In that case, a yacht which was anchored in a lagoon at Lord Howe Island was stolen surreptitiously by the yacht's sailing master and forward hand who both had returned to the yacht while the owner and remainder of the crew and passengers were present at a dance on the island. The vessel was apprehended by a cargo vessel with the sole member of Norfolk Island's police force on board. The judge did not decide the question whether or not the thieves were also pirates.

However, no unanimity exists among them concerning a fit definition of piracy, and the matter is therefore very controversial. If a definition is desired which really covers all such acts as are in practice treated as piratical, piracy must be defined as every unauthorised act of violence against persons or goods committed on the open sea either by a private vessel against another vessel or by the mutinous crew or passengers against their own vessel.

The common law definition of piracy was enlarged by statute, as was the Court's jurisdiction to deal with piracy. Originally, piracy by a subject was regarded as treason, whereas piracy by an alien was a felony. By 25 Edw. III, c. 2, the subject's piracy was treated as a felony. The law against piracy was however administered by the Court of Admiralty, applying the rules of civil law,[20] but by 28 Hen. VIII, c. 15, a charge of piracy could be determined by the common law courts, so that an accused on such a charge could be judged by his peers.[21] By 11 and 12 Will. III, c. 7 (the Piracy Act 1698), section 9, the revolt or mutiny against a lawful commander of a ship would also be treated as a piracy, even if there were no piracy.[22] By 8 Geo. I, c. 24, trading or confederating with or abetting pirates was deemed to be an act of piracy.[23] By 18 Geo. II, c. 30 (the Piracy Act 1744), clarifying the 1698 Act, any hostile act committed *'upon the sea, or in any haven, river, creek or place, where the admiral or admirals have power'* by a British subject or denizen against a fellow subject under commission of or assisting the King's enemies, would be treated as an act of piracy and the offenders could be *'tried as pirates, felons and robbers in the said court of admiralty'*.[24] Such alterations to the meaning of piracy are matters of municipal law alone so that there is a discrepancy between the notion of piracy as a matter of English law and as a matter of public international

---

[20]   R. Zouch, *The Jurisdiction of the Admiralty of England Asserted* (1st edn, 1663), 34.

[21]   M. Hale, *Pleas of the Crown* (1678), 77; Blackstone, *supra* note 5, Book IV, 71.

[22]   *R v McGregor* (1844) 1 Car & K 429, 431 (Lord Abinger, CB).

[23]   Blackstone, *supra* note 5, Book IV, 72.

[24]   The Piracy Act 1837 (7 Will. IV and 1 Vict. c. 88) provided that persons convicted of aggravated piracy (piracy with an intent to murder) would be guilty of a felony, and consistently with the earlier legislation, would be subjected to the death penalty. The death penalty for aggravated piracy and treason, the last remaining capital offences, was abolished in 1998: Crime and Disorder Act 1998, s. 36; see also Criminal Justice Act 2003, s. 304 and Schedule 32, Part 1.

law,[25] unless of course the latter develops by reference to such national modifications.

Nevertheless, it is clear that robbery or attempted robbery is not a critical feature of piracy. Any attack not involving a theft or attempted theft is capable of constituting an act of piracy.

11.4 VIOLENCE

A further aspect of piracy is the use of violence or force by the pirate. In *The Salem* [1982] 1 Lloyd's Rep 369, 373,[26] Lord Denning, MR succinctly described piracy as an instance of 'forcible robbery'. Sir Charles Hedges and Sir Hersch Lauterpacht were content to describe piracy in terms of the use of violence. Furthermore, the repeated references to robbery suggest that the use or intended use of violence or force is an essential aspect of piracy. Thus, in *Republic of Bolivia v Indemnity Mutual Marine Assurance Co Ltd* [1909] 1 KB 785, Kennedy, LJ (at page 802) approved the definition used by Carver, namely:

> Piracy is forcible robbery at sea, whether committed by marauders from outside the ship or by mariners or passengers within it. The essential element is that they violently dispossess the master, and afterwards carry away the ship itself, or any of the goods, with a felonious intent.[27]

In *Athens Maritime Enterprises Corporation v Hellenic Mutual War Risks Association* [1983] 1 QB 647, Staughton, J explicitly considered the role violence had to play in the domestic – i.e., non-public international law – sense of piracy. In that case, whilst the insured vessel was anchored in the Chittagong Roads within the territorial seas of Bangladesh, a number of men, armed with knives, boarded the vessel with the intention of stealing goods clandestinely but also with the intention of using force or the threat of force if the crew on board resisted or interfered with their plans. The armed men took mooring lines and equipment, but as they were preparing to leave the vessel, the sailor on watch sounded the alarm, whereupon members of the crew armed

---

[25] *In re Tivnan* (1864) 5 B&S 645, 687 (Blackburn, J). Apparently, in the sixteenth century in Spain, Philip II declared that fraudulent insurers and those who cut the nets of herring fishers were pirates: see the argument of Serjeant Manning in *Serva*, *supra* note 5, 61.

[26] Reversed on appeal, though not on this point: [1983] 2 AC 389.

[27] T. G. Carver, *Carriage of Goods by Sea* (4th edn, Stevens & Sons Ltd, 1905), 117.

themselves with knives, the master with a pistol and two officers with rockets. Upon one of the rockets being fired near them, the armed boarders took fright and jumped into the sea. The question before the Court was whether this involved a sufficient degree of violence so as to constitute piracy for the purposes of defining the scope of an insured peril under a marine insurance policy.

Staughton, J held (at pages 660–661) that 'theft without force or a threat of force is not piracy under a policy of marine insurance'. On the facts of this case, the judge held that the theft or robbery was completed surreptitiously without the use or threat of force and that where force was used to make good an escape following the theft or robbery, there was no relevant use or threat of force to constitute a piracy. For this purpose, Staughton, J relied on English criminal law. This, however, appears to be an unnecessarily formalistic approach to the question of piracy. It is difficult to discern any sensible reason why a gang of men who board a vessel, armed and prepared to use or threaten violence, in order to carry out a theft, should not be treated as pirates or should be treated only as pirates if, by chance, they are confronted by resistance before the theft is completed. It is also difficult to believe that any business or popular understanding of piracy would depend on such technical distinctions as to whether force is used or threatened immediately before or immediately after the theft is completed. In any event, the judge must have been wrong in holding that the violence was used after the loss, because whilst the armed men's crime was still being executed, there cannot be said to have been a loss in the sense of a deprivation which satisfies the tests of an actual or constructive total loss.[28]

11.5 DISCONNECTED TO A STATE

The judgment of Mr Justice Story in *The Malek Adhel* 43 US 210 (1844) is revealing in that it identifies as a defining aspect of piracy the fact that the pirates must operate outside the bounds of the state or quasi-state.[29]

---

[28]   See Chapter 12.5.1. However, it is possible that there might be a partial loss by deprivation, even though the Marine Insurance Act 1906 makes no specific provision for an indemnity for such a partial loss (other than by s. 75): see *Integrated Container Service Inc v British Traders Insurance Co Ltd* [1984] 1 Lloyd's Rep 154, 160–162.

[29]   In *The Magellan Pirates* (1853) 1 Sp Ecc & Ad 81, 83–84, Dr Lushington did not agree that a state could not be guilty of piratical acts, citing the Barbary pirates, at least if the state is a 'barbarous state'. Cf. *Le Louis* (1817) 2 Dods 210.

Mr Justice Story's approach therefore identifies as an essential character-istic the absence of any lawful authority permitting the acts of aggression (as may be sanctioned for example during conditions of war).

This echoes the comments made in a *Charge to the Grand Jury* (1680) Burr 255, where Sir Leolin Jenkins said (at page 256):

> The next thing is robbery; and that committed on the high sea is piracy, for piracy at sea is made up of the same ingredients as robbery on land, for it is piracy to assault a ship, carry away a ship or goods out of a ship, unless it be in necessity, for upon necessity a man may take victuals or tackle out of a ship, if the ship can spare the same, or if payment be made or undertaken to be made for the same, for then he is excused by the statute 28 Hen VIII, 15. Also a man is excused if he takes a ship or goods by a legall commission in time of war of by reprisalls; but otherwise he shall be esteemed a pirate; and pirates are so odious in the eye of the law that they are adjudged the enemies of mankind; he is out of the protection of all laws, shall neither have benefit of clergy or benefit of sanctuary, but wherever taken shall be judged to death whatever country he is of.

Where those engaged in hostilities against ships are acting for or in the interests of a particular state, no matter how much censure their conduct deserves, their conduct is not piratical. So, in *Le Louis* (1817) 2 Dods 210, Sir William Scott considered (at pages 247–248) that those engaged in the slave trade were not pirates:[30]

> It is not the act of freebooters, enemies of the human race, renouncing every country, and ravaging every country in its coasts and vessels indiscriminately, and thereby creating a universal terror and alarm; but of persons confining their transactions (reprehensible as they may be) to particular countries, without exciting the slightest apprehension in others. It is not the act of persons insulting and assaulting coasts and vessels against the will of the Governments and the course of their laws, but of persons resorting thither to carry on a trade (as it is there most unfortunately deemed), not only recognised but invited by the institutions and administrations of those barbarous communities.

Such an absence of authority may characteristically be encountered on the high seas, which by definition belong to no one state. However, it does not follow that conduct which would otherwise be described as

---

[30] Though they are enemies of humankind: *Filartiga's case* 630 F 2d 876, 890 (Kaufman, J), cited by Mance, LJ in *Jones v Ministry of the Interior of the Kingdom of Saudi Arabia* [2005] 1 QB 699, para. 62. Certain aspects of the African slave trade were to be treated as piracy, though there could be material differences: see *Serva, supra* note 5.

piratical should not be so regarded merely because it takes place within the jurisdiction of a particular state – such as on a river – and not within the jurisdiction of the British Admiralty. In *The Magellan Pirates* (1853) 1 Sp Ecc & Ad 81,[31] Dr Lushington held (at pages 84–87) that insurgents at a Chilean convict settlement who captured two vessels, one British and one American, whilst in port, murdered the owners either in port or on land, and carried away the vessels on to the high seas, were all piratical acts, including the murders which may have been carried out on land.[32]

In *Republic of Bolivia v Indemnity Mutual Marine Assurance Co Ltd* [1909] 1 KB 785, 790–791, Pickford, J was prepared to consider whether a seizure of insured goods on a tributary of a tributary of the Amazon River on the border between Brazil and Bolivia might constitute piracy. On appeal, however, the members of the Court of Appeal were divided as to whether piracy could be perpetrated on a domestic or inland waterway. Kennedy, LJ (at page 802) agreed with the judge, particularly where the policy was by its terms insuring a cargo on a 'riverine' policy – where the departure and destination in the policy were specified to be on a river – against piracy risks. However, Vaughan Williams, LJ considered that piracy must be limited to the high seas (at page 799):

> Whatever the definition of piracy may be, in my opinion piracy is a maritime offence, and what took place on this river, running partly in Brazil and partly in Bolivia, far up country, did not take place on the ocean at all. That distant place was not the theatre on which piracy could be committed. It is a region which cannot be said to be, like the ocean, under the jurisdiction of no particular power. It was under the jurisdiction of either Brazil or Bolivia. That part of the river is not the highway of the world, where ships of all nations can go protected only by the law of nations. It is a place where, if any ships go, they go, not on the sea, but on a river running in occupied territory which is under the government of a specific nation which has jurisdiction there.

In *Athens Maritime Enterprises Corporation v Hellenic Mutual War Risks Association* [1983] 1 QB 647, the Court considered whether a municipal conception of piracy depends on the relevant attack taking place outside or inside territorial waters. In that case, the relevant theft from the victim vessel took place whilst the vessel was anchored in the

---

[31]   An insurance claim relating to the piracy the subject of this decision was considered in *Dean v Hornby* (1854) 3 E&B 180.

[32]   This may well be in part explained by the fact that the legislation which Dr Lushington was considering (13 & 14 Vict c. 26) refers to pirates operating 'afloat or ashore'.

Chittagong Roads within the territorial seas of the Republic of Bangladesh. Staughton, J held (at page 658) that piracy – as that term was used
in a marine insurance policy – could not be committed anywhere within
the jurisdiction of the Admiralty Court, such as navigable inland waterways, but did hold that piracy could take place within territorial waters,
as this conforms with popular notions of acts of robbery or depredation
being 'at sea'.

This view is supported in the case of marine insurance policies, as the
judge recognised, because rule 8 of the Rules of Construction, set out in
the First Schedule to the Marine Insurance Act 1906,[33] provides that 'The
term "pirates" includes passengers who mutiny and rioters who attack the
ship from the shore'. Accordingly, attacks on a ship from the shore may
be treated as piratical, provided of course the vessel is located 'at sea'.
The corollary should be that attacks upon coastal property by a vessel
could also be acts of piracy.

This, however, may (or may not) stretch the popular notion of the
vessel being at sea if she is at berth. As the judgments of Pickford, J and
Kennedy, LJ suggest, where marine insurance policies are intended to
cover not only 'perils of the seas', but also 'perils of ... rivers lakes or
other navigable waters',[34] it is not difficult to associate piracy with inland
waterways, and certainly navigable rivers.[35]

---

[33]   The Rules of Construction were inserted specifically as an aid to constru-
ing the SG form of marine policy – also included in the First Schedule – which
was the form of policy used in the marine insurance market at the time of the
Act's passing. 'SG' probably refers to 'ship and goods' (see J. Gilman *et al.*
(eds), *Arnould's Law of Marine Insurance and Average* (17th edn, Sweet &
Maxwell, 2008), paras 2–21, 2–22). The SG form provided insurance cover in
the following terms: 'Touching the adventures and perils which we the assurers
are contented to bear and do take upon us in this voyage: they are of the seas,
men of war, fire, enemies, pirates, rovers, thieves, jettisons, letters of mart and
countermart, surprisals, takings at sea, arrests, restraints, and detainments of all
kings, princes, and people, of what nation, condition, or quality soever, barratry
of the master and mariners, and of all other perils, losses, and misfortunes, that
have or shall come to the hurt, detriment, or damage of the said goods and
merchandises, and ship, &c., or any part thereof.'

[34]   The insured peril is so described in the Institute Hulls Clauses. See
Chapter 12.4.

[35]   A number of the world's great rivers have suffered from river piracy.
Indeed, the Thames Police Office was instituted in 1798 to deal with such piracy.
Piracy has been encountered on the Mississippi, the Amazon and the Nile. In one
case noted by Dr Lushington in *The Magellan Pirates* (1853) 1 Sp Ecc & Ad 81,
84, a person who fired upon a vessel 100 yards from shore was regarded as a
pirate. In this case, Dr Lushington quoted W. O. Russell, *A Treatise on Crimes*

11.6 THE IMPORTANCE OF MOTIVES

The definition of piracy which is adopted in public international law or as part of the domestic law of individual nations, however, is not the only sense which has a legal relevance. Where parties to a commercial contract refer to the risk of piracy, for example in an insurance, transport or sale contract, the English Courts may interpret piracy by reference to the popular or business understandings of piracy, giving effect to the objectively ascertainable intention of the contracting parties, irrespective of technical legal definitions.

Thus in *Republic of Bolivia v Indemnity Mutual Marine Assurance Co Ltd* [1909] 1 KB 785, a crew of Brazilian malcontents used an armed vessel to navigate on the Amazon River for the purpose of resisting Bolivian authority and establishing an independent republic in the territory, and as part of this activity seized goods being carried on the river which belonged to the Bolivian government to supply Bolivian soldiers. With respect to a claim under an insurance policy for an indemnity for the lost goods, the question arose whether or not the loss was one by piracy. At first instance, Pickford, J resisted applying technical definitions of piracy and held (at pages 791–792) as follows:

> As I have said, I have to look at the more popular or business meaning of the word 'piracy,' and I do not think that can be better expressed than it is in Hall's International Law, 5th ed. p. 259, where it is said: 'Besides, though the absence of competent authority is the test of piracy, its essence consists in the pursuit of private, as contrasted with public, ends. Primarily the pirate is a man who satisfies his personal greed or his personal vengeance by robbery or murder in places beyond the jurisdiction of a State. The man who acts with a public object may do like acts to a certain extent, but his moral attitude is different, and the acts themselves will be kept within well-marked bounds. He is not only not the enemy of the human race, but he is the enemy solely of a particular State.' That I think expresses what I have called the popular or business meaning of the word 'pirate'; and I find that several, though not all, of the definitions cited in the note on p. 260 of the same work bear out that idea. No doubt there are definitions which do not embody that idea, but that I think is the common and ordinary meaning; a man who is plundering indiscriminately for his own ends,[36] and not a man who is simply operating

and Misdemeanors (3rd edn, 1843), Book II, 84: 'If a robbery be committed in creeks, harbours, ports, etc. in foreign countries, the Court of Admiralty indisputably has jurisdiction of it, and such offence is, consequently, piracy.'

[36] In *The Magellan Pirates, supra* note 35, 83, Dr Lushington questioned whether the indiscriminate nature of the crimes committed on the high seas was an essential element of piracy.

against the property of a particular State for a public end, the end of establishing a government, although that act may be illegal and even criminal, and although he may not be acting on behalf of a society which is, to use the expression in Hall on International Law, politically organized. Such an act may be piracy by international law, but it is not, I think, piracy within the meaning of a policy of insurance; because, as I have already said, I think you have to attach to piracy a popular or business meaning, and I do not think, therefore, that this was a loss by piracy.

The Court of Appeal unanimously approved Pickford, J's decision in defining piracy by reference to the perpetrators' subjective motives, as opposed to their outward conduct and their obvious effects. This judgment identifies the 'essence' of piracy as residing in the pirates' aims: a pirate acts from a motive of personal gain or personal vengeance. The essential characteristic of piracy is that the pirate's motives are not of a public, political, religious or ideological nature.

In *Banque Monetaca and Carystuki v Motor Union Insurance Co Limited* (1923) 14 Ll L Rep 48,[37] the vessel *Filia* was seized off the Black Sea coast of Turkey by a band under the command of the Turkish Nationalist, Osman Agha. A claim was made for an indemnity for the loss of the vessel under a war risks insurance policy, which excluded from cover losses caused by piracy. Roche, J held (at pages 50–51) that even though Osman Agha was 'a person of a low character, and ... was and had been a brigand', he controlled the region in which the seizure took place as a virtual dictator and undertook the seizure from a political motive in support of the Kemalist Turks' conflict against the Greek army. The band 'were killing from hatred and revenge and not from a scheme of brigandage'. Accordingly, the judge held that Osman Agha was not a pirate, at least on this occasion, even though on other occasions he acted as a mere brigand.[38]

This essential aspect of piracy bound with the pirate's interior motives creates one of the most surprising and potentially elusive distinctions between pirates and terrorists. Terrorists act out of motives which are characteristically political or religious or driven by ideology. National and international legislation may impose very different approaches in

---

[37] Commented upon in Ormerod, *supra* note 3, 14.

[38] In *The Magellan Pirates*, *supra* note 35, 83, Dr Lushington said that an insurgent against a government would not be a pirate with respect to that insurgency but that such an insurgent may commit piratical acts against other persons. In *Serhassan (Pirates)* (1845) 2 W Rob 354, 357, the Court declared: 'nor can it be imagined that the title of pirate attaches solely to persons following an avowed piratical occupation upon the high sea'.

dealing with pirates and terrorists – it is clear that they are different in type – and yet in many cases the only difference between them lies in their inner motives.[39]

11.7   ESTABLISHING A STABLE DEFINITION OF A PIRATE

Most of us would probably be able to identify a pirate if we saw one. The necessity of a stable definition is, however, critical both to public and private laws which apply in the event of a piratical attack. After all, unless we know when a pirate is a pirate, we will not know if we are confronting a so-called 'enemy of humanity'.

The purpose of definitions of words used in commercial contracts, such as insurance or shipping contracts, is to give effect to the understanding of those words shared by the 'ordinary commercial community'. Accordingly, in *Athens Maritime Enterprises Corporation v Hellenic Mutual War Risks Association* [1983] 1 QB 647, Staughton, J eschewed any technical or public international legal definitions in favour of a commercial meaning.[40]

With this approach in mind, the authorities referred to above reveal that a pirate – as understood at least at the level of English civil or commercial law – is able to be defined with some degree of precision. It may be said that there is piracy where:

---

[39]   For example, payments of ransom to pirates are not illegal under English law or contrary to English public policy (*Masefield AG v Amlin Corporate Member Ltd* [2011] 1 WLR 2012), but payments made to terrorists are treated as illegal (Terrorism Act 2000, ss. 15–17). On differing views as to the role of motive in distinguishing pirates and terrorists at public international law see: R. Geiss and A. Petrig, *Piracy and Armed Robbery at Sea* (OUP 2011), 61.

[40]   The English Courts have taken somewhat inconsistent approaches to the construction of particular perils. The Courts have held that, like 'piracy', 'robbery' (*Canelhas Comercio Importacao e Exportacao Ltd v Wooldridge* [2004] Lloyd's Rep IR 915, para. 11; cf. *Athens Maritime Enterprises Corporation v Hellenic Mutual War Risks Association* [1983] 1 QB 647, 660–661) and 'war' (*Spinney's (1948) Ltd v Royal Insurance Co* [1980] 1 Lloyd's Rep 406) are to be construed in their popular, non-technical sense. However, the Court has also held that the words 'theft' (*Dobson v General Accident Fire & Life Assurance Corp plc* [1990] 1 QB 274) and 'riot' (*Athens Maritime Enterprises Corporation v Hellenic Mutual War Risks Association* [1983] 1 QB 647, 661–662; though note Public Order Act 1986, s. 10) are to be construed in their legal, technical sense.

1.   A person carries out a theft or attack upon a ship or other form of maritime property and/or the persons on board the ship or property and, possibly, coastal property. The theft or attack may be carried out by persons on board that ship or property, from another vessel, or from the shore. The theft or attack, however, need not be successfully completed.

2.   The theft or attack is carried out 'at sea'. This would include thefts or attacks within a nation's territorial seas. It is suggested, however, that piracy could equally take place on the inland waterways of a state.

3.   The theft or attack is carried out with the use of violence, the threat of violence or the intention to use violence, even contingently.

4.   The person carrying out the theft or attack does so without the authority or complicity of a state.

5.   The person carrying out the theft or attack does so with motives of personal gain or to satisfy personal senses of vengeance or hatred. If the motives are public, political, religious or ideological in some other sense, the theft or attack will not be treated as piratical.

This definition is to be contrasted with that adopted as part of the law of nations in article 101 of the United Nations Convention on the Law of the Sea (UNCLOS), as adopted by the United Kingdom in section 26 of the Merchant Shipping and Maritime Security Act 1997 and discussed in Chapter 6. By article 101:

> Piracy consists of any of the following acts:
>
> (a) any illegal acts of violence or detention, or any act of depredation, committed for private ends by the crew or the passengers of a private ship or a private aircraft, and directed –
>   (i)   on the high seas, against another ship or aircraft, or against persons or property on board such ship or aircraft;
>   (ii) against a ship, aircraft, persons or property in a place outside the jurisdiction of any State;
> (b) any act of voluntary participation in the operation of a ship or of an aircraft with knowledge of facts making it a pirate ship or aircraft;
> (c) any act of inciting or of intentionally facilitating an act described in subparagraph (a) or (b).

The definition of piracy adopted at public international law is reasonably conformable with that adopted by English law in its civil or commercial sphere. There are drafting infelicities in article 101 – for example, the word 'illegal' begs the question whether or not the conduct in question is in fact unlawful[41] – but the international and common law legal senses are more similar than dissimilar. The obvious differences are that at public international law: (a) the piratical attack must take place on the high seas or outside the jurisdiction of a state, (b) the attack must be made by one ship (or aircraft) against another ship (or aircraft), and (c) it is not entirely clear on its face whether state-sponsored piracy would be captured by the definition in article 101.[42] The common law definition is not so confined.

Both the civil and international legal definitions still may be stretched and tested in novel circumstances. Either definition might brand as piracy the use of violence by a ship which starts as self-defence against a piratical attack but which exceeds a reasonable, proportionate level of force required for the purposes of self-defence or where a naval vessel engages in violent acts in excess of the authority granted by the state concerned.[43] UNCLOS makes it clear, at least in the latter case, that naval vessels cannot commit piracy unless they mutiny.[44] Nonetheless, it demonstrates, at least as a thought experiment, that although we look for stable definitions of piracy, they will have to adapt to new experiences.

---

[41]   On the debate in public international law see: D. Guilfoyle, *Shipping Interdiction and the Law of the Sea* (CUP 2009), 42–43 (arguing the definition excludes State-sponsored piracy); Rubin, supra note 5, 366–367 and 380.

[42]   See further: Guilfoyle, *supra* note 41, 37–38; UNCLOS, Art. 102.

[43]   In *Serva, supra* note 5, 115, in answer to the submission that an English captain who captured a vessel alleged to be involved in the slave trade might be described as acting as a pirate because he captured the vessel unlawfully, Baron Alderson said: 'Surely that would not be so? Unless it were shewn that he acted with mala fides. A mere mistake of the law would not make him a pirate.' It would also be an instance of a state exceeding its authority, not normally a case of piracy: see the quote from Wheaton's *Elements of International Law* at page 133 of the report.

[44]   UNCLOS, Art. 101(a) (as quoted above, referring to a 'private ship') and Art. 102 ('acts of piracy, as defined in article 101, committed by a warship... whose crew has mutinied and taken control of the ship or aircraft are assimilated to acts committed by a private ship or aircraft').

12. Insurance protection against piracy

Peter MacDonald Eggers QC

12.1 INTRODUCTION

With the rise of piracy in the modern world in Somalia and elsewhere,[1] the risks encountered by shipowners, cargo-owners, traders, crew members and passengers of sustaining a loss by piracy is one for which there should be adequate protection. Such protection may be arranged by suitable risk-allocation provisions in transport and sale contracts or by appropriate insurance cover.

If a piratical attack occurs, such contractual assignments of risk become critical to the contractual parties. Once pirates attack or seize a vessel, those interested in the maritime adventure (i.e., the voyage of a ship and cargo) – those who own the property and those who will financially benefit from the adventure – will alert their contractual counterparts. Almost invariably, this will involve notifying the attack or seizure to the parties' insurers.

The insurance industry has had to respond to attempted and successful piratical attacks using legal principles developed since the foundation of the industry and insurance law itself. Piracy was in the past a prevalent risk insured against and, in recent years, has become prevalent again. The operation of an insurance contract and the essential elements of a valid insurance claim can be usefully considered against the background of a piratical attack on a ship and cargo. Today, such attacks occur in particular areas around the world. A typical attack can occur when a ship with cargo on board is transiting the Gulf of Aden or the Indian Ocean and the ship is attacked by Somali pirates who threaten and seek to take possession of the vessel, not with a view to keeping the vessel and cargo

---

[1] In 2010, there were almost twice as many piratical attacks as there were in 2006 (445 attacks compared to 239). See International Maritime Bureau (IMB), *Piracy and Armed Robbery against Ships Annual Report 2006–2011*. As at 29th July 2012, the IMB reported that there had been 189 attacks worldwide, of which 20 had resulted in hijackings.

permanently, but for the purpose of ransoming the hijacked property (the ship and cargo) and of course the crew members on board the ship.

Insurance policies differ depending on the subject-matter of the insurance (i.e., the interest which the insurance is intended to protect) and the nature of the risks or perils against which the insurance will respond (e.g., piracy, fire, earthquake, negligence). In connection with a piratical attack, the two obvious subject-matters of an insurance policy are the ship and cargo. The ship will usually be insured under a 'hull and machinery' policy and the cargo will be insured under a 'cargo' policy. There are, however, other interests which may be insured, for example the profits arising from the adventure (e.g., the hire or freight due to be paid to the shipowner or the sale price which the cargo-owner expects to earn at the voyage's destination), the lives of the crew members (who may be insured under a life insurance or accident insurance policy) and the liabilities to which the shipowner or the cargo-owner may be exposed. The risks or perils against which these interests may be insured are considered below.

12.2 THE ELEMENTS OF A VALID INSURANCE CLAIM

A contract of marine insurance represents a contractual promise by the insurer to the assured that he or she will indemnify the assured against marine losses. In other words, the insurer undertakes to make good or compensate the loss sustained by the assured, provided that the loss is proximately (that is, sufficiently closely) caused by an insured peril.[2] In this chapter, a piracy marine insurance claim will be considered by reference to: (a) the making of the marine insurance contract; (b) piracy as an insured peril; (c) the loss; and (d) the assured's duty to mitigate the loss and the recovery of mitigation expenses (sue and labour).

12.3 THE CONTRACT OF MARINE INSURANCE

As mentioned above, a contract of property insurance – such as an insurance policy protecting a ship or cargo – contains terms which either describe the risk or peril insured against or impose obligations on the assured as to what the assured should or should not do with respect to the

---

[2] Marine Insurance Act 1906 (MIA), ss. 1 and 55. See *Castellain v Preston* (1883) 11 QBD 380; *Soya GmbH v White* [1983] 1 Lloyd's Rep 122, 126.

insured property. Before considering piracy as an insured peril, it should be noted that hull or cargo insurance policies will often incorporate a standard market wording, typically represented in the London marine insurance market by the various wordings produced originally by the Institute of London Underwriters and now known as the International Underwriting Association.[3] Such wordings are known as 'Institute' wordings and standard insurance provisions for ship and cargo are referred to as the Institute Hull or Cargo Clauses.

The insurance contract may contain warranties or conditions requiring the assured to trade the vessel only within permitted areas (a 'trading warranty').[4] Recently, given the frequency of piratical attacks off the coast of Somalia, London insurance market committees have recommended that insured vessels should keep a particular distance from the Somali coast and should avoid other designated areas, where piracy is most commonly encountered. In addition, provisions are now commonly included in insurance contracts requiring insured vessels trading through high-risk areas to conduct their voyages at certain minimum speeds, with a minimum freeboard, in convoy and/or in compliance with anti-piracy measures, such as Best Management Practices for Protection against Somalia Based Piracy (currently version BMP4). Any failure to comply with a trading or operating warranty of this type would have one of two consequences. First, it could discharge the insurer from liability from the date of the breach of warranty (subject to any 'held covered' provision),[5] even if the breach is subsequently remedied.[6] Alternatively, it may render

---

[3] J. Gilman *et al.* (eds), *Arnould's Law of Marine Insurance and Average* (17th edn, Sweet and Maxwell, 2008), paras 2-23–2-24.

[4] See, e.g., *Uhde v Walters* (1811) 3 Camp 16; *Provincial Insurance Co of Canada v Leduc* (1874) LR 6 PC 224; *Birrell v Dryer* (1884) 9 App Cas 345; *Simpson SS Co v Premier Underwriting Association* (1905) 10 Com Cas 198; *Bank of Nova Scotia v Hellenic War Risks Association (Bermuda) Ltd (The 'Good Luck')* [1992] 1 AC 233.

[5] By a 'held covered' provision, the cover afforded by the policy will continue notwithstanding any breach of warranty or condition subject to notice being provided to the insurer and subject to an additional premium reflecting the change in the risk being agreed (*Liberian Insurance Agency Inc v Mosse* [1977] 2 Lloyd's Rep 560, 567–568). See, e.g., clause 3 of the Institute Time Clauses – Hulls (1995).

[6] Assuming that the warranty is a 'promissory warranty' within the meaning of sections 33–34 of the MIA.

the insurer off-risk if the relevant loss occurs whilst the assured is in breach of the trading warranty.[7]

This type of obligation finds its counterpart in the assured's duty of disclosure prior to the conclusion of the insurance contract pursuant to the mutual duty of 'utmost' good faith.[8] If the assured fails to disclose (or misrepresents) his or her plans concerning the vessel's use close to recognised areas of piratical activity, the insurer may be entitled to avoid the insurance contract and avoid liability thereunder, subject to two provisos. First, the information concealed or misrepresented must be material (in the sense of being of a nature which would influence the judgement of a prudent insurer). Second, the insurer must have been induced to enter into the contract by reason of this non-disclosure or misrepresentation. The existence of a trading warranty in the policy, however, may excuse the assured from any obligation to disclose the insured vessel's trading plans.[9]

12.4 PIRACY AS AN INSURED PERIL

The essence of an insurance contract is that it protects an insured person against fortuitous events. This is inherent in the notion of 'risk'. In other words, the insurance covers risks, not certainties. The widest cover afforded by an insurance contract is an insurance against 'all risks', that is the insurer will indemnify the assured against loss or damage caused

---

[7] See *De Maurier (Jewels) Ltd v Bastion Insurance Co. Ltd* [1967] 2 Lloyd's Rep 550, 558–559; *GE Frankona Reinsurance Ltd v CMM Trust No 1400 (The 'Newfoundland Explorer')* [2006] EWHC 429 (Admlty); [2006] Lloyd's Rep IR 704, para. 23; *Sugar Hut Group Ltd v Great Lakes Reinsurance (UK) plc* [2010] EWHC 2636 (Comm); [2011] Lloyd's Rep IR 198, paras 40–54.

[8] MIA, ss. 17–20. Insurance contracts, almost uniquely among the broad spectrum of commercial contracts under English law, attract not just a duty to abstain from misrepresentation (which might be described as a duty of good faith) but also a duty to make full and accurate disclosure even in the absence of questions from the other contracting party (hence the description of the duty as one of the utmost good faith or *uberrimae fidei*). See Peter MacDonald Eggers, Patrick Picken and Simon Foss, *Good Faith and Insurance Contracts* (3rd edn, Informa 2010), ch. 1.

[9] MIA, s. 18(3)(d); *Cantiere Meccanico Brindisino v Janson* [1912] 3 KB 452, 462; *The Dora* [1989] 1 Lloyd's Rep 69, 91–92; *J Kirkaldy & Sons Ltd v Walker* [1999] Lloyd's Rep IR 410, 423; *Garnat Trading & Shipping (Singapore) Pte Ltd v Baominh Insurance Corporation* [2010] EWHC 2578 (Comm); [2011] Lloyd's Rep IR 366, paras 152–155; aff'd [2011] EWCA Civ 773; [2011] Lloyd's Rep IR 667.

by all fortuitous events (which represent the materialisation of a 'risk' or 'peril').[10] This does not mean that any loss or damage sustained by a ship or cargo will be covered, only loss or damage caused fortuitously or accidentally (even if it is likely or foreseeable) and not as a certainty.[11] Many insurance contracts, however, will provide cover against a limited number of risks or perils. For example, many policies on ships (hull policies) will insure against 'perils of the seas', fire, explosion and piracy. Traditionally, in the marine insurance market (which insures ships and cargoes) different policies will insure marine risks on the one hand (such as 'perils of the seas') and war and political risks on the other hand (such as war, revolution, insurrection, capture, seizure, detainment). Historically, piracy is usually insured against in marine policies, not war risks policies, but with the rise of piratical attacks, many war risks policies provide express cover for piracy (as well as associated risks such as malicious mischief, sabotage, vandalism and terrorism).[12]

Even if the insurance policies provide cover against a wide number of perils, it is common for there to be substantial exclusions from cover. In particular, as the insurance against ordinary marine risks on the one hand and the insurance against war and strikes risks on the other hand are often insured in separate contracts subscribed by different underwriters, each of the contracts will have exclusions to ensure that the loss falls within the scope of one of the marine risks cover or the war or strikes risks cover, but often not both. This was not always the case, as the SG form of policy[13] insured against both marine and war risks.

Thus, hull marine risks (i.e., risks to which ships are exposed whilst navigating the seas, other than war, political and strikes risks) are commonly insured under the Institute Time Clauses or Institute Voyage Clauses 1995 (or less commonly the International Hull Clauses 2003) and hull war and strikes risks are often insured under the Institute War and Strikes Clauses 1995. Cargo marine risks (i.e., risks to which cargoes

---

[10]   *British & Foreign Marine Insurance Co v Gaunt* [1921] AC 41, 47, 51–52, 57–58.

[11]   *C A Blackwell (Contracts) Ltd v Gerling General Insurance Co* [2007] EWHC 94 (Comm); [2007] Lloyd's Rep IR 511, paras 44–48; *Marina Offshore Pte Ltd v China Insurance Co (Singapore) Pte Ltd* [2006] SGCA 28; [2007] 1 Lloyd's Rep 66, para. 56 (Singapore Court of Appeal). See Bennett, 'Fortuity in the law of marine insurance' [2007] LMCLQ 315.

[12]   Note that the Marine and Aviation Insurance (War Risks) Act 1952, s. 10(1) defines 'war risks' as including piracy.

[13]   The SG form was introduced in the eighteenth century and is the form set out in the First Schedule to the MIA. See *Wilson v Nelson* (1864) 5 B&S 354.

are exposed whilst being carried at sea) are almost invariably insured under the Institute Cargo Clauses (A), (B) or (C) 1982 or 2009.[14] Cargo war risks are insured under the Institute War Clauses (Cargo), and cargo strikes risks are insured under the Institute Strikes Clauses (Cargo).

The description of insured perils differs within the marine, war and strikes covers. Insured perils may either be defined by reference to the identity or description of the actor giving rise to the loss or defined by reference to the nature or consequence of the act giving rise to the loss.[15] Reviewing the forms of cover available in respect of hull and cargo risks:

1. Under the Institute Hull Clauses, there is express cover for loss and damage caused by 'piracy' and also against 'violent theft by persons from outside the vessel' and 'barratry of Master Officers or Crew',[16] as well as cover for fire and explosion. There is an exclusion from cover for loss and damage caused by 'capture seizure arrest restraint or detainment (barratry and piracy excepted), and the consequences thereof or any attempt thereat', by 'strikers, locked-out workmen, or persons taking part in labour disturbances, riots or civil commotions', by 'any terrorist or any person acting from a political motive' and by 'the detonation of an explosive' or 'any weapon of war' caused by 'any person acting maliciously or from a political motive'.

2. Under the Institute War and Strikes – Hulls Clauses, there is express cover for loss and damage caused by 'capture seizure arrest restraint or detainment, and the consequences thereof or any attempt thereat', by 'strikers, locked-out workmen, or persons taking part in labour disturbances, riots or civil commotions' and by 'any terrorist or any person acting maliciously or from a political motive'. There is an exclusion from cover for loss and damage caused by 'piracy' (although this exclusion is provided not to affect

---

[14] The (A) Clauses insure against 'all risks' and the (B) and (C) Clauses insure against specified perils.

[15] Cf. *Cory v Burr* (1883) 8 App Cas 393, 398 (Lord Blackburn).

[16] Rule 11 of the Rules of Construction (Sched. 1 to MIA) provides: 'The term "barratry" includes every wrongful act wilfully committed by the master or crew to the prejudice of the owner, or, as the case may be, the charterer.' As piratical attacks may be carried out by members of the crew, such conduct may be both piratical and barratrous. See *Marstrand Fishing Co Ltd v Beer* (1936) 56 Ll L Rep 163; *The Cythera* [1965] 2 Lloyd's Rep 454, 464; *The Salem* [1982] QB 946, 959; [1983] 1 Lloyd's Rep 342.

cover in respect of strikers and riots), and for 'loss damage liability or expense covered by the Institute Time Clauses – Hulls'.

3.   Under the Institute Cargo Clauses 2009, the (A) clauses provide cover for 'all risks' of loss or damage, with an exclusion for loss or damage caused by 'capture seizure arrest restraint or detainment (piracy excepted), and the consequences thereof or any attempt thereat', caused by 'strikes, lock-outs, labour disturbances, riots or civil commotions' and persons taking part in such activities, caused by 'any act of terrorism being an act of any person acting on behalf of, or in connection with, any organisation which carries out activities directed towards the overthrowing or influencing, by force or violence, of any government whether or not legally constituted', or caused by 'any person acting from a political, ideological or religious motive'. Under the (B) and (C) clauses, there is no directly relevant peril which would automatically cover piracy, but there is cover for fire, explosion, and sinking, grounding, stranding and capsize of the vessel. There is also additional cover available under the (B) and (C) clauses which insures against loss or damage caused by 'deliberate damage to or deliberate destruction of the subject-matter insured or any part thereof by the wrongful act of any person or persons'. The (B) and (C) clauses adopt the same exclusions as the (A) clauses.

4.   Under the Institute War Clauses (Cargo) 2009, there is cover for loss or damage caused by war risks and by 'capture seizure arrest restraint or detainment', arising from war risks. Under the Institute Strikes Clauses (Strikes) 2009, there is cover for loss or damage caused by 'strikers, locked-out workmen, or persons taking part in labour disturbances, riots or civil commotions', by 'any act of terrorism … ', and by 'any person acting from a political, ideological or religious motive'.

These standard wordings define the scope of cover by reference to: (a) the actors, including pirates, terrorists and persons acting out of a political, ideological or religious motive; (b) the quality or nature of the actors' act, such as capture or seizure; and (c) the consequence of the act such as fire, explosion, or theft.

Where the actors are specified as the relevant peril or risk insured against or excluded, it is a simple matter of determining whether or not the person causing the loss or damage falls within the description of the actor in question. There is cover for piracy where the actor in question acts violently for his or her personal ends, attacking a vessel from within the vessel, from another vessel or from the shore, without the authority or complicity of a state, often in connection with a robbery.[17] By contrast, where the motives of the actor are not for the personal ends of the actor – such as personal gain – but of a public, political, religious or ideological nature, the loss or damage will (in insurance law at least) not have been caused by a pirate, but by a terrorist or other person acting maliciously.[18]

Where the nature of the act is the relevant peril or risk, the identity of the actor does not matter, unless the policy provides otherwise. Pirates can undertake a seizure of a vessel or cargo.[19] A 'seizure' has been described as 'every act of taking forcible possession either by lawful authority or by overpowering force',[20] or 'belligerent or non-belligerent forcible dispossession'.[21] It is less clear whether a pirate can execute a 'capture', which has been defined as 'every act of seizing or taking by an enemy or belligerent',[22] which suggests the actions of a state in wartime.

The Institute Hull Clauses seek to put a clear dividing line between marine risks (where capture or seizure are excluded, other than piracy or barratry) and war risks (where piracy and marine risks generally are excluded). The Institute Cargo Clauses similarly allocate piracy to the marine risks cover and not to the war risks cover.

The curiosity lies with the risk of '*riot*'. Section 1 of the Public Order Act 1986 provides that: 'Where 12 or more persons who are present together use or threaten unlawful violence for a common purpose and the

---

[17] See Chapter 11.

[18] See Terrorism Act 2000, s. 1, as amended by the Counter-Terrorism Act 2008. See European Union Committee – Minutes of Evidence, 11th March 2009, Money Laundering and the Financing of Terrorism, Annex A.

[19] *Dean v Hornby* (1854) 3 E&B 180; *Masefield AG v Amlin Corporate Member Ltd* [2011] EWCA Civ 24.

[20] *Cory v Burr* (1883) 8 App Cas 393, 405; *Bayview Motors Ltd v Mitsui Marine and Fire Insurance Co Ltd* [2002] EWCA Civ 1605; [2003] 1 Lloyd's Rep 131, paras 27–34.

[21] *Kuwait Airways Corp v Kuwait Insurance Co SAK* [1999] 1 Lloyd's Rep 803, 814–815. In *The Saldanha* [2010] EWHC 1340 (Comm); [2011] 1 Lloyd's Rep 187, the relevant charterparty contained an off-hire clause providing that 'Should the Vessel be seized, arrested, requisitioned or detained during the currency of this Charter Party by any authority ...'. Gross, J said (at paragraph 35) that – 'Plainly [this clause] did not extend to cover seizure by pirates', because an 'authority' refers to the lawful authority of a state.

[22] *Cory v Burr* (1883) 8 App Cas 393, 396, 405; *Forestal Land, Timber & Railways Co v Rickards (The Minden)* [1940] 4 All ER 96, 109. Where 'capture and seizure' is insured against, see *Osmium Shipping Corporation v Cargill International SA ('The Captain Stefanos')* [2012] EWHC 571 (Comm); [2012] 2 Lloyd's Rep 46, para. 25.

conduct of them (taken together) is such as would cause a person of reasonable firmness present at the scene to fear for his personal safety, each of the persons using unlawful violence for the common purpose is guilty of riot.' Section 10(2) provides that: 'In Schedule 1 to the Marine Insurance Act 1906 (form and rules for the construction of certain insurance policies) "rioters" in rule 8 and "riot" in rule 10 shall, in the application of the rules to any policy taking effect on or after the coming into force of this section, be construed in accordance with section 1 above unless a different intention appears.' Rule 8 of the Rules of Construction set out in the First Schedule to the Marine Insurance Act 1906 provides that: 'The term "pirates" includes passengers who mutiny and rioters who attack the ship from the shore.'

These Acts establish a connection between the meaning of *'pirates'* and the meaning of *'rioters'* in that at the very least *'rioters'* who attack a ship from the shore – so long as they act out of a motive of personal, non-ideological gain – will be treated as pirates. It is to be observed that the definition of *'riot'* in section 1 of the Public Order Act 1986 is so elastic that it would appear that pirates classically so called (e.g., a pirate ship attacking another ship at sea) may also satisfy the definition of a rioter. In *Athens Maritime Enterprises Corporation v Hellenic Mutual War Risks Association* [1983] 1 QB 647, 661–662, Staughton, J held that the armed men who boarded the insured vessel in the Chittagong Roads and stole goods and used force after the completion of the theft, were neither pirates nor rioters, merely because violence was used only after the loss had occurred (although the judge's conclusion about the loss having already occurred before the use of violence is questionable).[23] Many instances of piracy in its classical form (a hijacking at sea) may be highly organised and seem the opposite of a riot, which denotes a civil commotion or civil unrest.[24] If an act of piracy is in truth an act of riot, the indemnity shifts from the marine risks cover (under the Institute Hull and Cargo Clauses) to the Strike risks cover (recalling that the piracy exclusion under the Institute War and Strikes Clauses – Hulls was not to prejudice the cover in respect of strikes and riots and that the marine risks cover excludes cover in respect of riots).

---

[23]   See Chapter 11.3.

[24]   A 'civil commotion' has been described as lying somewhere between a riot and a civil war. See *Republic of Bolivia v Indemnity Mutual Marine Assurance Co Ltd* [1909] 1 KB 785, 801; *London & Manchester Plate Glass Co Ltd v Heath* [1913] 3 KB 411; *Levy v Assicurazioni Generali* [1940] AC 791, 800; cf. *Spinney's (1948) Ltd v Royal Insurance Co* [1980] 1 Lloyd's Rep 406, 428, 434–435, 437–438.

Where the peril is defined by reference to the consequence of the act, for example where pirates cause fire, explosion or sinking, etc., there will usually be cover where the loss and damage is caused by the fire, explosion or sinking, etc., even if caused by pirates, provided that the actors are not identified as excluded perils.[25]

12.5 THE LOSS

12.5.1 Nature of the Loss

In order to have a recoverable claim under a marine insurance contract, there must be a loss, because, by reason of section 1 of the Marine Insurance Act 1906, the marine policy is a contract of indemnity (namely, a contract which compensates the assured in respect of loss sustained by reason of loss of or damage to the insured subject-matter, such as ship or cargo). Unless there is a loss, there will be nothing to indemnify. Losses under a property insurance policy take different forms. The classification of such losses depends on the impact on the insured subject-matter or on the scale or degree of the loss.

With respect to the impact on the subject-matter of the insurance, losses can be characterised in three principal ways. First, there is a loss associated with physical damage to the subject-matter of the insurance (whether it be hull or cargo). Thus, if a ship's plating distends by reason of a collision or if a ship runs aground or sinks, it will invariably undergo a physical alteration of such a nature as to impair the vessel's utility or value, even if the damage is relatively minor. Without such a physical alteration to the subject-matter insured, there will be no physical damage.[26]

Secondly, there is a loss associated with the assured being deprived of possession or use of the subject-matter of the insurance (namely, the ship or cargo insured). This is so, even if the subject-matter insured suffers no

---

[25] A peril of 'fire' will cover fire caused by a malicious person: *Tempus Shipping Co Ltd v Dreyfus & Co Ltd* [1930] 1 KB 699, 708; *Slattery v Mance* [1962] 1 QB 569; *The Alexion Hope* [1988] 1 Lloyd's Rep 311. However, note the anomalous position concerning a fire caused by an explosion: *Boiler Inspection & Insurance Co of Canada v Sherman-Williams Co Ltd* [1951] AC 319.

[26] *Ranicar v Frigmobile Pty Ltd* [1983] Tas R 113, 116 (Tasmanian Sup Ct); *Promet Engineering (Singapore) Pte Ltd v Sturge (The Nukila)* [1997] 2 Lloyd's Rep 146; *Quorum A/S v Schramm* [2002] 1 Lloyd's Rep 249, para. 90.

physical damage. The classic example of this is where a third party, such as a pirate or a thief, steals the insured vessel or cargo, so that the assured can be said to be deprived of the possession or use of the insured subject-matter.

Thirdly, there is a peculiar type of loss which applies only under cargo policies, namely the loss of the adventure. Where, by reason of the operation of an insured peril, it is practically or commercially impossible for the assured to procure the safe arrival of the insured cargo at the policy destination, there may be an indemnifiable loss under a marine cargo policy (as a constructive total loss). This is so, even if the cargo has not itself sustained physical damage.[27]

As regards the scale or degree of loss, there are two types of loss as provided for in section 56 of the Marine Insurance Act 1906. There are total losses and partial losses. They are mutually exclusive in the sense that whatever is not a total loss is treated as a partial loss.[28] There are two kinds of total loss: an actual total loss and a constructive total loss.[29] These definitions of total loss are exhaustive in the sense that if a loss does not constitute an actual total loss or a constructive total loss, the loss will be a partial loss.[30]

12.5.2   Actual Total Loss

An 'actual total loss' is defined by section 57(1) of the Marine Insurance Act 1906: 'Where the subject-matter insured is destroyed, or so damaged as to cease to be a thing of the kind insured, or where the assured is irretrievably deprived thereof, there is an actual total loss.'[31]

---

[27]   *Arnould's*, *supra* note 3, paras 29–45, 29–51. Similarly, in the case of hull insurance, where a vessel is a constructive total loss, for example, because the cost of repairing the vessel exceeds the value of the vessel, but it is not practicable for the vessel to be repaired and so is sold, the vessel may well become an actual total loss.

[28]   MIA, s. 56(1). Partial losses comprise particular average losses, general average losses or particular charges: ss. 64–66.

[29]   MIA, s. 56(2).

[30]   *Irvin v Hine* (1950) 83 Ll L Rep 162, 166–168.

[31]   The definition of an actual total loss applicable under the law of marine insurance does not apply with all its rigour under the law of non-marine insurance, where a more flexible test applies, not least because there is no doctrine of constructive total loss under non-marine insurance law. Bennett, *The Law of Marine Insurance* (2nd edn, OUP, 2006), para. 21.47, footnote 84: 'In non-marine insurance, which does not have a concept of constructive total loss, there is some authority that the concept of irretrievable deprivation is interpreted

This statutory definition, as well as section 58 of the Marine Insurance Act 1906, specifies four different types of actual total loss:[32]

1. Where the subject-matter insured is destroyed.
2. Where the subject-matter insured is 'so damaged as to cease to be a thing of the kind insured'.
3. Where the assured is irretrievably deprived of the subject-matter of the insurance.
4. Where the ship concerned in the adventure is missing and after the lapse of a reasonable time no news has been received of the ship.[33]

The first two types of actual total loss are instances of actual total loss by physical damage. The latter two types are instances of actual total loss by deprivation of possession or use.

Each of these cases is predicated on the notion that it would be impossible (as opposed to being merely impracticable) to restore the subject-matter of the insurance. It is this aspect of an actual total loss which distinguishes it from a constructive total loss.[34] As Chalmers

---

more generously and requires nothing more than that the assured has taken all reasonable steps to recover the property and recovery remains uncertain or unlikely ... Put another way, there will be an actual total loss where an informed observer would conclude that there was only a mere chance of recovery as opposed to any realistic likelihood of recovery ... These tests do not apply to actual total loss in marine insurance law.'

[32] Whether there has been an actual total loss must be assessed as at the date of the commencement of legal proceedings in respect of the insurance claim. Therefore, if the subject-matter of the insurance is subsequently restored or becomes salvageable, the subject-matter remains an actual total loss notwithstanding. See *Tunno v Edwards* (1810) 12 East 488; *Goldsmid v Gillies* (1813) 4 Taunt 803; *The Anita* [1970] 2 Lloyd's Rep 365, 383; *Arnould's Law, supra* note 3, para. 28–04). Nevertheless, there may be occasions where one has to wait a reasonable time to determine whether there has been an actual total loss (*Scott v Copenhagen Reinsurance Co (UK) Ltd* [2002] EWHC 1348 (Comm); [2002] Lloyd's Rep IR 775, paras 67–73; [2003] EWCA Civ 688; [2003] Lloyd's Rep IR 696, paras 34–50, 76–83; *Masefield AG v Amlin Corporate Member Ltd* [2011] EWCA Civ 24.

[33] MIA, s. 58.

[34] See *George Cohen, Sons & Co v Standard Marine Insurance Co* (1925) 21 Ll L Rep 30; *Panamanian Oriental Steamship Corporation v Wright* [1970] 2 Lloyd's Rep 365; and *Fraser Shipping Ltd v Colton* [1997] 1 Lloyd's Rep 586.

and Owen said in *The Marine Insurance Act 1906*, (2nd edn, 1913), at page 92:[35]

> In the majority of cases the distinction between actual total loss and constructive total loss corresponds with the distinction which had been drawn between physical impossibility and mercantile impossibility. A merchant trades for profit, not for pleasure, and the law will not compel him to carry on business at a loss. A commercial operation is regarded as impracticable, from the mercantile point of view, when the cost of performing it is prohibitive.

In *Masefield AG v Amlin Corporate Member Ltd* [2011] EWCA Civ 24; [2011] 1 WLR 2012, the vessel *Bunga Melati Dua* with cargoes of bio-diesel on board was hijacked by Somali pirates in the Gulf of Aden and was taken to Somali waters in August 2008. The pirates demanded a ransom in return for the release of the vessel, cargoes and crew. A ransom was eventually agreed and paid by or on behalf of the shipowner. The vessel, cargoes and crew were safely released six weeks after the vessel had been seized. The owner of the cargoes claimed an indemnity under its cargo policy issued by the defendant for the actual or constructive total loss of the cargoes. The cargo-owner argued that in determining whether there had been a total loss, the Court could not take into account the prospect of recovering the vessel and cargoes by reason of the payment of a ransom, because such a payment was contrary to English public policy. The cargo-owner also argued that there was a rule of law that the seizure of a vessel or cargo by pirates constituted an automatic actual total loss. The defendant submitted that the existence of an actual total loss had to be determined by applying the factual tests in section 57 (the test of 'irretrievable deprivation' being the relevant test for the purposes of this case).

The Court rejected the cargo-owner's arguments and held that the cargoes were not totally lost. In particular, Rix, LJ said (at paragraph 56):[36]

> piratical seizure in the circumstances of this case, where there was not only a chance, but a strong likelihood, that payment of a ransom of a comparatively small sum, relative to the value of the vessel and her cargo, would secure recovery of both, was not an actual total loss. It was not an irretrievable deprivation of property. It was a typical 'wait and see' situation. The facts

---

[35]   Quoted by Rix LJ in *Masefield AG v Amlin Corporate Member Ltd* [2011] EWCA Civ 24, para. 17. See also *Moss v Smith* (1850) 9 CB 94, 102–103.

[36]   See *Marstrand Fishing Co Ltd v Beer* (1936) 56 Ll L Rep 163, 172 (Porter, J).

would not even have supported a claim for a CTL, for the test of that is no longer uncertainty of recovery, but unlikelihood of recovery. That is itself recognised by the insured's dropping of its CTL claim. There is no rule of law that capture or seizure is an ATL. The subject-matter is not amenable to a rule of law at all: it is all ultimately a question of fact. The typical case of capture, by a nation's warship, subject to condemnation as a prize, is not an ATL, although it may mature into one. Piratical seizure, in the absence of a policy of ransom, may amount to an ATL, where the pirates escape with their prize for their own use and there is no prospect whatever of finding or recovering vessel or cargo: but where a chance of recapture remains even such a seizure will not give rise to an immediate ATL, and in any event that is very far from this case.

Like 'irretrievable deprivation', an actual total loss by physical damage is concerned with similarly absolute degrees of loss, namely where the subject-matter insured is destroyed,[37] or where it 'cease[s] to be a thing of the kind insured'.[38] In order to constitute an actual total loss, it is not sufficient for the insured subject-matter to be damaged, even severely damaged, if it remains technologically possible to repair the vessel, even if the cost of repair would be exorbitant.[39]

12.5.3   Constructive Total Loss

The doctrine of constructive total loss is unique to marine insurance law (although it may well be applied to other types of insurance contract by agreement).[40] Section 60(1) of the Marine Insurance Act 1906 defines a constructive total loss in the following terms: 'Subject to any express provision in the policy, there is a constructive total loss where the subject-matter insured is reasonably abandoned on account of its actual

---

[37]   If the vessel or cargo is reduced to ashes, then the subject-matter of the insurance has been 'totally destroyed or annihilated' and will be an ATL (*Roux v Salvador* (1836) 3 Bing NC 266, 286). As Lord Watson declared in *Sailing Ship 'Blairmore' Co v Macredie* [1898] AC 593, 603: 'A mere congeries of wooden planks or of pieces of iron could not without reconstruction be restored to the form of a ship.'

[38]   Although, in this instance, questions of commercial identity are considered: *Asfar v Blundell* [1896] 1 QB 123; *Berger and Light Diffusers Pty Ltd v Pollock* [1973] 2 Lloyd's Rep 442, 456.

[39]   *George Cohen, Sons & Co v Standard Marine Insurance Co* (1925) 21 Ll L Rep 30; *Fraser Shipping Ltd v Colton* [1997] 1 Lloyd's Rep 586.

[40]   *Moore v Evans* [1918] AC 185; *Kuwait Airways Corp v Kuwait Insurance Co SAK* [1996] 1 Lloyd's Rep 664, 686. Cf. *Scott v Copenhagen Reinsurance Co (UK) Ltd* [2003] EWCA Civ 688; [2003] Lloyd's Rep IR 696, paras 34–50, 76–83.

total loss appearing to be unavoidable, or because it could not be preserved from actual total loss without an expenditure which would exceed its value when the expenditure had been incurred.'

Section 60(1) therefore identifies two types of constructive total loss, namely where the subject-matter insured is reasonably abandoned[41] (a) on account of its actual total loss appearing to be unavoidable, or (b) because the subject-matter insured could not be preserved from an actual total loss without an expense which exceeds the value of the subject-matter insured after the expense has been incurred.[42]

The definition of a constructive total loss does not end there, because sub-section 60(2) proceeds to identify two particular instances of a constructive total loss where the subject-matter insured is either a ship or cargo, namely where:

1.   The assured is deprived of possession[43] of the ship or goods. In that event, there will be a constructive total loss where it is unlikely that

---

[41]   Abandonment, in this sense, is concerned with giving up the insured subject-matter as 'lost' as opposed to the abandonment of the subject-matter to the underwriters within the meaning of sections 61 and 63 of the MIA. The former notion of abandonment precedes or gives rise to a constructive total loss whereas the latter notion is a consequence of there being a constructive total loss. See *Court Line v The King* (1945) 78 Ll L Rep 390; *Masefield AG v Amlin Corporate Member Ltd* [2010] EWHC 280 (Comm), paras 55–57.

[42]   Under section 27(4) of the MIA, the value of the subject-matter insured is the actual sound or repaired value. However, in most cases the policy will stipulate that the value will be the agreed or insured value (assuming the policy is a valued policy). It is notable that under clause 21 of the International Hull Clauses 2003, the relevant 'value' is 80% of the agreed or insured value. Increased value policies will pay a total loss claim if there is a constructive total loss under the underlying hull policy. See *The WD Fairway* [2009] EWHC 889 (Admlty); [2009] 2 Lloyd's Rep 191.

[43]   The deprivation of possession of the vessel or cargo means that the assured is deprived of the right to use the vessel or cargo as he or she chooses. Therefore, if the assured or the vessel's master remains in physical custody of the vessel or cargo but is not, for example, permitted to remove the vessel or cargo from a particular place or port, the assured will be treated as having been deprived of possession because he or she has been deprived of the free use and disposal of the vessel or cargo. See *Fooks v Smith* [1924] 2 KB 508; *Polurrian Steamship Co v Young* [1915] 1 KB 922; *Panamanian Oriental Steamship Corp v Wright* [1970] 2 Lloyd's Rep 365; *The Bamburi* [1982] 1 Lloyd's Rep 312, 317–321; *Royal Boskalis Westminster NV v Mountain* [1997] LRLR 523, 533–534.

the assured will recover the subject-matter insured within a reason-able time[44] or where the cost of recovering the vessel or cargo would exceed its value when recovered.

2. The ship or goods have been damaged. In that case, there will be a constructive total loss where the cost of repair (together, in the case of cargo, with the cost of forwarding the cargo) exceeds the value of the subject-matter insured.

The relationship between sub-sections 60(1) and 60(2) has been the subject of some judicial interest. One view is that sub-section 60(2) is merely illustrative of sub-section 60(1). The other view, and that pre-ferred by the courts, is that sub-section 60(2) provides a definition of a constructive total loss independent of that in sub-section 60(1) so that an assured could rely on either sub-section 60(1) or sub-section 60(2) in order to establish a constructive total loss.[45] The latter view is plainly right, given that a constructive total loss may exist under sub-section 60(2) without any abandonment (i.e., such an abandonment occurs when the assured has given up the subject-matter insured as lost). The existence of a constructive total loss must be assessed as at the date on which the notice of abandonment is tendered in accordance with section 62 of the

---

[44] The words 'within a reasonable time' are not included in section 60(2) but they have been read into the provision by the Courts: *Polurrian Steamship Co v Young* [1915] 1 KB 922, 937; *Petros M Nomikos Ltd v Robertson* [1939] AC 371, 383; *Royal Boskalis Westminster NV v Mountain* [1997] LRLR 523, 534.

[45] *Polurrian Steamship Company v Young* [1915] 1 KB 922, 936–937; *Robertson v Petros M Nomikos Limited* [1939] 1 AC 371, 382, 391–392; *Rickards v Forestal Land, Timber and Railways Co Ltd* [1942] AC 50, 83–84; *The Bamburi* [1982] 1 Lloyd's Rep 312, 314; *Clothing Management Technology Ltd v Beazley Solutions Ltd* [2012] EWHC 727 (QB); [2012] Lloyd's Rep IR 329, paras 34–36. In *Masefield AG v Amlin Corporate Member Ltd* [2011] EWCA Civ 24, para. 18, the policy was subject to clause 13 of the Institute Cargo Clauses 1982 providing that a claim for a constructive total loss could be made only in the circumstances referred to in section 60(1) and made no reference to the circumstances set out in section 60(2). The parties in *Masefield v Amlin* agreed that clause 13 had the effect of restricting the circumstances in which a constructive total loss could be claimed. This is correct as a matter of construction, given the explicit language of clause 13 and the Court's assessment of the relationship between sections 60(1) and (2). For other views, see Bennett, *supra* note 31, para. 21.76; *Arnould's Law, supra* note 3, para. 29–43 (note 230).

Marine Insurance Act 1906 (assuming such a notice was required) and as at the date on which legal proceedings are commenced.[46]

12.5.4 Ransom Cases

Where pirates seize a vessel and decide to keep the vessel, there may well be a total loss, an actual total loss if the deprivation is irretrievable and a constructive total loss if the recovery of possession is unlikely within a reasonable time. If, however, the pirates seize a vessel and demand a ransom for the return of the vessel, the existence or non-existence of a total loss may have to await the outcome of the ransom negotiations. There may be a total loss if the vessel is regarded as irretrievable or its recovery is unlikely or if the ransom demanded exceeds or is likely to exceed the value of the vessel.[47]

Thus, in *Dawson's Field Arbitration Award* (March 1972), three aircraft were hijacked in 1970 by the Popular Front for the Liberation of Palestine and the hijackers threatened to blow up the aeroplanes if certain guerrilla prisoners were not released (a fourth aircraft had already been destroyed in Cairo). An insurance claim was made under a non-marine insurance policy.[48] The arbitrator, Mr Michael Kerr QC, held that the aircraft were not lost when they were hijacked, but only when they were destroyed (after the hijackers' demands were not met). In his Award, Mr Kerr QC said as follows:[49]

---

[46] *Pesquerias y Secaderos de Bacalao de Espana SA v Beer* (1946) 79 Ll L Rep 417, 433; *Royal Boskalis Westminster NV v Mountain* [1997] LRLR 523, 534; cf. *Rickards v Forestal Land, Timber and Railways Co Ltd* [1942] AC 50, 84–85.

[47] Somali piracy ransoms have increased on an average of US $670,000 per vessel/cargo in 2007 to US $4.5 million in 2011 and total more than US $135 million for that period: House of Commons Foreign Affairs Committee, 'Piracy off the coast of Somalia' HC 1318 (5 January 2012) ('House of Commons Report'), 3 <http://www.parliament.uk/business/committees/committees-a-z/commons-select/foreign-affairs-committee/publications/> accessed 14 September 2012. The evidence before the Committee was that the cost of ransoms to insurers each year is US $350 million (*Ibid.*, 17).

[48] The meaning of a 'total loss' under a non-marine insurance policy is different from the definition of an actual total loss under a marine insurance policy, because there is no doctrine of constructive total loss under non-marine insurance law: Bennett, *supra* note 31, para. 21.47 (note 84).

[49] See also *Kuwait Airways v Kuwait Insurance* [1996] 1 Lloyd's Rep 664, 687–689 (*per* Rix J). Note *Arnould's* comments: *supra* note 3, para. 28–03 (note 9) and para. 24–17 (note 177). Rix, LJ revisited his comments in *Masefield AG v Amlin Corporate Member Ltd* [2011] EWCA Civ 24.

'Wait and see' is therefore to some extent always an essential ingredient of a claim for a total loss in circumstances involving deprivation of possession, unless (perhaps) there is a deprivation within the terms of specifically enumerated perils such as 'capture' or one can infer from the circumstances that there was a clear intention at the time of the dispossession permanently to deprive the owner of possession and ownership. This is quite different from a 'ransom' situation such as in the present case ... In my view, as was said by Parker J. (as he then was) in Webster v. General Accident ... every case in which there has been a dispossession must depend on its own facts as to whether and at what stage a total loss has occurred. One must consider the facts concerning the dispossession, the apparent intention of the person or persons concerned, whether or not or to what extent the whereabouts of the subject-matter are known, and allow for the lapse of a period of time to form a view about the prospects of recovery; i.e. whether the loss is total or partial ... I therefore reject the contention that these aircraft were total losses before they were blown up.

In *Scott v Copenhagen Reinsurance Co (UK) Ltd* [2003] EWCA Civ 688; [2003] Lloyd's Rep IR 696, a case concerned with the Iraqi seizure of a British Airways aeroplane, Rix, LJ said (at paragraph 76):[50]

it is impossible on the judge's findings to say that BA was irretrievably deprived of its aircraft from the first, whatever the content of that test may be. It was a 'wait and see' situation. Care must no doubt be taken with that expression, because it is capable of being used in two senses. In its real sense, it refers to a situation which is subject to a process of development and change. Will a ransom be paid and honoured and the property recovered? Will the property be released? That is the sense in which it was used by Mr Kerr in Dawson's Field and again by the judge in this case ... In the present case, however, the 'wait and see' concept is used in its real sense.

This analysis of ransom cases was approved by Rix, LJ in *Masefield AG v Amlin Corporate Member Ltd* [2011] EWCA Civ 24; [2011] 1 WLR 2012, as is evident from the passage quoted above. Accordingly, it will often not be possible to determine whether there is a total loss where a vessel is seized by pirates and a ransom is demanded by the pirates until the ransom negotiations are concluded or possibly where the ransom negotiations are so protracted as to render the recovery of the vessel within a reasonable time unlikely.

---

[50] Rix, LJ also referred to another meaning of 'wait and see', being a situation where the deprivation is complete and further evidence has yet to emerge.

12.5.5   Measure of Indemnity

In the event of a total loss, whether actual or constructive, the assured will be entitled to an indemnity assessed as the agreed value or the insurable value of the subject-matter insured, depending on whether the policy is a valued or unvalued policy.[51]

Under sections 69 and 71 of the Marine Insurance Act 1906, the measure of indemnity for a partial loss (i.e., a loss which is not a total loss) is the cost of repair or the depreciation in value under a hull policy, depending on whether the ship is repaired, and the depreciation in value under a cargo policy. Both provisions appear to contemplate that there is physical damage to the insured subject-matter. There appears to be no indemnity available for a partial loss by deprivation (even assuming that such a partial loss exists).[52] The consequential losses associated with the delay caused by the temporary deprivation may be insured under financial loss policies (e.g., loss of hire insurance).

12.6   MITIGATION OR SUE AND LABOUR

12.6.1   The Duty to Mitigate and the Recovery of Mitigation Expenses

Section 78(4) of the Marine Insurance Act 1906 provides that 'in all cases' the assured and his agents shall be obliged to take such reasonable measures for the purposes of averting or minimising a loss insured under a marine policy. Whilst section 78(4) speaks of a 'duty', this is in effect no more than a statement of the law that if the assured or his agents fail to take reasonable measures to avert or minimise a loss, that failure may be the proximate cause of the assured's loss, in whole or in part, so that the assured would be unable to prove that the loss or that part of the loss is caused by an insured peril and would be prevented from recovering an indemnity in respect of such loss under the policy. It is comparable to the 'duty to mitigate' arising in respect of ordinary contracts.[53]

---

[51]   MIA, ss. 67–68. The 'insurable value' of the subject-matter insured is assessed in accordance with section 16.

[52]   Cf. *Integrated Container Service Inc v British Traders Insurance Co Ltd* [1984] 1 Lloyd's Rep 154, where the Court of Appeal considered that a partial loss by deprivation could occur, but gave no indication of what measure of indemnity would apply to such a loss.

[53]   See *British & Foreign Marine Insurance Co v Gaunt* [1921] AC 41, 65; *National Oilwell (UK) Ltd v Davy Offshore Ltd* [1993] 2 Lloyd's Rep 582, 619;

The 1906 Act recognises that the assured will be entitled to recover the charges and expenses incurred in taking reasonable steps to mitigate, namely:[54]

1. Where there is a sue and labour clause in the policy allowing the recovery of such mitigation expenses under section 78(1) of the Marine Insurance Act 1906.
2. Where the expenses are incurred as 'the direct and natural result of the casualty', they might be recoverable as 'particular charges' under section 64 of the Marine Insurance Act 1906.[55]
3. Where the expenses amount to a general average expenditure under section 66 of the Marine Insurance Act 1906.

Against this background, the question arises whether an assured faced with a ransom demand from a pirate in exchange for the safe return of the insured property would be obliged to pay that ransom demand in accordance with the duty set out in section 78(4) of the Marine Insurance Act 1906 and whether any ransom paid, whether or not pursuant to the

---

State of the Netherlands v Youell [1997] 2 Lloyd's Rep 440, 458; [1998] 1 Lloyd's Rep 236, 244–245; *King v Brandywine Reinsurance Co (UK) Ltd* [2004] EWHC 1033 (Comm); [2004] 2 Lloyd's Rep 670, paras 141–142; [2005] EWCA Civ 235; [2005] 1 Lloyd's Rep 655, paras 112–115; *Masefield AG v Amlin Corporate Member Ltd* [2011] EWCA Civ 24; [2011] 1 WLR 2012, para. 76.

[54] In addition to the methods of recovery set out, it may be possible that ransom is paid and recoverable by a salvor (operating independently of contract) which may be indemnifiable under MIA, s. 65. As to whether such expenses are always recoverable independently of one of the three methods referred to below, see *Emperor Goldmining Co v Switzerland General Insurance Co* [1964] 1 Lloyd's Rep 348 (Sup Ct NSW); *The Netherlands Insurance Co Est 1845 Ltd v Karl Ljungberg & Co AB* [1986] 2 Lloyd's Rep 19, 22–23 (Privy Council); *contra*, *Yorkshire Water v Sun Alliance & London Insurance Ltd* [1997] 1 Lloyd's Rep 1; *Integrated Container Service Inc v British Traders Insurance Co Ltd* [1981] 2 Lloyd's Rep 460, 464–465; [1984] 1 Lloyd's Rep 154; *King v Brandywine Reinsurance Co (UK) Ltd* [2004] EWHC 1033 (Comm); [2004] 2 Lloyd's Rep 670, para. 143; [2005] EWCA Civ 235; [2005] 1 Lloyd's Rep 655, paras 112–115. See also MacDonald Eggers, 'Sue and labour and beyond: the assured's duty of mitigation' (1998) 2 LMCLQ 228; Clarke, 'Wisdom after the event: the duty to mitigate insured loss' (2003) 4 LMCLQ 525.

[55] In *Royal Boskalis Westminster NV v Mountain* [1999] QB 674, 717–718, Phillips, LJ approved the view expressed in *Arnould's Law of Marine Insurance and Average* (16th edn, Stevens and Sons, 1981), para. 914A, that particular charges may be recovered independently of a sue and labour clause. See also the current edition of *Arnould's* , *supra* note 3, para. 25–24.

said duty, would be recoverable as a sue and labour expense, particular charges or general average expenditure.

This in turn depends on the question whether or not the payment of a ransom is contrary to English law (or any other applicable law) and/or contrary to English public policy.

12.6.2 Legality of Ransom Payments

In the absence of any illegality or contravention of public policy, the position appears to be reasonably clear that the assured may well be obliged to take reasonable mitigating steps pursuant to section 78(4) and/or, in many cases, be entitled to recover an indemnity under the policy for any ransom paid by the assured for the return of the insured property.

The assured will be under a duty to pay a ransom to pirates pursuant to section 78(4) if it was reasonable so to do, having regard to the value of the property at risk and the amount of the ransom. That the assured may well be under such a duty was recognised by Phillips, LJ in *Royal Boskalis Westminster NV v Mountain* [1999] QB 674, who said (at pages 719–720):[56]

> Mr. Aikens informed us that this assumption that ransom expenses are recoverable under a marine policy reflects the approach of the market today, in circumstances where a resurgence of piracy has resulted in a number of such claims ... The terms in which the duty under section 78(4) is expressed are wide enough on their natural meaning to embrace expenditure necessary to procure the release of a vessel that has been seized and I see no reason of policy or practice why they should not do so. If that is right, then it would be strange indeed if such expenditure did not fall within the sue and labour clause. In my judgment the assumption of the editors of Arnould that payment of a ransom, if not itself illegal, is recoverable as an expense of suing and labouring is well founded.

Phillips, LJ's judgment thus acknowledged that the payment of ransoms to pirates is neither illegal nor contrary to policy.

In *Masefield AG v Amlin Corporate Member Ltd* [2011] EWCA Civ 24; [2011] 1 WLR 2012, it was common ground between the parties that the payment of ransoms to pirates was not illegal as a matter of English

---

[56] Pill LJ raised but did not answer the question whether the payment of ransoms was contrary to English public policy.

law.[57] In 1782, the Ransom Act (22 Geo. III c. 25) outlawed the payment of ransom in respect of British ships taken by the King's enemies or 'persons committing hostilities against his Majesty's subjects'. This Act was repealed by section 1 of the Naval Prize Acts Repeal Act 1864.[58]

The position with respect to the payment of ransoms to pirates is to be contrasted with:

1. The payment of money (including, presumably, ransoms) to terrorists where the payer knows or has reasonable cause to suspect that the money will be used for the purposes of terrorism, in which case the payment will be illegal.[59]

2. The payment of a bribe to a person which is intended to induce that person improperly to perform a relevant function or activity which is to be performed in good faith, impartially or in accordance with obligations of trust, where the relevant function or activity is one of a public or representative nature, or arises in the context of a business or a person's employment, which bribes are illegal.[60]

---

[57] Cf. US Executive Order 13536: Paulsen and Lafferty, 'Hijacked: The Unlikely Interface Between Somali Piracy and the U.S. Regulatory Regime' (2011) 85 *Tulane Law Review* 1241–1256.

[58] There was subsequent legislation prohibiting the ransoming of vessels taken as prize, but this legislation has also been repealed. The Naval Prize Act 1864, s. 45 permitted Orders in Council to be made, in relation to any war, prohibiting or allowing the ransoming of British ships or cargoes taken as Prize by Her Majesty's enemies. This provision was repealed by s. 152(4) and Schedule 7 of what is now the Senior Courts Act 1981. The Naval Discipline Act 1957, s. 23(b) and the Armed Forces Act 1971, s. 3 (amending the Army Prize Act 1955 and the Air Force Act 1955) rendered it an offence for any person in command of any of Her Majesty's ships, vessels or aircraft unlawfully to enter into any agreement for the ransoming of a ship, vessel, aircraft or goods taken as prize. This legislation was repealed by the Armed Forces Act 2006, s. 132 and Schedule 17. The relevant 'prize offences' provisions of the 2006 Act (ss. 37 and 38) contain no such prohibition.

[59] Terrorism Act 2000, ss. 15–17. For the definition in international law see: International Convention for the Suppression of the Financing of Terrorism (adopted 9 December 1999, entered into force 10 April 2002) 2178 UNTS 197, Art. 2 (making it an offence if any 'person by any means, directly or indirectly, unlawfully and wilfully, provides or collects funds with the intention that they should be used or in the knowledge that they are to be used, in full or in part, in order to carry out' a terrorist act. The reference to 'unlawfully and wilfully' may, perhaps, exclude payments made under duress.)

[60] Bribery Act 2010.

These cases are distinguishable from the payment of ransoms to pirates, because terrorists differ from pirates by reason of the terrorists' ideological motives,[61] and because pirates are not being induced to perform a function or activity of trust within the meaning of the Bribery Act 2010: the pirates are acting for themselves with private, albeit nefarious, intent.[62]

12.6.3 Public Policy

The question, nevertheless, arises and may well repeatedly arise, whether the payment of a ransom to pirates is contrary to (English) public policy. If so, any ransom paid in breach of such public policy would not be recoverable as sue and labour as a matter of law. This issue arose in *Masefield AG v Amlin Corporate Member Ltd.*[63] The cargo-owner contended that the Court was not permitted to have regard to the prospect of recovering the insured cargoes by reason of the payment of a ransom to the pirates because such ransoms were contrary to English public policy and/or it was contrary to English public policy to expect the assured to make such payments in accordance with its duty to mitigate. The affront to public policy, it was argued, resided in the fact that such payments would encourage further piratical attacks and the escalation of ransom demands. The cargo-owner also relied on the advice by British government ministers not to yield to ransom demands.

Both David Steel, J at first instance and the Court of Appeal rejected this argument, holding that the payment of ransom to pirates was not contrary to English public policy, for different reasons. Before considering their reasons, it is worth considering the principles applied by the Courts in determining whether or not there is a rule of public policy, a rule which exists in the absence of any applicable statutory or common law rule.

---

[61] Terrorism Act 2000, s. 1 as amended by the Counter-Terrorism Act 2008. See also European Union Committee Minutes of Evidence (11 March 2009) 'Money Laundering and the Financing of Terrorism', Annex A. See also Chapter 11. Cf. Proceeds of Crime Act 2002, s. 328.

[62] In *Masefield AG v Amlin Corporate Member Ltd* [2011] EWCA Civ 24, Rix, LJ declared (at para. 74) that it was common ground that bribery was distinguishable from ransoms paid to pirates: 'The payment of a ransom in response to threats to life or liberty is not prima facie a bribe, done for the purpose of obtaining an improper advantage.'

[63] [2010] EWHC 280 (Comm); [2010] 1 Lloyd's Rep 509; [2011] EWCA Civ 24; [2011] 1 WLR 2012.

The Court must approach issues of public policy with great caution and should in principle intervene by pronouncing a new, previously unarticulated rule of public policy, only if in the event that the Courts do not intervene, there would be 'substantially incontestable' harm to the public and there are clear and cogent reasons for intervening. The fundamental approach to issues of public policy was explained by Lord Atkin in *Fender v St John Mildmay* [1938] AC 1, 12:

> the doctrine should only be invoked in clear cases in which the harm to the public is substantially incontestable, and does not depend upon the idiosyncratic inferences of a few judicial minds.

In *McLoughlin v O'Brian* [1983] 1 AC 410, 426, 428, Lord Edmund-Davies stated that 'any invocation of public policy calls for the closest scrutiny' and will have to meet the standards of 'clarity and cogency'. The importance of these pre-conditions for formulating a new rule of public policy is that the interests of the public are ordinarily a matter for Parliament, not for individual judges. So, Parke, B in *Egerton v Brownlow* (1853) 4 HLC 1 observed that: '[i]t is the province of the statesman, and not the lawyer, to discuss, and of the Legislature to determine, what is best for the public good, and to provide for it by proper enactments'.[64]

Parliament is best suited to deal with such issues, not least because there may be two or more different approaches to any issue falling within the scope of public policy, and Parliament is much better placed to determine which of contrasting views should be upheld. Thus, in *Johnstone v Bloomsbury Health Authority* [1992] 1 QB 333, 346–347, Stuart-Smith, LJ said that where there were two *bona fide* views on a particular issue, it would be unwise for the Court to apply any public policy considerations.

In *Masefield v Amlin*, David Steel, J considered that there was 'no clear and urgent reason for categorising the activity as contrary to public policy',[65] because the payment of ransoms to pirates was not illegal and given that there had been legislation in the past prohibiting ransom payments (at least in part) the repeal of such legislation militated against any supposed rule of public policy. Further, the judge discerned the impact on kidnap and ransom insurance of any rule of public policy prohibiting the payment of ransoms.[66] The judge also said:[67]

---

[64]   *Per* Lord Atkin, *Fender v St John Mildmay* [1938] AC 1, 10.
[65]   [2010] EWHC 280 (Comm), para. 60.
[66]   *Ibid.*, para. 62.

So far as harm is concerned it is true that payments of ransom encourage a repetition [of ransom demands], the more so if there is insurance cover: the history of Somali piracy is an eloquent demonstration of that. But if the crews of the vessels are to be taken out of harm's way, the only option is to pay the ransom. Diplomatic or military intervention cannot usually be relied upon and failure to pay may put in jeopardy other crews.[68]

After David Steel, J's judgment, in April 2010, the House of Lords European Union Committee published its 12th Report of Session 2009–2010 bearing the title 'Combating Somali Piracy: the EU's Naval Operation Atalanta'. EU Operation Atalanta was set up to combat piracy on 10th November 2008 and has been in operation since December 2008.

In its Report, the Committee examined the mandate and effectiveness of EU Operation Atalanta, as well as the key challenges facing it and how to address them. The Report was prepared following an inquiry by the Foreign Affairs, Defence and Development Sub-Committee with the benefit of both oral and written evidence given between February 2009 and March 2010 by witnesses representing the government, the military and industry (in particular, the insurance and shipping industry).

One of the issues considered in the Report is that of the payment of ransom to pirates. In particular, at paragraphs 54–56, the Committee reported that:

Lord Malloch-Brown (then FCO Minister) acknowledged the reality that ransom payments were made by ship owners to save the life of their crews, and confirmed that such payments were not illegal under international law. However, the Government would not endorse, condone or participate in such a transaction, in line with the common EU position ... Baroness Kinnock of Holyhead confirmed that the payment of ransoms was not a criminal offence under UK law; the Government's position was that such payments should be discouraged as they would only exacerbate the piracy problem ... The insurance industry confirmed that the payment of a ransom was insurable and it was not illegal to insure such a payment.[69]

---

[67] It appears that the Crown is not under a duty to protect British subjects abroad against pirates: *China Navigation Co v Attorney-General* [1932] 2 KB 197 at 213 per Scrutton, LJ and at 246 per Slesser, LJ.

[68] The danger to 'other crews' arises because if ransoms are not paid, pirates may cease to keep hostaged crews from more serious harm.

[69] The final statement reflected the evidence of three underwriters: Mr Croom-Johnson (of Aegis), Mr Roberts (of Lloyd's Market Association) and Mr Voke (of the LMA Marine Committee and of Chaucer). The underwriters and the Committee both referred to the decision of Mr Justice David Steel.

The minutes of evidence given before the Committee are attached to the Report. In particular, at Q79, Lord Malloch-Brown is recorded as saying that:

> The handling of hostage situations is a national responsibility. It is a curious, you might argue, anomaly of international law that paying a ransom is not illegal. Ship owners say that the ability to pay ransom is absolutely critical to saving the lives of their crews and are universally in favour of it, despite the fact that it, of course, amounts to both an incentive for further hostage taking and a huge tax on their operations. We are very clear that while we recognise this practice goes on, we will not be a party to it. We do not endorse or condone it, we do not participate in it, but it is a reality of this situation.

After recording the evidence, the Committee concluded (at paragraphs 57–58, which conclusions are repeated at paragraphs 82–83):

> Hostage taking and ransoms
>
> 82. We support the status quo whereby the payment of ransom to pirates is not a criminal offence under United Kingdom law. We recommend that the Government continue to monitor the potential risks of monies reaching terrorists.
>
> 83. We understand that skilled ransom negotiators can help to keep risk to life and vessels, as well as ransom payments, to a minimum. Where ship owners intend to pay a ransom to recover their vessel and crew, we recommend that they use experienced and effective ransom negotiators. Where insurance policies do not already insist on experienced negotiators, they should do so.

A similar conclusion was reached by the House of Commons Foreign Affairs Committee in January 2012.[70]

In January 2011, the Court of Appeal in *Masefield v Amlin* held that no rule of public policy such as that contended for by the assured existed. The reasons given by Rix, LJ were as follows (at paragraph 71):[71]

> There is thus something of an unexpressed complicity: between the pirates, who threaten the liberty but by and large not the lives of crews and maintain their ransom demands at levels which industry can tolerate; the world of commerce, which has introduced precautions but advocates the freedom to

---

[70] House of Commons Report, *supra* note 47, paras 113–115, noting indeed that the UK had placed a 'technical hold' on US proposals in the UN Security Council to place two pirate kingpins on the list of persons subject to international sanctions under Security Council Resolution 1844.

[71] [2011] EWCA Civ 24; [2011] 1 WLR 2012.

meet the realities of the situation by the use of ransom payments; and the world of government, which stops short of deploring the payment of ransom but stands aloof, participates in protective naval operations but on the whole is unwilling positively to combat the pirates with force. Mr Williams described it as a 'fragile status quo'. In these morally muddied waters, there is no universally recognised principle of morality, no clearly identified public policy, no substantially incontestable public interest, which could lead the courts, as matters stand at present, to state that the payment of ransom should be regarded as a matter which stands beyond the pale, without any legitimate recognition. There are only elements of conflicting public interests, which push and pull in different directions, and have yet to be resolved in any legal enactments or international consensus as to a solution, save that of wary watchfulness, the deployment of naval resources as a form of law enforcement or policing operation, and a regard for 'a comprehensive approach, seeking to address political, economic and security aspects of the crisis in a holistic way'.

It may be added that the primary objective of a ransom payment is to save the lives of the crew members and to recover the property seized. Such payments cannot be regarded as necessarily morally objectionable and will invite public sympathy. This is especially so given that there are no national or international solutions available in the absence of a ransom being paid. As David Steel, J observed with respect to Somali piracy in *Masefield v Amlin*, 'Somalia is a failed state with no effective government or law enforcement' so that the recovery of seized vessels, cargo and crew by diplomatic or military means is beset by difficulties, 'leaving aside the risk to captured crews'. This means that the 'only realistic and effective manner of obtaining the release of a vessel is the negotiation and payment of a ransom'.[72]

The importance of the payer's reasons for paying a ransom was acknowledged in *Royal Boskalis v Mountain* [1999] QB 674, 739, where a sue and labour claim was made in respect of expenses and charges incurred by the assured to secure the release of hostages and an insured dredging fleet seized by the Iraqi government following the invasion of Kuwait in 1990, and the underwriters argued that the claim should be reduced proportionately to reflect the fact that the sue and labour exertions had been motivated in part by a desire to save human life, and not solely for the purpose of averting or diminishing any loss of the insured property. Phillips, LJ stated that:

Preservation of life cannot be equated with preservation of property. Provided that the expenses can reasonably be said to have been incurred for the

---

[72] [2010] EWHC 280 (Comm), paras 12–13.

preservation of the property, it does not seem to me either sound in principle or desirable that the assured should be penalised if they were sufficiently concerned to save not only their property but also those lives.

There the position rests (at least for now). It follows that any ransom paid by an assured, being neither illegal nor contrary to public policy, should be recoverable as a mitigating expense, assuming it was reasonable and assuming there is a contractual or legal right of reimbursement.[73]

The public policy position has recently been re-affirmed by the House of Commons Foreign Affairs Committee, in January 2012,[74] where it was concluded that:

It is true that the high payments encourage and fund further piracy. However, the Government should address this through the recovery of ransoms and prosecution of those who have profited rather than by blocking payments, which would endanger seafarers' lives and would be likely to result in driving the practice underground. We commend the Government for its work at an international level to ensure that the payment of ransoms is not made illegal. *We conclude that the fact that ransom payments in 2011 have already totalled $135m, another all-time record, should be a matter of deep concern to the British Government and to the entire international maritime community. We conclude that the Government should not pay or assist in the payment of ransoms but nor should it make it more difficult for companies to secure the safe release of their crew by criminalising the payment of ransoms.*

12.7 CONCLUSION

Piratical attacks upon ships and cargoes are very often insured against. The increase in such attacks has highlighted numerous issues in most aspects of the law governing marine insurance claims. It has also revealed the contours of the law of piracy and its interaction with the law of marine insurance.

---

[73] See Soyer, 'Coverage against unlawful acts in contemporary marine policies', in D. Rhidian Thomas (ed.), *The Modern Law of Marine Insurance* (Vol. 3) (Informa, 2009), paras 7.42–7.51.

[74] 'Piracy off the Coast of Somalia', Tenth Report of Session 2010–2012 dated 5th January 2012, paras 111–115 (emphasis in original). This is not to understate the UK government's public position of not granting concessions to hostage-takers: see the Response of the Secretary of State for Foreign and Commonwealth Affairs, dated 19th March 2012, Cm 8324.

13. Piracy and carriage of goods by sea

Keith Michel

13.1 INTRODUCTION

This chapter concerns the carriage of goods by sea. This is the branch of commercial law which concerns charterparties and bills of lading, these being the primary contractual documents that govern the rights and obligations of shipowners, charterers and the owners of cargo carried by sea. In particular the chapter aims to analyse the concept of piracy as a contractual risk and the way in which such risk is defined and allocated between the parties to the contract of carriage. The consequence of a party accepting or seeking to exclude the contractual risk of piracy forms the underlying basis of that risk being insured as discussed in Chapter 12.

It has become a matter of notoriety that shipowners and those engaged in international trade over the last five years have faced largely unprecedented problems consequent upon the hijacking of cargo vessels and the kidnap and ransom of their crews off the coasts of Somalia and out in the Indian Ocean. These events have been contrasted with earlier threats to maritime trade and security, in particular attacks carried out in the Malacca Straits and South China Sea more than a decade before, where the motive of the attackers was not a ransom payment but the theft of both vessels and cargo for illicit trade often by the creation of 'phantom ships' with murderous intentions towards the unfortunate crews. Robbery and theft of vessels' equipment have also been a major feature of attacks on merchant vessels, notably off West Africa and continue to pose threats in an increasing number of other locations.

It is, however, the advent of Somali piracy that has dominated the attention of the maritime industry in recent years both in the context of marine insurance as discussed in the preceding chapter and in the context of contracts of carriage as discussed in this chapter. The gravity of the present position was recognized in the judgments of both Steel J at trial and Rix LJ in the case of *Masefield AG v Amlin Corporate Member Ltd*, previously discussed in Chapter 12.[1] At trial there was uncontested expert evidence that *inter alia*:

> There has yet to be a case where a merchant ship has been hijacked by Somali pirates, where the ship, its crew and cargo (where laden) has not been subsequently released ... the safest, most timely and effective means to secure the release of a ship's crew in such circumstances has proven to be, in case after case, to negotiate and subsequently pay a ransom.[2]

In the Court of Appeal Rix LJ commented:

> There is something of an unexpressed conspiracy: between the pirates, who threaten the liberty but by and large not the lives of crews and maintain their ransom demands at levels which industry can tolerate; the world of commerce, which has introduced precautions but advocates the freedom to meet the realities of the situation by use of ransom payments; and the world of government which stops short of deploring the payment of ransom but stands aloof, participates in protective naval operations but on the whole is unwilling positively to combat the pirates with force.[3]

It is against this background that it is necessary to review the legal concept of piracy in the context of contracts of carriage by sea.

13.2 CONTRACTS OF CARRIAGE – STRUCTURE AND FUNCTION

An act of piracy will generally take place when a vessel is operating under either a time or voyage charterparty and a contract of carriage evidenced by a bill of lading. The impact of piracy on the operation and performance of each of these types of contract of carriage is explained below.

13.2.1 Time Charter

A time charter comprises a contractual agreement under which a shipowner hires his vessel to a time charterer for a fixed period of time. The shipowner contracts to deliver a vessel to the time charterer which is fully insured, properly crewed, has appropriate equipment for the trades

---

[1] See Chapter 12.5.2.
[2] [2010] 1 Lloyd's Rep 509, 513.
[3] [2011] 1 Lloyd's Rep 630, 644.

required and meets all current safety, maintenance, engineering and security standards.

The time charterer pays monthly or semi-monthly hire to the shipowner and pays for the vessel's fuel, in consideration of which the time charterer is permitted to arrange the vessel's commercial trading operations. Such operations, however, have a number of legal and contractual boundaries which include the obligation to order the vessel only to safe ports, to load and carry only lawful and non-dangerous cargoes and to adhere to such navigational or political limits as the time charter or the vessel's insurers may impose. If compliance with the time charterer's orders exposes the vessel or her owners to loss, damage or liability to others, the shipowner may be entitled to recover damages from the time charterer under what is known as an employment and indemnity clause. The time charter will also contain relatively standard 'liberty' clauses permitting the master of the vessel or her owners to avoid areas where the vessel may be exposed to undue risks such as the outbreak of war or hostilities and to allow an alternative method of completing a particular voyage without a breach of contract occurring.

13.2.2   Voyage Charter

A single voyage or consecutive voyage charter differs from a time charter in that the shipowner charters the vessel out for only a single voyage or consecutive voyages, where routinely the ports of loading and discharge are named in the charterparty as are the cargoes to be carried. The shipowner's obligations as to the requisite technical and operational standard of the vessel on delivery will be the same as in a time charter but the shipowner under a voyage charter will pay for the vessel's fuel and will be paid freight for each voyage rather than hire.

The regime as to port safety under a voyage charter may differ from that under a time charter where the ports or berths at the loading and discharging ports are named but the charterer's obligations as to lawful and non-dangerous cargoes will broadly be the same. The voyage charter will also generally contain 'liberty' clauses in similar form to those found in a time charter.

13.2.3   Bills of Lading

The bill of lading, whether issued under a time or voyage charter, is the commercial document which will evidence and contain the terms of the vessel's contract of carriage between the named loading and discharge ports. Those terms will routinely include the incorporation (as a matter of law or contract) of a set of rules governing international sea carriage such as the Hague Visby Rules. These will set out the rights, obligations and liabilities of the shipowner and the owners of the cargo carried and will contain other terms excluding or limiting the shipowner's liability for loss or damage to cargo during the voyage.

13.3 PIRACY – MATTERS OF DEFINITION

As has been noted in Chapter 11 the definition which English civil law attributes to the concept of piracy will be similarly applied from a legal, evidential and causative standpoint, whether the incident relates to a claim or dispute under a policy of marine insurance or under a contract of carriage. It may nonetheless be useful at this point to consider the facts of three cases in order to assess how the courts have evaluated the evidence in the light of the requirement that piracy be for 'private ends' and the 'public/private' dichotomy this creates.

13.3.1 The *Petro Ranger* Case

The case of *The Petro Ranger* concerned an attack in Southeast Asia in 1998. The vessel had been chartered to carry a cargo of gasoil and kerosene from Singapore to Ho Chi Minh City in Vietnam. The vessel disappeared during what should have been a two day voyage. Some ten days later the vessel was located at a Chinese port where she was found discharging a quantity of cargo into a lighter. On investigation it was found that the vessel had been boarded by attackers who had over-powered the crew, repainted the vessel's name and created false registra-tion papers and forged bills of lading. Before being located, a substantial quantity of cargo had been discharged elsewhere and was never found.

The charterparty contained a mutual exceptions clause excluding the liability of owners and charterers if 'loss or damage or delay in performing' arose from 'act of pirates'. Both in the arbitration and subsequent trial in the Commercial Court it was accepted that the evidence of the violent attack on the vessel, her enforced passage to China and the theft of her cargo amounted to an act of piracy within the exceptions clause.[4] This case is further discussed below.

---

[4] *Petroships Pte Ltd v Petec Trading and Investment Corporation* [2001] 2 Lloyd's Rep 348.

13.3.2   The *Alondra Rainbow* Case

A similar but even more dramatic case concerned the *Alondra Rainbow*. In October 1999 the vessel loaded a cargo of aluminium ingots in Indonesia for discharge in Japan. Shortly after her departure, an armed gang of attackers hijacked the vessel, threatened the crew with death and transferred them to another vessel before they were set adrift in a life raft, fortunately to be rescued by a fishing boat some ten days later. It later transpired that the cargo of aluminium ingots had been transhipped or discharged.

An international alert was put out for the missing vessel which resulted in the Indian authorities several weeks later locating a vessel matching the description of the *Alondra Rainbow* although it appeared that her name and flag had been changed and there had been an attempt to alter her configuration. As a consequence of an armed and successful intervention by the Indian Coastguard the vessel was recovered and the assailants captured and detained. A prosecution for the crime of piracy ensued.

At trial it was found that whilst India was a signatory to the UN Convention on the Law of the Sea (UNCLOS), the Convention had not at that time been incorporated into national legislation nor was India then a signatory to the Convention on the Suppression of Unlawful Acts against the Safety of Maritime Navigation 1988 (SUA Convention).[5] Furthermore the Indian Penal Code did not prescribe specific offences of piracy or vessel hijacking. Notwithstanding this, a successful prosecution resulted as a consequence of the authorities invoking the use of old British Admiralty laws, as they existed at the time of Independence in 1947, which outlined a series of offences akin to piracy with which the offenders could be charged within the ambit of the Indian Penal Code.

13.3.3   The *Salem* Case

The third case is that of the *Salem*.[6] In the words of Lord Denning in the Court of Appeal:

---

[5]   United Nations Convention on the Law of the Sea (adopted 10 December 1982, entered into force 16 November 1994) 1833 UNTS 397 (UNCLOS); Convention for the Suppression of Unlawful Acts against the Safety of Maritime Navigation (adopted 10 March 1988, entered into force 1 March 1992) 1678 UNTS 222 (SUA Convention); see further Chapters 6 and 8.8.1, note also Chapter 2.6.2.

[6]   *Shell International Petroleum Company v Gibbs* [1983] 1 Lloyd's Rep 342.

A gigantic ship was used for a gigantic fraud. She was Salem a super tanker. Behind this gigantic fraud there were of course gigantic swindlers. The captain and chief officer were only the tools in their hands to do the dirty work. The wicked minds behind it were those of a group of cosmopolitan crooks. They have never been caught.[7]

The conspiracy involved the clandestine delivery of a cargo of crude oil to South Africa in 1979. The perpetrators procured a contract to deliver a cargo of Saudi Arabian crude oil to Durban and used this contract to procure finance to purchase a tanker, the *Salem*. The vessel was chartered out to an innocent charterer who arranged for the vessel to load a cargo in Kuwait for an apparent laden voyage to Europe.

In the event, the vessel sailed to Durban, false documentation including forged bills of lading were procured and the receivers in Durban were persuaded to accept the cargo of Kuwaiti crude on board instead of the cargo contracted from Saudi Arabia. The conspirators collected the price of the cargo and the vessel was subsequently scuttled off West Africa.

A wide range of issues came before the courts, but of particular significance were the further comments of Lord Denning in the Court of Appeal which were quoted with approval by Staughton J in *The Andreas Lemos*:

Pirates and thieves[:] These perils have been very narrowly construed. There were no 'pirates' here because there was no forcible robbery. There were no 'thieves' because there was no violent means.[8]

13.3.4 Conclusion

The three cases discussed concern different factual scenarios but have as a common theme the requirement that the evidential and causative elements of the definition of piracy be considered by a court or arbitration tribunal before the legal consequences of the events in question can be assessed – in a charterparty context in *The Petro Ranger*, in the context of criminal proceedings in the *Alondra Rainbow* and in the context of a commercial cargo insurance policy in the *Salem*.

---

7 [1982] 1 Lloyd's Rep 369, 371.
8 [1982] 1 Lloyd's Rep 369, 373.

13.4 PIRACY AND WAR AS INSURED PERILS – THE DEFINITIONS COMPARED

In such cases, in order to establish an act of piracy under a policy of marine insurance or a contract of carriage strict legal and evidential criteria are required to satisfy the civil and public law definition. There has been considerable discussion in the insurance market in recent years as to whether piracy should be reclassified as a war rather than a marine risk. Indeed, new charterparty liberty clauses drafted specifically to respond to piratical attacks have as their origin the form of traditional war risk clauses. It is instructive therefore to assess how the definition of war under English insurance law compares with the definition of piracy. The new clauses referred to are for use in private commercial contracts of carriage and are not at present part of any international treaty or convention regime.

The principal difference is that the legal test applied in order to establish an act of war is much less strict. There have, as a consequence, been very few decided cases on the meaning of piracy, whereas as Staughton J noted in his judicial arbitration award in *The Bamburi*: 'The political and commercial history of the Western world for the last two hundred years is reflected in the cases on war risk insurance.'[9]

The English courts have evolved what has been termed a 'common sense' approach to an assessment as to whether an individual incident was caused by an act of war or civil war or 'warlike operations', an insured peril that was extensively reviewed by the courts in cases involving loss or damage to merchant vessels during the two World Wars.

The authority most often cited to support this approach is *The Nailsea Meadow*.[10] The vessel's charter contained a clause entitling both owners and charterers to cancel the charter 'if war breaks out involving Japan'. On the invasion of Northern China by Japanese armies in 1937, owners gave notice of cancellation which was upheld. At trial Goddard J stated:

> they were using the word 'war' in this clause and must be taken as intending it to be construed as war in the sense in which an ordinary commercial man would use it. I have not a doubt that a captain of a tramp steamer arriving at Shanghai and finding the state of things ... would have no difficulty in recognising that a state of war existed.[11]

---

[9]   [1982] 1 Lloyd's Rep 312.
[10] *KKK v Bantham Steamship Company Limited* [1938] 61 Lloyd's Rep 131.
[11] [1938] 61 Lloyd's Rep 131, 138.

In the Court of Appeal, Sir Wilfred Greene MR agreed, stating: 'the word "war" found in this charterparty ... must be construed ... in what may be called a common sense way'.[12]

This approach was reflected in the comments of Lord Phillips MR in the Court of Appeal in *The Northern Pioneer*.[13] This case also involved a charterparty cancellation clause which provided that either owners or chartererers had the right to cancel in the event of 'the nation under whose flag the vessel sails becoming involved in war'. An arbitration tribunal had held that the deployment of aircraft by the Federal Republic of Germany in support of the NATO operation in Kosovo in 1999 did not amount to an 'involvement' in war by a nation state. Lord Phillips summarized the tribunal findings: 'There is no technical meaning of the word "war". It must be construed in a common sense way ... .'[14] That comment affirms the essential definitional difference between the evaluation of an act of 'war' and an act of 'piracy' in the context of a contract of carriage. The criteria for an act of piracy are closely prescribed as has been seen in both the public and private law aspects of its application.

As a consequence, the English courts have been able to adopt a wider approach to assessing whether an act of 'war' has occurred. This has not been available in a comparative assessment of 'piracy' to date and it is submitted will not be so unless a new internationally agreed wider definition of piracy is adopted as was advocated by the Comité Maritime International in its attempts to introduce a new Model Law a decade ago.

The wider approach is reflected in the words of Mustill J in *Spinney's Case*, which involved consideration of the outbreak of violent disorder in the Lebanon in 1976:

> Methods of pursuing political aims and of waging an armed struggle do not stand still. A situation existing today might fall outside a definition formulated in the past, not because the Judge or scholar who proposed it considered that the situation should be excluded but simply because the possibility that it might exist had not crossed his mind ... [15]

Such an approach may lead to changed attitudes to previously accepted practices. In *The Storra*[16] the descendants of a sailor killed in 1943 when the merchant vessel on which he was serving was attacked and sunk by

---

[12] [1939] 63 Lloyd's Rep 155, 164.
[13] [2003] 1 Lloyd's Rep 212.
[14] [2003] 1 Lloyd's Rep 212, 214.
[15] [1980] 1 Lloyd's Rep 406, 429.
[16] *R (on the application of Fogg) v Secretary of State for Defence* [2006] 3 WLR 53.

German E Boats in the English Channel challenged the practice that only naval vessels should be granted the protected status of a War Grave.

Newman J upheld the application saying:

> If merchant vessels sank with loss of life in 'military service' then the vessels and the remains of those who died are capable of being protected ... having regard for the aim and object of the Act (The Protection of Military Remains Act 1986) ... namely according respect for the dead and protecting the sanctity of human remains, being considerations at the forefront of the values of a civilised society ... [17]

It is now appropriate to consider against the background discussed, and insofar as this is currently possible, the legal consequences of attacks on vessels which have been the unfortunate victims of Somali kidnap and ransom.

13.5 VESSEL HIJACKING, KIDNAP AND RANSOM – IMPACT ON CONTRACTS OF CARRIAGE

Apart from the grim misery afflicted on innocent crew members whose workplace and home have been the subject of callous incursion by intruders, one of the main concerns of all those interested in the fate of an individual vessel that has been seized is loss of time and delay in the operation of the contractual voyage. These two categories of risk, loss of time and delay, are dealt with further below. Whilst there have been numerous piratical seizures and a number of private arbitrations to which the parties' particular claims and disputes have been referred in recent years, as at the date of publication there have been few reported court cases. These include *Masefield v Amlin*, which has been discussed above in a marine insurance context, and, discussed below, *The Saldanha*, a case arising under a time charter.[18]

13.5.1 Loss of Time – Off-hire Clauses

Under a time charter, hire is a payable continuously from the time of the vessel's delivery to time charterers until the time of her redelivery to owners at the end of the charter, unless a permitted deduction from hire can be made by the charterers' reliance upon an off-hire clause. Such a

---

[17] *Ibid.*, 81.
[18] [2011] 1 Lloyd's Rep187.

clause, according to its particular terms, will permit charterers lawfully to deduct an amount of hire equivalent to the time lost to the charterers as consequence of the vessel being physically unavailable for operational service caused by one of a number of 'off-hire' events.[19]

In *The Saldanha*, which was time chartered on an NYPE form (a standard form of contract), the off-hire clause included amongst the listed off-hire events: 'average accidents to ship or cargo' and 'default and/or deficiency of men'. The clause also contained a provision providing that the vessel would be off-hire as a consequence of 'any other cause preventing the full working of the vessel'. The vessel in passage from Indonesia to Europe was hijacked by pirates in the Gulf of Aden and held for a period of some three months before her release. Charterers refused to pay hire for the period of the vessel's seizure by pirates seeking to bring themselves within the terms of the off-hire clause, in particular those particular elements of the clause quoted above.

The trial judge Gross J rejected the time charterers' claims and held that none of the listed off-hire events was appropriate to cover the circumstances of the case. He considered that the circumstances of the seizure did not amount to 'default of men' as there was nothing to suggest on the evidence that the conduct of the master, officers and crew had in any way contributed to the loss of time. He said that these words should be narrowly interpreted as having their traditional meaning, that of the master, officers and crew refusing to perform all or part of their employment duties owed to the shipowner.[20] The judge also rejected any reliance on the 'any other cause' provision. Adopting the approach of Rix J in *The Laconian Confidence*,[21] he considered that the seizure of the vessel was an extraneous cause. In that regard he said: 'all in all whether regard is had to piracy, the effects of piracy or both, to my mind, the incident remains a totally extraneous cause, falling outside the scope of the sweep-up wording'.[22]

A different result occurred in a subsequent case, *The Captain Stefanos*,[23] wherein the vessel had been hijacked by Somali pirates for some three months. The charterparty, on a similar standard form, provided that the vessel would be off-hire where time was lost on account of the vessel's '... capture/seizure ... by any authority ... '. The owners contended that the vessel remained on-hire throughout on the grounds

---

[19] See also *The Mareva AS* [1977] 1 Lloyd's Rep 368.
[20] [2011] 1 Lloyd's Rep 187, 191–192.
[21] [1997] 1 Lloyd's Rep 139.
[22] [2011] 1 Lloyd's Rep 187, 194.
[23] [2012] 2 Lloyd's Rep 46.

that the words 'capture/seizure' were qualified by 'any authority', and that the pirates did not constitute any such authority. The charterers said that the words were unqualified and that a seizure by pirates was an off-hire event. The dispute was referred to an arbitration tribunal which upheld the charterers' case and held that the vessel was off-hire, a decision affirmed by Cooke J on appeal to the High Court.

In a time charter context the only other method of deduction from hire is by time charterers seeking to invoke the doctrine of equitable set off. It is submitted however that reliance on the doctrine in a case such as *The Saldanha* would not be permitted within the narrow confines that the courts have laid down as the basis of this equitable relief.[24]

Similarly the rule of law that prohibits any deduction from freight payable to owners under a voyage charter or contract of carriage evidenced by a bill of lading means that claims for loss of time consequent upon a vessel seizure by pirates could not be advanced by seeking to make a set off or deduction from freight contractually due.[25]

13.5.2 Delay – Which Party Bears the Risk?

The question of which party – shipowners or time charterers – bore the risk of loss of time caused by piratical attack on the basis of the particular charter terms in *The Saldanha* was therefore found to fall on the charterers.

In an earlier case, by way of comparison, the incidence and acceptance of risk of loss of time caused by compliance with new national security regulations put in place by the United States Government following the attacks of 9/11 was held to be a matter affecting the legal status of the vessel and thus fell on the owners rather than time charterers. The *Doric Pride* was instructed to load at New Orleans under a time charter. The vessel was then ordered by the United States Coast Guard not to proceed up the Mississippi River until a security inspection had taken place. As this was the vessel's first call at a United States' homeland port she consequently became a 'High Interest Vessel' under the new regulations. The security inspection was delayed through the fault of neither owners nor charterers by an unrelated collision upriver.

Charterers contended that the delay was for owners account as the time lost should count as off-hire and the event fell within the wording and circumstances envisaged by the following wording in the 'War risks'

---

24 Cf. *The Nanfri* [1978] 2 Lloyd's Rep 132 (CA).
25 Cf. *The Aries* [1977] 1 Lloyd's Rep 334.

clause: 'Should the vessel be ... detained by any authority ... the payment of hire shall be suspended.' The trial judge, Michael Crane QC, held that the owners had consented to the risk of the vessel being subject to a security detention by permitting the vessel to be traded to the United States on a time charter basis. He stated:

the risk of boarding and inspection by the USCG under laws enacted after the World Trade Centre attack was a risk general to any vessel calling at any US Gulf port, particularly if she was calling at a US port for the first time. The risk did not flow from any act or omission of charterers or their nomination of a particular loading port ... [26]

The decision was upheld by the Court of Appeal.[27]

The case of the *Doric Pride* therefore provides guidance on the issue of loss of time consequent upon required compliance with external regulation. The concept of compliance with third party instructions is one of the central features of traditional war risks clauses in charterparties and this has been carried into the form of newly drafted piracy clauses in similar terms as discussed below.

13.5.3 Delay Amounting to Frustration

Whether the piratical seizure of a vessel, the period of time which she is detained and, for example, her possible use as a 'mother ship'[28] will allow the doctrine of frustration to be invoked will depend on the terms of the contract of carriage and certain general principles of law. These principles have found expression in many decided cases, the theme of which can be traced in the following brief extracts from some of the leading judgments.

In *The Chrysalis*, a Gulf War case, Mustill J stated: 'a declaration of war does not prevent the performance of a contract; it is the acts done in furtherance of the war which may or may not prevent performance, depending on the individual circumstances of the case'.[29] The essential criteria of the operation of the doctrine was summarised by Lord Radcliffe in *Davis Contractors Ltd v Fareham UDC*: 'frustration occurs whenever the law recognises that without default of either party a contractual obligation has become incapable of being performed, because

---

[26] [2005] 2 Lloyd's Rep 470, 476.
[27] [2006] 2 Lloyd's Rep 175.
[28] See Chapter 3.2.
[29] [1983] 1 Lloyd's Rep 503, 511.

the circumstances in which performance is called for would render it a thing radically different from that which was undertaken by the contract … '.[30] This test was applied by Lord Denning in *The Eugenia*, a case decided consequent upon the closure of the Suez Canal by the Government of Egypt in 1956:

> To see if the doctrine applies, you have first to construe the contract and see whether the parties have provided for the situation that has arisen. If they have provided for it, the contract must govern. There is no frustration. If they have not provided for it, then you have to compare the new situation with the situation for which they did provide. Then you must see how different it is. The fact that it has become more onerous or expensive for one party than he thought is not sufficient to bring about a frustration. It must be more than merely onerous or more expensive. It must be positively unjust to hold the parties bound.[31]

In the case of *The Petro Ranger*, the facts of which have been discussed above, the shipowners argued in the arbitration that the voyage charter had been frustrated on the basis of a radical change in circumstances. The arbitrators initially rejected the owners' claim but were requested to state their further reasons for this decision on a later application to the court.[32]

13.5.4   Employment and Indemnity

One of the central provisions in a time charter, as has been noted, is the employment and indemnity clause. This may comprise slightly different wording in the various forms of time charter but the relevant clause in the Baltime (1939) form,[33] a widely used form of time charter, demonstrates the essential criteria:

> The Master shall prosecute his voyages with the utmost despatch and shall render customary assistance with the Vessel's crew. The Master shall be under the orders of the Charterers as regards employment, agency and other matters. The Charterers shall indemnify the Owners against all consequences or liabilities arising from the Master, officers or agents signing Bills of Lading or other documents or otherwise complying with such orders …

The justification for the clause was summarised by Devlin J: 'If (the shipowner) is to surrender his freedom of choice and put his master under

---

[30]   [1952] AC 166, 185.
[31]   [1963] 2 Lloyd's Rep 381, 390.
[32]   [2001] 2 Lloyd's Rep 348, 355.
[33]   As amended in 2001.

the orders of the charterers, there is nothing unreasonable in stipulating for a complete indemnity in return.'[34] The width of that indemnity needs to be set against the evidence of the order and its causative effect in respect of the loss or liability for which the indemnity is sought. In the words of Donaldson J:

> A loss may well arise in the course of compliance with the time charterers' orders, but this fact does not, without more, establish that it was caused by and is in law a consequence of such compliance, and in the absence of proof of such causation, there is no right of indemnity.[35]

A court or arbitration tribunal will therefore be required to assess each case of piratical seizure, kidnap and ransom on its own facts in order to determine whether in accordance with the test discussed above such facts demonstrate the necessary causal link between the charterer's orders to the vessel and the events in question.

13.6 THE CONTRACTUAL VOYAGE

Whether acting in compliance with time charterers' orders or proceeding between ports of loading and discharge named under a voyage charter or in a bill of lading, the master's obligation is to proceed on the contractual voyage with due despatch and not to deviate from the course of that voyage other than in the limited circumstances permitted in the contract of carriage or on occasion if permitted by the common law. The voyage will generally comprise the direct geographical route that is most appropriate for the particular vessel and cargo at the time of year, subject to matters of safety and navigation.

In that regard it is noteworthy that the House of Lords in *The Hill Harmony* held that time charterer's orders to the master to proceed on a certain route are to be regarded as a matter of 'employment' rather than a matter of 'navigation'. In the words of Lord Hobhouse:

> ... the charterers were, by ordering the vessel to proceed by the shortest and most direct route, requiring nothing more than was in any event the contractual obligation of the owners. Therefore the question whether the order

---

[34] *Royal Greek Government v Ministry of Transport* [1950] 83 Lloyd's Rep 228, 234.
[35] *The White Rose* [1969] 2 Lloyd's Rep 52, 59.

was an order as regards the employment of the vessel is academic. But it was in truth such an order.[36]

The obligation to proceed directly on the voyage or navigational route is also routinely made subject to liberty clauses in the contract of carriage permitting the master in certain circumstances to take steps, including a possible change of course, in order to avoid the risk of encountering perils that may expose the vessel to undue risk.

Liberty clauses in the traditional 'war risks' form and the more recent 'piracy clauses' in similar form are discussed below. The cases on 'war risk' clauses and port safety have frequently considered the question of the conduct of the master in response to the vessel's encounter with external threats or risks or navigational difficulties faced during the course of a contractual voyage.

Generally, when assessing the issue of the reasonable conduct of the master the courts have tended to uphold decisions made at the time on safety or like grounds. This approach found expression in the words of Neill LJ in *The Houda*:

> ... I am satisfied that in a war situation there may well be circumstances where the right, indeed the duty, to pause in order to seek further information about the source of and validity of any orders which may be received is capable of arising even if there may be no immediate physical threat to the cargo or the ship.[37]

Like issues may arise where a master fails to comply with contractual obligations or the instructions of third parties such as flag states, marine or war risk insurers or naval forces as to joining or proceeding in convoy to minimize the risk of pirate attacks and the vessel is hijacked as a consequence. Each such case will turn on its individual facts, the provisions of the contract of carriage and matters of causation. The extent to which any negligence or failure on the master's part has contributed to the losses will be subject to evidential enquiry into the events that have occurred.

The courts in earlier times had to make similar judgements when the availability of evidence may have been less immediate but the contractual issues little different. In *The Teutonia*,[38] an 1872 case that has attracted much comment down the years, the master's conduct was upheld. The vessel, which was Prussian owned, was operating under a voyage charter

---

[36]   [2001] 1 Lloyd's Rep 147, 158.
[37]   [1994] 2 Lloyd's Rep 541, 549.
[38]   [1872] LR 4 PC 171.

that included the option to call at continental ports between Le Havre and Hamburg. The vessel arrived off Dunkirk where she had been ordered by charterers to be informed of the outbreak of war between Prussia and France in June 1870. The master put back into the English Channel to verify the position. The shipowner instructed the master not to proceed to Dunkirk but to proceed to Dover. On arrival in Dover the master learned that war had formally been declared on that day rather than four days beforehand when the vessel had arrived off Dunkirk. The court held that there had been no breach of the contract of carriage as the decision to put back into the English Channel and subsequently to proceed to Dover was reasonable. A case on similar facts considered by the courts today would, it is submitted, be likely to include in addition considerations of port safety and the operation of a traditional war risks clause both of which are discussed below in a piracy context.

13.7　PORT SAFETY

In most cases where there has been a vessel hijacking and kidnap and ransom of the crew, being sadly the hallmark of Somali piracy, such attacks have occurred in the open sea. In such cases the question of choice of or responsibility for the chosen route on a contractual voyage during which a piratical attack occurs has been discussed above. Although an attack within the approaches to a port may be less likely, at least in the context of Somalia, the scope and application of the port safety regime is nonetheless a relevant consideration.

The definition and effect of port safety has been the subject of lengthy and extensive judicial scrutiny over many years. Its scope and application has evolved to meet the occurrence of new and changing events in the same way as the definition of 'war' has evolved in a similar way.

In the World War I case, *Palace Shipping Company v Gans Steamship Line*, Sankey J stated in relation to the evaluation of the status of a port in wartime: '... the word "safe" used in conjunction with "port" implies that the port must be physically and politically safe ... '.[39] This proposition has found expression in many subsequent cases and was considered by Sellers LJ when he set out his well-known definition of port safety in *The Eastern City* in the Court of Appeal:

> If it were said that the port would not be safe unless, in the relevant period of time the particular ship can reach it, use it, and return from it, without in the

---

[39] [1916] 1 KB 138, 141.

absence of some abnormal occurrence, being exposed to danger which cannot be avoided by good navigation and seamanship, it would probably meet all circumstances as a broad statement of the law.[40]

This definition has led to enquiry in many subsequent cases involving port safety issues as to the characteristics of a particular port where loss or damage to a vessel has occurred whether arising from navigational issues or hostilities. Such enquiries have resulted in the courts evaluating the physical and structural 'set up' of a port, as analysed by Lord Denning MR in the Court of Appeal in *The Evia*.[41] In other cases the specific evidential assessment of matters of safety related to the risk posed by external threats such as the threat of attack by armed guerrilla forces in *The Saga Cob*[42] or air to ship missiles in *The Chemical Venture*.[43]

Similar evaluations would, it is submitted, occur in relation to port safety in the context of threats posed to merchant vessels either within a named or nominated port or its approaches. In relation to the question of a port or its approaches becoming potentially unsafe through the risk of pirate attack after orders had been received to proceed there in a time charter context, it is further submitted that Lord Roskill's 'secondary' obligation as stated in *The Evia* in the House of Lords would become relevant: '... there may be circumstances in which, by reason of a port, which was prospectively safe when the order to go to it was given, subsequently becoming unsafe ... (the safe port clause in question) imposes a further and secondary obligation on the charterer'.[44] Such further obligation would require the charterer to: '... cancel his original order and, assuming that he wishes to continue to trade his ship, to order her to go to another port which at the time when such fresh order is given is prospectively safe for her'.[45]

---

[40]   [1958] 2 Lloyd's Rep 127, 131.
[41]   [1982] 1 Lloyd's Rep 334, 338.
[42]   [1991] 2 Lloyd's Rep 398.
[43]   [1993] 1 Lloyd's Rep 508.
[44]   [1982] 2 Lloyd's Rep 307, 320.
[45]   *Ibid.*

13.8 STANDARD CLAUSES DEALING WITH WAR RISK GENERALLY AND PIRACY SPECIFICALLY

13.8.1 War Risks Clauses

Most time and voyage charterparties and some bills of lading contain 'war risks' clauses, many of which appear in similar form and with similar provisions.

As has been noted, the purpose of these clauses is to set out a regime which will permit the parties to the contract of carriage to respond in a mutually agreed way to a situation where the occurrence of 'war risks' prevents or impedes the ability of the parties operationally to carry out the voyage in question on the originally agreed basis. The clauses routinely contain rights and liberties available to the parties to continue to perform the contract of carriage on an agreed alternative basis where the events akin to war and hostilities impact or may impact on the voyage or charter but do not necessarily render its continued performance impractical.

It is also noteworthy that some of the traditionally drawn war risks clauses do contain references to 'piracy' or 'acts of piracy' in addition to references to 'war' or 'hostilities'. The decisions of the courts over many years, particularly in response to events of the two World Wars, have been concerned principally with matters of 'war' and related risks. The clauses were not drawn as a specific response to 'piracy', which is the principal concern of the new 'piracy' clauses considered in the next section, although as noted some 'war risks' clauses do contain references to 'acts of piracy'.

The applicable principles can readily be discerned from forms such as the Shelltime 4 time charterparty, another widely used form, where clause 35 (employing the text of the Chamber of Shipping War Risks Clause 1952) states:

(a) The Master shall not be required or bound to sign bills of lading for any place which in his or Owners reasonable opinion is dangerous or impossible for the vessel to enter or reach owing to ... war, hostilities, warlike operations, civil war ...

(b) If in the reasonable opinion of the Master or Owners it becomes, for any of the reasons set out in clause 35(a) ... dangerous, impossible or prohibited for the vessel to reach or enter ... any place to which the vessel has been ordered ('a place of peril') ... the Charterers shall ... have the right to order the cargo, to be loaded or discharged ... at any other place within the trading limits of this charter ...

Whilst a common 'protective theme' can be seen from the text of 'war risk' clauses appearing in the principal time and voyage charterparty forms, close attention to the specific rights and liberties contained in an individual clause is needed in order to assess the ability of one or other party successfully to operate its terms in the 'war' scenario that the vessel might be facing. Such a scenario comprising 'war risks' is found in the Conwartime 93 terms incorporated in clause 20 of the revised Baltime (2001) form (another widely used form of time charter):

> War risks shall include any war (whether actual or threatened), act of war, civil war, hostilities, revolution ... warlike operations, the laying of mines ... acts of piracy, acts of terrorists, acts of hostility or malicious damage ...

The clause continues by prohibiting charterers, unless the written consent of the owners is obtained, from ordering the vessel to 'any port, place area or zone where in the reasonable judgement of the master or owners the vessel may or is likely to be exposed to "war risks"'. As the clause states, the concept of 'piracy' is included in this 'war risks' clause and 'piracy' is included in similar terms in the 'War Clauses', clause 31(e) of the New York Produce Exchange form of time charter.

In a voyage charter case, *The Product Star*,[46] the court had to consider the legal and evidential issues relating to the refusal of the master to proceed to load at the United Arab Emirates' port of Ruwais in 1987, on the grounds that the lower Arabian Gulf through which the vessel had to pass had become 'dangerous' within the meaning of the war risk clause. This was notwithstanding that the port was named in the charter; that the vessel had made several uneventful calls at the port and the charterers had paid the additional war risks premium for the vessel in accordance with charter terms. Judge Diamond QC held that the owners were not entitled on the basis of the evidence before the court to rely on the terms of the Conwartime 93 war risks clause (discussed above) to justify their decision to refuse to comply with charterers' orders to proceed to the port of Ruwais on the grounds that it had allegedly become unsafe. The judge said:

> First it must be shown that the owners bona fide, that is to say honestly thought reaching the port to be dangerous: second, that there was a sufficient degree of danger involved in reaching the port that a reasonable owner informed of the relevant facts could reasonably consider the port to be dangerous ... What is a significant level of safety, or for that matter danger must be judged by the surrounding circumstances which existed at the date of

---

[46]   [1991] 2 Lloyd's Rep 468.

the contract ... I would construe the word 'dangerous' as meaning 'dangerous by reference to the standards and circumstances existing at the date of the charterparty'.[47]

The issues raised in *The Product Star* were considered in the recent decision of Teare J in *The Triton Lark*.[48] The court, on appeal from an arbitration tribunal, was asked to decide the legal consequences of an owner declining charterers' orders to proceed from Hamburg to China via Suez and the Red Sea because in the owners' view compliance with such orders would expose the vessel to Somali piracy within the terms of the Conwartime 93 clause incorporated in the charter.

Instead the vessel proceeded to China via the Cape of Good Hope which the owners contended was permitted by the terms of clause (8) of Conwartime 93, on the basis that if 'anything is done or not done' in accordance with the earlier provisions of the clause (as discussed above) 'such shall not be deemed a deviation, but shall be considered as due fulfilment of this Charterparty'. The court upheld the owners' case on deviation but said that the test to be applied to clause 2 of Conwartime 93, where the owners take the view that the 'Vessel ... may be, or are likely to be exposed to War Risks', should be assessed on the basis of 'real likelihood' rather than 'serious risk'.

At a subsequent hearing in *The Triton Lark* case[49] concerning the meaning of 'exposed to (acts of piracy)' within the relevant clause, Teare J held that this referred to a situation which was dangerous. He said that when ordered to go somewhere, the owner or master should address the question as to whether there was any 'real likelihood' that the vessel would be exposed to acts of piracy in the sense that the place be considered dangerous on account of acts of piracy. What constitutes 'dangerous' would depend upon both the degree of likelihood that acts of piracy might occur, and the severity of consequences to the vessel, cargo and crew should that peril occur.

Similar issues arose in *The Paiwan Wisdom*[50] where owners declined charterers' orders for the vessel to proceed from Taiwan to Kenya, on the grounds that she would be exposed to 'acts of piracy' within the terms of the Conwartime 2004 War Risks clause incorporated into the time charter. The charterers disputed this and, following a reference to arbitration, the tribunal upheld the owners' decision, stating that the

---

47 *Ibid.*, 478.
48 [2012] 1 Lloyd's Rep 151.
49 [2012] 1 Lloyd's Rep 457.
50 [2012] 2 Lloyd's Rep 416.

owners were not precluded from relying on the clause in the event that there was no material change in the risk of proceeding with the voyage between the date of signature of the charter (when the vessel's trading limits were agreed) and the date of the order to proceed. On appeal to the High Court, the case came before Teare J who also upheld the owners' case, stating that the relevant war risks clause did not contain any requirement that the risk to the vessel should have escalated between the two dates.

Issues of compliance in the context of instructions received from third parties may also be relevant to the operation of war risks clauses. Clause 35(c) of Shelltime 4 gives the vessel liberty to comply with 'any directions or recommendations ... given by the government of the state under whose flag the vessel sails...or any other government or local authority ... or by any committee or person having under the terms of the war risk insurance on the vessel the right to give any such directions or recommendations'. In a similar vein, The BP time charterparty in clause 30.6.3 permits the vessel to act in compliance with '... any Resolution of the Security Council of the United Nations, any Directives of the European Community'.

13.8.2   Specific Piracy Clauses: The BIMCO Model Clauses

The Baltic International Maritime Council (BIMCO), as it has done on other occasions, has developed and produced a series of proforma piracy clauses for use in time or voyage charterparties, the current versions having been published in 2009. These clauses adopt the main principles found in the traditional form of 'war risks' clauses as discussed above, but also include specific operational, liability and compensatory provisions that have been designed on a contractual basis to meet the commercial reality of vessel hijacking and kidnap and ransom threats specific to Somali piracy as analysed in the case of *Masefield v Amlin* reviewed earlier.

The BIMCO time charter clauses

The key concepts may be summarised as follows with reference to the relevant sub-clauses. The vessel is not 'obliged' to proceed on any voyage where 'in the reasonable judgement of the Master and/or the Owners' it would be 'dangerous ... due to any actual, threatened acts of piracy and/or violent robbery and/or seizure' (all of which events fall within the definition of 'piracy') 'whether such risk existed' at the time of entering the charter or 'occurred thereafter'. Clause (a) provides that the vessel is given liberty to leave or avoid any such area of danger.

It is noteworthy that this wording ('acts of piracy and/or violent robbery and/or seizure') encompasses a wider range of threats faced by vessels than what might be covered under the 'traditional' definition of piracy as earlier discussed. The clause therefore seeks to reflect perhaps a more practical approach to the reality of the physical threats faced by vessels and crews. Indeed, the approach taken was foreshadowed a decade ago when the Comité Maritime International (CMI) attempted to introduce an international Model Law on piracy containing more widely defined 'maritime crimes'. (That initiative, however, met with limited success at the time.) The wider definition of the moment in time when the risk of a piratical attack is identified contained in this drafting is also noteworthy. Such language may allow a court to take perhaps a broader approach to the assessment of 'danger' than was permitted in the case of *The Product Star*.

Clause (b) of the BIMCO clauses provides that if 'the Owners' decide not to continue with the voyage because of the danger of piratical attack, they are to inform the time charterers who are 'obliged' to issue 'alternative voyage orders'. Any such 'alternative' orders also require time charterers to provide an indemnity to the owners against any claims that may be advanced by the 'holders of the Bills of Lading' caused by the vessel awaiting new orders or by performing an alternative voyage. It is expressly stated that 'any time lost' in compliance with new orders shall 'not be considered off-hire'.

If notwithstanding the above the owners' consent to the vessel proceeding on the original contract voyage or 'the vessel proceeds to or through an Area exposed to the risk of Piracy' the owners are given a number of 'liberties'. These include the taking of 'reasonable preventive measures to protect the Vessel' including *inter alia* 'proceeding in convoy', taking appropriate navigational precautions and 'engaging security personnel or equipment', clause (c)(i), and compliance with the instructions of 'third parties' including *inter alia* underwriters ((c)(ii)), the flag state ((c)(iii)) and supranational organisations such as the Security Council of the United Nations ((c)(iv)).

In the event that the vessel is required to comply with such 'third party' instructions time charterers are obliged to indemnify the owners against 'any claims from holders of bills of lading' unless covered by specific insurance. The clause also seeks to achieve a balance between owners and time charterers by including an apportionment between the parties in respect of time lost, costs and expenses incurred as a consequence of a pirate attack and in the event of the vessel being seized. It is to be noted that the clauses proposed by BIMCO and others in the market are in the nature of proposed or recommended terms. It will be for the parties to each individual contract to decide whether to include or modify the terms to reflect their commercial aims.

If the vessel does proceed 'to or through an Area where due to risk of Piracy additional costs will be incurred', including the cost of 'additional personnel and preventive measures', such reasonable costs are for the charterers' account. The same position is adopted in relation to payment by the owners of any 'crew bonus or additional wages' and the payment by the owners of any 'additional premiums or additional insurance cover'.[51] The clause therefore aims to reflect the general time charter structure previously reviewed, where costs associated with the charterers' commercial operation of the vessel will be for them to bear.

As to the payment of hire and loss of time, clause (d)(i) provides that the vessel shall remain on-hire where time is lost 'waiting for convoys' and on account of other operational or navigational measures which are taken to 'minimise risk'. The same position as to loss of time is adopted when the vessel is 'attacked by pirates' when again the vessel is to remain on-hire.[52]

A further clause deals with the position if the vessel 'is seized by pirates'. In that event owners are to keep charterers closely informed of efforts made to have the vessel released. Hire is to remain payable 'throughout the seizure'. However, time charterers' liability to pay hire shall cease 'as of the ninety-first (91st) day of the seizure' and will resume again only when the vessel is released.

Lastly, clause (g) provides that any action taken in compliance with the clause overall 'shall not be deemed a deviation, but shall be considered as due fulfilment' of the charterparty.

As can be seen, the BIMCO Piracy Clause for Time Charterparties adopts the principal criteria of war risks clauses routinely found in time charterparties but adapts these, and issues relating to loss of time, hire and off-hire and additional costs and expenses, to the specific commercial and operational threats posed by pirate attacks.

BIMCO voyage charter clauses

The BIMCO Piracy Clause for Voyage Charterparties is drafted in similar terms, adapted to the different legal and commercial structure of a voyage charter.

Clause (a) provides that: 'If, in the reasonable judgement of the Master and/or the Owners' any part of the route which is 'normally and

---

[51]   Clause (d)(i),(ii) and (iii).
[52]   Clause (e).

customarily' used for the contractual voyage becomes 'dangerous' on account of the risk of 'Piracy' (the definition of which is the same as in the time charter clause) 'the Owners shall be entitled to take a reasonable alternative route to the discharging port'. If owners so decide, charterers are to be immediately informed. A similar provision is made for an alternative voyage to the loading port for the purposes of a consecutive voyage charter. If an alternative route is taken pursuant to clause (a) which exceeds 100 miles the owners are entitled to adjusted additional freight at the charterparty rate. If the owners incur 'additional costs' (as defined in the time charter clause) or have to pay 'additional premiums or additional insurance', the owners may recover half the cost in each case from the charterers (clause (c)(ii) and (iii)).

Clause (b) contains similar terms to clause (c) of the time charter clause relating to compliance with third party instructions, but there are a number of consequential differences in the structure of the costs and compensation regime.

In the event of a pirate attack or seizure 'any time so lost' shall be 'shared equally between the Owners and the Charterers' at an amount equivalent to half the demurrage rate agreed in the charter (being the rate of detention damages set out in the charter which the charterer agrees to pay day by day to the owner based on the time by which the actual time for loading and discharging the vessel exceeds that which has been agreed – what is known as the 'contractual laytime'). It is to be noted that these provisions are tailored specifically to the commercial basis of operation of a voyage charter, being an entitlement to additional freight for a longer voyage and payment for demurrage at half rate entitling the owner at least to a partial recovery for time lost as would have occurred if the contractual laytime for loading and discharging had been exceeded.

Lastly, in order to link issues of cargo ownership under the bill of lading to the voyage charter terms, clause (e) provides:

> This clause shall be incorporated into any bill of lading issued pursuant to this charterparty. The Charterers shall indemnify the Owners against all consequences and liabilities that may arise from the Master signing bills of lading as presented to the extent the terms of such bills of lading impose or result in the imposition of more onerous liabilities upon the Owners than those assumed by the Owners under this clause.

Clause (f) in the voyage charter form is in like terms as clause (g) in the time charter equivalent.

13.8.3 Exceptions Clauses

Exceptions clauses in charterparties and bills of lading comprise a contractual regime that seeks to exclude the liability of one or both parties to the contract of carriage for any loss damage or delay where such is caused by one or more of a series of listed events. Such clauses may exclude liability for acts of piracy, either on the facts of a case or because they have been specifically drafted to have that effect. The courts regard these clauses as separate and distinct in law from the terms and operation of 'war risks' clauses of the traditional type described and, it is submitted, would similarly interpret the effect of the newer piracy clauses reviewed in the previous section. Exceptions clauses are also interpreted as separate and distinct in law from time charter provisions governing the payment of hire or off-hire clauses as well as provisions regarding payment of freight and demurrage under a voyage charter or bill of lading.

In the case of *The Petro Ranger* discussed above, it will be recalled that one of the issues that arose was whether an 'act of piracy' had occurred such as would exclude the liability of the shipowner under the following general exceptions clause:

> ... And neither the Vessel nor Master or Owner nor the Charterer shall, unless otherwise in this charter expressly provided, be responsible for any loss or damage or delay or failure in performing hereunder arising or resulting from ... acts of ... pirates...

In the arbitration and in court it was accepted (and conceded by charterers) that on the evidence the theft and disposal of cargo discharged from the vessel, prior to the intervention of the Chinese authorities, was an act of 'piracy' covered by the exception.

The concept of 'piracy' as an exception to liability is found in several standard form time charterparties, including, for example, clause 22(a) of the STB Tanker Time Charterparty, and similarly in several voyage charter forms, including clause 36 of Norgrain 89 and clause 29(a) of ExxonMobil Voy 2000.

In the context of bills of lading there is no specific exception for 'piracy' contained in the list of the carrier's exceptions in Article IV rule 2 of the Hague Rules although it is to be noted that an exception for 'piracy' has been included in Article 17.3(c) of the Rotterdam Rules.

13.9 CONCLUSION

There have, as noted, been few reported court decisions arising from incidents of Somali piracy. Nonetheless it is fair to say that the court in those cases has approached the specific issues arising in the same way as courts in the past have approached the advent of other events impacting on risks and liabilities arising under contracts of carriage. Courts in the future will no doubt approach matters on a similar basis but, in addition, may be required to consider the effect in individual cases of the inclusion of specific clauses that have been drawn up in an attempt to reflect the operational and commercial realities that piratical seizures have forced upon the maritime community.

PART IV

Conclusions

14. Policy tensions and the legal regime governing piracy

Douglas Guilfoyle

14.1 INTRODUCTION

This volume set out to examine the public and private law responses to modern piracy in context and some of the legal challenges piracy presents to both government and commercial actors. This has given rise to a number of recurrent themes. First, there is the problem of definition. Second, there is the palpable fact that piracy is situated: local conditions of geography, economic opportunity and governance all shape piracy. Third, multilateral efforts to repress piracy off Somalia in particular raise questions about the tension between efficiency (how do we reduce the rate of successful pirate hijackings and ensure that captured pirates are sent for trial?) and broader questions of justice, due process and human rights. Fourth, the legal response to piracy has always involved a tension between state sovereignty or jurisdiction on the one hand and collective responses on the other. Piracy on the high seas would be impossible to suppress or prosecute effectively if an attacked ship had to await the intervention of a naval vessel of either its flag state or that of its attacker. This has led to the traditional exception to the freedom of the high seas which allows all states to police acts of piracy on the high seas. Nonetheless, states continue to guard jealously their sovereign jurisdiction over similar crimes in territorial waters. States are also very reluctant to allow exceptions made for piracy to become generalised to other areas of maritime law, as seen in the cautious approach of the Security Council in authorising counter-piracy action in relation to Somalia. Finally, we might ask when the state fails, does the market intervene? Piracy is often portrayed as an alternative market enterprise enabled by state failure, and one could also think of the turn by industry towards private armed security as it became apparent that navies could never provide perfect protection from pirate attacks off Somalia,[1] especially as pirates adapted their tactics to the responses of navies. These themes are examined in turn below.

14.2 WHAT IS 'PIRACY'?

Piracy is not a subject that has ever been noted for its definitional clarity. Martin Murphy aptly observes that there is always a temptation on the part of 'winners' in any particular economic order to brand 'losers' who resort to predation as pirates.[2] While classical authors certainly described the pirate as *hostis humani generis* (an enemy of all humankind) this has always been more a term of rhetorical condemnation than legal art.[3]

Contemporary international law as reflected in the United Nations Convention on the Law of the Sea (UNCLOS) defines a number of acts to be piracy, the essential one being an act of violence, detention or depredation committed on the high seas by a private vessel against another vessel for private ends.[4] As noted throughout this volume, the prerequisite that such acts be on the high seas excludes similar acts within territorial waters (or ports or rivers) which are normally classified as 'armed robbery at sea'.[5] However, as has also been noted, two other offences constitute piracy under UNCLOS: voluntary participation in a pirate craft (including one intended for future acts of piracy) and facilitating or inciting piracy. Both these expanded definitions of piracy 'do not explicitly set forth any particular geographic scope'.[6] The question, in particular, of whether universal jurisdiction over piracy

---

[1]   See Chapters 8 and 10.

[2]   Chapter 4.5; compare the authoritative historical survey of its unstable legal meaning: A. Rubin, *The Law of Piracy* (2nd edn, Naval War College Press, 1998).

[3]   E.g., J. Bingham (rapporteur), '[Harvard] Codification of International Law: Part IV – Piracy' (1932) 26 *American Journal of International Law Supplement* 739, 770 (attributing the term to Cicero) and 774, 796, 806–807.

[4]   United Nations Convention on the Law of the Sea (adopted 10 December 1982, entered into force 16 November 1994) 1833 UNTS 397 ('UNCLOS'), Art. 101(a).

[5]   Even when not involving robbery or, indeed, arms.

[6]   United Nations Division for Ocean Affairs and the Law of the Sea, 'Piracy: elements of national legislation pursuant to the United Nations Convention on the Law of the Sea, 1982' IMO Doc LEG 98/8/1 (18 February 2011) 4 at n.15. See Chapter 9.3 and A. Murdoch, 'Recent Legal Issues and Problems

extends to 'facilitating' piracy through acts committed ashore remains both open[7] and controversial.[8]

These geographical or jurisdictional distinctions at public international law exist for a number of reasons, discussed below, but may only serve to divide a single phenomenon into a number of artificial legal categories. Somali pirates cruising for prey are engaged in one criminal enterprise whether they strike in the territorial sea or on the high seas, but only the latter is 'piracy' in a strict international law sense. Similarly, we generally refer to maritime predation in Nigerian waters as 'piracy' in a loose or common-sense way, despite only a minority of such attacks occurring seaward of the territorial sea.

The approach to piracy in private law, at least in common law jurisdictions, favours a broader definition. Piracy under the law of insurance certainly encompasses high-seas violence of the type captured by the core UNCLOS definition but also extends to attacks in port, or even attacks originating from the shore.[9] While we might think this a preferable approach for the law to take, it is unlikely to be replicated at the level of public international law. It is one thing for an insured and an insurer to agree between themselves as private parties that an act of 'piracy' may occur in port; such an interpretation affects only private interests (and reflects a popular understanding of piracy without regard to technical definitions and public interests). For public international law to take such a view would be to extend significantly the reach of the universal jurisdiction which accompanies the crime of piracy and would be fiercely resisted by coastal states in some of the world's most piracy prone areas. As Robert Beckman has noted, for example, Southeast Asian states 'jealously guard their sovereignty and...are very unlikely to agree

---

Relating to Acts of Piracy of Somalia', in C. R. Symmons (ed.), *Selected Contemporary Issues in the Law of the Sea* (Nijhoff, 2011), 139 at 157–158.

[7]   Murdoch, *supra* note 6, 139 at 157–158. In at least one case a US Court has convicted a pirate negotiator who committed no acts on the high seas: Roger L. Philips, 'Negotiator Sentenced to Multiple Life Terms: SCOTUS on the horizon' (15 August 2012) <http://piracy-law.com/2012/08/15/negotiator-sentenced-to-multiple-life-terms-scotus-on-the-horizon/> accessed 21 August 2012.

[8]   See, for example, the debate at: Douglas Guilfoyle, 'Committing Piracy on Dry Land: Liability for Facilitating Piracy' (*EJIL: Talk!*, 26 July 2012) <http://www.ejiltalk.org/committing-piracy-on-dry-land-liability-for-facilitating-piracy/> accessed 21 August 2012.

[9]   See Chapter 11.4.

to other states patrolling waters or exercising police power in maritime zones under their sovereignty'.[10]

14.3 PIRACY OR 'PIRACIES'?

Definitions and labels, however, do not necessarily help solve problems and may even lead to their misdiagnosis. The single word 'piracy' suggests a unitary phenomenon and implies a readily transferrable set of both criminal business models and law-enforcement practices. A theme of this volume has been to ask to what extent both 'piracy' and 'counter-piracy' are transferrable. Broadly, the conclusion suggested by the 'context' chapters in Part I must be that piracy is always highly contingent on local conditions of geography, politics, governance and poverty. We are confronted not with *piracy* but *piracies*. The flexible private law approach of risk allocation adapts better to this reality than public law and institutions.

On the counter-piracy side of the equation we can readily overstate the transferrable lessons from one instance of piracy to another. The complex bilateral webs of agreements facilitating the criminal justice disposition of Somali pirates captured by one state, transferred (in some cases) to another for state trial, and then (perhaps) to a third to serve their sentence are unlikely to arise outside the context of major multi-national counter-piracy deployments.[11] So far, Somalia is the only example of such a situation. The Southeast Asian response to piracy, coordinated regional patrols by the littoral states and the establishment of an Information Sharing Centre, may be exported to other environments but we should be cautious about expecting similar results. As Robert Beckman notes, other contributing factors to a decline in regional piracy may include the 2004 Asian tsunami, the strengthening of local law-enforcement agencies and the conclusion of a peace in Aceh.[12] It is easy to overstate the impact of regional institution-building on piracy to the detriment of other factors. Further, the problem of piracy in the Malacca Strait occurred in a relatively confined geographical area compared to the expanse of the Indian Ocean. Nonetheless, the Southeast Asian experience does provide a compelling example of the truism that both the strength of local governance institutions and the economy ashore are critical in reducing

---

[10] See Chapter 2.2.
[11] See, in particular, Chapters 5 and 8.
[12] Chapter 2.3.3.

piracy.[13] A successful counter-piracy strategy has to acknowledge that suppressing piracy requires both adequate law enforcement ashore and viable alternative livelihoods for those who might engage in it. Perhaps another lesson, already learned in other theatres of maritime law enforcement and which piracy has proven once again, is simply the importance of cooperation *within* governments if different agencies are to cooperate in maintaining a criminal justice chain from capture to prosecution.[14]

14.4   THE TENSION BETWEEN EFFICIENCY AND JUSTICE

These considerations all point to the intrinsic difficulty of addressing maritime criminality only by taking action at sea, as inevitably the roots of such crimes lie ashore. Nonetheless, the preponderance of the international effort in the Somali case appears to have been focused on precisely such maritime actions, which, while necessary, can never be sufficient of themselves to end piracy. Even taken on their own terms, efforts to suppress Somali piracy at sea have been fraught with difficulties, as noted below. While there has been clear agreement that counter-piracy is a law-enforcement exercise, not a laws-of-war operation,[15] this has not always been consistently reflected in the relevant legal instruments – most notably the Security Council resolutions on point. The Security Council is most used to dealing with matters of peace and security and authorising the use of force on the international plane between states. The language and mindset of law enforcement took a little while to replace the language and mindset of military operations in the relevant resolutions. Curiosities still remain in this regard, including the Security Council's reference to 'applicable...humanitarian law' in counter-piracy operations ashore in Somalia and in its seeming grant of a summary power of disposal of private property merely reasonably

---

[13]   Although piracy is a 'market dependent' crime requiring some level of local governance, there is a risk that (up to a point) improving governance may exacerbate piracy: 'Brigands seeking harbours: Why pirates like a little law and order', *The Economist* (20 April 2011) <http://www.economist.com/node/18586874> accessed 17 August 2012) and Olaf J. de Groot, Matthew D. Rablen and Anja Shortland, 'Gov-aargh-nance – "even criminals need law and order"', Working Paper No. 11–01, Centre for Economic Development & Institutions (Brunel University, February 2011) <http://ideas.repec.org/p/edb/cedidp/11–01.html> accessed 17 August 2012.

[14]   See Chapters 7 and 8.

[15]   Chapters 3 and 6 to 8.

suspected of being intended for use in an act of piracy.[16] The latter, in
particular, seems to prioritise military efficiency over ordinary notions of
criminal justice.[17] The temptation towards efficient solutions must be
strong. Organised crime can always adapt more quickly than laws can be
made to help suppress it; this is especially the case in the international
arena, where the pace of law-creation or reform is typically much slower
than at the national level.

Further, Western states capturing pirates are typically unwilling to
prosecute them before their own courts and will send them for prosecution in the region. While this may be justified on numerous grounds
including cost-effectiveness (trials in the region are certainly less expensive), concerns have also been raised about the appropriateness of
European states sending suspects to face justice before national systems
with different (and potentially lower) standards.[18] Criticisms have
focused not only on human rights concerns, but more recently on the
extremely variable sentencing practices that result.[19] As discussed further
below, the collective response to Somali piracy might be thought broadly
efficient in that it *does* work insofar as trials do occur and it *does* deliver
new resources to regional legal systems conducting those trials. However,
one may legitimately ask if there is a risk of justice lagging behind
efficiency in such cases.

14.5 THE TENSION BETWEEN SOVEREIGN JURISDICTION AND COLLECTIVE RESPONSES

More than anything else, perhaps, the problem of piracy wherever it
occurs illustrates the tensions between state sovereignty and collective
responses. In the case of Southeast Asia, this dynamic perhaps played out
in quite a constructive manner. As the outside world became increasingly
interested in and concerned by piracy in the region – culminating in the
listing of the Malacca Strait by Lloyd's Market Association as a 'war risk

---

[16]   On humanitarian law see Chapters 7.3 and 8.2; on confiscation of property
Chapters 3.3.5 and 8.7.

[17]   Chapter 8.7.

[18]   Chapter 8.8.2.

[19]   Eugene Kontorovich, 'The Penalties for Piracy: An Empirical Study of
National Prosecution of International Crime' (Northwestern University School of
Law Public Law and Legal Theory Series, No. 12–16, 3 July 2012) <http://
papers.ssrn.com/sol3/cf_dev/AbsByAuth.cfm?per_id=274349#show2103661>
accessed 17 August 2012.

area' – that interest prompted action at the regional and national level.[20] In that case the states involved clearly saw it as preferable to deal with the local problem themselves in order to forestall (further) external intervention. It is interesting to note, in this context, that the final and critical political spur to action was provided by commercial actors, and insurers at that.

Great emphasis has been placed in the Somali context on maintaining the legal fiction of the effective sovereignty of the Somali state. Everything that has been done within Somalia's territorial waters or land territory has occurred under the double-authority of a Security Council authorisation and the permission of the Transitional Federal Government.[21] As noted, the authorising Security Council resolutions scrupulously avoid suggesting that piracy *per se* justifies such potentially wide-ranging intervention within a state or its territorial waters.[22] This was obviously necessitated by the concerns of some states that counter-piracy might become a new realm of Security Council intrusion into states' sovereign domain.

Less concern has been expressed over the potential interference with freedom of navigation posed by the extensive counter-piracy presence off Somalia. Typically, states are jealous of their jurisdiction over their flag vessels and tend only 'grudgingly' to accept the right of visit over their vessels when established in treaty law.[23] Even though high-seas enforcement jurisdiction over piracy is long-established, one might have thought there would be more nervousness about the sheer scale of the operations being conducted off Somalia. Of course, the obvious rejoinder is that those with whose freedom of navigation patrolling navies are most likely to interfere are smaller regional vessels, not the international merchant fleet. Indeed, the concerns expressed by regional states have generally *not* been about the stopping and searching of the local fishing fleet, but

---

[20] Chapter 2.3.3.

[21] Which has been frequently described as 'neither transitional, nor federal, nor a government'. See, e.g., J. Peter Pham, 'Somalia: Strategic Realities and Realistic Stratagems' (Word Defense Review, 2 July 2009) <http://worlddefensereview.com/pham070209.shtml> accessed 17 August 2012.

[22] Chapters 3.3.3 and 6.3.

[23] Robert C. F. Reuland, 'Interference with Non-national Ships on the High Seas: Peacetime Exceptions to the Exclusivity Rule of Flag-state Jurisdiction' (1989) 22 *Vanderbilt Journal of Transnational Law* 1161, 1170; compare Natalie Klein, *Maritime Security and the Law of the Sea* (Oxford University Press, 2011) 114.

whether counter-piracy may form a pretext for the long-term militarisation of 'their' waters. Thus, many in India saw in the modest Chinese deployment of three warships to convoy vessels through piracy-affected waters 'as the first step onto a slippery slope to a permanent [Chinese] naval presence in the Indian Ocean'.[24] Similar concerns regarding the presence of foreign navies have been expressed by states bordering the Gulf of Aden.

The efficacy (or perceived efficacy) of the collective response to Somali piracy also depends in part on the willingness of states to prosecute suspected pirates and imprison convicted pirates. However, the decision to prosecute remains, quite clearly, a sovereign one. The reluctance of states to make open-ended commitments in advance to prosecute pirates has left us with quite a porous and *ad hoc* system of transnational criminal justice cooperation in Somali counter-piracy efforts.[25] That said, this *ad hoc* approach has been, on many accounts, rather more effective in securing prosecutions than one might expect. Overall, however, the lack of institutionalisation perhaps makes the response to Somali piracy particularly vulnerable to shifting international priorities.[26] It is a system of cooperation that can be thrown off balance at any point by a significant party either withdrawing or scaling back its commitment to the collective effort. Indeed, this is precisely what has occurred given Kenya's continuing reluctance to accept responsibility for any significant new number of piracy trials since late 2010.[27]

In stark contrast, Nigerian armed robbery at sea and in its internal waters by various groups (which can and do occasionally act as pirates in an international law sense) has attracted little by way of a multilateral response.[28] Superficially, one might suggest that the fact that the majority of attacks occur within Nigeria's territorial sea and internal waters means it has relatively little impact on the international community. Yet this cannot be right. Illegal bunkering, for example, inflicts very significant

---

[24]   James R. Holmes, 'The Interplay between Counterpiracy and Indian Ocean Geopolitics', in Bibi van Ginkel and Frans-Paul van der Putten (eds), *The International Response to Somali Piracy: Challenges and Opportunities* (Nijhoff, 2010) 153, 163.

[25]   See Chapters 8.4 to 8.8 and 7.1.2 in particular.

[26]   Chapter 3.4.2.

[27]   See, e.g., House of Commons Foreign Affairs Committee, 'Piracy off the coast of Somalia', HC 1318 (5 January 2012) ('House of Commons Report'), para. 96 <http://www.parliament.uk/business/committees/committees-a-z/commons-select/foreign-affairs-committee/publications/> accessed 14 September 2012.

[28]   Although see Chapter 5.3.1.

losses on major multi-national corporations in Nigeria and feeds a black market for oil not only in the region but internationally.[29] It may simply be the case that as an oil-producing state Nigeria is shielded from outside pressure so long as the price of doing business with it does not become unacceptably high.[30] As Martin Murphy has pointed out, this may simply encourage the hollowing out of the state's infrastructure by privileged elites who will remain unthreatened so long as the enclaves relevant to international trade remain tolerably orderly and functional.[31] Such predation, ironically, is legitimated by state structures and is generally not branded as either piracy or criminality.

14.6   WHEN THE STATE FAILS, THE MARKET INTERVENES?

It is also tempting to suggest that a lesson of piracy is that when the state fails, the market intervenes. After all, piracy is essentially an alternative market activity: a crime aimed purely at profit. Somali piracy is often seen as the legacy of state failure in Somalia, and Southeast Asian piracy declined alongside the establishment of more effective state repression. The picture is, of course, more mixed. Piracy requires not just the absence of effective state repression but the presence of enough stability for local markets to work (in order to sell stolen goods, or receive and spend ransom payments). There is a governance 'sweet spot' for piracy: piracy needs enough governance to allow markets to function but not enough to get in the way of piracy as a business.[32] Thus, strengthening a weak state may, in the short run, result in a *better* climate for piracy during the transition to a fully effective state (if the latter is ever achieved).

Market actors may also have an impact on the profitability or viability of piracy as a practice. I have already noted the impact of the Lloyd's Market Association's designation of the Malacca Strait as a 'war risk area' on the littoral Straits. Here we had functional governments which were sensitive to their international reputation as well as local conditions for piracy that were at the upper end of the governance 'sweet spot'; thus there was realistic government action that could be taken in a short time that had a measurable impact on piracy. Pressure from commercial actors

---

[29]   Chapter 4.9.
[30]   Chapter 4.12.
[31]   *Ibid.*
[32]   See Chapter 3.1; compare *The Economist, supra* note 13.

is likely to have less impact in Nigeria where decision making elites are somewhat shielded from international pressure and little or no impact in Somalia where government lacks sufficient repressive capacity. Indeed, in the Somali case improvements in governance might only push the situation deeper into the 'sweet spot' by providing more stable conditions for piracy as a business but still insufficient state capacity to repress piracy as a crime. That is, in states in the process of becoming stronger and better organised: '[c]riminality might increase as markets create new opportunities and can become endemic unless bureaucrats are incentivised to tackle rather than tolerate or protect criminal organisations'.[33]

Commercial actors may also influence the profitability of piracy through choices about where and under what conditions a vessel will sail. Liberty and time-charter clauses in contracts governing the carriage of goods by sea may give the captain of a vessel the freedom to avoid (or require him or her to avoid) areas where piracy is a significant threat.[34] Insurers have also played a role in promoting the adoption of the IMO-sanctioned Best Managements Practices (BMP), by rewarding compliance with lower premiums.[35] BMP compliance appears to reduce the risk of a vessel being taken by pirates noticeably. Finally, of course, the presence of private armed security aboard a vessel is – where the flag state permits it – a commercial choice which may have a significant impact on the success rate of pirates (or at least the risks they face).[36] All of these decisions taken by private actors in the shipping industry may cumulatively affect the odds of pirates finding prey.

However, when pirates do succeed in taking hostages, the difficult question of ransoms arises. If the response of the world's governments cannot perfectly secure the safety of all shipping in the Gulf of Aden and the Indian Ocean (and it never plausibly could), then in the final analysis the only recourse of the private sector is the paying of ransoms. However, it is also quite clear that paying ransoms fuels piracy.[37] It is easy enough, then, to suggest that there should be a law against paying ransoms. The key objections to criminalising ransom payments are that it is too late now, and would require international uniformity of approach. To stop

---

[33] De Groot, Rablen and Shortland, *supra* note 13, 21.

[34] Chapter 13.2 and 13.8.2.

[35] Chapter 3.3.

[36] See Chapter 10.

[37] L Ploch *et al.*, 'Piracy off the Horn of Africa', Congressional Research Service (27 April 2011) 6–7, 12 <http://www.fas.org/sgp/crs/row/R40528.pdf> accessed 5 September 2012; House of Commons Report, *supra* note 27, paras 55–58.

paying ransoms while pirates hold hostages (and at present Somali pirates *always* have numerous hostages) is to risk those hostages' lives.[38] Further, the ransom incentive could only effectively be eliminated if all maritime states took the same policy – which seems unlikely. At present, under UK law the paying of ransoms is not considered contrary to public policy by the courts and is not illegal under statute.[39] Indeed, the UK has in international fora resisted having pirate leaders added to lists of individuals targeted by UN sanction regimes,[40] presumably in order to prevent ransom payments becoming illegal under international law.

At time of writing, the good news is that in the first eight months of 2012 there were only nine successful pirate attacks off Somalia, compared with 34 in 2011 and 64 in 2010.[41] This may, however, only increase the desperation and violence of Somali pirates as their business model becomes further squeezed.[42]

14.7 CONCLUSIONS

A significant difficulty in addressing piracy is understanding what we are facing. This practical problem can become obscured in definitions and preconceptions. As noted throughout this volume, there is no one form of piracy and suggestions that lessons can be readily transferred from one context to another should be resisted. Piracy is always flexible, adaptable and rooted in its local conditions. Efforts to suppress piracy need to be similarly tailored and contextual.

Efforts at countering piracy off Somalia have shown at times admirable flexibility and a focus on coordinating existing jurisdictions and resources.[43] Nonetheless, there remains a tension between efficiency and justice in a world of scarce resources. What is being done off Somalia is necessary to contain piracy; but only greater efforts within Somalia and the Gulf of Aden region will be able to repress it effectively. The risk is that if international naval forces are able to suppress piracy to a level we

---

[38] House of Commons Report, *supra* note 27, Evidence Annexe 48 (at Q290) and 63 (evidence of the Chamber of Shipping).

[39] See in particular Chapter 12.6.3.

[40] House of Commons Report, *supra* note 27, para. 114.

[41] Thom Shanker, 'U.S. Reports That Piracy Off Africa Has Plunged' (*New York Times*, 28 August 2012) <http://www.nytimes.com/2012/08/29/world/africa/piracy-around-horn-of-africa-has-plunged-us-says.html?_r=1&smid=tw-share> accessed 5 September 2012.

[42] Chapter 3.2.

[43] See, in particular, Chapter 5.

can 'live with', international efforts will stop there. If state repression cannot prevail, we can expect the market to step in where it can. This, in turn, will require new and flexible structures – be they in insurance contracts or arrangements for private armed security or the adoption of soft-law instruments such as Best Management Practices.[44] Such commercial measures may actually provide both more uniformity and flexibility of response than state driven measures.

That said, in addressing a complex problem like piracy or maritime violence a plurality of actors, definitions and approaches noted in this volume is not always intrinsically a disadvantage. A variety of approaches may need to be taken by both public and private actors to constrain the space in which piracy can operate as a prelude to putting pirates out of business. With luck, this is what we have seen occur in the cases of piracy both off Somali and in Southeast Asia – although there appear to have been relatively little such effort to date in the case of Nigerian maritime violence.[45] Other factors (environmental, economic and security-related) will, of course, remain vital. Nonetheless, law as an organising tool for both the private and public sector remains important.

---

[44]   On Best Management Practices see Chapters 3.3.7, 5.3.1, 10.3.1, 10.4 and 12.3.
[45]   On various regional initiatives see: UNSC Res. 2018 (31 October 2011), UN Doc. S/RES/2018.

Index